THE BEST OF TIMES,
THE WORST OF TIMES

Also by Michael Burleigh

The Racial State: Germany 1933–45

Death and Deliverance

Germany Turns Eastward

The Third Reich: A New History

Earthly Powers

Sacred Causes

Blood and Rage

Moral Combat

Small Wars, Far Away Places

MICHAEL BURLEIGH

THE BEST OF TIMES, THE WORST OF TIMES

A History of Now

MACMILLAN

First published 2017 by Macmillan
an imprint of Pan Macmillan
20 New Wharf Road, London N1 9RR
Associated companies throughout the world
www.panmacmillan.com

ISBN 978-1-5098-4788-4 HB
ISBN 978-1-5098-4792-1 TPB

1 3 5 7 9 8 6 4 2

A CIP catalogue record for this book is available from the British Library.

Typeset in Sabon LT Std by Palimpsest Book Production Limited, Falkirk, Stirlingshire
Printed and bound by CPI Group (UK) Ltd, Croydon, CR0 4YY

In Memoriam Geordie Kidston

(1964–2016)

Contents

Prologue

This book is about the shift from a brief period of US dominance lasting two decades following the end of the Cold War in
1989–91, towards a present in which power is palpably dispers-
ing among other great powers of which China is the most
important. I neither regret nor welcome this fact. It is.

Such transitions, and how global institutions and ideas adapt
to them, are invariably disruptive. Sometimes the clash of rising
and declining powers results in what is known as the Thucyd-
ides Trap. Named after the ancient Athenian historian, it refers
to the moment at which an ascendant Athens challenged an
established Sparta, or, in modern times, imperial Germany's
challenge to the British Empire at the dawn of the twentieth
century. Some detect such tensions between the US and China
today, though they can be overblown and some of the past
'traps' (including the Cold War) did not involve major war
between the main protagonists.

Usually these transitions *follow* catastrophic wars, as peace
is restored, so our present inverted experience is atypical and
unlike the international new orders established in 1648, 1814,
1918 or 1945. It has been complicated, too, by what is called
globalization. This is shorthand for how the global penetrates
the more local, in the guise of capital flows, cut flowers from
Colombia and Kenya or vegetables from Peru, digitization, refugees, terrorists and tourists. The digital aspect of this is the
most important since it enabled companies to offshore the least
profitable part of their business – fabrication and assembly – to
low-wage economies, while retaining highly lucrative design and
marketing for themselves, with the entire process managed and
orchestrated online. Some claim it has also led to a difference of

consciousness and culture within populations, pointing to the mutual incomprehension of people rooted in 'somewhere' near where they were born and those rootless 'citizens of the world' who can live 'anywhere', though surely alienation between bustling metropolises and the deep country is nothing new. Two events gave enormous impetus to this present transition: the 2003 invasion of Iraq and the financial crises after 2008 that shook the West's confidence in its ability to shape the world. The first led to strategic retrenchment, after the hubris of the Bush Junior years, while, together with globalization, the financial crisis has highlighted inequalities within as well as between nations and triggered a left and right populist reaction. But these are not the only influences afoot.

Most obviously, the Middle East is in chaos, with its state failure and terrorism menacing Africa, China, Europe, Russia and the US. Russia and Turkey have succumbed to authoritarianism and the European Union is in crisis, reverting back to its 'Carolingian' core. Presidents Vladimir Putin and Donald Trump both seem eager to deal with competing European sovereign nation-states rather than with Brussels and the EU. The traditional West is fractured with some eastern EU states succumbing to illiberalism and the much-vaunted 'Anglosphere' presumes that, for example, Britain or Canada has much in common with such pseudo democracies as India or South Africa. Relations with Europe cooled in May 2017 after Trump delivered a salty lecture to Nato leaders gathered in Brussels, in which he refused to explicitly endorse Article 5 and then barged aside the Prime Minister of the alliance's newest member, Montenegro, followed quickly by his refusal to commit the US to the Paris Agreement on climate change, thereby leaving the US in the company of Nicaragua and Syria. A certain *froideur* has even crept into relations between Trump and Australia.

The disruptive, scattergun inattention of President Trump is obvious enough, and it is already showing signs of damaging US soft power and tourist visitor numbers to the US, even as a promised $53 billion military build-up will not address any pertinent threats from American adversaries and rivals. More tanks and ships are irrelevant to the informational subversion and agile use of military power employed by the Russians and more missiles are impotent in the face of the multiplying soft power of Beijing. Trump's erratic and transactional view of all alliances is likely to provide rival powers with many opportunities to divide and rule a West already reeling from attacks by domestic populists, some of them actively sponsored by Putin. The European Union is riven with divisions at all points of the compass, and is a geopolitical nullity, an empire of virtue in fact. Unless the new partnership known as 'M&M' or 'Merkron', meaning Chancellor Merkel and President Macron, changes that.

A few days before Donald Trump's dark 'Mid-West as Mogadishu' inaugural address in January 2017, President Xi Jinping of China delivered an altogether brighter account of the world, quoting Charles Dickens's *A Tale of Two Cities* to the effect that we are living in the 'best and worst of times'. He committed China to globalization, free trade and maintenance of the post-war international order, themes which were picked up again at the huge One Road Initiative conference in Beijing in May 2017. Chinese Premier Li Keqiang was also handily present in Berlin and Brussels when Trump renounced a climate-change deal that was aspirational and which contained no sanctions in the event of backsliding and non-compliance.

But it is far too simplistic to imagine that a more self-assertive China is simply going to assume the costly role of global leadership that the US may be vacating, most obviously in tackling man-made climate change. Are the Chinese really interested in curbing climate change when they are selling India one new thermal coal power plant every three weeks for the next five years and consuming a lot of imported coal themselves?

Globalization has suited the Chinese very well, and their business-driven diplomatic approach means that they enjoy good relations with such deadly foes as Iran and Saudi Arabia, Israel and Iran, to take some examples. Are the Chinese going to assume a bigger role in the various miasmas of the Middle East just to protect their oil supplies? Isn't American talk of China becoming a 'Responsible Stakeholder', as Robert Zoellick requested in 2005, 'a new way for Western nations to pressure and constrain China', as a top Chinese scholar responded? Recent

years have also witnessed alarmist rumbling in the US much indebted to the American seapower geostrategist Alfred Thayer
Mahan (1840–1914) about a looming showdown between
China and the US in the Pacific or further afield, which has sometimes been echoed by chauvinistic Chinese naval officers. As in
the case of swallows, one modest Chinese naval base in Djibouti
does not make a summer. China's main focus is achieving hegemony in its own Asia-Pacific backyard, extensively defined, most
definitely by 2049 when the People's Republic celebrates the
centenary of the Revolution, not in squandering its blood and
treasure beyond that realm in ways all too familiar to Americans
from recent decades. Two things the Chinese are not are idealistic
or stupid. What they are hoping to achieve, with the chaotic
Trump in the White House, is to add international engagement,
colossal overseas infrastructural investment and a predictable
solidity to the limited things China is already renowned for,
namely autocratic governance and remarkable economic growth,
which even at roughly 6 per cent is much greater than anything
the US has been managing. Projecting hard power on a global
scale in not among Beijing's ambitions.

China seeks a larger role within the UN, having led the
World Health Organization since 2006, while lobbying unsuccessfully to run UN peacekeeping missions too, as the largest
contributor of troops and second largest budget contributor. A
Chinese paramilitary police general has become the newly
elected head of Interpol. Dissatisfied with voting weights in the
IMF, China has also created a new Asian Infrastructure Investment Bank, in which its veto is as crucial as that of the US in
the IMF. It did this because in 2010 the US Congress refused to
alter IMF voting weights – as both the Bush and Obama administrations sought – that left Beijing with the voting power of
France, an economy five times smaller than China's. In joining
various international clubs, China will seek to rewrite the rule-
books. Among the budget cuts China will demand of any
international agency it joins will be anything to do with protecting human rights. It will invariably seek to mitigate sanctions
imposed on rogue actors (when it does not actively subvert
them, as it has done with North Korea) and it will oppose

humanitarian interventions in the name of respect for absolute state sovereignty. Nonetheless, with Trump in the White House, China will present a plausibly moderate and reasonable face to the wider world, notably as a defender of free trade and international institutions. China has certainly offered to mediate disputes in regions where it has traditionally not been engaged. But some suspect this is primarily designed to bolster domestic belief that China is a world power. The results of Beijing's mediation offers have also been modest. At the same time, China has launched its vast One Belt, One Road (formerly OBOR but now ORI for short) development plan to build and connect infrastructure across Asia to the Middle East and Europe so as to boost growth and trade. It will also join two of the world's most powerful economies in Europe and East Asia, home to nearly three-quarters of the world's population and one-third of its landmass. With a projected investment of up to $150 billion a year, and perhaps $1 trillion in total, this will eclipse such earlier US-led ventures as the post-war Marshall Plan, whose $13 billion cost translates into $130 billion in current values.

If the US provokes a conflict with China (for provocation is not a one-way street) it is doubtful whether traditional US allies in the Antipodes, the Gulf, Europe or even Israel will be rushing to her support. No one in Europe wants a conflict with Iran either, were the Trump administration to arrange one as it huffs and puffs at various enemies.

This is a very present-centred book, since I am not a 'futurologist' and I lack the gift of prophecy. There is some history in it, mainly to get to the essentials of particular cultures but also sometimes to illustrate the irrelevance of historical analogies, which can often be actively harmful, but it is not a work of history. Writing about a story that is evolving has clear limitations, but is not necessarily problematical. While I emphatically do not think Donald Trump is like Hitler (and in fact devote some paragraphs to denigrating such comparisons), it is worth recalling that the best biography of the German leader was published in 1936, written by the journalist Konrad Heiden, who had fled the country two years earlier. Besides, Trump is just a symptom of some of the changes my book seeks to describe, so whether he reaches the end of his term or is replaced by Vice-President Mike Pence is almost irrelevant. Perhaps he will establish a dynasty, with Ivanka Trump taking over in 2024?

In what follows I seek to explain how we passed from the relative stability of 1989–2011/13 to the bewildering present of 2017. Although many people feel anxious and gloomy about the state of the world, I see grounds for optimism beyond the comparative rarity of famines, excepting those that are man-made in Africa and Yemen, in such things as ongoing agreements on climate change and nuclear non-proliferation.

The US economy is vast, innovative and diverse, with positive demographic trends, and the US is not in decline. Its democratic culture, robust press and rule of law will survive its current 'presidicament'. Authoritarian populism is currently enjoying an upswing, with the Russian version widely admired by fellow-travelling Western conservatives, but one only has to imagine the lives of ordinary people under such regimes, without the benefits of the rule of law, to dispel such fond illusions. Whatever the fate of the EU, Europe will continue to be a great civilization that affords most of its citizens a very decent way of life. It is not about to be transformed into 'Eurabia' by an 'Islam' that is bitterly divided itself, as some alarmists fear. Elections in Austria, the Netherlands and France (and the one in Germany in September 2017) have shown that there is nothing ineluctable about the populist wave, though after the resignation in May 2017 of the Austrian government they are not out of the woods yet. It is worrying that young people are among the chief supporters of the Austrian Freedom party, and that the Front National drew most support from people under forty. At some point, fresh people will find novel solutions to the current degeneration of mainstream politics on the left and right, and the challenge from insurgent populists whose electoral fortunes are more mixed than one sometimes imagines, judging from the AfD, the Finns and Ukip. They do not handle governmental responsibility very well, and their leaders may actually prefer lucrative careers as media celebrities. Perhaps the most urgent political task, assuming confidence is restored in immigration controls and economic growth returns, will be how societies will navigate the impending Fourth Industrial Revolution, which will massively disrupt white-collar work in ways already depressingly familiar to the 'old' blue-collar workforce and those who grow up among the wastelands it has left. Will greater resort to social media result in a revivified public sphere or atomized 'slacktivists' obsessed with one craze after another, while the political equivalent of meteorologists read the political weather and policies are adjusted before they have even been implemented? None of us will remain untouched by this.

While Africa and Latin America make crucial guest appearances, they are not central to this story, though a book which took them as a point of departure would be fascinating, of course, not least because European and US politics seem to be undergoing a Latin American phase. The perspective is not much indebted to my local optics, however intriguing British domestic politics may currently be, since the point is to describe multipolarity and how other global actors view the world and the major issues of our times. In the case of some major conflicts, I have deliberately included enough evidence to enable readers to make up their own minds, even if this means they will reach conclusions different from my own. As a political historian, I've included what I think people ought to know, by establishing the deep context of the countries and regions in narrative form, with special attention to how they interact with one another and view the world from perspectives that are very different from those of the West. Throughout I have used brief excursions along particular paths to colour the dry essential story, for example on the relationship between celebrity and politics, or how China magics up a Pacific island from a coral reef. Although the book includes plenty of human drama, I have deliberately avoided reportage-style 'human interest' story-telling in favour of analysis, numbers and facts which transcend the fate of individuals, the cannon fodder, so to speak, of much media reportage. Inevitably, then, this is an open-ended narrative. The conclusion points only to what I imagine will happen next, as 2017 becomes 2018, and then 2020. Anything more speculative is left to futurologists and prophets who might know better than I whether we are destined to enjoy the best of times or the worst. Remember the rest of Dickens's opening sentences:

> . . . it was the age of wisdom, it was the age of foolishness, it was the epoch of belief, it was the epoch of incredulity, it was the season of Light, it was the season of Darkness, it was the spring of hope, it was the winter of despair, we had everything before us, we had nothing before us, we were all going direct to Heaven, we were all going direct the other way – in short, the period was so far like the present period, that some of its noisiest authorities insisted on its being received, for good or for evil, in the superlative degree of comparison only.

1

Two Shocks That Made Our World 'Incandescent with Moral Clarity': The Post-Cold War Present

Saddam Hussein was the dictator of a medium-sized Middle Eastern country. He joined a series of such men, beginning with Iran's Mohammad Mossadeq and Egypt's Gamal Abdel Nasser in the 1950s and ending with Libya's Muammar Gaddafi, who were magnified into Hitler proportions before attempts were made to destroy them. This comparison is routinely made to demonize an enemy so as to preclude diplomatic resolutions of crises. Diplomacy becomes 'appeasement' or 'another Munich' as if the world were permanently stuck in 1938.[1]

Saddam's biographical details need not detain us. By 1979 he had achieved total command of the Ba'ath Party and Iraq, which the British had earlier cobbled together from three provinces of the Ottoman Empire. In 1980 Saddam led his forces into the costly and inconclusive eight-year war with Iran, in which he was backed by Western (and Gulf) powers against the Shia Islamic revolutionary regime of Ayatollah Khomeini. A quarter of a million Iraqis died, though a quarter of these were Kurds whom Saddam's forces killed, sometimes by using chemical weapons, for collaborating with Iran. Saddam's use of such munitions to neutralize Iranian 'human wave' attacks was a major spur to the Iranian decision in 1982 to revive the Shah's nuclear programme.[2]

In the war's aftermath, Saddam sought to liquidate $40 billion of debt to the Gulf monarchies by invading Kuwait, the smallest and nearest creditor. He declared it Iraq's nineteenth province. A 500,000-strong US-dominated coalition force assembled in

Saudi Arabia for Operation Desert Storm. The presence of Western troops in the Kingdom outraged zealous Saudis. Saddam was forced out of Kuwait by the swift US-led First Gulf War in January–February 1991, though not before igniting its oil wells and then violently suppressing uprisings by the northern Kurds and southern Shiites once back in Iraq. The First Gulf War vindicated about fifteen years of work by America's military leaders – led by General Creighton Abrams – on how America could overcome the ruination that the Vietnam War had inflicted on the US military and the deep divisions it caused in US society.

The successful campaign in Iraq also resulted in something whose importance becomes clear only in retrospect. An act of collective defence on behalf of little Kuwait had a 'good deed' tacked on to its aftermath. This entailed meddling in Iraq's internal affairs in perpetuity. 'Operation Provide Comfort' would see the US policing the skies over northern and southern Iraq for the next twelve years.[3]

Provided one watched only Western television news, the First Gulf War seemed like a teenager's video game. It inflicted more physical damage on Iraq in six weeks than the Iran–Iraq War had done in eight years. The UN's Martti Ahtisaari spoke of the 'near apocalyptic results', with a hundred bridges down, power stations destroyed and trains, TV and radio stations, flour mills and every type of factory pulverized from the air.[4]

Crippling UN sanctions, imposed originally in 1990 to prise Iraq out of Kuwait, were maintained to achieve additional goals which became ends in themselves: identification and destruction of Iraq's WMD programme, payment of war reparations and an end to Saddam's brutal repression of Iraqi citizens. Iraq could no longer import dual-use items (chemicals, fertilizers, pesticides) or agricultural machinery and water-purification systems, while an embargo on oil sales meant that Iraq could not easily import food and medicines. The UN itself estimated that a third of Iraqi children were suffering from malnutrition. Easily corrupted oil-for-food deals did little to alleviate the shortages of food and drugs, while UNSCOM's cat-and-mouse search for WMD ensured sanctions were maintained for thirteen years. US patience was running out too. In late 1998 President Clinton launched four days of bombing of supposed WMD sites. That December Congress passed the Iraq Liberation Act, for exiled opposition politicians had charmed many of their US colleagues into voting that $99 million be earmarked for the future over-throw of Saddam Hussein.[5]

This last gesture reflected aggressive lobbying by an ideo-logical claque that was never going to be satisfied with the demise of Soviet communism in 1990–91 or the business-first approach to Communist China before and after the bloody hiatus of Tiananmen Square. Pragmatic realism was almost as much of a sin in 'neoconservative' circles as the 'appeasement' they constantly denounced. For in many ways the neocons operated like a neo-Jacobin sect, though their backgrounds were often Trotskyite, in which compromise and nuance were anathema in a very unconservative way. Despite the neocons' moralizing posturing, they presumed that every right-minded person must agree, and were prepared to use all manner of dirty tricks to ensure that this was so. For instance, as the prominent political scientist Francis Fukuyama discovered when he broke with the neocons, they quickly ceased to regard ex-members as 'one of us'.[6]

The most visible figures in the movement include: Irving Kristol and his son William; Norman Podhoretz, Midge Decter and their son John Podhoretz, who run the journals *Commentary* and the *Weekly Standard*; journalists Charles Krauthammer, Irwin Stelzer (also a business adviser) and Max Boot; and Catholic public intellectual George Weigel, who adds theological heft. Others, including Robert Kagan, Ken Adelman, Daniela Pletka, John Bolton, Eliot Cohen and Elliott Abrams, operate in the interstices between think tanks and government. Their regular outlet is the editorial pages of the *Wall Street Journal*. The chief US institutional bastions of neoconservatism include such think tanks as the American Enterprise Institute, the Hudson Institute and the Henry Jackson Society. In the UK, the Murdoch press, the niche *Standpoint* magazine, the Henry Jackson Society (again) and the Policy Exchange think tank are the main outposts, with the utterly courteous journalist-politician Michael Gove as a link between all three. The Canadian-born

David Frum, whom we'll soon encounter, is a link between the US neoconservatives and the British element since he is chairman of Policy Exchange.

The neocons thought that preponderant US military power should be used to spread Washington's benign imperium wherever opportunity arose. In other words a Cold War strategy of containment was to be replaced by one of global messianic transformation conducted in a spirit of what Norman Podhoretz called 'incandescent moral clarity', something he shared with Robespierre. Under three successive presidents the claque never quite captured power, though not for want of trying and with some individual exceptions such as Richard Perle, an adviser to both Ronald Reagan and George H. W. Bush. The neocons were critical of Reagan and his two successors, believing that Reagan used military power too episodically and then struck deals with the Soviet 'evil empire', that Bush Senior and his advisers were amoral realists and timid in not finishing off Saddam Hussein entirely in 1991 and concluding that Clinton was only a 'halfway imperialist' after his botched humanitarian interventions in Somalia and Haiti and his casualty-averse reliance on air power alone in Bosnia and Kosovo. At first it seemed as if George W. Bush would continue this dismal record against a very visible backdrop of man's capacity for inhumanity. There was both an intellectual and geopolitical context to the ascendancy of the neocons under Bush Junior.

Francis Fukuyama's proclamation of the impending 'End of History' (or general convergence into the Western liberal camp) coincided with a messy decade of humanitarian crises, Balkan and Sudanese ethnic cleansing and genocide in Rwanda. The CNN television effect brought every atrocity into the Western living room, invariably without deeper analysis, not of 'causes', but of what 'doing something' – as reporters implicitly urged – might entail. The 'harrowing' images never incorporated the equivalent of a health warning on a cigarette packet or wine bottle regarding the perils of armed intervention should things not go to plan.

Such images assisted those elites who actively chose to expand Western democracy and the realm of universal rights, regardless of any retaliatory action this might provoke. Like it or not, other societies were going to be transformed, provided one could unearth even a small local constituency to support it, usually exiles with scant contact with their homeland. The feeling that after the collapse of Soviet-style communism the moment had come to expand democracy was felt across the US political divide. President Clinton's National Security Advisor Anthony Lake explained this shift in 1993: 'The successor to a doctrine of containment must be a strategy of enlargement – enlargement of the world's market democracies.'[7]

But then came the Al Qaeda terror attacks on 9/11. A new President who had promised to be humble and restrained in using American power, and who disliked the roles of Globocop and nation-builder in chief, had to man up to the mood of the hour. Bush was not a profound thinker and he was intellectually lazy. This left plenty of scope for older men around him who dealt in certainties in a persuasive way.

Americans were shocked by the tactic – homicidal, mainly Saudi, Islamists using hijacked aircraft as guided missiles to kill nearly 3,000 people – and by the dawning realization that enormous military power and ramified intelligence services had failed to protect them. Within twenty-four hours of the attacks President Bush asked his chief counterterrorism official to find out if Saddam was involved. 'But Mr President, Al Qaeda did this,' he replied. 'I know, I know but see if Saddam was involved. Just look. I want to know any shred.'[8]

Bush's speechwriter David Frum invented an 'axis of evil' between three unconnected hostile states, Iraq, Iran and North Korea (two of which were sworn enemies), though this was not grandiose enough. The next clarion call was to 'eradicate' evil from the world, something as surely futile as trying to rid the human mouth of plaque.* There was no end to what might be done after Saddam: 'we may willy-nilly find ourselves forced by

---

* Frum went on to be Chairman of the British neocon think tank Policy Exchange under its neocon director Dean Godson. Frum will be succeeded by Alexander Downer, the former Australian foreign minister and High Commissioner to the UK, later in 2017.

the same political and military logic to topple five or six or seven more tyrannies in the Islamic world'.[9]

But first a five-week campaign (involving only 400 CIA agents and American paramilitaries on the ground) expelled the Taliban who had hosted Al Qaeda in Afghanistan. This was a legitimate act of self-defence after the US was attacked. NATO contributed an International Security Assistance Force. But this was always a sideshow to a main event whose legality was much more dubious since it involved preventive war. In its seventeenth year, the campaign in Afghanistan is the longest in US military history and the Taliban are resurgent.[10]

Rather than focusing on Afghanistan, where Al Qaeda was based, the Bush administration turned to Iraq. For George W. Bush, this was personal. In 1993 the Kuwaitis had intercepted an alleged Iraqi-inspired plot – involving a male nurse and Basra whisky smugglers as executants – to assassinate Bush's father on a visit. In January 1998 fourteen leading neocons, led by Robert Kagan and William Kristol, had publicly written to Clinton urging him to overthrow Saddam; firing a dozen cruise missiles at Saddam's intelligence service headquarters, as Clinton did after the attempt on Bush Senior, was not the response they wanted.

Since vengeance is not a 'good look' for shining citadels on hills, the removal of Saddam was just one element of a wider transformation of the Middle East that was supposed to culminate, as if by magic, in a durable Israeli–Palestinian peace on the part of governments made answerable to their own peoples. The latter would no longer be distracted by regimes who used the existence of Israel for domestic political reasons.[11] Very helpfully, two smart-set media philosophers, the aristocratic Canadian Michael Ignatieff and the French millionaire Bernard-Henri Lévy, were more than willing to give this creed a plausible humanitarian rinse. In the UK the task fell to neocon hacks who lacked the celebrity these two brought to the cause. The cause and its execution had as much plausibility as shaking a kaleidoscope in the hope that it would produce a Raphael or Titian.

Saddam had stupidly opted for an Israeli-style 'ambiguity' regarding possession of WMD, despite Iraq's programmes having been discontinued. Both the military planning and congressional authorization that left the precise timing to Bush were in place by October 2002, though Paul Wolfowitz, the Deputy Secretary of Defense, had wanted to have a crack at Iraq within a week of 9/11. Despite reports from the IAEA and UNMOVIC (as UNSCOM became in 1999) that no WMD had been found, barefaced lies, based on doctored intelligence and the testimony of defectors linked to Iraqi exiles, claimed that Saddam had an active WMD capability and, moreover, links with the Al Qaeda terrorists who had attacked New York and Washington in 2001.[12]

The brazenness with which the Bush administration combined national self-assertion with supposedly high humanitarian ideals grated with European leaders such as Jacques Chirac and Gerhard Schröder, who imagined they had forsaken sordid nationalism for a higher level of European moral consciousness. Since their armed forces hardly counted in modern warfare, they could be ignored. Bush was almost torturously inarticulate, but he had a powerful voice on tap and one gifted with the faux passion of the courtroom. The British Prime Minister Tony Blair, a deluded idealist, fused his destiny with that of Bush on the realist grounds that the UK should always cling to the US as a means of self-assertion at the top table. 'Destiny,' he said portentously to Congress, which had awarded him a Gold Medal, 'puts you in this place in history, in this moment in time, and the task is yours to do'. In reality, as Stephen Glover later wrote in the *Daily Mail*: 'there is no special relationship', and Bush and Rumsfeld were indifferent as to whether the British came along for the ride.[13]

A swift and violent high-tech campaign collapsed Saddam's regime; looting and lawlessness ensued. This was not just a matter of making off with petty-cash boxes, but of rendering seventeen of Baghdad's twenty-three ministry buildings inoperative, as even the electric wiring was stripped from their walls. The total cost of looting was put at $12 billion.[14]

Mounting a shock-and-awe spectacle proved the easy part. The rather different activities of nation-building and state-building were tests the US comprehensively failed. There was a chasm between hatred of despotism – symbolized by statues of Saddam being toppled – and the deeper cultural resources needed to create a functioning democracy anywhere in the Middle East.[15] The terms of US engagement, and hence of America's entire foreign policy, were rewritten too. As Michael Mandelbaum, an astute foreign-policy expert, has said, the occasional hobby of interfering in the domestic affairs of other states became a full-time job, though recent US experience in Somalia, Haiti and the Balkans surely recommended restraint.

The future fate of Iraq was in the hands of a President who until 2003 was unaware of Shia and Sunni, and the 'Vulcans' – the collective moniker for Dick Cheney, Donald Rumsfeld, Condoleezza Rice and the neoconservative ideologues Paul Wolfowitz and Douglas Feith in the Pentagon – the lead agency in Iraq. The sobriquet derived from a statue in Rice's Alabama hometown of the Roman fire god rather than from Mr Spock, the wise alien on the Starship *Enterprise*. Spock would have been a better choice.

An occupation regime chosen for its ideological conformity, rather than expertise on Arab affairs, prepared for its task by reading about the occupations of Germany and Japan after the Second World War. This is an almost perfect illustration of how knowledge of the Second World War is unhelpful to contemporary affairs since both Germany and Japan were entirely floored and subject to huge occupation armies which soon had former mass murderers back in situ running the police in Bremen and Düsseldorf, not least because they were anti-communists. Such analogies, and the puritanically obsessive de-Nazification/ de-Ba'athification that flowed from them, were flawed, and impossible to implement with an army of occupation about a fifth the size of what might have been required had the analogies been even vaguely accurate.

Despite being founded on anti-imperialism, albeit with occasional lapses, the US seemed very like an empire by this point.[16] As a disdainful Bush aide explained to a critical journalist: 'We're an empire now, and when we act, we create our own reality. And while you're studying that reality – judiciously as you will – we'll act again, creating other new realities, which you can study too, and that's how things will sort out. We're history's actors . . . and you, all of you, will be left to just study what we do.'[17]

The generals who lead the vast US regional commands Cent-com, Africom, Pacom etc., which in the case of Centcom encompasses 500 million people, are akin to imperial Roman consuls. Occupied Iraq's two incoming imperial governors, L. Paul Bremer III and General Jay Garner, were not Arabists and had no experience either of a post-conflict society or of 'nation-building' – the talismanic term of the hour.

Callow Britons scooped up from the margins of NGOs and the Foreign Office latched on to the Americans, in line with the Macmillan-era conceit of playing worldly wise Greeks to dim American Romans. A few excitable historians urged the Americans to brush up on their knowledge of when Britannia ruled the darkies and the waves. The British had no influence on Pentagon occupation policy, despite their desperation to exhibit a largely one-way 'special relationship'. They have been aptly compared to people sitting in the second carriage of a train someone else was driving, while being dismissed as imperial 'lackeys' by more sceptical Europeans. Even their much-vaunted expertise in pacifying insurgencies with a softly, softly approach essayed in Northern Ireland became risible in the eyes of the Americans as the British Army was hounded out of Basra and Afghanistan's Helmand province.[18]

Intense sectarian violence erupted between Sunnis and Shias, exacerbated by a viciously effective Al Qaeda element that fused with bitter former Ba'athists, especially after Saddam was hanged in a basement of the Iraqi Ministry of Defence in 2006 by a late-night Shia lynch mob. Between the invasion and June 2012 an estimated 116,409 civilians were killed, according to the NGO Iraq Body Count, while US commanders revisited the history of French colonial counter-insurgency warfare so as to get a grip on a ghastly situation.[19]

US forces remained in Iraq under a UN Security Council mandate until November 2008, and thereafter under a bilateral security agreement specifying their withdrawal from the cities during 2009, and from Iraq by the end of 2011. When the last US combat units left in December of that year, having failed dismally to build a nation, the official fiction was that they left behind a 'sovereign, stable and self-reliant' Iraq. A total of 4,424

US military personnel had died in Iraq, with nearly 32,000 more wounded. In fairness, the US had fitfully functioned as a useful honest broker between rival Iraqi factions and tribes, and after peaking at 3,709 Iraqi civilian dead in October 2006, following a surge of US troops in January 2007, the *monthly* death toll declined to 500 in mid-2008 and then to around 300 thereafter. By 2013, two years after the US withdrawal, the annual death toll was 8,955, or an average of 746 per month.[20]

The Iraqi state is governed by a constitution approved by a referendum in October 2005, which, disastrously, transposed Lebanon's power-sharing arrangements onto Iraq, intensifying ethnic and sectarian divisions. It does not help either that the kleptocratic governing class (including the 325-seat National Assembly) are isolated, for security reasons, in the six square miles of air-conditioned luxury that is Baghdad's Green Zone which the Americans established within a former palace complex of Saddam's.

Shia, Sunni and Kurds vote along ethnic sectarian lines. Following the departure of US forces, the majority Shia supported the National Alliance, led then by Prime Minister Nouri al-Maliki. He was an activist in Dawa (the Call), and was arrested several times by Saddam before fleeing to Syria and then Iran, where during a seven-year sojourn he was close to the Revolutionary Guard and Hizbollah. He was allegedly co-responsible for a 1981 bomb attack on Saddam's embassy in Beirut in which the Iraqi ambassador and sixty people died. In 2006 Maliki was jobbed into the office of Prime Minister by the US Ambassador Zalmay Khalilzad, George W. Bush and Tony Blair, after a CIA analyst reported there was nothing to disqualify him. Maliki's previous job had been on a committee to purge Ba'athists, a policy he eagerly pursued as Prime Minister.

On coming to power Maliki expunged Sunnis from the bureaucracy, notably in the new Iraqi National Intelligence Service. As commander-in-chief he controlled both an army of a million men and the police force, while his cronies operated more sinister Shia sectarian militias. The most effective elements of the Iraqi army were deployed protecting Maliki himself. The collapse of this army during ISIS's initial rampage led to Maliki being ousted, under US and Iranian pressure, and his replacement in September 2014 by the engineer Haider al-Abadi, who some view as the last Prime Minister of a unitary Iraq.

Saddam's Iraq was not transformed into a bulwark of democracy and liberal economics (the dream of American neocons) that would then surge through the wider region so as to protect the security of Israel, a vulnerable state that is armed to the teeth. A much-weakened Iraq made Iranian and Saudi rivalry for regional dominance explicit in Lebanon, Syria, Yemen and elsewhere, as the next chapter will show, by inadvertently boosting the power of Iran. Prolonged US failure in occupied Iraq daily advertised the limits of US power. While there was much public war weariness – arguably contributing to the election victory of the faux 'isolationist' Donald Trump in November 2016 – most Americans still bought into an at once sentimental and aggressive militarism that had become pervasive under Bush. Trump does too. Invariably, the tuxedo-wearing classes at veterans' fundraiser gala events are not the parents of Hispanic and Scots-Irish boys who have had their limbs blown off in Afghanistan and Iraq.[21]

•

The Iraq debacle had even greater consequences in world affairs. Heavy-handed US intervention in Iraq and Afghanistan confirmed Russian suspicions that the new American-dominated post-Cold War order enabled the US to act like a rogue state under the flag of high principles. There was already a strong feeling in the Russian elite of having been double-crossed when their country was floundering.

President Bush Senior's Secretary of State James Baker had vaguely promised Soviet leaders that in return for allowing the reunification of Germany, NATO would not expand into Russia's former satrapies in central and eastern Europe, let alone the Baltic. Nothing was formally agreed, however, and the powerful Polish-American head of the Senate Ways and Means Committee would have certainly blocked such a move. With Clinton in the White House from 1993 onwards these decisions fell to his new team, first Warren Christopher and then from 1997 onwards

Madeleine Albright as Secretaries of State. One lobby consisted of the charismatic leaders of the newly liberated states of central and eastern Europe, who justifiably did not trust the Russians, as well as Germany, which wanted a buffer zone to its east. The second lobby were US defence industries which stood to make enormous sums of money selling the prospective NATO accession states US equipment like the F-16 fighter aircraft and whatever was needed to enhance interoperability with Western systems.[22]

Boris Yeltsin's Russia was to be reassured with a nebulous Partnership for Peace, which gave Moscow a seat, along with twenty-one other PfP nations, but no voice at the top table. The opportunity to use something like the Helsinki Conference on Security and Cooperation in Europe (CSCE) to recast both NATO and the former Warsaw Pact alliances was not taken. After calculating how many Polish, Czech, Hungarian American votes he needed the year before, in 1997 Clinton announced in Madrid that, at US urging, NATO would admit the Czech Republic, Hungary and Poland. They joined the alliance in 1999, and were followed by nine further states in the next decade, while Russia was excluded.[23]

While Western intelligence agencies desperately sought other lucrative missions such as combating drug traffickers or Russian gangsters, NATO needed a much larger role to justify enormous defence budgets. After the demise of the big red dragon, NATO rapidly discovered a jungle filled with poisonous snakes, conveniently on its own doorstep. In the name of humanitarian intervention, NATO was used to fight two wars inside former Yugoslavia, which had not attacked any NATO member and which was not part of the NATO area. Although Yeltsin played a role in bringing Serbia's murderous leaders to heel, the Russian public, and many of those waiting in the wings for Yeltsin to go, were deeply hostile to the transformation of NATO into a missionary war-fighting tool. One of them was Vladimir Putin.[24]

Russia (and China) suspected that, even in its diluted present form, the Responsibility to Protect (R2P) doctrine, adopted by the UN in March 2005, thinly concealed a Western Right to Intervene wherever it liked against weak states without major protectors.[25] This creed was backed up by vocal international

human rights lawyers and their NGO lobbies, who paradoxically would then denounce wars their own conceit had indirectly
fomented or, worse, had given perverse incentives to increasingly
brutalize before the US bombers arrived. As the public often
knows, impassioned calls to do 'something' are often as irresponsible as doing 'stupid shit', as President Obama would put it.[26]

By 2013 the war in Iraq had cost $1.7 trillion, with Bush
borrowing the money rather than raising taxes to pay for it. By
2050, when the big disability and pensions costs will manifest,
over a decade of war will ultimately cost the US between $4 and
$6 trillion, in line with how Second World War costs peaked in
1993. The lower figure would cover what the American Society
of Civil Engineers says needs to be spent upgrading America's
crumbling infrastructure.[27] These costs will coincide with, and
are dwarfed by, demographically induced health and social
security costs which by 2050 will leave a minimum $52 trillion
gap in funding, or roughly four times US GDP, unless Plan B is
to increase taxes by 150 per cent.

Such harsh facts have inhibited popular support for any
major overseas interventions, which under President Obama
shifted to a casualty-free (at least for Americans) war in the
shadows waged by special forces, spies and drones. The main
beneficiaries of war weariness were ultimately not the anti-war
demonstrators of the left, but the US nationalist, 'paleo conservative' and realist non-interventionist right, who regard any
Middle Eastern 'quagmires' as a waste of blood and treasure. Its
intellectuals know how to question such serviceable analogies
and clichés as 'appeasement', 'axis', 'credibility', 'present danger'
or 'threat', which were strewn along the paths to war, though
such voices are still marginalized in a transatlantic commen-
tariat disproportionately dominated by neocons. The latter
faithfully reflect the views of a few powerful newspaper propri-
etors rather than the few readers one might meet.

During the years after the invasion of Iraq and Afghanistan
much-vaunted American soft power also took a major hit. Much
of this was related to the dark sides of the 'Global War on
Terror', but the atrophy of the US political system, culminating
in the sordid election campaign in 2016 and the presidency of a

coarse billionaire reality-TV star, had its effects. Since authoritarian rival powers have no compelling model to offer anyone not beholden to their regimes, this constellation has left a dangerous space in what is otherwise a multipolar world, whose old structures need to be radically refashioned and revivified to ensure future stability.* But before we pursue these geopolitical themes, there is one further crisis (for it is ongoing) which also massively damaged Western hegemony.[28]

•

The second shock whose reverberations we are still experiencing had similarly longer-term origins: the financial crash of 2008 and the ensuing Great Recession as the financial meltdown mutated into the ongoing eurozone crisis.

In September and October 2008, the Western world's core financial system collapsed. Long after Bear Stearns, Lehman Brothers and Northern Rock are but a vague memory, the world has still not recovered, and the economic crisis has generated political responses that are equally disturbing. The major economies of the Western world remain between 15 per cent and 18 per cent smaller than they were in 2005–2006, blighting the lives and prospects of millions.[29]

Since the crisis was financial in origin it is reflexive to blame 'bankers', a term so undifferentiated as to be of limited use, a bit like blaming 'soldiers' for the mistakes of 'generals'. What happened was not simply a matter of individual greed, but a series of incremental failures that involved consumers, auditors, ratings agencies and regulators, central bankers and politicians. This is not to claim that everyone and no one was to blame, for inordinate individual greed played its part. Banks have not paid what are projected to be about $300 billion in fines for the fun

---

* US magazines such as *National Interest* and *American Conservative* often contain excellent critiques of the concepts used to justify foreign wars of choice. The neocon presence in British newspapers is especially odd (except as a memento of the 'special relationship'), since this organized and shouty claque has almost zero support in British society and scant traction anywhere else in Europe.

of it. The most egregious offences included deliberately subvert-
ing international sanctions on Iran, laundering money for
Mexican drug cartels and rigging the Libor interbank rate. Some
US justice agencies regard these fines as an alternative revenue
stream, especially if the banks are European like Deutsche,
HSBC and Paribas. The US case against Barclays for mortgage
security offences is just cranking into gear as I write while
Deutsche has been hit by another huge fine for illegal 'mirror'
trading operations with Russians.

Even within investment banks – the biggest villains – it is
important to make distinctions between the analysts, salespersons and traders, not to mention IT and personnel, those on the
corporate and equity sides, not forgetting the specialism of derivatives, and hierarchies of managers and executives, with each
division competing with the next, as well as with rival banks. For
many the day starts at 5 a.m. and ends at 7 p.m., much of it spent
watching charts, graphs and numbers on Bloomberg screens,
with constant instructions on the phones and office squawk box
from 7 a.m. onwards. Banking is not a job for life since under-
performance results in employers shedding entire 'deciles' as they
lop off the 10 per cent biggest failures or axe entire departments.
The mandatory unbundling of fees paid by investors for 'research'
by banks and brokerages could quite easily wipe out the entire
group called analysts, the small herd that reports on the performance of the same companies. Institutional failure also results in
mass layoffs, for it is untrue that bankers emerged unscathed
from the crash. In the wake of the 2008 crisis, RBS alone shed
41,000 jobs. Automation reduces headcounts too. But to understand what caused the financial crisis one has to look at the top,
which is where what the economist John Kay has called the
'financialization' of our lives commenced.

Important players sent key signals reflecting a combination
of complacency and laissez-faire ideology, doubtless after the
persistent interference of financial lobby groups. In contrast to
his sober predecessor Paul Volcker, the warning from Alan
Greenspan, chairman of the US Federal Reserve 1979–87, about
asset bubbles was so coded and diffident that markets shrugged
it off. 'How do we know when irrational exuberance has unduly

escalated asset values?' was the question he left hanging in the air as he concluded a speech in late 1996. He was referring to the inflating bubble in internet and technology stocks, which duly crashed three years later.

The turmoil caused by the 9/11 attacks required an infusion of money to shake loose a system that had seized up. Two rounds of tax cuts in 2001 and 2003 took $3.2 trillion out of the economy over ten years, and left Obama (who came to power in 2009) facing a $1 trillion annual deficit when he took office. Interest rates had also been cut to 1.75 per cent and by 2003 to 1 per cent. The jury is still out on whether Greenspan kept rates too low for too long, a question that need not detain us.[30]

Globalization has resulted in some economic convergence between rich and poor countries, but it has also heightened inequalities within them. It enabled finance capital to go where it would, often avoiding regulation and taxation in the process, which usually meant to places too poor to generate their own capital. Vast sums flowed outwards into 'emerging markets' (with crises in Korea, Indonesia and Thailand in 1997, Russia in 1998 and Brazil the following year) while the low-interest-rate regime coincided with, and was fuelled by, a vast glut of mainly Chinese enforced savings flooding into US government bonds.[31]

Unlike earlier financial crises, this was not a case of an unsustainable boom such as the internet stock bubble resulting in a sharp bust, though after the dot-com collapse hot money moved from technology stocks to complex mortgage-backed derivatives as investors sought out safe, fixed-income yield.[32] Growth in the major economies was roughly as normal in the five years before the 2008 crash. So much so that with what appeared to be stable, sustainable growth, the bullish Labour Chancellor of the Exchequer, Gordon Brown, repeatedly proclaimed an end to 'Tory' cycles of boom and bust, even though the New Labour government had bought into a differently moralized version of Thatcher and Reagan's no less moralizing belief in the virtues of free-market capitalism. Later others would speak of the 'Great Moderation'.[33]

But there was a fateful imbalance between countries that spent too freely – as if there was no tomorrow – such as the US, the UK and parts of Europe, and China and Germany, where spending was too low but where many people rent their homes and credit cards are comparatively rare. Speaking of which, the German word for debt is *Schuld*, which also means guilt. In the sinner group, cheap money sustained a consumer-credit and mortgage binge, especially as many people saw their wages stagnating and borrowed their way to the good life. Cheap credit encouraged consumers to shift the cost of living onto plastic cards and loans. Why not, since property prices seemed to always move upwards? Whereas the average US home had risen in value by an average of 1.4 per cent per annum in the period 1970–2000, from 2000 to mid-2006 annual appreciation was 7.6 per cent, and then 11 per cent in the final year's spurt before the crash. Amoral realtors, often touting mortgage deals on commission, like characters in the film *The Big Short*, pumped oxygen into this bubble. Then it burst. By 2011 average US house prices were 33 per cent below their peak, and one in four homeowners was in negative equity. Ten million lost their homes.

In a low-interest-rate environment banks and insurers sought novel ways to increase returns, by diversifying out of their core businesses. For that to happen, many checks had to be deliberately relaxed while the lessons of the earlier 'Savings and Loans' banking debacle in the late 1980s were ignored.

Governments competed to encourage their large financial sectors because of the corporation and income taxes (and ancillary employment) they would yield. Successive US administrations, including those led by Carter, Clinton, Reagan and Bush Junior, made their own contributions to what unfolded. Responding to financial lobbies acting on behalf of what were often major political campaign donors, they loosened regulation. One major effect was to encourage the creation of universal or 'mega' banks that fused retail and investment banking, by ending the mandatory separation of the Glass–Steagall Act regime that had prevailed from 1933 to 1999.

This was largely the handiwork of Bill Clinton, who in 1994 had already allowed interstate banking. The latter meant smaller, more prudent lenders who knew their customers and who were gobbled up by the likes of Citibank, Wells Fargo and Bank of

America, which could elude tight state regulation. Superficially this seems odd for a liberal politician.

Clinton was a 'New Democrat', part of the baby-boomer generation whose educational attainments (Oxford Rhodes scholar in Clinton's case) brought them close to the media and money elites even as they grew distant from the blue-collar unionized Democrat base. Their liberalism subtly shifted from what the state could do to a globalized philanthropy, in which interest in the domestic working poor shifted to a desire to eradicate disease and hunger in faraway places. The baby-boomer rock 'n' rollers were also in charge now. Symbolically, the Rolling Stones played a private eighty-minute set for 500 Deutsche Bank executives in Barcelona in July 2007. Singer Mick Jagger quipped: 'Thank you for having us. The best part is, it's [the band's $5.4 million fee] coming out of your bonuses.' In the new order, the plutocrats (especially those in Silicon Valley) were relaxed about gender, sexuality and race, while the old union core often had old-fashioned attitudes. Regardless of whether Clinton's cabinet was a kind of rainbow of hyphenated ethnicities, it had more million-aires than the cabinet of his ultra-patrician predecessor Bush Senior. And after raising more money from Wall Street than his Republican rival John McCain, Obama's cabinet would have more millionaires than that, while in turn the Trump admini-stration is full of billionaires.[34]

It was Clinton's former Goldman Sachs Treasury Secretary Robert Rubin, and his successor, former Harvard President Larry Summers, who pushed through an end to the anachron-istic 'Depression-era' Glass–Steagall Act with the Financial Services Modernization (or Gramm–Leach–Bliley) Act in 1999, thereby enabling financial holding companies to operate in many fields far from traditional banking. The justification was that otherwise US banks would not be competitive with big foreign players. Summers, it should be recalled, had knocked a third off Harvard's own colossal endowment by dabbling in derivative instruments. By 2005 Harvard salaries were frozen, ancillary staff were cut, and prestige construction projects were cancelled.[35]

Other Clinton innovations were to enable executives to take

stock options in lieu of pay, and to deregulate energy and telecoms firms, including Enron. Vast industrial companies like General Electric and General Motors also got in on the banking act, moving surplus cash onto the $12 trillion market for 'repurchase agreement' or 'repo' loans. Bear Stearns came a cropper after having to refinance $50 billion of repo loans every night. Cosying up to the 'filthy rich' as well as Bono, Fleetwood Mac and Nelson Mandela was all part of Clinton's 'triangulation' of Democrat Party politics, as was the $650,000 his wife would earn for three speeches to Goldman Sachs before losing the US election.

The aim was to grow the party's appeal beyond a shrinking unionized, industrial working class, to the new liberal profes-sionalized middle classes, while finding some common ground with a Republican-dominated Congress. The North American Free Trade Area or NAFTA was the ultimate expression of this approach, with globalization presented as being ineluctable, and 'change' as the new mantra. If American workers would not put up with twelve-hour shifts and stagnant wages, the employers could move the factory to Monterrey in Mexico.

In a vast country, things are more nuanced than that sug-gests, since those who produced computers, cosmetics, machinery and petrochemicals in Texas had a boom time exporting to Mexico. In Texan towns like Dallas, Fort Worth and Laredo 382,000 jobs, and another three quarters of a million through-out the US, depend directly on exports to Mexico.[36]

But in general terms, the Party of the New Deal had become the best friend of Wall Street. Speaking of which, a Blairite 'New Labour' cover version came to power across the Atlantic, fol-lowed by the Cameron conservative remix of that, as British politics degenerated into the equivalent of a pop song that mir-rored these American developments. A professional political class who knew pop music better than history spent their time essaying exciting 'counter-intuitive' ideas (many involving their new best friends in Silicon Valley) and playing games with their friends in the media, all the while becoming estranged from the people who vote every four years.[37]

Whether in Europe, Russia or the US, television has probably destroyed national cultures more than any other medium. Obviously there are exceptions, like *The Wire*, but even the good stuff, *Breaking Bad* or *The Sopranos*, merely celebrates dreadful people, amidst entire days given over to shouting, soaps and shopping or refighting World War Two.

Mark Burnett, a British former commando who served in the Falklands, progressed via posts as a nanny in Beverly Hills to pioneering a cheap form of 'reality' entertainment, with a show called *Survivor*, whose first season aired in 2000. Amateur contestants and cheap film technology meant that such stuff could be rapidly churned out. The Dutch variant franchise *Big Brother* simply exhibited contestants 24/7 in a communal house. The commando's version involved stranding sixteen lucky contestants on a Malaysian island so as to watch them suffer and then fall out. Burnett's TV show was such a success that he wrote a book, called *Dare to Succeed: How to Survive and Thrive in the Game of Life*. One day, he decided to film the finale of the run at a New York ice rink. Afterwards he chatted with the man who had allowed him to use this space, though he did not own it. The man was Donald Trump.[38]

Trump was and still is a larger-than-life figure, whose businesses included hotels, casinos and construction, which entailed close contact with men whose names end in vowels. Curiously, Trump would always use poured concrete in his buildings rather than structural steel, though other tycoons avoided the concrete since the Gambino and Castellano crime syndicates controlled its supply. Other close associates, such as Joseph Cinque, whose American Academy of Hospitality Services gave Trump businesses many awards, though the tycoon's daughter and butler were trustees, had back stories that included the monikers 'Joey No Socks' and 'The Preppy Don' together with three bullet scars on his midriff. Another long-time 'adviser', who spells his Russian-Jewish surname Felix Satter when it only had one 't' on his birth certificate, had convictions for ramming a cocktail glass stem into someone's face and for real estate fraud, though he did not go to jail.[39]

The commando and Trump hit it off so well that they soon

cooked up the idea of a new show in which teams of contestants would vie for the favour of a big businessman by devising money-making stratagems. Those who failed to impress Trump would be dismissed with 'You're fired!' To save Trump time and motion, the show would be filmed in a studio mocked up as a boardroom in Trump Tower. In a climate where people were worried about losing their jobs (many of which involved temporary contracts), such a show spoke to genuine underlying anxieties about how to succeed.

Commencing in 2004, *The Apprentice* was designed to 'paint' a picture of how 'beautiful American business is', as Trump volunteered to a credulous media. The winner would get a $250,000 contract to manage a Trump project for a year. No mention of advertising revenues of $700,000 per minute once the audience quickly rose to 20 million or of the 'product placements' such as fashion and perfumes branded by Ivanka Trump.

The main attraction was Trump himself, whose billionaire lifestyle was displayed in the opening sequences, with the O'Jays' R&B hit 'For the Love of Money' as theme song, despite Trump having been bankrupt six times and at one point having a net worth of minus $250 million. A mouthy New Yorker with vivid gestures, like the striking 'cobra' jab he used to fire the unlucky, Trump was good TV. But eventually the show was undercut by a strategic rival, hosted by the jailbird homemaker Martha Stewart, which sucked air out of the deflating original and audiences for the final series slumped to 4 million. But by then the show had served one vital purpose. It had made Donald Trump a national celebrity. He was quick to spot the uses of social media in a culture dominated by photographs of one's breakfast and the ubiquitous selfie as a means of bypassing the dead-tree mainstream press. But he is also a pathological narcissist and not alone in that. The more insignificant we become, corks bobbing on a sea of global forces, the more we must assert our presence, slowing death to a freeze frame of our every doing, and sharing each random thought and reaction with, in Trump's case, 34.6 million Twitter others.[40]

Media ownership has become one avenue to political power, as exemplified by Silvio Berlusconi and his Italian Mediaset empire, or the former policeman Thaksin Shinawatra, whose

Shin phone and TV group contributed to him becoming Prime Minister of Thailand between 2001 and 2006. But modern populists like Trump do not need to own the media, especially since they spend so much time accusing it of being corrupt or fake except when it is owned by such old muckers as Rupert Murdoch. Instead, they are adept at harmonizing their style to the manner already favoured by TV producers and directors, as anyone who has had any dealings with BBC news programmes knows. The latter prefer pithy soundbites and the maximum polarization of opinion. If you express bland balance on any issue to the 'researchers' who pick guests, you can be sure you won't be appearing, which some regard as a welcome relief. A few insults and a blazing row live on air don't go amiss either, which is why someone like Nigel Farage, who failed several times to become his party's second MP, seemed to be on TV every night. Social media amplify the performance. Farage's derogatory remarks to the leaders of the EU in the parliament at Strasbourg have made him a YouTube star all over the US, where he has latched on to the mega-celebrity of Trump like one of those pilot fish that attach themselves to sharks. Logically enough Farage's post-political career is with Talk Radio and Fox News.[41]

•

The entertainment industry was like froth on the surface of one of the biggest economic crises of modern history. Banks were central to what happened. The biggest of the new megabanks were 'systemic', meaning the whole economy could crash with them if they failed, unless the taxpayer picked up the tab first. The ten megabanks in the US had assets equivalent to 60 per cent of GDP, their UK equivalents in a much smaller economy were 450 per cent of GDP. Incredibly, Royal Bank of Scotland was the biggest bank in the world under its thrusting and later-knighted chief executive Fred Goodwin. This reflected a wider national hubris involving oil and financial services. Trading on the historic reputation of 'canny' Scots being good with money, Goodwin's RBS acquired the much larger NatWest group, sundry US asset management firms, and finally the sprawling ABN Amro. As a result of this corporate megalomania, by 2008 RBS had a balance sheet of £1.9 trillion, more than the UK's GDP, thereby (along with North Sea oil) indirectly fuelling the ambitions of the Scottish Nationalist Party for independent statehood.[42]

As the saying goes, the road to hell was also paved with good intentions. Clinton sought to make home loans available to people with non-existent or patchy credit histories. The US Department of Housing and Urban Development (HUD) was actively involved in promoting this extension of home ownership. Others with existing mortgages gambled, with the connivance of predatory lenders, on ever-ascending property values to extract more and more equity to cover their lifestyles since their wages and salaries were stagnant. Equity could be withdrawn from one's home to redecorate, buy a new car, go on a luxury cruise, or build a mini buy-to-let property empire.

Scrutiny of the relationship between loans, affordability and value vanished as banking degenerated into an industrial process involving the sale of synthetic financial products. Keen to outshine the performance of their glitzy investment banking colleagues – often short, bald, fat nonentities who became celebrities – humble retail-bank salesmen entered into the spirit of the times by tacking on such superfluous products as payment protection insurance (which rarely paid out) to various kinds of loans so as to earn commission. Why not replicate the trick by extending it to car loans and the like too, a present cause of concern about overheating?

Best of all, a vast 'shadow banking' sector grew apace, wherein the normal rules of bank capitalization no longer applied, and remoteness from the underlying assets was complete. This was like a mystery galaxy next to the known solar system. Those more mathematically gifted than me say that algorithms used by physicists to explore turbulence in water were misapplied to finance. Complexity inevitably benefited the finance professionals who could master the acronyms and jargon, though when stripped down to essentials, these things are not hard for any layman to grasp.

The bright sparks who engineered novel financial products called derivatives found creative ways to bundle mortgages into traded securities called CDOs or collateralized debt obligations, part of a $9 trillion sector which at its peak was 60 per cent of the entire US banking system. Nothing could go wrong since the bundles were aggregated from across the nation, thereby avoiding any localized house price crash due to flooding or a plague of termites. CDOs were like sausages. They included just enough meat and spice to mask whatever else was involved in the mix.

Ratings agencies like Moody's and S&P awarded these bundles AAA credit ratings, thus attracting, among others, staid German pension-fund managers who could not legally acquire securities without this top rating in a climate where low interest rates limited profitable alternatives. The ratings agencies earned about $200,000 per bundle of CDOs they rated, even if no one really knew what lurked in these bundles or how to price them. Ironically, in 2006 the IMF viewed Securitized Investment Vehicles or SIVs as a way of mitigating and spreading risk as so much money piled into mortgage loans: 'the dispersion of credit risk by banks to a broader and more diverse set of investors, rather than "warehousing" such risk on their balance sheets, has helped make the banking and overall financial system more resilient'.[43] Major ratings agencies have paid huge fines to atone for their dubious activities in 2008. For example, in early 2017 Moody's settled for $864 million, while Standard & Poor's paid $1.375 billion in 2015.[44]

The fusion of different cultures also played a part. In the US, a mega-rich class of Rockefeller 'old money' atoning for the sins of robber-baron progenitors was displaced by a more ruthless class of operator who had problems even understanding terms like 'fiduciary responsibility', especially if a corporate lawyer could parse them out of it. In the class-riddled UK the interaction of oiks and toffs was calamitous. In 1995 the Singapore-based rogue derivatives trader Nick Leeson singlehandedly collapsed the venerable Barings Bank after concealing trades that had gone disastrously awry. The better class of personage on the executive or 'C' floor did not have the incentive (or often, as in this case, the intelligence) to grasp the source of profits from which big bonuses came, beyond fitfully musing why the Singapore office of Barings was so remarkably successful.[45]

So it was with CDOs on a vaster scale not to mention credit default swaps, which were used to hedge against CDOs defaulting.

When a (British) Deutsche Bank senior executive was asked by a Commons select committee to explain what a CDO might be, he haughtily replied: 'I have not come before this committee as an expert in CDOs.' If this was the case with a senior executive, imagine how bewildered were the worthies who populated corporate boards of governance, by-products devised by thirty-year-olds with PhDs in maths or physics. Shareholders counting their dividends were not motivated to be curious either, though their subsequent losses should have made them so. Speaking of them, the average length of time fund managers held stock was four months rather than the eight years a few decades previously.

The CEOs of ramified companies regarded each moving part as a tradeable asset too, as they monitored the corporate stock prices which delivered their salaries and 'performance' bonuses, even if the firm lost money, sometimes rolling over repo loans just before quarterly results were published. Mandatory quarterly reporting was introduced in the US in 1934, but only in 2005 in the UK, and critics claim it encourages both short-termism and 'pump and dump' cynicism. The big losers were the shareholders. If executives were awarded stock options then the value of existing holdings was diluted. Best of all, although such options were an expense, there was no obligation to declare it for tax purposes, so that the likes of Cisco, Microsoft or Starbucks could seem far more valuable than they were.[46] During the nineties compensation for senior executives rose from an average $2 million to $10.6 million or by 442 per cent. Even when top US Treasury officials were debating emergency infusions of liquidity, or how to sell what was left of Lehman Brothers to a wary Barclays, the bank chiefs' first concern was how this would affect their 'compensation', despite their responsibility for the biggest financial disaster in modern history.[47]

Sins of omission were pervasive in 2008, though no lone rogue was involved. Europeans were dismissive of a disaster caused by 'Anglo-Saxon' capitalism, though their own regional *Landesbanken* and *cajas* and pension funds eagerly joined the Wall Street carnival, while also funding speculative property booms in Ireland and Spain. This would bring some of them to the brink of ruination, and some – like Northern Rock – went off the cliff, with the first British bank run in a hundred and fifty years. Auditors signed off on accounts that had huge risks buried in impressive-sounding financial instruments whose future returns were booked as current assets and profits on which huge bonuses were paid. By the time of the crash, the US derivatives market was worth $600 trillion.

The ecology of error was pervasive and involved institutional rather than individual corruption. Huge accountancy firms like Arthur Andersen combined humdrum auditing with lucrative consulting, despite the obvious conflict of interest, that would see Arthur Andersen's reputation (carefully established since 1913) destroyed by such corporate scandals as Enron and WorldCom which led to the loss of its operating licence. In the nineties its senior partners scooped trebled per-share payments, with the firm employing 85,000 people worldwide. Nowadays it employs 200 in Chicago, whose days are spent liquidating what remains of the business.

Then there were the regulators. In the US, regulatory agencies were both dispersed and proprietorial to each sector, especially after the 2000 Commodities Futures Modernization Act dispensed with the need to even keep records in some novel markets. Who was responsible for products that combined the features of equities and insurance policies, that in reality would have sat better with the gambling regulators?[48] Mervyn King, a former Governor of the Bank of England, has vividly explained how derivatives magnified the problems of sub-prime mortgages once the housing market slumped:

> It was rather like watching two old men playing chess in the sun for a bet of $10 ... and then realizing that they are watched by a crowd of bankers who are taking bets on the result to the tune of millions of dollars. The scope for introducing risk into the system rather than sharing it around is obvious. And that is why Warren Buffett described derivatives as 'financial weapons of mass destruction'.[49]

Lord King might have extended his metaphor. Imagine that some billionaires (perhaps the managers of our mutualized pensions) joined the outer throng of millionaires, taking bets in the billions on the bets of the millionaires, without being able to see the two chess players all the fuss was about. Why not blindfold half the gamblers too, or include a side bet about next week's weather or the Derby winner?

The combination of brokerage and corporate advice within investment banks resulted in analysts and salespersons boosting shares to the retail clients they were supposed to advise impartially, because their corporate banking colleagues one floor up or down represented those companies and wanted such business as share issues and IPOs from which they reaped huge fees – fees which dwarfed the modest sums that brokers buying and selling stocks yielded in an age of electronic trading. Metaphorical Chinese walls proved as moveable as the physical walls in banks that accountants could reclassify as moveable furniture to reap greater depreciation deductions in tax returns. But that was only the beginning of it.

If the brokers knew what they were selling was 'crap' then they could advise other clients (or their colleagues) to short the same stock, borrowing shares for a notional or margin sum and then collecting a fat profit when they sold at a lower price shares they had effectively rented. Realizing that CDOs were a giant Ponzi scheme, some enterprisingly sceptical bankers bet as much as $5 billion against them, with the knowledge of their managers, while their colleagues were still selling these securities to investors. The smart team at Deutsche Bank even wrote a song about the 'fools' still buying the 'crappy CDO business'. A treasure trove of retrieved emails illustrates the extreme cynicism to the losses of others that was common in such high-testosterone working environments. With a few exceptions including British novelist Sebastian Faulks's *Week in December*, imaginative fiction generally failed to describe this culture as you have to live the life to know it.[50] Their colleagues at Goldman Sachs were even more adept at 'directional bets', that is shorting CDOs which their clients were buying, or, as Senator Carl Levin asked Goldman's CEO Lloyd Blankfein during a hearing: 'Do you think [your clients] know that you think something is a piece of crap when you sell it to them and then bet against it, do you think they know that?'[51]

Some astute people saw the gathering storm clouds. One was

the real-estate speculator known as Sonny to reporter Ron Suskind, a billionaire with serious money invested with Lehman Brothers. In 2006 Sonny pulled his money while selling off his property portfolio. He knew. Say someone put a 10 per cent deposit down on a $900,000 Miami beachside condo in March 2006. Sixty days later the purchaser had to pay the balance of $810,000. Instead, he or she walked away from the deal, losing $90,000, which was much less than the $300,000 hit the condo's value had taken since the initial signature two months before. Alarms sounded in the strangest of places.

One Saturday three wealthy couples set off on a 110-foot yacht called *La Rêve* for a three-day cruise. The owner, Sal Nero, who ran a hedge fund, was plagued by calls out on the ocean. One of his guests, Robert Wolf of UBS, asked what was wrong: 'The nightmare is here,' Nero told him. The giant French insurance group AXA was not allowing clients to redeem funds while its triple A-rated CDOs plunged to worthlessness. While Nero disappeared to make a flurry of 'sell' calls, Wolf phoned a promising young senator, who was relaxing on his forty-sixth birthday. Wolf explained to Barack Obama, for it was he, that UBS, Lehman, Goldmans, Citigroup, Merrill Lynch, Morgan Stanley and Bear Stearns were all leveraged up to the gunwales with 'no margin, no cushion, to take a significant loss'. Wolf added: 'Listen, Barack . . . I think what we're looking at could be a once-in-a lifetime kind of thing . . . This is a market-driven disaster that could crush Wall Street and with it the whole US economy.' Obama hired him on the spot as an adviser. When the shit really hit the fan, Obama was one of those who genuinely grasped the enormity of what had happened. This gave him a huge advantage over his 2008 election rival, the elderly Republican John McCain and his clueless running mate Sarah Palin.[52]

When the party finally stopped, it seemed as if the global banking system would implode, as the scale of concealed obligations and interconnections became apparent in a blizzard of IOUs and banks stopped lending to each other or to consumers and businesses. It was like watching dominoes fall. The first to go was Lehman's, the fourth largest investment bank in the US. Next up was Merrill, a smallish bank, but a very large brokerage with the life savings of four million customers, which was merged with Bank of America ten minutes before midnight. Then Morgan Stanley, and at the top Goldman Sachs, each of these big three being three times the size of Lehman's.[53] In the UK, RBS had to be bailed out with £42.5 billion from the taxpayers, with more of their money shovelled into Lloyds Bank after it unwisely digested HBOS in a further example of striving for scale. The problem was that bank bosses could not keep a close eye on these ramifying empires, which often included relatively small but risky investment banking presences that could bring the entire edifice crashing down, rather as a tiny parasite can fell even the biggest beast. The eye for detail focused on corporate logos and office carpets or the colour of the bank's fleet of cars.[54]

•

Dealing with the recessionary aftermath of this colossal crisis fell to President Barack Obama, who wisely backed the measures George W. Bush approved in the dying months of his presidency, such as the $426 billion Troubles Assets Relief Program, or TARP, to buy up mortgage-backed securities, an initiative Republicans were resisting. Perhaps overambitiously, in power Obama sought to achieve vast health insurance reform (the health industry is 17.5 per cent of US GDP) at the same time as financial reform and dealing with a deep recession in which huge corporations like Chrysler and GM were going to the wall. Three bold initiatives proved too much for a leader whose flaw was to govern through a rolling seminar in which every decision was then comprehensively relitigated.[55]

As a professor of law, Obama assembled a team that resembled Kennedy's 'best and brightest', except Obama's team were cleverer and had not fought in wars. It included such key players as Tim Geithner and Larry Summers, who were predisposed to take the line of least resistance with the banks, brokerages and insurers responsible for the catastrophe. They continued to bail out the banks, with minimal demands in return, and injected an almost $800 billion stimulus into the economy, a sum which doubled when combined with stimulatory tax breaks. The Republicans did their best to counteract this by insisting on cuts to the federal government workforce during a recession. Unemployment climbed 10 per cent by 2009, not falling below 8 per cent until 2012.

A politically toxic and heavily symbolic moment came in March 2009 when, despite a massive $85 billion TARP bailout of money owed by insurance giant AIG to derivative trade counterparties, its financial services division executives awarded themselves $165 million in bonuses. This reinforced the view that there was one law for the rich and another for the struggling poor with their food banks.[56]

Obama's reforms of the financial services sector included establishing a Bureau of Consumer Protection as part of the wider July 2010 Dodd–Frank Wall Street Reform and Consumer Protection Act. This covered almost everything from ATM cards to predatory mortgage lending, though Wall Street's army of Washington lobbyists blocked several crucial amendments and Trump has said he wishes to undo Dodd–Frank. Nonetheless, derivative instruments were somewhat clarified by having to be exchange-traded, while regulation of the entire sector was streamlined, and there were mandatory stress tests of banks for systemic risk. As Martin Wolf has said, banking is now as regulated as the nuclear industry, for it can blow us all up too, though whether 30,000 pages of rules (in the US) or 60,000 pages (in the EU) help seems doubtful, since few can master them. It will clearly be odd if US consumers have greater access to relaxed credit than the Europeans or that the latter's banks will have to maintain greater capitalization reserves as a result of Trump's policies.[57]

With the aid of more armies of creative corporate lawyers, big finance quickly found new avenues to explore. One involved the $3.5 trillion of virtually free money from quantitative easing, which the banks could use to buy Treasury bonds yielding 3 per cent, though even more profit could be made by investing in emerging markets rather than a sluggish domestic economy. One hundred per cent mortgages are back and low interest rates can be defied by the latest bubble of peer-to-peer lending, in which the discredited banks are heavily invested. Reaching the un-banked poor is another potentially lucrative avenue. Car-leasing schemes may increase car sales, but they are also creating a huge

pool of used cars with depressed values. CEO pay is still stratospheric, and through corporate inversions, many US firms
simply took themselves overseas, whether for cheap labour or
to avoid 35 per cent corporation tax. Ironically, abroad and
especially in the developing world, they often benefited from
the free-market fundamentalism which the US had prescribed
through the IMF, even though at home successive Democrat
presidents had endeavoured to curb it.[58]

•

In August 2007 the European Central Bank published an analysis
of risks to global financial stability. It mentioned the US, China,
Japan, Saudi Arabia and Russia, but not Europe itself. In May
2008 the European Commission celebrated the ECB's tenth
anniversary. A glossy book reported that 'Governments coordinate their economic policies to ensure that all economies work
harmoniously together . . . The single currency itself acts as a
protective shield against external shocks . . . Existing coordinating mechanisms mean that decisions can be taken quickly and
smoothly – both in economic good times, and in the event
of economic and financial difficulties.'[59]

In 2008–10 the financial crisis exposed the inability of
Greece, Cyprus, Portugal, Ireland and Spain to refinance or repay
government debt (notably in Greece), or to bail out banks
that had overextended loans to feed property frenzies, as was the
case in Ireland and Spain. In a sense this was Lehman Brothers
again, but on a national scale. It had dire implications for
French and German banks that had purchased these government
bonds, as well as other banks that had lent to the banks buying
the bonds. Some banks had insured themselves against Greek
default, others had not, on the assumption that sovereigns tend
not to default, or that somewhere along the line taxpayers
would come to the rescue.

In the event, the European Central Bank and International
Monetary Fund stepped in, with the EU Commission in a supporting role, for at this point the governments of France and
Germany essentially took command. This was because only
sixteen of the EU's states belonged to the eurozone and the

Maastricht Treaty rules prohibited using the EU's relatively small budget to bail out countries. The IMF was encouraged to take part in order to bring a less 'political' technocratic and international approach to the party, although poor African states soon balked at bailing out countries whose living standards their own people could only dream of.[60]

The debt crisis was amplified by the rigidities of the common currency or euro, the most fateful big push on the part of euro enthusiasts. The ancient Roman denarius was often invoked; the failed Latin Monetary Union (1865–1914/27) was less familiar. Long in gestation, with such failures as the 1970 Werner Plan discarded along the way, monetary union was given added urgency by German reunification in 1989–91 as the German Question returned with a vengeance, after the abrupt demise of the predictable Bonn Republic. An American friend has wittily compared it to the dance duo of Fred Astaire and Ginger Rogers, in which it was said he gave her class and she gave Astaire sex appeal. In this case, the French conferred political respectability on Germany, while Germany's economic power amplified France's diminishing international influence.[61]

Paradoxically, the more the Germans tried to reassure their anxious neighbours that the leopard had changed its spots, the more some suspected a repeat of Chancellor Gustav Stresemann's tactic in the Weimar era of restoring German power through its apparent diffusion. In line with the thinking behind the initial 1951 European Coal and Steel Community, Germany would relinquish her Deutschmark currency so as to win French acquiescence to her becoming a more powerful nation of 80 million people without reviving the German Question which since the time of Bismarck had resulted in three major wars, two of them global.

Currency union was the handiwork of a very small technocratic elite working according to the incremental *méthode Monnet*, named after the French visionary fixer Jean Monnet, taking one step backwards, or sideways, and two steps forward. Although this was very much an elite project, ordinary people were told it would ease their travels since no currency needed to be changed, and once in the Schengen Area there was no need to show an ID card or passport. Businesses large and small would be freed from complex exchange rate calculations, even as they were smothered by EU regulations.

Sincerely felt but irrelevant rhetoric silenced expert exposure of obvious pitfalls which occurred under a regime in which countries lost the ability to set exchange or interest rates for themselves. Another key issue that was ignored was how such a currency bloc would react to an asymmetric shock to one or all of its members, if there were no fiscal unity and transfer mechanisms to compensate an entire country, as there are with distressed regions within properly sovereign states.[62] The shock duly came about as demand for the bonds of weaker economies drove down the interest rates required to sell them, thereby encouraging borrowing on a colossal scale. When investor sentiment turned, the bonds of 'peripheral' states became harder to sell, and the gap between their interest rates and the rates on the most creditworthy bonds (Germany's) increased sharply. This brought northern European banks that had purchased the bonds of the 'peripherals' to the brink of ruination. These underlying economic realities, about which Europeans were warned, were camouflaged with much grave and vague talk about avoiding a regression to the era of major European wars, as well as the prospect of establishing a benign and virtuous soft superpower to rival the harder-edged US or China. Each EU advance involved lawyers bending international treaties to their maximum limits so as to avoid anything as messy as a popular vote. When referenda were held, they were often rerun until the 'right' result was achieved.[63]

Monetary union between the original eleven member states began with the adoption of a common currency peg in 1999, and after a period of convergence, physical notes and coins were introduced on 'E-Day' or New Year's Day 2002. Political imperatives invariably meant that strict convergence criteria were relaxed, as a unified Germany itself had done in 2001, 2002 and 2003. Though the Maastricht Treaty rules for euro adoption stipulated a maximum 3 per cent budgetary deficit and debt no greater than 60 per cent of GDP, Italy joined despite a 7.7 per cent deficit (in 1995) and a debt to GDP ratio of 117.4 per cent in 1997. Having been admitted to the EU in 1981, so

as not to exclude the land of Aristotle and Plato, as Valéry Gis-
card d'Estaing insisted, Greece adopted the euro in 2001–2002
after the 'magician' in charge of its national statistics agency
transformed an 8.3 per cent deficit into a 1.5 per cent deficit by
disappearing the losses of the state railways and arms purchases
– Greece being the fourth largest importer of arms in the world.
Eyes were averted from the corruption and political clientelism
of Greece, not to mention that it did not have a forestry or land
registry and tax collection was nugatory.[64]

Although the German government did indeed relinquish the
DM for political rather than economic reasons, it also ensured
that its version of fiscal prudence (the budgetary thrift of a
stereotypical Swabian housewife) was included in the DNA of the
European Central Bank. The German creed combined the social
market economy (worker participation on company boards, for
example) with a zealotry about rules that largely reflected Germany's catastrophic experience of hyperinflation in the early
1920s. The very different roles of the Bundesbank and the Banque
de France also illustrate the cultural divide between a federalized
Germany, where the Bundesbank is very powerful, as central
banks are in Switzerland and the US, and a highly centralized
France where the national bank is under political control.[65]

The European Central Bank had a much more restricted
remit than the US Federal Reserve and, more importantly, the
European Union has no equals to the range of US federal agencies able to intervene in ailing states. The politics of pork ensures
that vast Pentagon money can be spread around even the most
improbable of places, while the Federal Deposit Insurance Corporation ultimately bails out banks.* But then the US really is a
nation-state.[66]

The terms of joining the euro area also incorporated the
crucial German stipulation that it was not a 'transfer union',
meaning that rich countries like Germany and the Netherlands
were not going to bail out their more profligate southern neighbours. Hostility to a transfer union was rife among German

---

* Many Europeans will be wondering why so many US inner-city areas
resemble Beirut on a bad day, of course.

taxpayers, and was independently guaranteed by Germany's powerful Constitutional Court, though Germany itself had bent deficit ceilings when it suited.

Reuniting Germany on a 1:1 Deutschmark/Ostmark basis proved massively costly, not to mention modernizing the old GDR, which eventually required a special solidarity or 'Soli' tax. This meant that, unlike previous hegemons such as the US with its reconstructive Marshall Plan, Germany refused to write off the debts of others. Though it is also important to note that German economic thought (and policy) was dominated by belief in the centrality of rules to free markets, in accountability and responsibility, in the risk of moral hazard when bailouts encouraged more reckless borrowing, and that a bit of pain is necessary to recovery. German moralizing has been somewhat undercut by widespread evidence of 'Vorsprung durch Cheating' in several sectors.[67]

One of the reasons for the indebtedness of the European periphery was the huge trade surpluses Germany accumulated. Germany had undergone structural reforms under Chancellor Gerhard Schröder in the early 2000s (the so-called Hartz I–IV reforms) whose effects were to liberalize Germany's labour practices in a more competitive direction, just as the euro made German products relatively cheap. The Germans also produced high-value goods like luxury cars and machine tools, which individuals and companies aspired to buy, whereas much of southern Europe faced cheaper competition from China. Speaking of which, Germany was never excoriated for 'dumping' Audis and BMWs in the manner of China's cheap-as-chips furniture, toys, TVs, screwdrivers and hammers.[68]

Since the Germans refused to pump up their own consumption while importing more from the peripheries, Germany duly built up huge trade surpluses which were then lent on easy terms to the European periphery to finance expanding fiscal deficits. Not only German banks benefited. So did construction companies that put in a lot of modern infrastructure, or German arms firms which targeted Greece's relatively large defence budget. Although Germans denounce Greek corruption, bribery was involved when Ferrostaal won a Greek order for four diesel-electric submarines with Howaldtswerke-Deutsche Werft. The corrupt Greek socialist Defence Minister involved, Apostolos Tsochatzopoulos, was eventually jailed. It was discovered that €1.5 billion had been skimmed off arms contracts and Ferrostaal were fined €140 million. After Greece went into meltdown, German corporations (which sometimes had major regional government shareholders) grabbed cheap assets in fire sales and the Chinese swooped in too on the docks at Piraeus.[69]

More than a decade in gestation, the euro became currency in 1999 before either fiscal or a politically inconceivable political union had been achieved, in disregard for the evolution of the United States of America, which to some European federalists was the rival model to be improved on. This flawed element of a European project whose solution to any problem or setback was always 'more Europe' made it impossible for governments to devalue their way back to competitiveness, while the absence of common fiscal institutions made it impossible to direct funds to distressed countries, as the US federal government would do if there were mass unemployment in the Midwest. Language barriers also meant that there was much less worker mobility than is common in the US, though the UK became a little like Texas, which acts as 'America's America' in the job market. Exiting the euro (for which there was no formal provision) was widely seen as likely to result in a general financial catastrophe. Although only nineteen of the twenty-eight EU countries are in the eurozone, and some European states are not in the EU, it was feared that if the euro imploded, the European Union itself would collapse or regress into a pure trading association.

Faced with popular hostility towards a project which, like the EU itself, had been suspicious of democracy from its inception, adding the nation-state to the list of bad things to be overcome, the EU Commission has so far rescinded laws designed to prohibit ecologically unsound coffee machines, kettles and hairdryers while adding a modest pan-European investment scheme that depends on private sector multiplication. Far better experts than I have ruminated on Greece or Germany (or both) leaving the eurozone, or of it being divided into hard northern and soft southerly bi-currency zones, an E+

and an E–, so to speak or in the first case a 'neuro'. We'll come back to that and the political effects in the final chapter.

Inertia and muddling through have been the preferred solutions, not least because Europe's countries do not have synchronized election systems, never mind common financial institutions or a common government. Someone would pay a heavy political price if their own people were the losers of radical reform. How could any German chancellor explain that it was the Germans' turn to take a hit, or a French president that France was about to lead a southern second-division euro? Leaving aside the political sensitivities of where to 'put' France, after the Anglo-Welsh vote for Brexit in June 2016, the EU feared a cascade of Grexit, Frexit, Italexit, Nexit and so on, though with the possible exception of Italexit this has become a receding moral panic.

The management of Greece was transferred from its succession of struggling dynastic centrist left or right parties to a 'troika' comprising the European Central Bank, Europe's Finance Ministers (Ecofin) and the IMF, which increased the perception of foreign dictation, especially since the Germans seemed the most implacably legalistic about eurozone rules. Use of the Russian-derived epithet was dropped in favour of the more anodyne 'the institutions'. The experience of foreign dictated austerity, with no economic improvement in sight, also undermined the attractions of a future common government, for manifestly the voices of some powerful countries would count for more than the minnows.

Inevitably, the hard left (and their hard-right nationalist ANEL partners) came to power in Greece in January 2015 on a wave of popular despair and resentment and were then repeatedly re-elected to defy the troika. The new Prime Minister, Alexis Tspiras, imagined he could reverse austerity and get some of the debt written off, while Greece would remain in the Eurozone which the majority of Greeks wanted. Some of the Syriza hardliners wanted to bring about a general overthrow of western capitalism from their peripheral Balkan bastion. Although they often talked darkly about a Greek deep state, this did not include the Communist trades unions and militant students on their own side who eagerly invoked 'the people' so as to marginalize any Greek supporters of the EU as the last hope of an unreformed Greek polity. The latter were traduced as 'collaborators', 'fifth columnists' and 'traitors' who went along with the troika's 'fiscal waterboarding'. Syriza managed to reduce Greece to the status of Venezuela on the Aegean, as withdrawals from ATMs were rationed to €60 per day. After following the Greek crisis every day for months, I can report that the war of nerves has left me with a twitch at the mention of Yanis Varoufakis or Euclid Tsakalotos that makes me resemble Herbert Lom's Inspector Dreyfus in the Pink Panther comedies. In the end the vainglory of Varoufakis and Syriza's unpredictability was their undoing as they became all too predictable to Germany's Finance Minister Wolfgang Schäuble, who spoke of Greece having a 'time-out' from the Eurozone and meant it. Greek debt currently amounts to €320 billion, or 180 per cent of GDP, and the repayment schedules stretch into the 2060s. Ordinary Greeks have probably seen about 10 per cent of the unimaginable sums deluged on debt repayment.

It suited many to focus on Greece, especially after its naive Syriza politicians were pitted against the stolid likes of Jeroen Dijsselbloem, 'Eurofin' ministers' chair and Dutch Labour Party Finance Minister, and the redoubtable Schäuble, the latter an avid federalist. In Greece, black marker pens were used to give images of Merkel and Schäuble added Hitler moustaches. National stereotypes, not all of them wrong, resurfaced. German politicians were indignant about 'Greek' clientelism, fraud and tax dodging that appeared almost daily in *Bild Zeitung*, as well as talk of a German 'Fourth Reich' in its equivalents in Greece and elsewhere. Syriza politicians even managed to stoke domestic opposition to agreements they had solemnly struck to get more bailouts, a game that continues as I write, while the courts have given suspended custodial sentences to those few Greek statisticians who dared to expose how a 15 per cent deficit had been massaged down to 3.7 per cent by less scrupulous colleagues.[70] There was less moralizing talk about Finland, where there was no clientage and corruption but whose economy contracted by 8 per cent after the decline of forestry and Nokia, necessitating a devaluation that membership of the euro made impossible. Ireland had also practised fiscal responsibility before a housing bubble driven by bank lending policy triggered a mini version of what happened in the US after 2008.[71]

While Greece, Ireland and Spain underwent stringent austerity, the ECB joined the US Federal Reserve, the Bank of England and the Bank of Japan in massive programmes of quantitative easing. Unimaginable sums of electronic money were injected into their financial systems, while interest rates were kept low in the hope that this would spark a twitch in the equivalent of a patient in a coma. So far the results have been modest and patchy, with low growth and persistent unemployment, though some foreign investors are being lured back. Average unemployment in Greece is 23 per cent, rising to 44 per cent in the 15–24 age cohort. A fifth of the population lack such basic services as heating or telephones. Fifteen per cent of people live in dire poverty, eating from bins and sleeping on benches or in doorways. In rural areas, buses have disappeared along with clinics and schools. Handfuls of elderly people comprise entire villages. Although pensions have been lowered and taxed (and VAT on food increased to 24 per cent) multiple generations have to live on their €300 a month.[72]

There has been success in Ireland, and parts of Italy and Spain, but one doubts whether their young emigrants would agree. Like an overused drug, QE may have reached its palliative limits. It also primarily benefited ailing banks rather than struggling people. By 2015 non-eurozone Europe had a GDP 8.1 per cent higher than in 2007, and US output has risen by 10 per cent. Eurozone GDP had risen by 0.6 per cent between 2007 and 2015, and only by an annual average rate of 0.8 per cent in Germany, where both poverty and income inequalities, though a world away from the hungry children and begging pensioners of Greece, are more evident than outsiders often realize.[73]

•

A balance sheet recession has proved more insurmountable than the boom-and-bust business cycle recessions of the past. An excess of debt on the books, even though, as in the case of Greece, it will never be repaid, led to Mexican stand-offs between creditors and debtors, and an outbreak of national stereotyping as the rhetoric grew heated. Any signs of recovery are so fragile that central bankers hardly dare to shift interest rates by even minor increments and some countries have negative rates. Germany's non-financial sector has built up €455 billion in savings because of anaemic global growth and multiple geopolitical risks.[74]

Punitive austerity policies blighted the prospects of entire generations of young people. Europe's secular nineteenth-century shift from the countryside to the cities went into reverse, especially in countries where multiple inheritance within extended families leads to part shares in ancestral village homes, as people could no longer afford to pay urban mortgages and rents. In multigenerational households adult children and their parents lived on the grandparents' pensions (which were ruthlessly slashed), those in Greece subsisting on fruit and vegetables rather than fish and meat. Half a million Greeks emigrated. The desperate and enterprising sought a new life, and not just in London. Some desperate young Portuguese left for Brazil or Mozambique, in a bizarre reversal of colonial experiences.

Although the baby boomers may go to their graves in relative comfort, the crash has heightened intra-generational inequalities that may prove enduring. Age joined such fractures as gender, race or sexuality that had already split the traditional class-based politics of the old left. Anger about the absence of transgender bathrooms or the latest campus hysteria did not cut it with the long-term disadvantaged of Pennsylvania, or people whose definition of being poor is being told by the boss when to pee.[75]

The perception that wealthy elites (the wealthiest 1 per cent) had prospered from globalization – and indeed from the bailouts – created a political backlash in the shape of left- and right-wing populisms, to use a term that, while having real historical roots (in the US), is sometimes seen as patronizing and unsatisfactory. But the fact remains that in the US by 2016, median household incomes had not risen since 1999. Many Americans favoured protectionism to insulate angry or disadvantaged people from powerful global forces such as migration, digitization and the tyranny of technocracy, though in the 2016 US presidential election Trump's supporters were marginally better off financially than Clinton's. Many of them were angry about the ways in which equality had supplanted reciprocity, whereby you have to contribute to social security and welfare schemes before you are entitled to take something out. That obviously mainly applied to recent migrants.[76]

People rooted in 'somewhere' revolted against people who could have been from 'anywhere', as David Goodhart, founder and former editor of *Prospect* magazine, has written. The 'country' party in various countries rejected the precious and pretentious concerns of metropolitan rather than 'court' elites, who in their preoccupation with 'humanity' seemed clueless about fellow countrymen who might have been from another planet.* The media, universities (and most pollsters except for those in France) proved incapable of accurately predicting this earthquake since they were part of that elite too.[77]

This conflict has led to politics in Europe and the US assuming an oligarchic flavour more usually associated with Latin America, charismatic outsiders adept at media performance (notably on TV) denouncing the old Establishment and questioning the probity of fundamental institutions, from central banks via the courts to the mainstream media. Even the trustworthiness of election results was impugned, especially after the Russians began meddling in them. In March 2017 the Dutch electoral agency insisted on manual counting to prevent the Russians interfering with electronic tallying. Ironically, much of Latin America is gradually eschewing this same populist model.[78]

The financial and eurozone crises also went global. Waves of money that had flowed into emerging markets between 2003 and 2010, as an alternative to diminished returns in the developed world, have washed back, while what are often hydrocarbon mono economies have been further hurt by the collapse in the price of oil and natural gas from $110 to around $50 a barrel.

---

* There was also a disconnect between study of the past and a present to which the past may not be much of a guide anymore. Much modern European history is 'mediated' to ordinary Americans by scholars whose primary emotional focus is fascism, Nazism and the Holocaust, though there are obviously excellent specialists in fields like France, Germany, Spain or Russia. Judging from the resurgence of the populist right (and a neo-Nazi subculture and the American 'alt-right'), decades of academic work on these subjects has not served us well if its aims were immunization.

The downturn of commodity super cycles has more glaringly exposed the corruption, graft and inequality that wealth based on politically mediated access to extractive commodity rights concealed. This sparked political crises in several countries including Brazil, Chile, Mexico, South Africa and Venezuela. In China, where various bubbles have built up in banking, housing and the stock market, so much money has been sloshing around what is a highly unequal society that the Communist Party has been running a major anti-corruption drive lest ordinary people become restive. In a bold departure, the Party has even dramatized this subject on television.[79]

Some Western hedge-fund tycoons predict an 'apocalyptic' denouement to China's giddy rise, but, so far, it is the hedge funds themselves that are undergoing an apocalypse.[80] Their fusion of high fees and failed bets has resulted in mass withdrawal of money by endowment and pension funds, with the 'hedgies' transformed into private offices that can invest only their own money. Contrast their hubris with Chinese Vice-Premier Wang Qishan's cool observation to US Treasury Secretary Hank Paulson about the financial crisis: 'You were my teacher, but now here I am in my teacher's domain, and look at your system, Hank. We aren't sure we should be learning from you anymore.'[81]

The American Century, which Henry Luce proclaimed in 1941, proved to be a short one by the second decade of the twenty-first. Some believe that Pax Americana is over. Disastrous aftermaths of wars in Afghanistan and Iraq (as well as Libya) ended the passing delusion of a world dominated by a sole superpower, in which the US could throw its weight around with impunity. The economic realities of the Great Recession and the imminence of an 'entitlements' crisis, as more baby boomers enter old age with fewer workers to support them, mean that the US will not be able to sustain the expansive 'national security' strategy of the decades between 1945 and 2011, especially its luxury-extra humanitarian nation-building and preventive war variants before and after 9/11.[82]

With US self-belief punctured, and the country turned inwards, other actors have become more assertive on the world stage, with the G20 and G2 (China and the US) displacing the G7 as the key forums, and China and Russia demanding roles commensurate with their economic might and/or quest for 'considération' and respect as great powers.[83] It is important to stress that their community of interest is limited and that they are also rivals with long histories of mistrust. Attempts to insert a wedge between them, as Japan's PM Shinzo Abe did in December 2016, when his high hopes of a Putin visit yielded very little, and which Donald Trump is likely to try too, are probably going to disappoint.

Russia proved to be more than 'Upper Volta with nuclear weapons' – the colonial era name for the impoverished African nation that is now called Burkina Faso – under the Mephistophelean President Putin. China's rise is no longer occluded. It wants to play a bigger role in existing global institutions, bidding to take over running UN peacekeeping operations while creating rival organizations that operate on its terms. In January 2017 President Xi Jinping staunchly defended globalization while offering to lead the struggle against man-made climate change whose reality Trump denies. That the Chinese see value in doing this, and by and large benefit from the international economic system, is probably the most positive feature of our times, even if a rift between Europe and the US may be one consequence.

Some have claimed that it is the liberal democracies that are in retreat in a world of advancing authoritarianism and demagogic left and right populism, though in practice Chinese and Russian market authoritarianism do not appeal in the West or beyond the ranks of fellow authoritarians. In one sense, the end of the Cold War advantaged Russia since it became a more slippery ideological opponent. The outgoing President Obama noted acidly that Putin's foreign fellow travellers would include about a third of the supporters of the erstwhile party of Ronald Reagan: 'There was a survey some of you saw where – not this just one poll, but pretty credible source – 37 percent of Republican voters approve of Putin. Over a third of Republican voters approve of Vladimir Putin, the former head of the KGB. Ronald Reagan would roll over in his grave.' For, in a sign of how strange these times are, it is true that many on the Western right do not conceal their admiration for the socially conservative and Christian Putin as he pursues Islamists 'into the shitter' to kill them and poisons his enemies in the centre of London. The evangelist Billy Graham's son is now an honoured guest among Orthodox circles in Russia, while the FSB has helped to establish gun ownership associations so as to better liaise with their friends in the National Rifle Association.[84]

While Russia and China (and others) are rapidly modernizing their armed forces, to the point where they have key deterrent capabilities in cyber, space, and missile technologies, a fiscally strapped West has had to make defence cuts, with few NATO countries meeting the desired percentage of GDP minimum expenditure. This has deepened the mistrust between Americans, who contribute 70 per cent of NATO's budget, and Europeans, who want to spend money on education, health and welfare. There might be more intra-European mistrust were Germany to actually spend 2 per cent of GDP on arming herself, for the neighbours have keen memories. NATO certainly will be in trouble if 490 million rich Europeans fail to pay to defend themselves against a Russia that has one-third of their combined population and a ninth of the EU's joint GDP, but which could end up dominating a fractured post-EU Europe, which both Putin and Trump wish to see.

Perhaps 'the West' with which we began does not really exist any more, despite plaintive and invariably British romantic yearnings for an 'Anglosphere' which may perplex all those many African-American, Hispanic and Asian Americans.* And South Africa was dropped from the sphere, too, once it got black majority rule. The crises of Iraq after 2003 and the Great Recession after 2007 have had massive repercussions in the West. But, as we shall see, many other regions were also undergoing their own turmoil.

---

* The term 'Anglosphere' was dear to the likes of Russian historian Robert Conquest, who died in 2015. As is usual, the devotees of a cult (Eric Hobsbawm was another object of veneration) have all the demerits of their guru without the talents of the exemplar. It also involves such sleights of hand as imagining that India is a democracy rather than a place where a lot of people vote.

2

Gulf Rivals

The violent removal of Saddam Hussein in 2003 simplified the balance of forces in the Gulf region by removing a negative element who had had his geopolitical uses. A 1983 handshake with special envoy Donald Rumsfeld, who brought a pair of golden cowboy spurs for the Iraqi dictator he wished to arm against Iran, was one symbol of this.

The 2003 invasion, which Rumsfeld masterminded, exposed the main rivalry around the Gulf, and throughout the Middle East, between Iran and Saudi Arabia. They are waging proxy wars in Bahrain, Iraq, Lebanon, Syria and Yemen. Outsiders are not obliged to take sides, though some have, including the US and Russia. They do so partly because so much of the world's crude oil is produced around the Gulf, and exported through such choke points as the Straits of Hormuz, whose shipping channel is much narrower than the twenty-one-mile-wide straits themselves.

Most obviously this is a sectarian clash, between Sunni Arabs (including the Saudis) and Shia Iranians, though that is to simplify the realities of the participants, all of which have substantial minorities from the other faith. In the case of Bahrain a Sunni monarchy rules the Shia majority. The sectarian labels also conceal different intensities of belief, as well as the view that reason should temper theological fundamentals, or that religion needs to be saved from contamination by politics, a view common in Iran.

But it is also a clash between a quasi-democratic and in many respects Westernized Iranian Islamic Republic of nearly 80 million people, which regards itself as heir to a Persian empire dating back to 700 BC, and Gulf autocracies of more recent provenance. These are tribal rentier states that have been superficially retouched with modernity and the largest is Saudi

Arabia, with about 30 million people. After Venezuela, it has the world's second largest reserves of crude oil.[1]

An almost annual catastrophe illustrates the depth of Saudi–Iranian animosity. The legitimacy of the Saud monarchy rests on custodianship of the two holy places, Mecca and Medina, which Muslims visit at least once in their life in the annual pilgrimage called the Hajj. It is here that the conflict between Iran and Saudi Arabia has become lethal. In 2015 450 Iranians died, along with 1,850 others, in a mass stampede caused by Saudi organizational incompetence. In 1987 450 pilgrims were killed in clashes with Saudi security forces, 275 of the dead being Iranians. In the later incident, the Saudis delayed repatriating the mangled corpses of the victims and compensation issues were not resolved. As a result, Iranians were effectively disbarred from the 2016 Hajj; many went instead to the Shia holy city of Karbala in Iraq. This may have disappointed Iran's intelligence services, which use the Hajj to propagate Iran's revolutionary ideology and to disburse money in opaque ways to its clients who include Saudi Arabia's Shia minority.[2] The hosts also use the Hajj to meet people they formally oppose. For example in July 2015 the King met with Muslim Brotherhood pilgrims from Egypt and Turkey as well as leaders of Hamas from Gaza, including politburo chief Khaled Mashal, in a bid to lure Hamas away from Iran.[3]

Hatred towards Saudi Arabia runs deep in Iran, as symbolized by Supreme Leader Khomeini denouncing King Fahd as a 'traitor to God' in his final testament. Castigating the 'small and puny Satans' of Riyadh, his successor Ayatollah Ali Khamenei called on the Muslim world to remove Saudi custodianship of the two holy places and the Hajj. The Saudi Grand Mufti, Sheikh Abdul-Aziz Al Sheikh, promptly ruled that Iranians are not really Muslims but the descendants of pagan Zoroastrians, which indeed they are. Then, in January 2016, the Saudis decided to include the Shia cleric Sheikh Nimr al-Nimr among the forty-six men (most of them Al Qaeda members) it executed. His offence was to call for the overthrow of the Sauds, though charges of involvement in terrorism were spuriously added. After playing a cat-and-mouse game with the authorities, Nimr was apprehended in 2012 and sentenced to death in October

2014. Angry Iranians burned down the only recently opened Saudi embassy in Tehran.[4]

The Kingdom continues to clash with Iran. On 4 April 2016 Riyadh banned Iran's Mahan Air from its air space, ostensibly on safety grounds but really because Tehran uses it to ferry Islamic Revolutionary Guard Corps Quds Force personnel and weapons to Iraq and Syria and then Lebanon. That followed a ban on tankers carrying Iranian crude entering Saudi (or Bahraini) territorial waters. Iran has responded by intensifying cyber attacks, though nothing on the scale of the 15 August 2012 attack that left 30,000 Windows-based computers at Saudi Aramco defunct for two weeks after a virus called Shamoon invaded their operating systems. Another obvious target is the Abqaiq crude processing plant in Eastern Province, which handles 70 per cent of initial processing of Saudi crude before it reaches Arabian Gulf or Red Sea terminals.

Wherever you travel in the greater Middle East or Africa, the Saudis are widely reviled, for imagining that money can buy anyone any time, as well as for their manifest hypocrisy regarding alcohol and sexual mores. Except perhaps by those who solicit Saudi money, which is disbursed through the Kingdom's embassies on a colossal scale. They try to temper this with ostentatious plays for the allegiances of the regional Arab street, notably by backing the Palestinians, a cause in which Iran and Hizbollah are also invested. Palestinian support for Saddam's occupation of Kuwait and Sunni fear of Iran have also had an effect. Nowadays covert contacts between Israel and the Gulf States are multiple, with Israeli tech firms monitoring Saudi social media on behalf of their royal paymasters.[5]

Riyadh's closest allies are the members of the Gulf Cooperation Council, which was founded in Abu Dhabi in 1981, though at least three of them have amicable relations with Iran too. It is rife with animosities and plots but its members act like a wolf pack to remain in power. Their mutual security agreements allow them to 'exchange' (extradite) anyone suspected of terrorism, and they have many murky British ex-forces types advising on internal security. They have all toned down their anti-Semitism to develop security relationships with Israel, though that is not popular among their own peoples, let alone the diaspora Palestinians who often fill elite jobs.

Bahrain is the poorest and most vulnerable of the GCC states. On the 'day of rage' in February 2011, 150,000 Shia took to the streets to protest lack of reform by the minority Sunni Al Khalifa rulers. This resulted in Saudi Arabia sending 1,500 troops (and 500 from the UAE) across the King Fahd Causeway to Manama, the capital of Bahrain, where they joined the local national guard in violently suppressing the protests. Pakistani troops followed. The Al Khalifa used a human-rights investigation to mask what was going on. But the Bahrain Independent Commission of Inquiry subsequently reported that protestors had been hooded, electrocuted, threatened with rape and killed, and none of them had any connections with Iran. Nobody was dismissed or prosecuted, and British security experts were hired to keep a lid on future trouble, along with PR apologists whose journalist hirelings fabricate connections between the Bahraini Shia and Iran.[6]

Gas-rich Qatar is the most maverick GCC member, resented by its fellows as a haven for Muslim Brotherhood and representatives of Hamas and the Taliban. They may have been there at US urging, because the US needed a backchannel and Qatar provided it. In July 2017, Bahrain, Saudi Arabia and the UAE cut Qatar's external communications, presenting a thirteen-point ultimatum that was designed to be rejected, rather like the one Austria-Hungary sent to Serbia in July 1914. The demands included expulsion of the Muslim Brotherhood leaders and the closure of al-Jazeera TV. Although support from President Trump probably encouraged Crown Prince Mohammed bin Salman down this path, ironically the Secretaries of Defense and State rushed to protect Qatar, which is home to a huge US airbase. Some suspect that the conflict is also motivated by Dubai's desire to stifle commercial competition from Doha. The longer it drags on, the global 'brands' of all belligerents are damaged. Kuwait is the most politically liberalized GCC state. The United Arab Emirates is the most militarily potent and best connected in the West, where like Qatar it has huge investments. Only Sultan Qaboos of Oman maintains a wise equidistance between Saudi Arabia and Tehran, though these latter relations immedi-

ately attracted the attention of spies from the UAE. Qaboos's
benevolent autocracy brokered the initial contacts between Iran
and the US which led to the July 2015 Joint Comprehensive
Action Plan (JCPOA) between Iran and the so-called 5+1 powers
(including the US, Russia, the EU and China) which has retarded
Iran's nuclear weapons programme. Since the bachelor and
childless Sultan is gravely ill, the future of Oman will hinge on
how the succession is managed.

Iran's major advantage over the Gulf monarchs is that it has
developed instruments to project power. The Revolutionary
Guard and its Quds Force are battle tested and know how to
share expertise and advice. Iran's closest allies are Hizbollah in
Lebanon, the Assad regime in Syria, the Shia government of Iraq
and President Putin's Russia.[7] But none of these are 'clients' and
the notion of a 'Shia crescent' operating in the region is a propaganda theme spread by the Gulf monarchies and the Israelis,
friends bonded by a common Iranian enemy.

In 1990, for example, Shia in Kuwait supported the Sunni
Al-Sabah family even though it fled Saddam's occupation. None
of the Shia 'crescent' members want to adopt Iran's doctrine of
divinely guided clerical government, and Iraqi Shia have their
own founts of spiritual authority in Najaf and Karbala that rival
those of Iran.[8] The Saudis tried also to exert influence in Lebanon
through businessman and PM Rafik Hariri, until his assassination
in 2005, probably by Syria. Riyadh dangled $3 billion in front of
Beirut to purchase French arms, but Lebanese Shia and their
Maronite Christian allies showed they could not be bought, and
in fury the Saudis cancelled the deal. In late 2016 Saudi diplomacy suffered a further setback when, after a two-year stalemate,
Hizbollah secured the election of the Maronite Christian general
Michel Aoun as Lebanon's President – a convert to the cause of
Syria's Assad – against a rival candidate backed by the Saudis.[9]

With its large chequebook, Saudi Arabia has other friends and
allies ranging from North Africa monarchies to Pakistan, whose
nuclear bomb programme they financed. The Saudis were horrified
when the Muslim Brotherhood came to power on the back of
Hosni Mubarak's defenestration by the youthful protestors on
Tahrir Square. The Saudis backed both neo-Nasserite army officers

and the quietist Salafi Nour Party, until the Brotherhood-backed President Morsi was himself eventually ousted in a democratic coup. A relieved Riyadh provided the new thinly disguised military regime of President Abdel Fattah el-Sisi with $23 billion in aid.

Money does not always buy you love. Egypt was an ancient and proud culture millennia before Islam appeared. While Sisi has certainly destroyed the Muslim Brotherhood there, he refused to send troops to die in the Saudi war in Yemen, and he wants the Syrian rebels purged of Islamist (Brotherhood and Al Qaeda) elements before anything else. When the Egyptians supported a Russian UN Security Council resolution to this effect, the Saudis immediately cut off the 700,000 tons of fuel they had promised them for the next five years. Sisi simply responded, 'Egypt bows to no one but God alone,' and turned instead to Iraq. Egypt did, however, enthusiastically join in the demarche to Qatar. The Iraqis had by then clashed with Riyadh over their refusal to repatriate imprisoned Saudi jihadists they had scooped up on the battlefields. This was music to the ears of Tehran as, once again, Saudi Arabia's petulant diplomacy failed. The Saudis have also backed General Khalifa Haftar against Islamists in Libya's multisided civil war, and the opponents of the Islamist Ennahda Party in Tunisia.[10]

Vertiginous defence spending that recently hit 8–10 per cent of GDP also buys other friends. In the case of Britain or France, the supermarket-style maxim 'buy our arms and get our foreign policy for free' prevails. The Serious Fraud Office in London uncovered remarkably lavish funding of the exotic honeymoon of Prince Bandar bin Sultan's daughter (£250,000 to be precise) doled out before the £43 billion Al Yamamah arms contract, an investigation which was shut down by Tony Blair on grounds of national security.[11] A British university press of some repute also pulled every copy of a book about Saudi funding of Al Qaeda after a Saudi banker issued a writ.

The US also sells Saudi Arabia armaments, but fracking has drastically reduced America's need for Saudi crude oil, 40 per cent of which now goes to China. The 2015 nuclear deal with Iran also meant that the Obama administration was very unpopular in Riyadh. Obama had also told the Kingdom's rulers that they were 'free-riders' on US defence efforts, a theme to which

Republican candidate Donald Trump also warmed. Worst of all, in his lengthy foreign policy interview with *Atlantic Monthly*, President Obama told King Salman to 'share the region with Iran' in a cold peace like that between Egypt and Israel. Obama also criticized Riyadh's (deplorable) human rights record.

Saudi Arabia retains an army of lobbyists in Washington, orchestrated by SAPRAC (the Saudi American Public Relations Affairs Committee) to augment the influence of such friends as Texan oilmen and State Department Arabists. But the relationship has significantly cooled since the attacks of 9/11. There were persistent suspicions that the US government had suppressed a heavily redacted report on Saudi involvement with three of the 9/11 hijackers through 'clerical diplomats' in the Kingdom's US consulates. During the presidential election US congressmen and senators waved aside President Obama's veto and passed the Justice Against Sponsors of Terrorism Act (JASTA) in September 2016. A parallel effort to block a $1.15 billion arms deal because of murderous Saudi conduct of the war in Yemen was rejected in the Senate.[12] It is also the case that Saudi Arabia's decision to raise oil production was a deliberate attempt to put US shale producers (or the banks that fund them) out of business. This is strange for a supposed friend.[13]

Ordinary Americans have made up their minds that any alleged benefits of strategic cooperation with the Saudis (which remain secret) are far outweighed by Saudi global propagation of Wahhabism, the theological mulch in which Islamist terrorism thrives. Many also find the sybaritic lifestyle of Saudi royals repellent. JASTA opens the floodgates to endless litigation and the risk of asset freezes while courts deliberate.[14] If anything, calls from the American right in such journals as *National Interest* to ditch the Kingdom are even more relentless than those from the left.[15]

Before and after the passage of JASTA, Riyadh huffed and puffed that it would respond by liquidating $750 billion of Treasury securities (in reality it only holds $117 billion of US government bonds compared with China's $1.3 trillion trove) before US courts can freeze these and other assets as law suits are mounted. About two-thirds of the Kingdom's $587 billion sovereign wealth funds are held in US dollars too. Difficult to disengage, liquidating these would destabilize the global economy (for which Riyadh would be blamed) while the Saudi riyal would plunge along with the US dollar. Since American opinion has turned against the Saudis over terrorism, it is now hard to imagine what the results of such a strategy would be, especially on top of Saudi efforts to ruin the US fracking industry. It would also jeopardize building up the Saudi Sovereign Fund to $3.5 trillion on the back of part-privatizing 5 per cent of Saudi Aramco, which is the key to modernizing and diversifying the Saudi economy and ensuring domestic stability. This gambit is not universally popular among patriotic Saudis who regard Aramco as the Kingdom's crown jewels.[16] Unless Trump alters the rules, the JASTA act makes a New York IPO less likely than one in London, where current rules insisting on 25 per cent rather than 5 per cent of a company's shares being floated so as to protect shareholders have been creatively adapted to secure the enormous fees entailed in a deal where Aramco's management is utterly opaque. As Groucho Marx said: 'These are my principles. If you don't like them, I have others.' [17]

China and Russia have been the main beneficiaries of despair at President Obama's coolness. Riyadh likes the 'hear and see no evil' attitude of the Chinese on human rights, especially as China has surpassed the US as Saudi Arabia's main oil customer. The unwillingness (and inability) of the Chinese to project global power will not give that relationship much clout. Recently, like many Arab rulers, the Saudis have visited Moscow, despite President Putin's support for Assad in Syria.

The Saudis are inveterate double-dealers. Some fifty Wahhabi clerics on the state payroll enjoined Muslims to wage holy war against the Russians because of Putin's military intervention in Syria, ongoing since 2015. The Russians will not have forgotten a crass threat by ex-spy chief Prince Bandar to activate Chechen terrorists during the Sochi Winter Olympics if Russia did not drop Assad. Bandar said to Putin:

> As an example, I can give you a guarantee to protect the
> Winter Olympics in the city of Sochi on the Black Sea next
> year. The Chechen groups that threaten the security of the

Games are controlled by us, and they will not move in the Syrian territory's direction without coordinating with us. These groups do not scare us. We use them in the face of the Syrian regime but they will have no role or influence in Syria's political affairs.

Some allege that Putin said he would retarget Russia's nuclear missiles on Riyadh.[18]

The international nuclear deal with Iran led to fears that Iran had been unleashed though it is a narrow arms-control agreement much like the ones the US concluded with a then hostile Soviet Union, which also did not cover Soviet conduct domestically or elsewhere. Even before the Joint Comprehensive Plan of Action was concluded in July 2015, many governments and businesses courted Iran. There was a rush of European bankers, aircraft, automotive, retail and oil executives to Tehran. Residual US sanctions still make dollar-denominated bank transactions risky, because multiple US agencies have not removed sanctions, and having an Iranian visa complicates travel to the US for foreigners who deal with Iran, especially since Trump has empowered every little Hitler at US border controls. Hawks in Congress and the Trump administration may now try to wreck the agreement, especially as his cabinet includes generals whose troops were killed by sophisticated shaped IEDs which the IRGC supplied to Iraqi Shiite militias. These sent streams of molten metal through armour plate and people.

With the JCPOA in the bag, Iran is acting more assertively (and sometimes aggressively), partly to compensate for hardline elements of the regime. They opposed concessions over Iran's nuclear programme, and fear the domestic reverberations of contacts with the West. In the wake of the deal, Iran's ability to restore its share of global oil production has been impressive. As a senior US ConocoPhillips executive remarked, even without any Western technology to modernize its oil industry after years of sanctions, Iran has returned as a major oil producer (approximately 3.6 million barrels per day) in a remarkably rapid time.

Iran calculates that during the period of grace it enjoys as the international community seeks to bed down the nuclear agreement, it can afford to make aggressive moves, especially as Iran will have to be included in any peace negotiations over Syria, one of the main sources of the waves of refugees troubling Europe, Turkey, Jordan, Lebanon and elsewhere. Tehran also exerts considerable influence on Shia-dominated Iraq, seemingly able to engineer the appointment and replacement of prime ministers through its influence on the powerful Dawa Party. It also has links with Shia militia groups, who in the mid-2000s it armed with sophisticated IEDs to attack Western coalition forces.

Things are different nowadays. Shia militia commanders are present at briefings inside Taqaddum air base in Anbar province, where US special forces liaise with Iraqi security forces. Two powerful figures direct these Shia militias. One is sixty-year-old Qassem Soleimani, head of the IRGC Quds Force, and the other his deputy, sixty-three-year-old Jamal Jaafar Ibrahimi, aka Abu Mahdi al-Mohandes, 'the engineer'. The latter's backstory includes terror bombings in Kuwait and supplying the Sadrist militias in Iraq with shaped explosives to attack coalition occupation forces.

These Iraqi militias are part of the larger (mainly Afghan, Iraqi, Lebanese and Pakistani) Shia force that Iran has deployed to bolster Syria's embattled President Bashar al-Assad. So great is Iran's influence that it can change Iraqi strategy against ISIS. Initially Mosul was to be enveloped in a horseshoe posture, leaving a western exit for both refugees and fleeing ISIS fighters. Since Iran feared the latter would debouch to Syria, where they and the Russians have turned the war there in favour of Assad, the Iranians insisted on complete encirclement, with their proxy militias poised to turn the road west from Mosul into a kill-box. The French government supported this strategy since it would eliminate the terrorist commanders who in 2016 ordered attacks in Brussels and Paris.[19]

Iran's hand is evident in murkier areas too. Iran's Chief of the General Staff, Major General Mohammad Hassan Bagheri, is an exponent of the 'threat for threat' doctrine of strategic deterrence, and boosted intelligence and subversion in the Gulf, including swift-boat incursions into disputed littoral waters with Kuwait and Saudi Arabia as well as covert dabbling in Bahrain.

In August 2015 Bahrain's security forces raided a warehouse being used as a bomb-making factory and found 1.5 tonnes of high-grade explosives. Five men were detained, who subsequently admitted – probably after being tortured – that they were funded and trained in terrorism by the IRGC and the Iraq Hizbollah Brigades. Bahrain gave the Iranian chargé d'affaires seventy-two hours to leave the country and recalled its ambassador to Tehran.[20]

In the same month, the Kuwaiti authorities uncovered large amounts of explosives smuggled from Iran, while the US embassy in Riyadh warned US citizens of threats to compounds in Eastern Province, where many expats work in the oil fields. There is a high probability that Iran will escalate tensions using Shia proxies in Eastern Province, whether through attacks on oil installations or by organizing riots and subversion through the restive Shia population. They are under attack from ISIS bombers, attacks the Sunni Saudis do little to interdict since they regard the victims as 'heretical snakes'. It did not help that the Saudis judicially murdered Shia divine Sheikh Nimr al-Nimr. Iranian proxies could also strike Saudi interests in Iraq, Lebanon and Kuwait.[21]

At the same time, Iran has revisited ambiguities in the Joint Comprehensive Plan of Action which Supreme Leader Ali Khamenei and Iran's parliament approved. In an open letter on 21 October 2015, President Rouhani delineated new conditions for acceptance of the nuclear accord Iran had signed up to, namely written declarations by the US and EU to the effect that sanctions are completely lifted and that if they are not – for any reason including ballistic missile tests or Iranian support for terrorism or human rights violations – then the agreement will be nullified. The Iranian majlis (parliament) quietly made this a matter of law before approving the deal. Since the US, at least before Trump, and EU do not want the nuclear deal to collapse, it is likely that they will abandon the link between dismantling centrifuges and down-riching of uranium and the gradual alleviation of sanctions. The EU has a major interest (supported by the US) in diversifying its energy dependence on Russia's Gazprom, and gas from the Caspian Sea area (and the eastern Mediterranean) would be one way of doing this.

Ideologically, Iran's clerical regime needs the Great Satan to justify its own creation story, beginning with the American puppet Shah Reza Pahlavi, who the mullahs belatedly helped depose in 1979. Khamenei regards trade liberalization as the thin end of the wedge for further subversive American influences, including those accompanying imported consumer goods. Owing to the autarchic 'resistance economy' of recent years, the Revolutionary Guard has built a considerable economic empire that it will be loath to forfeit as the economy is de-monopolized and deregulated as a condition of modernization. The nervousness of the regime is evident in a spate of arrests of journalists accused of subversively 'beautifying' the image of America on behalf of US intelligence agencies as well as dual nationals who allegedly spy for them.

Because many Westerners neither like nor trust Saudi Arabia, whose state-subsidized creed is an international menace, it does not mean that Iran is any less sinister in its own right, however much visitors admire the country's rich culture or businessmen are eager to deal with it. But maybe it is not quite as sinister as its local enemies maintain, a perspective outsiders should not uncritically adopt as if it were their own. Iran spends 3 per cent of GDP on defence, whereas the Saudis spend 10.4 per cent and Israel 5.8 per cent.

This is an example of how Middle Eastern governments seek to shape the views of opinion-formers. Having been accustomed to the smooth reasonableness of a senior Gulf figure (not a Saudi) at periodic briefings, it was surprising to be exposed to the paranoia beneath as he explained collective Gulf Arab concerns. They, he explained in rational mode, are reconciled to the fact of the successful nuclear deal with Iran, worried about a lack of specifics and disappointed about the failure to broaden the talks to include Israeli nuclear bombs. They know that some countries, led by Germany, will rush to do business with Iran when sanctions are fully rescinded as Tehran is insisting. Banks are especially worried by the New York District Attorney's control of Wall Street banking licences, for doing business with Iran involves considerable potential risk.

Reasonably enough, the Gulf States are anxious about the disconnection between the emollient President Rouhani and

Foreign Minister Zarif (whose deputy is a leading member of the IRGC) and the 'true face' of Iran: the Revolutionary Guard. Everyone is part of the theocracy since any social democrat or liberal Iranians have either been killed long ago (along with the Tudeh Party communists) or are in exile, where they have completely integrated into their host countries, being well educated, urban and middle class. Of course, while 'the regime lives in a medieval century, the Iranian people live in the twenty-first', said the Gulf spokesman at one briefing. The prospect of a nuclear deal paving the way for future regime change is pie in the sky, he added.

'They' are also concerned that the agreement will bring de facto acknowledgment of Iran as the regional leader. They absolutely reject Iran's interference in 'Arab affairs' (though Iran is surely a country bordering the Gulf and has its own ethnic Arab minority). They fear that a more 'muscular' Iran will use the $140–150 billion (figures plucked out of the air) that will be unblocked from asset freezes to make mischief in the region. Iran getting its hands on big money to make big trouble is their chief fear. Once again 'the Arabs' feel a loss of dignity as Iran seems to do what it likes in their backyard.

Above all, they suspect Iran of trying to lever Shia minorities into the ineradicable position Hizbollah has already achieved in the domestic politics of Lebanon. An acid test for Iranian good faith would be if Iran/Hizbollah allowed the Lebanese presidential elections to occur without them exercising their baleful influence. (In the interim Lebanon does indeed have a new President.) That is about as likely as snow in the Sahara, said the spokesman. Of course, unlike Erdoğan's Turkey, Iran is not a 'model' for anyone other than devout Shia.

The Gulf States are using warplanes to bomb the Shia/Zaidi Houthi in Yemen. Some pilots have experience of combat in Iraq, Libya, Kosovo and Afghanistan. They claim this has prevented the Houthi from moving 300 Scud missiles to the border with Saudi Arabia (apparently Saudi satellites picked up launch pads being constructed there). They claim their navies have stopped Iran resupplying the Houthi, while flights are being closely inspected. Commandos with combat experience from

Afghanistan have done sterling work. The official said nothing about the Latin American mercenaries the Gulf States have reportedly hired to fight for them in Yemen.

He claimed that Iran has had up to five thousand IRGC 'advisers' in Yemen, though when challenged by a BBC man, this figure first fell to two thousand and then just three secret agents who were picked up before the current conflict by Yemeni forces and then delivered to Iran via Oman. His auditors were sceptical about the lack of hard proof regarding an Iranian proxy conspiracy since most detailed studies of the Yemeni Houthi claim the links are more exiguous. The absence of a land border makes it hard for Tehran to exert the influence it has in Afghanistan and Iraq. Ships are easy to detect and stop.

Triumphalism regarding the failure of Iranian intelligence to spot the hundreds of combat aircraft mobilizing against the Houthis should be balanced against the fact that Gulf money (and diplomacy) did not prevent Egypt or Pakistan from failing to provide ground troops in Yemen as the GCC expected. Pakistan's PM Nawaz Sharif did the David Cameron trick of consulting his parliament (over bombing Syria's chemical munitions), which then voted down Pakistani military involvement. 'We would have been happy with an ambulance with the Pakistani crescent on it,' commented our speaker, who would not forget the duplicity of Islamabad any time soon. Of course, Tehran can make a world of trouble for its eastern neighbour, as Islamabad knows very well.

While military efforts to check the Houthi (and former Yemeni President Saleh) are ongoing, there is likely to be a big development plan in addition to the usual bribes to Yemeni tribesmen. This will be much larger than the $27 million in humanitarian aid already being dispensed in Yemen and more like the aid programme to President Sisi's Egypt. Attempts will also be made to thrash out a political settlement, to avoid Yemen being ruled by a small religious sect (the Zaidi Houthi) in conjunction with an ousted President Saleh, who misruled Yemen for forty years as he dexterously 'danced on snakes'.

The Gulf States want an agreement to make containment of Iran effective that stops short of either a formal treaty or an extension of the US nuclear umbrella (both politically impossible in the US). They seek a permanent qualitative advantage over Iran, and not just through more weapons sales.

They were pleased with the new team in Riyadh, stressing the competence of Deputy Crown Prince Mohammed bin Salman, despite his youth – he is only thirty-one. They believe that Saudi Arabia is going to be much more assertive in rolling back Iranian influence. This costs money, in addition to the subsidies the monarchy is doling out to buy social peace (the Shia in Eastern Province are a real worry). This means tapping the sovereign wealth fund at an increasing rate. There is fundamental disagreement with HM Government's 'it's good to talk' strategy in Libya (in line with British UN envoy Jonathan Powell's idiosyncratic Irish perspective), but praise for France (and Italy), which see Libya as respectively a terrorism threat (especially vis-à-vis the Sahel) and a migration crisis. The official was concerned about Britain's suppression of its official report on the activities of the Muslim Brotherhood. This is how foreign governments seek to shape our perceptions of foreign conflicts. One hopes such efforts are not simply ingested, although reading some newspapers, where these views are uncritically regurgitated, it is obvious they are.[*]

•

Saudi Arabia's strategic position is deteriorating, though it likes to advertise its martial might. The Ra'ad Al Shamal – Northern Thunder – military exercises held there in 2016 sounded impressively ominous. The Peninsula Shield Force, the GCC's military alliance, was joined at King Khalid Military City by troops from Jordan, Egypt, Senegal, Sudan, the Maldives, Morocco, Pakistan, Chad, Tunisia, Comoros Islands, Djibouti, Malaysia, Mauritania and Mauritius. This was the tangible manifestation of a thirty-four Muslim nation anti-terror alliance which Saudi Defence Minister and deputy Crown Prince Mohammed bin Salman announced at the end of 2014. It was news to Indonesia

---

[*] This section draws on my contemporaneous notes of this session. Other participants may have different recollections.

and Pakistan, who said they had never heard of the alliance, despite being enrolled in its imposing membership list.

The aim of the three-week-long exercise, and hence the symbolism of the name, was to warn Iran, Syria and Russia that their evolving alliance will not be uncontested. The arrival of a few Saudi fighters at Turkey's Incirlik air base was supposed to send the same message, reflecting the Kingdom's pretentious adoption of a 'two war doctrine'. Riyadh means war in neighbouring Yemen and Syria by the way, not Europe or the Middle East and Asia Pacific, as the US two simultaneous wars doctrine proclaims with more substance, since the US could just about do this.

Riyadh's war in Yemen has not worked and has been hugely expensive, costing roughly $700 million per month. It was let down by Saudi's traditional allies Egypt and Pakistan, who refused to donate cannon fodder. In Syria, the Saudi-backed 'Army of Islam' has been hammered by Russia around Aleppo and by elite Iranian regular army airborne troops, deployed abroad for the first time to augment IRGC Quds Force 'volunteers'. Hizbollah may not jump ninja-style over car bonnets for the cameras, but even equipped with slingshots (in fact they are very heavily armed) south Beirut's finest would cut these Saudi SF troops to pieces.

Every day that sanctions on Iran lapse, Tehran grows stronger, while the Western public rightly queries Saudi's indiscriminate conduct of the air war and its own dubious involvement in it. Yemen is suffering mass starvation while a cholera epidemic in twenty-one of its twenty-two provinces has so far resulted in a quarter of a million cases. Nor is Saudi Arabia innocent of meddling in Iran's backyard, quite apart from its involvement in the Syrian tragedy and Yemen. Iran's own complex ethnic geography provides opportunities. Like Turkey with the Kurdistan Workers' Party or PKK, Iran has discovered that its enemies can thrive inside Iraq's autonomous Kurdish region, though this is fraught with risks for its capital, Erbil.

On 9 July 2016 Prince Turki bin Faisal (head of Saudi intelligence 1977–2001) addressed a Paris rally of the People's Mujahadeen of Iran (Mujahadeen-e-Khalq or MEK). Ten days later a former head of the IRGC accused Riyadh of setting up military bases for the MEK in autonomous Iraqi Kurdistan, where the Saudis had opened a new consulate in Erbil. The Iranians earlier accused the Saudis of fomenting anti-Iranian Baluchi separatism over the border in Pakistan. Where else may the Saudis be meddling, in addition to the activities of the 'clerical diplomats' operating within their embassies and consulates? Despite the MEK being a totalitarian sect, which the US listed as a terrorist organization until 2012 when Hillary Clinton 'delisted' it, some US hawks imagine that it might be used to overthrow the Iranian regime, even though most Iranians regard it as a bunch of brainwashed violent terrorists.

•

The Kingdom of Saud was founded, at the third attempt, in 1932 by Abdul-Aziz bin Saud (known as Ibn Saud), whose desert forefathers had joined forces in 1744 with the religious zealot Muhammad ibn Abd al-Wahhab. The latter had revived the harsh unyielding Islam of the thirteenth-century theologian Ibn Taymiyyah. Living at a time of Mongol domination, when there were many opportunistic conversions to the faith, Taymiyyah arrogated the right to determine who was or was not a true believer. This crucial religio-political alliance of convenience persists today, for the ulema (clerical council) is dominated by the Al ash-Sheikhs, who are direct descendants of al-Wahhab. The state pays their salaries, whether they support the monarchy or not. The Sauds were also adroit at intertribal marriage, and in 1929 crushed their own fanatic army the Ikhwan, once it had neutralized their tribal rivals, though dreams of the Ikhwan live on.

The fortunes of the Sauds were transformed after vast oil reserves were discovered around the Persian Gulf, oil that began to flow in 1941. US President Roosevelt quickly recognized Abdul-Aziz as a strategic partner. Abdul-Aziz's son Saud ruled from 1953 to 1964, when his half-brother Faisal overthrew him. Faisal was assassinated in 1975 by a nephew and was succeeded by King Khalid (1975–82) and then King Fahd (1982–2005). Under Fahd, Saudi Arabia became the largest oil producer in the world. Wealth became conspicuous at home and abroad. The Saudi Aramco compound at Dhahran, home to 11,000 people in the Shia-populated Eastern Province, is an oasis of efficiency and Western modernity in a country where most working Saudis are in the public sector. Generally speaking, the central Nejd region, home to the Sauds, is the most conservative province, while coastal Jeddah and the Hijaz is the most relaxed about modernity. Tribal loyalties are more important than membership of a nation.

Even superficial urban modernization appalled religious conservatives. In 1979 the grandson of a member of the Ikhwan and his followers stormed into and temporarily occupied the Grand Mosque at Mecca, being inspired by the Iranian revolution of that year. Although the perpetrators were slain or executed, many of their disciples were encouraged to go to Afghanistan to fight the Soviet invaders. Some would mutate into Al Qaeda. Another response of the Saudi ruling dynasty was significant too. In 1986 King Fahd ceased to be called 'His Majesty'. Instead he was to be referred to as 'Custodian of the Two Holy Places', to underline the regime's religious legitimacy. The arrival of US troops in the Kingdom on the eve of the First Gulf War further aggravated the zealous, including the exiled Osama bin Laden, who in 1996 issued his 'Declaration of War Against the Americans Occupying the Land of the Two Holy Places'.[22]

To combat rising religious extremism, the government vested more power in the Wahhabist ulema, who tightened their grip on domestic education and enforcement of public morals. The Ministry of Islamic Affairs seeded 'clerical diplomats' in Saudi embassies and consulates to oversee the huge sums being pumped into a global network of madrassas and mosques. With the aid of Korans churned out in Medina by one of the world's largest print plants,[23] these rote-learning factories have poisoned minds from Pakistan to the Philippines and retarded children in such countries as northern Nigeria and Pakistan, where it is the only form of 'education' open to disadvantaged Muslim children. This is also happening on Europe's doorstep, though the Saudis and Qataris have sponsored many enemies within too. Thanks to Saudi proselytism, the moderate Hanifi school of Islam practised in Albanian Muslim majority Kosovo (which ironically would not exist as an independent state without Western intervention) has been extinguished by a scowling Salafism, as extreme imams paid by the Saudis (and individual and NGO 'charities' from the UAE) have made their baleful influence felt, not least in the fact that the largest number of volunteers per head of European population fighting with ISIS are Albanian Kosovars, 314 to be precise. While a Salafist underground continued to operate inside Saudi Arabia, much of the terrorist energy was displaced to Afghanistan, where the Taliban regime replaced the mess left by the Soviets, and then to Bosnia, where in five years 1992–7 Riyadh itself gave more money to Islamists than it had given to the Palestinians in the previous fifteen.

Saudi jihadists also infiltrated neighbouring Yemen, where Al Qaeda in the Arabian Peninsula merged Saudi and Yemeni terrorists. For one by-product of Saudi Arabia's export of extremists was terrorist cells in dozens of other countries. Some of these perpetual strangers returned home to Saudi, where they accused the regime of establishing *mulk* – a secular ruler's estate, rather than an Islamic community – and hence of *bid'a*, meaning illicit occupancy of the two holy places.[24]

After Fahd suffered a debilitating stroke in 1995, Crown Prince Abdullah became acting monarch, assuming the kingship a decade later upon Fahd's death. In 2007 Abdullah established an Allegiance Council consisting of about thirty-five senior princes to create consensus among whoever would be chosen to succeed him in proceedings that are otherwise secret. The oldest surviving son of Abdul-Aziz bin Saud, Abdullah was presumed to be ninety years old when he died in 2015.

The succession to Abdullah brought into play Saudi Arabia's 7,000 princes, of whom 200 are direct descendants of Abdul-Aziz and thirty-seven his sons by more than twenty wives. Not all wives are equal. The seven sons of Ibn Saud with Hassa bint Ahmed of the Sudairi tribe (the 'Sudairi Seven') are paramount. Gerontocracy brought other problems. The heir presumptive to Abdullah, Crown Prince Sultan, died aged eighty-seven in 2011 and his replacement, Prince Nayef bin Abdul-Aziz Al Saud, expired in 2012 aged seventy-eight. Abdullah had to cope with limited manifestations of a Saudi Arab Spring. With $560 billion in the bank, in 2013 King Abdullah tried to purchase social peace by throwing $130 billion at various problems. Nearly a million Saudis were given unemployment assistance of $600 per month, and official monthly salaries were raised to $850, double the average private sector wage.

Vast monies were also poured into a new business park outside Riyadh as well as into new industrial cities (one of them dedicated to employing women). The Kingdom also found the money to send 140,000 young Saudis abroad on scholarships, hoping they would return to help modernize the economy, but without seditious ideas. It is revealing of Saudi values that it was easier to send 30,000 women as students abroad than to let a single one of them drive a car. When a limited number of women were allowed to serve on the 150-strong Majlis al-Shura advisory body, it was from a separate room, but in 2009 Abdullah at least nominated a woman as a deputy minister.

In 2015 the throne passed to Prince Salman, then aged seventy-nine, who has had two strokes, and is reported to suffer from Alzheimer's, making his concentration flag after forty-five minutes in meetings. He was best known for governing Riyadh province for forty-eight years and chairing the Descendants Council set up by Fahd in 2000 to iron out wayward members of the royal family by methods including stints in a mini prison. After dispensing $32 billion, or the equivalent of Nigeria's entire annual budget, in his accession handouts, King Salman moved to marginalize the incumbent crown prince, Muqrin bin Abdul-Aziz, promoting the fifty-five-year-old Interior Minister, Muhammad bin Nayef, as crown prince and his own son, Mohammed bin Salman (known as MbS), as deputy crown prince. Whereas Nayef is a security specialist, the recipient of the George Tenet medal for counter-terrorism no less, Prince Mohammed dabbles across the piste. As a Sudairi, this thrusting thirty-one-year-old is Minister of both Defence and Economics and has higher status than Nayef, whose mother was a foreign 'concubine'. To signal a parallel conservative turn, Salman quickly dismissed the female deputy minister.[25]

These men attended the Prince's School in Riyadh, and then occupied either one of the big ministries (for example Crown Prince Nayef succeeded his father as Minister of the Interior in

2012) or one of the thirteen regional governorships. MbS may
lack experience, as his critics mutter, but he is making up for it
with multiple titles, which is perhaps why he is widely known
as 'Prince Everyone'. As was entirely predictable, in late June
2017 Salman edged aside Prince Nayaf (who had already retired
in a sulk to Algeria for two months), replacing him as Crown
Prince with the thrusting Mohammad bin Salman. Rumours
were spread that in addition to being diabetic, Nayaf had PSDT
and had become addicted to painkillers after a jihadist tried to
kill him in 2009 with a bomb in the assassin's rectum, which
was detonated by mobile phone. Salman sealed the deposition
by kissing Nayaf, thereby confirming the common view that
'When MbS kisses you, you know something bad will happen.'
Since MbS is himself only thirty-one and could have many sons
of his own, this is not proving popular with the other princes.[26]

The Saudi political system is deeply autocratic, with no independent judiciary and no parliament. The law is Sharia. Any
changes have been cosmetic and designed to placate the West,
like the sixty-man Consultative Council which is stuffed with
compliant technocrats from the regions. Meetings of the tribal
majlis are brief, more about dispensing favours than influencing
decision-making, which is concentrated in few hands. The Sauds
have sought to inculcate a form of Saudi nationalism by reviving
both traditions and interest in the national football team. In
1985 King Abdullah created the Janadriyah Festival for the
National Guard to show off their riding skills, and in 2005 a
National Day when towns are decked out in green and white.
But for all the talk of 'dialogue', little will be changed or decided.

Instead, the Sauds exploit the rituals and paraphernalia of
tribalism – the majlis, the *ardah* sword dance, the *thobe* and
kufiya – as a way of neutralizing that tribalism. But beneath this
nostalgic fakery, Saudi Arabia is a very repressive place. And in
the wake of the Arab Spring, Prince Nayef increased the already
ample headcount at his interior ministry by 60,000 employees.[27]

Most obviously this has affected religious extremists, especially after 2003, when thirty-five people were killed in three
concerted attacks on compounds for foreigners. Many modern
Saudi women resent having to have a male legal guardian or a

chaperone every time they venture out. There is also a high toleration of male domestic violence. But repression also extends to anyone rash enough to write a dissenting blog or to issue the wrong Tweet.[28]

•

Between 80 and 90 per cent of Saudi state revenues derive from oil. The average basket price of a barrel of OPEC oil has declined from $106 in 2013 to $96 in 2014, $50 in 2015, and $41 in 2016. The average 2017 price is $51, though on 8 May as I wrote this it reached $47. In other words, Gulf oil revenues have halved. While no one knows where oil prices may head in future, there is mistrust between oil producers, an increase in production by non-OPEC nations, led by the US, and lower than expected global oil demand – roughly 96.3 million barrels per day in 2017, only 1.2 million more than the previous year. Should electric vehicles become popular, the demand for oil will fall precipitately.

The Kingdom sits on top of vast reserves, estimated at 260 billion barrels. But this is illusory, even if one trusts statistics that are closely guarded secrets and which seem remarkably constant despite profligate local use. Saudi Arabia domestically consumes over a quarter of its production, that is 3 million barrels a day, which is more than Germany, an industrial economy with nearly triple the population and an economy five times Saudi's own. Producing oil requires a lot of power: Aramco uses 10 per cent of the country's energy output alone. Petrol cost 12–16 US cents a litre until MbS hiked the price to 24 cents as part of his subsidy reduction plans.

Saudi Arabia also suffers from severe water shortages, with all ground water earmarked for agriculture, yet is profligate with water, consuming 936 per cent of its renewable water resources each year. The lion's share of domestic oil consumption is therefore used in desalination plants or natural-gas and oil-powered electricity generation to cope with air conditioning that is left on even when the consumers are avidly shopping in London or Paris during peak summer months. While all natural gas is reserved for domestic electricity generation, wastage through flaring runs at 15 per cent, and in the summer these power plants have to revert to oil, so great is the demand. There are frequent power outages in the summer that can be lethal, given ambient temperatures of 50°C. Domestic electricity demand is rising by 10 per cent per year.

The fall in the price of oil has badly hit the revenues of the Gulf states. The planned Saudi budget deficit for 2017 is $53 billion or 7.7 per cent of GDP. This means borrowing or tapping into foreign currency reserves. Saudi reserves have fallen from $725 billion in late 2014 to about $550 billion in late 2016. Bond issues have raised $17.5 billion in 2016 and $9 billion in 2017. There have also been cost-cutting measures and plans to introduce a GCC-wide VAT of 5 per cent from 2018.

Ostentatious gestures, for example cutting the salaries of a few ministers by 20 per cent, mean nothing in a country where the stipends and pensions of 7,000 mainly working-age royal princes are secret. While some princes receive a few thousand dollars a month, others get $250,000 or more, as well as the right to expropriate land from commoners. They also trade in blocks of visas for foreigners. They get free flights on the national carrier, and if they borrow money from a bank they are unlikely to pay it back.[29]

It is also an unequal society, with one economist estimating that 35 per cent of Saudis (who have large families) rely on incomes of less than $533 a month. Divorced or widowed women are in a particularly bad place. Slums are a reality too, behind the glittering facades. There is also a shortage of 1.5 million homes, because of rich people sitting on undeveloped land so as to benefit as its value rises while limiting construction in this sector, and a very undeveloped mortgage market.[30] A lack of housing means that young Saudi men and women cannot get married as home ownership is a sine qua non for union. Strict segregation of the sexes also fuels sexual frustration and anger that can take pathological forms.[31]

At current and projected consumption rates, the Saudis will need international oil prices to rise to $320 per barrel by 2030.[32] However, long-term estimates suggest that by 2038 Saudi Arabia will have become a net importer of oil, and that by 2043 it will be entirely consuming its diminished output domestically. Although at present Saudi Arabia is adding to pressure on rival producers by raising production to its limits, this strategic use of oil may not operate much longer, particularly as the agreement with Iran made in July 2015 means that Iran has returned to the oil market and will not cap output to suit Riyadh. The Saudis are desperately searching for shale oil deposits, and intend to build sixteen nuclear reactors by 2030, with China positioning itself to secure these contracts with adapted Westinghouse AP1000 reactors in the face of Argentine, French and Russian competition. So far these are just paper projects. In the meantime the Saudis are burning through their sovereign wealth funds at a rate that would exhaust them in five or six years, liquidating overseas holdings and allowing budget deficits to rise to 13.5 per cent of GDP in 2016.[33]

This is the background to Mohammed bin Salman's Saudi Vision 2030, a revamped McKinsey-style attempt to boost *non-oil* revenues from $43.6 billion in 2015 to $160 billion in 2020 and then $267 billion by 2030. The first stage involves issuing an IPO on 5 per cent of Saudi Aramco, which will yield $100–150 billion, but would value the whole company at a minimum of $2 trillion. This would then be moved into the Public Investment Fund, which with other assets would be worth $3 trillion. This would dwarf even Norway's huge sovereign wealth fund, the largest in the world.[34] Gold and uranium mining will also become part of the new energy ministry. A government-owned but publicly listed holding company will take over arms production, cutting dependence on the Americans, with BAE Systems, Boeing, Lockheed and Raytheon obliged to partner locally and to employ native Saudis. Some production as well as maintenance will be moved to KSA too. The Vision seeks to boost Islamic tourism, to which end Saudi archaeologists have been restoring pre-Islamic ruins. How this will play with the Wahhabi clergy who deplore idolatry and have erased much of the country's physical heritage remains to be seen. Alternatively, there are plans to turn fifty islands between Umluh and Al Wajh, together the size of Belgium, into de luxe resorts, though alcohol and dress issues have not been resolved.[35]

Vision 2030 is designed to modernize Saudi society while diversifying the economy away from hydrocarbons over the next fifteen years. The problem has been recognized since the 1970s and reform plans have come and gone. In 2012 King Abdullah also unfurled grand plans, which resulted in a giant solar project at the King Abdullah City for Atomic and Renewable Energy, but this has disappointed.[36] The search for diversification away from hydrocarbons partly reflects demographic imperatives and the maxim that the devil makes work for idle hands. Saudi Arabia suffers from a youth bulge, with two-thirds aged under thirty, and that population is set to grow to 40 million by 2030. A quarter of a million Saudis enter the workforce each year, far too many to be absorbed into the existing economy. Officially 'only' 11 per cent of Saudis are unemployed, though the real figure may be 27–29 per cent, and it rises to 60 per cent among under thirties. There is also a fundamental problem with the balance between the public and private sectors. The public sector employs 90 per cent Saudi citizens, but the private sector is 90 per cent staffed by foreigners. The 11.7 million expats include 4.3 million dependants. The Saudis have increased the fees for the latter's residency permits and visas in order to indirectly bring about the 'Saudization' of such sectors as health, shop work and tourism.[37]

Prince Mohammed's Vision involves eliminating subsidies on water and fuel, and deep cuts to the public sector, including privatizing education and health care. This shift proved so contentious that at the time of writing the pay cuts have been reversed with millions spent on backpay too. Among the more cynical Saudis, the Vision is defined as 'they give us 20 but take back 30'. For Saudis regard free services and generous state stipends as their right, in return for which they are loyal to the Sauds. Saudis prefer the indolence of putting in the odd hour in the public sector in a country where the private alternative is undeveloped but more demanding for people whose education has been rudimentary. While the Vision also seeks to relax restrictions on skilled expatriate workers with a Green Card system so that they can travel almost anywhere inside Saudi Arabia, a parallel 'Saudization' policy is probably doomed to fail. For while one can shame firms by advertising how many Saudis they employ, if the education system remains poor, those firms will still find ways to avoid hiring Saudis. For example, firms simply pay what are often family members to remain at home, and then hire foreigners to do the work of these payroll 'phantoms'. Corruption means it is relatively easy for employers to acquire visas for foreign workers.[38]

Keenly aware of what is being said on social media (Saudis are the biggest Facebook, Twitter and WhatsApp users in the Middle East), the self-styled 'Prince of Youth' wants to make some cultural changes without offending the Wahhabi clergy or religious Salafists who might threaten the monarchy. He has reined in the omnipresent Mutaween religious police, who tend to beat those they harass or detain. He has created a Ministry of Entertainment too, though as yet there are no public cinemas in Saudi Arabia, and though there is an opera house, no opera has ever been performed there. Allegedly a suburb in Riyadh will be dedicated to 'fun'.[39]

Contrary to traditional consensus decision-making, Vision 2030 was the handiwork of MbS and key technocrats. Those left out in the cold will not feel invested in making this vast project work especially if it jeopardizes Saudi Arabia's underlying social contract. Worse, though it seemed relatively easy to cut public sector profligacy and subsidies, it is much harder to create sustainable employment in which even 'educated' youth are poorly skilled and ill equipped to compete in a free labour market. Withdrawal of traditional rights (or what we might regard as handouts) could seem like breach of social contract to indigent Saudis. They won't relish flipping burgers in McDonald's either, a common problem for spoiled young men across the Middle East, even if Saudis are paid a state subsidized $1,460 a month to do such work whereas a humble foreigner gets a starting wage of $320.[40]

These are not problems that can simply be exported, a strategy the regime has often employed to rid itself of troublemakers. The judicious use of 'the right to exit' means that any impetus for reform is deflected outwards – to Bahrain for hedonism or Europe and the US for hedonism and study. Many Saudis live a secret life within gated communities or special facilities like the beach clubs on the Red Sea where the Mutaween cannot enter to see men and women in Western attire or consuming alcohol, tobacco and pornography. The Kingdom is the world's seventh greatest online consumer of porn (position number one goes to Pakistan), perhaps because even pictures of women's legs on imported cornflakes packets are covered with black stickers. On one notorious occasion in 2002 these zealous police forced schoolgirls back into a raging fire because they were improperly dressed when they fled and left their headscarves behind. Fourteen of them perished.[41]

•

Saudi Arabia faces various internal threats. One might involve one of the smaller Gulf monarchies succumbing to popular revolution, the ripest candidate being Bahrain. That would really pose a challenge for the US since its espousal of democratic and human rights would run up against it being the base of the US Fifth Fleet. Trouble in Bahrain could in turn infect Saudi Arabia's own oil-rich Eastern Province, home to the Kingdom's only major minority. The protests in Bahrain in 2011 transcended the sectarian divide, and it is not inconceivable they could also do so in Saudi Arabia.[42]

The 1979 Iranian revolution empowered and emboldened the downtrodden Shi'ite minority in Eastern Province, though in the interim many Saudi Shia have become deeply critical of Iran, especially if they have been there and experienced clerical government.[43] These 3.5 million people have been actively discriminated against; they are not allowed their distinctive names, calls to prayer, cemeteries or festivals including Ashura. They are discriminated against as heretics, called snakes and excluded from public office as well as any posts in the security apparatus. Unlike Sunni Saudis they have a tradition of street protests, which are repressed violently. The Shia town of Qatif is virtually under martial law. Qatif's suburb al-Awamiyah has witnessed several attacks on Saudi security forces, at least six of whom have died, the latest in July 2017. This led to the non-appearance at the Hamburg G20 summit of either King Salman or Crown Prince Mohammad, as was widely noted. The Saudi Shia have also been attacked by ISIS. In November 2014 seven worshippers in a Shia hall were killed and twelve wounded. But the fact that Shia unrest is regional and inevitably sectarian means they are unlikely to deliver the death blow that will fell the House of Saud.[44]

In a divided society, rival princes patronize rival factions. Some support conservative Islamists, others favour more liberal elements who want a relaxation of cultural puritanism. The regime can watch coolly as they attack each other on social media. These factions might assume more threatening forms if there was division at the top. This could involve a succession crisis when King Salman dies, or the failure – or success – of reform, some of which will go too far for one group and not far enough for others. An absolute monarchy can also abruptly rescind what it has granted. Carrying out such a vast social transformation as Vision 2030 is ambitious enough, but to do so while losing old allies and simultaneously pursuing a belligerent foreign policy seems foolhardy in the extreme.[45]

It is unlikely that an Arab Spring 2.0 will topple the House of Saud, not least because young Saudis are aware of the chaos that enveloped so many societies in its wake. They do not want to become like Egypt, Libya or Syria. But the system affords them no formal means of expressing a political view, let alone a choice. Instead they gather in *samoods* (resistance salons), behind closed doors. There are many dissenting voices in Saudi Arabia, judging from social media, but they have no political vehicle.

The monarchy is so fearful that democracy would bring *fitna* (strife) that Saudi Arabia has invested in a multilayered 900-kilometre fence to seal off the nearest source of democratic contagion in Iraq. An even longer fence is going up to isolate Yemen too, since buying off border tribes has not worked. The bin Laden construction group is hard at work in the mountainous ridges, though such a barrier will take years to complete.[46]

The Saudi regime fears the civil war between the centre and the periphery in neighbouring Yemen, which is why Prince Mohammed launched Operation Decisive Storm in March 2015. It has not led to the restoration of the exiled Yemeni President Abdrabbuh Mansur Hadi (he is in Riyadh), nor to the defeat of the alliance between the northern Houthi rebels and the forces of former President Ali Abdullah Saleh, who Riyadh helped ease out. In Yemen, Saudi Arabia has even modified its hatred for the Muslim Brotherhood, regarding the local branch, the Islah party, as a force for stability. Instead, from time to time the Houthi or Saleh lob Scud missiles and mortar shells into the largely empty spaces on Saudi Arabia's southern border. One intercepted missile was sixty-five miles out from Mecca itself. This war has cost Riyadh a lot of money and, if it is unsuccessful, even in its rebranded Operation Restore Hope guise, Prince Mohammad will be blamed as its chief architect. Many want him to fail. The fact that he has had to reverse his own austerity measures after public discontent was registered and despite no increase in the price of crude oil does not augur well for a Kingdom ruled by him.[47]

But the main challenge to the Saudi dynasty is the perennial one of religious conservatives, supporters of the Muslim Brotherhood and violent radicals who one might crudely call Salafis. They were angered by Saudi connivance in the destruction of Morsi's elected government in Egypt, and Saudi clerics who want to support much more extreme forces on the Islamist side in Syria have also been proscribed. They are unlikely to welcome close cooperation between intelligence agencies in Riyadh and Tel Aviv either, especially if Israeli technology is being used to monitor domestic dissent. Regardless of the conformity of the clerical Establishment, there are many firebrand clerics in Saudi Arabia who use social media to vent their puritanical rage against the evils of modern life that the princely regime licenses. One of them claims to have 10 million Twitter followers alone. At some point they will be joined by jihadis returning from Iraq and Syria, not all of whom can be given long prison sentences. They may conspire against the monarchical regime, especially now that Nayaf has been displaced by Mohammad, and is under house arrest in his home in Jeddah.

The House of Saud has seen off the Ottomans, Nasserism, communism and Ba'athism. One should not underrate its will to survive. But any major mistakes by the Sauds might lead to open defiance from any or all of the quarters discussed above (though without coordination between Sunni and Shia or liberals and

Salafis), and could result in the Kingdom splitting into rival spaces in line with the entropy that afflicts many states in the MENA region. That would soon reverberate on all of the Saudis' lesser clients in the Gulf and beyond, as well as on the world price of oil. There would be one main beneficiary: Iran.

•

Persia became Iran in 1935. The name alludes to ancient Aryans who preceded the Persians and whose Zoroastrian faith was much older than Islam.[48] As elsewhere in the world, Britain's crisis was Iran's opportunity. The suggested name change came from the Persian consulate in Berlin, so as to ingratiate Iran with Germany's 'Aryan' rulers. Government buildings in Tehran mimicked the Third Reich style too.

Heirs to many venerable empires, and a great artistic and literary culture, Persians regard themselves as several rungs above mere Bedouin, who they contemptuously refer to as desert-dwelling camel drivers and locust-eaters. Their Arab enemies call them Safavids after the Turkic dynasty that ruled Iran from the fifteenth century. In fact, Iran has a very diverse population.[49]

While all Persians are Iranians, they are only half of Iran's population, so not all Iranians are Persian. The biggest minority are 15–20 million ethnic Azeris, who Persians regard as muscle-bound dimwits, though the current Supreme Leader is one of their number, ethnic Kurds in the Zagros Mountains, about 2 million Baluchis in Sistan near Afghanistan and Pakistan, and 2.5 million ethnic Arabs in oil-rich Khuzestan neighbouring Basra in Iraq. The Arabs, Baluchis and Kurds are Sunnis. There is not a single Sunni mosque in Tehran. Christians, Jews and Zoroastrians are tolerated, but the Baha'i sect have been severely persecuted.

The majority of Iranians are Shia 'Twelvers', who Sunni Muslims regard as deviant heretics. The Sunni believe the succession to the Prophet should be based on competence rather than kinship, which historically meant who became the caliph was whoever fused religious and political authority. Shia reject the first three caliphs and start with Ali, Mohammed's cousin and son-in-law, whose own son Hosein was slain by the Umayyad caliph Yazid I at the battle of Karbala in 680.

Shiism is both more clerical and more hierarchical than Sunni Islam, and has more explicitly mystical and martyrological sides. Shiism more closely resembles the structures of Christianity than the arrangements of Judaism or Sunni Islam. Paradoxically, the importance of clerical power was facilitated by the fact that the greatest authorities lay in Ottoman Iraq, at Karbala and Najaf, rather than in Persia, where the authorities could have got at them. Since God would never leave mankind bereft of righteous instruction, Shias believe in the Twelve Imams, some of them identifiable jurists and imams, of whom the last (the Mahdi) is alive but 'occluded' or hidden.

But Iran also experienced what sociologists blandly call developmental dictatorship. The military strongman Reza Shah did much to modernize Iran, after he usurped the last of the Qajar dynasty in 1921, becoming successively Prime Minister (1923) and then Shah in 1926 after adopting the dynastic name Pahlavi. A former army sergeant, Reza curbed tribal influences as well as the Shia clergy, some of whom he massacred to make his point. Like his hero, Turkey's Kemal Atatürk, Reza Shah outlawed veils for women and beards for men, forcing the latter to adopt Western dress. In addition to increasing the mileage of roads and railways and domestic industry, he also expanded education and a secular legal system in what he insisted from 1935 onwards had to be called 'Iran'.

After Reza Shah was deposed and exiled in a 1941 Anglo-Soviet joint effort, the British replaced him with his diffident son Mohammed Reza Shah Pahlavi. Under him, the Anglo-Iranian Oil Company (AIOC) – from 1954 one of the constituent elements of BP or British Petroleum – had a field day, extracting enormous profits under skewed agreements while treating the local workers at the major Abadan refinery like helots toiling in a hellhole.

The majlis and the country's hundred or so newspapers became vocal sources of opposition to AIOC, and in particular an aristocratic nationalist politician called Mohamed Mossadeq became wildly popular. In 1951 Mossadeq became Prime Minister and nationalized AIOC's Iranian assets. After a protracted international dispute, which Mossadeq largely won in the court of world opinion, first SIS (unsuccessfully) and then the CIA (successfully) tried to overthrow him by manufacturing local opposition.[50]

The Shah ruled Iran until April 1979, in an autocratic and modernizing fashion. His 1963 White Revolution sought to emancipate women, who got the vote and could stand for parliament in 1963 (and become diplomats, judges or ministers), and to redistribute land to the peasantry. He improved education and literacy rates, essayed crash industrialization, and introduced a rudimentary social security system, rent and price controls and measures to combat government corruption. Land reform stripped the clergy of their larger endowments and earned the Shah a condemnatory fatwa.

His most implacable opponent was the exiled cleric Ayatollah Ruhollah Khomeini, who opposed these 'Westernizing' measures, which from 1963 also included affording the large numbers of US military personnel in the country legal immunity from Iranian courts. The sheer visibility of 'Pepsi Cola civilization' in the plusher purlieus of Tehran was already resented in the teeming slums, especially as Americans enjoyed legal immunity even if they knocked down a pedestrian in their car. Curbs on democratic rights and the press accompanied the Shah's reforms, and any opposition was repressed by the SAVAK secret police. In a bad mistake he tried to replace the traditional clerical ulema with state control of mosques and mullahs.[51] The Shah was overthrown in April 1979 by huge worker and student demonstrations mobilized by the Tudeh (Masses) Party, left-wing Islamists and liberals. But the ultimate beneficiary would be Ayatollah Khomeini, hitherto known to most Iranians as a disembodied voice on smuggled audiotapes who combined populism with anti-imperialism from his base in Neauphle-le-Château outside Paris.

•

Iran is a theocracy in which the senior clergy ultimately rule the roost, though the system is a complex one with rival power centres that seem constantly labile. Since there are few political parties, politics is organized around personalities and their clients. Clerical rule suggests the blackest reaction, but this is only partly true, though the system is bitchy and gossipy in the extreme.

Although the regime is responsible for such barbaric practices as publicly hanging drug dealers and homosexuals from cranes, it is also open to many scientific innovations, whether nuclear energy, robotics or embryonic stem-cell research, where its attitudes are more 'liberal' than the US or UK. It is an unusual clerical regime that allows abortion up to 120 days of pregnancy, and encourages family planning clinics that distribute condoms and birth-control pills to limit families to two children. In that respect, Iranian demography is approximating European family norms.[52]

Iran's governmental structures are complex and based on a fusion of divine and democratic sovereignty. The Supreme Leader is elected, and can be removed by an eighty-six-man elected Assembly of Experts which meets for two days at least twice a year. Iran has had two Supreme Leaders, Khomeini until his death in 1989 and Ali Khamenei ever since. Khomeini came very close to being the returned Twelfth Imam in the eyes of his supporters, who claimed to see the Ayatollah's face on the moon. Khamenei is the son of an ethnic Azeri cleric from Mashhad who studied under Khomeini in the vast seminary at Qom with regular stints in jail under the Shah. In 1981, he survived a bomb hidden in a tape recorder as he was preaching and became the republic's third president that year and, though he was not a widely respected theologian, Supreme Leader nine years later. He does not seem to enjoy his eminence.[53]

The Supreme Leader serves for life and appoints the members of the Supreme National Security Council, the commanders of the armed forces, all senior judges (who manage agencies that investigate corruption), the heads of the national TV network, the chief imams in the mosques and the members of defence and foreign-affairs councils. The Supreme Leader also has a powerful base, quite apart from his spiritual authority. He appoints all Friday prayer leaders and he decides what content is reported on state TV and in *Kayhan*, the main newspaper.

Khomeini set up a foundation called Setad, or the Headquarters for Executing the Orders of the Imam, to confiscate abandoned assets (mainly property) left by those who fled the revolution or who were convicted under its draconian laws. Trusts funded charitable donations to 'the downtrodden', war widows and orphans as well as his own modest staff at Beite Rahbar, the Leaders' House. Today Khamenei has five hundred staff and the foundation controls assets valued at $95 billion, most of it in property, which is bought and traded at soaring prices. Setad also has major interests in banks and pharmaceutical and telecommunications companies worth $40 billion. Subject to neither inspection nor law, Setad gives the Supreme Leader an independent economic base distinct from the government or IRGC.[54] The wider clerical establishment also operates a hundred 'bonyads' which are businesses set up as charitable foundations to secure tax exemption, which all clerics enjoy along with exemption from compulsory military service. The richest of these bonyads is the Astan Quds Razawi foundation around the holy Iman Reza shrine in Mashhad, run by its custodian, Ebrahim Raisi, one of two conservative candidates for the presidency in May 2017. It employs 19,000 people in a range of businesses including carpet manufacturing and canning plants for soft drinks.[55]

Iran's regular armed forces (545,000 personnel and known as the Artesh) are impressive only by regional standards, since the country spends on defence one-twentieth of what the US splashes out each year, and much less at 3 per cent of GDP than its Gulf neighbours. Iran's 'axis of evil' is limited by the minority Shia faith in a sea of Sunni, and it is not an 'existential' threat to either Israel or the US, either of which could erase Iran from the map.

The Supreme Leader has his own paramilitary army – the Sepah e Pasdaran (Iranian Revolutionary Guard). This was originally formed to protect the revolution at a time when the regular armed forces were deemed unreliable, notably after the Iran–Iraq War erupted and the air force was suspected of plotting a counter-revolutionary coup. The IRGC consists of 125,000 armed men, with a further 90,000 fifteen- to twenty-four-year-olds in the Basij militia or Mobilization Resistance Force, whose chief Khamenei appoints too. After their demobilization in 1988, the Basiji became the main element in the regime's public morality police, which includes involvement in rigging elections. There is also a separate Ashura command to deal with civil unrest and a radical clerical unit to keep the mullahs and seminarians in order. Together, these forces combine Shia spiritual ardour and military might.

The Guard are a well-equipped force, with their own air, naval and missile detachments and an elite Quds or 'Jerusalem' force (2,000–5,000 strong) which performs external missions. We will look at what it does in more detail below. The Ministry of Intelligence and Security (MOIS) is an organ of government whose head is approved by the Supreme Leader. An iteration of the Shah's US and Israeli created SAVAK, MOIS handles operations like the attempts to murder the writer Salman Rushdie and his foreign translators. It has murky connections to various terrorist groups, as do many of the neighbouring Gulf Arab states.[56]

The IRGC is also an economic juggernaut, controlling about 36 per cent of Iran's GDP, valued at $140 billion. It controls all borders and ports and hence much valuable smuggling, including arms, oil, alcohol and drugs from Pakistan and Afghanistan, as well as links to drug cartels in Central and South America (and West Africa) via Hizbollah's overseas Lebanese nexus. The Guard owns more than a hundred companies in construction and engineering worth $12 billion or so, including Khatam al-Anbiya which alone has 750 government contracts for infrastructure, oil and gas projects. The IRGC was also at the heart of the country's covert nuclear programme. Large parts of the economy have also been privatized, or rather devolved to a new class of apparatchiks who are also entrepreneurs ('entrepetrachiks') under the control of the Social Security Organization, a vast pension fund which provides half the population with health care, disability benefits and retirement provision.

An Expediency Council is supposed to mediate disputes between parliament and the twelve-man Guardian Council, consisting of clerics and clerical jurists appointed by the Supreme Leader. The Guardians vet every candidate for the presidency and parliament, and have a right of veto over new laws which are scrutinized for their religious conformity. In 2004 it disqualified 3,600 independent and reformist candidates in elections, and in 2008 rejected a third of the candidates it had previously approved and who were sitting members of the

260-seat parliament. In 2016 it purged some 12,000 candidates. In April 2017 it disbarred the bumptious Ahmadinejad.

But it would be wrong to imagine the regime has total control. The more democratic elements in the original revolution have not gone away, and those who chafe at religious controls on their lives have augmented them. Who they include can be gauged from the young women whose headscarves are tilted back in an action called 'mal-veiling' to reveal wisps of lustrous hair, or youngsters who want to play rock music or paint pictures. Naming a baby after a figure in pre-Islamic Persian mythology is an act of defiance too. Oddly enough, so is wearing a tie in a country where collarless shirts and no ties are a symbolic rejection of Westernization. This is why each election results in waves of voters who support reformist candidates like former President Khatami or the current President, Hassan Rouhani. Some argue that democratic elections are a useful way of channelling the energies of the population along routes that the regime can ultimately control.[57]

The Islamic Revolution in Iran was arguably the most widely supported revolution in modern history – estimates suggest it was backed by as much as 11 per cent of the population. It is the story of the rise of a theocratic dictatorship that succeeded in exploiting the innate superstitions in the populace to out-manoeuvre the sophisticated urban secular elements that had toppled the Shah's regime. The world watched as such Westernized figures as Mehdi Bazargan and Abolhasam Bani-Sadr were edged aside by the all-conquering Khomeini. The losers included liberals, the Communist Tudeh party, and those who like Ali Shariati had blended Shia Islamism and Marxism into a new theology of national liberation that owed much to Franz Fanon's sentimentality towards the world's wretched. It helped that the 444 days hostage crisis with the US, which erupted in November 1979, lent the new regime anti-imperialist credentials, damaging relations with the US almost in perpetuity. The eight-year-long war with Saddam Hussein's Iraq which broke out in 1980 enabled clerics with an international revolutionary agenda to pose as Persian patriots while bolstering the prestige of their Revolutionary Guard.[58]

The concept behind the regime is *velayat-e faqih* – which means the interim regency of expert jurists until the Twelfth

Imam (Mohammad al-Mahdi) reappears from his prolonged occultation since AD 941. It is somewhat akin to the idea of Plato's Philosopher King – the assumption being that the people are not sufficiently astute to rule through direct democracy and therefore need a wise ruler to guide them. The young Khomeini was a careful student of both Aristotle and Plato. This idea was not accepted by all parts of the original coalition that formed the regime, and therefore the regime that was formed was a hybrid theocracy-democracy that oscillates between these two poles.[59]

If the old triangular political system was based on the Shah, the clergy and the commercial Bazaar, the new one comprises the Supreme Leader, the clergy and the Bazaar. Like Wall Street the Bazaar is both a physical place, notably the enormous market in central Tehran, and a metaphor for a ramified commercial and trading class that is involved in international trade (via Dubai) and smuggling, as well as selling pistachio nuts, spices and Persian carpets.

The Supreme Leader (the title is *Rahbar e inqilab e-islami* – which means the Leader of the Islamic Revolution) became nothing more or less than a Shah with a turban and beard. Like the Safavid founder Isma'il Shah, Khomeini cultivated an image of being supernaturally inspired, with some esoteric relationship with Allah and the Imam 'Ali and is therefore to be regarded as infallible.

The new regime succeeded in consolidating power by mobilizing anti-US hysteria in the 1979–80 US embassy hostage crisis, and through an eight-year war with Iraq (1980–88). This was a boon to Khomeini since it enabled the regime to call on the patriotism of Iranians and to attribute the lack of improvement in the lot of the populace to the war and not his clerical regime. Anything up to a million Iranians were killed, whether by Saddam's bombing, missile and chemical weapons onslaught or in suicide attacks in which waves of young boys were sent into minefields with their (Chinese-manufactured) plastic keys to paradise. Relatives of these martyrs of the revolution are one of the main supports of the clerical regime, not least since they are the main beneficiaries of its charity. The death toll dwarfs any other wars of the late twentieth century, and makes Iranians wary of foreign adventurism. They will fight against Israel or for Assad down to the last Shia, be they Afghan, Lebanese or Pakistani.[60]

Khomeini's special status protected him from the consequences of having to agree to a ceasefire. He slyly made the then President Khamenei announce it, after stating that it was Allah's will that the war continue until Iraqi dictator Saddam Hussein was killed. When Khomeini died in 1989 *velayat e-faqih* began to fall apart. The constitution had to be amended in order to accommodate the facts that his chosen successor – Ali Khamenei – was not a high-level cleric (just a *hujjat al-Islam*) and that most of the High Ayatollahs do not accept the concept of *velayat e-faqih*, and like Ayatollah Seyyed Kazem Shari'atmadari had been silenced in 1980–81 for saying so. One of Khomeini's parting gifts was to fulfil the Shah's attempt to bring the clergy under state control, with 'becoming an ayatollah' more a matter of conformity than of intellectual rigour or spiritual depth. To make sure, Khamenei controls the seminaries and uses computer systems to keep clerics on a tight lead. If they transgress, they appear before the secretive Special Court of Clerics and are executed or imprisoned.[61]

Khamenei is the son of an Azeri cleric. His early influences were Marxism and the Egyptian Islamist ideologue Sayyid Qutb, whose work he translated. He is also widely read in Russian literature, even though his favourite novel is said to be Hugo's *Les Misérables*.[62] He became President of Iran after his predecessor was assassinated along with the Prime Minister. Though he held that office for eight years, this was wartime. The dominant PM, Mir Hossein Mousavi, and the Supreme Leader's deputy as commander-in-chief, Akbar Hashemi Rafsanjani, eclipsed President Khamenei.

Remarkably enough, the right-wing Khamenei was viewed as relatively pro-American (he now calls the US 'the arrogance') at a time when leftist Islamists were more hostile to the US. Becoming anti-American, as he did, served to neutralize them in parliament. Since then, Khamenei has skilfully extended his own centres of power to weaken two reformist presidents, Rafsanjani and Mohammad Khatami, as well as their conservative populist successor Ahmadinejad.

•

The essential dynamics of the Iranian system are unique. Iran is authoritarian, democratic, Islamic and revolutionary, and all these elements operate simultaneously. The political spectrum in and beyond parliament runs through reformists, pragmatists, conservatives and fundamentalists (who are usually called the 'Principalists'). The latter have since split, one faction associated with former President Ahmadinejad being dubbed the deviationists. There are also latent tensions between a decadent and sophisticated capital and the puritanical provinces (as there are in many Western states too, of course).[63]

Once the war with Iraq ended, pressures for reform to achieve what the revolution had promised increased. This swept Rafsanjani to power in 1989. He liberalized the economy (often to his clique's own advantage) and sought to restore relations with the West, while not relaxing the regime's social conservatism. On his retirement he ensured that the election of his reformist successor would not be rigged. In 1997, 70 per cent of voters, on an 80 per cent turnout, supported the moderate cleric Mohammad Khatami, who pushed the economic reforms further while relaxing domestic censorship (particularly in the film industry and press) and seeking an international 'dialogue of civilizations'.[64]

The reformers were handicapped by two factors, one external, the other internal. Any possibility of a rapprochement with the US after 9/11 – ordinary Iranians condemned the attacks and Iran cooperated with the US in Western Afghanistan – was snuffed out by President Bush's 2002 'Axis of Evil' speech in which his wordsmiths lumped together Kim Jong-il, Saddam and Iran in obvious ignorance of all three. This did not help the cause of reform in Iran, which felt itself under siege, with US troops to the west in Iraq and to the east in Afghanistan. Khatami also found himself subject to a constant war of attrition at home, with hardliners using corruption charges to pick off his ministers, while the MOIS intelligence service used a fake 'serial killer' to murder prominent reformist intellectuals. The serial killer turned out to be a rogue cell within MOIS.[65]

The second generation of any revolution tend to look at the promise of revolutionary utopia and ask themselves why things are not now perfect. In Iran there were two rival answers: the reformists suggested that the revolution has to be tweaked and some of its principles corrected, while the 'Jacobins' felt that the failure of the revolution lay in the flagging of revolutionary ardour, which therefore had to be returned to its pure essentials.

This second-generation revolutionary elite embodied by the Islamic Revolutionary Guard Corps (IRGC) became the newest pillar of power, weakening the three traditional vertices. Originally established to corral a variety of radical armed factions, the guard became the bloodhounds of the Revolution as well as a useful source of heroic and pious cannon-fodder to plug gaps in the regular forces fighting Saddam's Iraq in attritional battles that sometimes resembled the Somme. They control the Supreme Leader's office by virtue of their role as gatekeepers of incoming information and outgoing operational orders, and they have created an alternative military-industrial economy that weakens the Bazaar. At the same time, they restrict the clergy's independent collection of taxes (*khoms*) so they are now at the mercy of the regime for their stipends.

Mahmoud Ahmadinejad – a scion of the IRGC/Basij elite – was the first representative of this group to take power from the first generation of the revolution when he was elected President in 2005. The five foot two inch son of a blacksmith, he was liked by ordinary people for his piety and native cheek, as well as his bad haircut, simple nylon windbreakers and modest car. A former traffic systems engineer who changed his original surname to seem less provincial, Ahmadinejad became Mayor of Tehran in 2003. A principalist, his spiritual muse was Ayatollah Yazdi, a cleric who calls elections un-Islamic, compares dissidents with the AIDS virus and who openly urged Iran to acquire a nuclear bomb, something other Shia clerics regard as un-Islamic.

One of Ahmadinejad's first acts as mayor was to insist that the remains of wartime martyrs be reburied in parks in the wealthier suburbs of northern Tehran, to shame courting couples and rich people who had avoided the draft. This sparked riots. As President he succeeded by playing on the resentments of the rural poor and urban unemployed with his combination of exaggerated promises and religious fanaticism. Within two years his introduction of petrol rationing had made more than 60 per cent of those who had voted for him say they would not do so again.[66] Worse, he became a national embarrassment, at least to the educated Iranian middle class who know that Cyrus the Great and Reza Shah were friends of Iran's Jews, a minority who played a liberalizing role in the constitutional struggles of the early twentieth century too. In 2006 Ahmadinejad said that 'this Jerusalem-occupying regime must disappear from the page of time', which was translated crudely as 'Israel must be wiped from the map'. Next he hosted a conference of Holocaust-deniers, the participants including a former head of the Ku Klux Klan and ultra-Orthodox Hasidim who regard Israel as a presumptuous intrusion on the divine will.

The elections that preceded his second term (in 2009) were rigged and sparked a wave of unrest – the Green Revolution – which was viciously repressed by the Basij militias prowling on motorcycles. Its leaders, Mehdi Karroubi and the runner-up election candidate Hossein Mousavi, are still under house arrest. Economic discontents and absence of freedoms were primary drivers of these protests. After Ahmadinejad's re-election, Khamenei wearied of the strange little fellow's overweening pretensions, especially when the madcap President sought to 'clarify' the financial assets of the IRGC and Supreme Leader, notably wealth derived from smuggling. He also dismissed the Intelligence Minister who Khamenei had appointed and then vanished for twelve days when told to reappoint him. Next he accused parliament of being involved in corruption too. Khamenei used charges of 'sorcery' against the President's acolytes and then swung his support behind Hassan Rouhani in 2013.

About 40 million Iranians have internet access. The Great Persian Firewall enables the regime to shut out the global internet while the domestic net continues unimpeded. The Shenzen-based telecommunications group ZTE Corps supplied Telecommunications Co. of Iran with technology that enables the regime to monitor all landline, mobile and internet usage, and to investigate those using sophisticated networks like Tor to evade censors. Typically, the IRGC combine censorship of the net with selling the VPNs that enable crafty users to circumvent the censors. This enables the Ministry of Intelligence and Security to closely monitor critics and dissenters. But there is a rational calculation too. As in China, such electronic protectionism is used for the benefit of local cover versions of Western businesses, so that Iran has a thriving copy of Amazon and may soon have a Persian-language version of Baidu, the Chinese search engine that rivals Google. Persians are enterprising people.[67]

•

Iran is the last major emerging market to be effectively outside the world economy, a fact constantly boosted by Western businessmen and bankers. Apart from hydrocarbons, it has automobile, cement, petrochemicals, agricultural and mining sectors, including coal, copper, iron ore and uranium. The auto industry is already the thirteenth largest in the world, and in addition to the local market, mainly French manufacturers with joint ventures in Iran have high hopes of a wider regional market of 400 million people. Iran has the world's second largest reserves of natural gas (with 200–800 trillion cubic feet potentially awaiting exploitation) and is third or fourth in terms of proven oil reserves. Although Iran's refining capacities are antiquated (partly because of US sanctions imposed after 1979, reinforced since 2006 and then augmented by the EU in 2012 over the nuclear bomb issue), oil production has been ramped up pretty sharply since 2015 and will not stop until Iran has revisited 4 million barrels output per day.

Much of Iran's oil wealth is squandered on domestic subsidies in a country where fuel costs less than bottled mineral water. Each year $100 billion is spent on keeping local petrol at ten cents a litre. Paradoxically, Iran therefore still has to import fuel, and since 2007 petrol has been rationed. Further subsidies control the price of bread, cooking oil and rice. In December 2010 parliament passed Ahmadinejad's Targeted Subsidies Law, designed to phase out subsidies on food and fuel over the next five years. Direct payments of $45 per person to 90 per cent of Iranian households were one way of mitigating discontent about the ending of the subsidy regime, though it proved impossible to discriminate between poor people who needed these payments and the rich who did not.

Sanctions had major impacts on Iran, despite Western hawks denouncing them as being ineffective. In the wake of 9/11 in particular, US agencies were in fact very effective in closing Iran's access to the international banking system. Even now, banks deal with Iran at their peril, as HSBC and Paribas discovered.

The effects of sanctions on ordinary Iranians were grim, and served to accentuate the lifestyle of a jeunesse dorée driving Porsches. The rial suffered severe depreciation and inflation rocketed to 40 per cent. The price of chicken trebled in a year, so Iranian TV stopped broadcasting any historical drama or soap operas in which chicken feasts were too prominent.[68] In 2015 inflation halved to around 20 per cent and the budget deficit is falling. Every cloud has a silver lining. Unlike the Gulf rentier states which rely on oil and gas revenues that have en-abled them to dispense with income tax, VAT and representative institutions, Iran has a relatively efficient tax system. Rouhani's administration hopes to extend this over the IRGC empire, having already forced exempt religious foundations to pay taxes. Currently tax income exceeds oil revenues, even though 40 per cent of the economy goes untaxed, and the number of taxpayers is likely to increase thanks to a new integrated tax system recommended by Deloitte Canada and a French IT firm.[69]

The need to husband oil and gas exports is one of the reasons the Iranians sought nuclear power, as represented by the Russian-built reactor at Bushehr that came online in 2010. It also reflects Iran's strategic ambitions, and a need for modernistic prestige akin to the old Soviet Union's investment in Sputniks and Soyuz. Iran pursued both uranium and plutonium tracks. But there were also uranium high-enrichment activities (beyond any conceivable Iranian medical isotopic need) and a parallel attempt to manufacture key elements of a bomb, as well as a parallel ballistic missile programme. The latter was excluded from negotiations.

The key issues were not so much the theoretical capability, but whether Iran had successfully 'weaponized' a miniature warhead for a ballistic missile, and how long it would take to assemble a live weapon. Evidence of all or anything of this was welcome news for the hawkish war parties in the US and Israel, even though, from late 2006, Iran was subject to a tightening noose of UN, US and EU sanctions. The price was mainly paid by French and German companies trading with Iran. For example, Peugeot had to close an entire plant, which virtually destroyed the livelihood of a French town. Not so good for the hawks was the 2007 consensus view of all seventeen US intelligence agencies that Iran had abandoned its quest for a nuclear weapon in 2003.

The idea of Iran having a nuclear bomb strikes morbid terrors into the Gulf Arabs and Israel, whose Prime Minister, Benjamin Netanyahu, regards the prospect as an 'existential' threat, huffing and puffing against it, as well as eliminating key scientific personnel and using cyber weapons (such as the Stuxnet virus) against German-supplied industrial operating systems. In 2012 the US made him back down from threats of military strikes by avowing their military support for Israel.*

As the so-called 'spy revolt' by the likes of Meir Dagan and Yuval Diskin, respectively heads of Mossad and Shin Bet, showed, most of Netanyahu's intelligence chiefs do not share his morbid apprehensions, especially those who spent their careers frustrating Iran's nuclear ambitions. Nor did former chiefs of staff like Shaul Mofaz.[†] Despite the celebrated 1981 raid on Iraq's Osirak reactor, Israel was not in a position to disable the many hardened and dispersed targets that Iran had, and it lacked operational mid-air refuelling tankers. Iran's Russian-supplied S-300 missiles are also a deterrent, as they are in Syria.[70] Instead, Netanyahu outrageously interfered in US domestic politics against Obama, and with a view to the US finishing any war with Iran that Israel started. Following the last US presidential election, Israel's current line is to say the nuclear deal is 'good' for the next seven years, since the IAEA monitoring regime is so strict that the Trump administration would be 'foolhardy and reckless to scuttle it now', but thereafter the US should be ready to strike or let Israel do the job.[71]

---

* I attended this conference in Herzliyha, where US Envoys John Negroponte and Michèle Flournoy delivered the bad tidings in the most silky of ways to an audience that included Netanyahu, Ehud Barack, various diplomats and army and intelligence chiefs.
† Of course, these objections tended to be raised after these men retired.

Iran's Supreme Leader gave the team political cover for 'heroic flexibility' in talks against hardliners who feared any wider liberalization a deal might bring. In the event, the Iranians agreed to a fifteen-year moratorium on their nuclear programmes in return for gradual lifting of sanctions. The deal put at least a year between having the capacity (for knowledge cannot be erased) and the ability to build a weapon. Enough activity was left in place to satisfy widespread Iranian belief that having a civil nuclear capacity was their sovereign right. For the time being this seems to have also halted the prospect of nuclear proliferation across the region, a theme Israel emphasized heavily too. Talk of a 'polynuclear' Middle East, commencing with Saudi Arabia getting an off-the-shelf bomb from Pakistan, remains mere talk, as both states would be sanctioned for proliferation and Saudi Arabia lacks modern missiles to deliver the warhead.[72]

Iran endeavoured to circumvent sanctions that cost the country $45–50 billion in lost oil revenues a year while $100 billion more was frozen in Western banks. It reoriented its oil exports to Japan, China, India, South Korea and Pakistan, though all haggled about price, and India tried to offload contaminated wheat in return for oil supplies. Iran resorted to reflagging and renaming tankers (again thwarted) and removing tracking devices, though a sanction against insuring tankers was a big problem. The IRGC may have welcomed sanctions since it acquired a major slice of the ensuing autarchic resistance economy that developed in compensation. President Rouhani has sought to reduce this power, partly because IRGC involvement in any business automatically incurs sanctions. Either way, the recovery of Iran's oil exports has been very rapid, so that they are currently only 200,000 barrels per day short of the pre-sanctions levels in 2011, or about 3.2 million bpd, and they hope to reach 4 million bpd soon.[73]

•

Although the war with Saddam's Iraq meant the adoption of an Iran First strategy, in which defending the Republic was paramount, from its inception until the present Iran has also believed that offence is the best form of defence. The main vehicle for this has always been the IRGC's Quds force, and a murky nether-world of terrorists of whom the best known was Imad Mughniyah – Hizbollah's mastermind of the 1983 Beirut US Embassy and barracks bombings and a lethal 1993 attack on the Israeli embassy in Buenos Aires – who the CIA and Mossad killed in Damascus in February 2008 with a car bomb as he exited an Iranian embassy reception celebrating the twenty-ninth anniversary of the Revolution. But Iran also has major allies beyond the friendly government it has in Baghdad and its Hiz-bollah friends in Lebanon. Leaving aside its bonds with Caracas, the clerical regime has paradoxically allied itself with a Russia that sees itself as the champion of conservative Christian values, and China, which is ruled by an atheist Communist Party.

Although the Iranian regime is Shia, it has always had uni-versal pretensions, though these were muted during the war with Iraq. It clearly wishes to destroy the Saudi and Gulf mon-archies, and to be a major player among the Arab republics to the west. It hates and fears the US in equal measure, believing that the 'Great Satan' is bent on regime change in Iran by back-ing colours revolutions (uprisings named after specific colours), ethnic separatism and/or the encouragement of 'dual sover-eignty', whereby institutions seek autonomy from the clerical hierarchy dominated by the Supreme Leader. This explains why Iran has swum into the orbit of Russia and China, neither of which preach about human rights, as well as – like the Iranians – creating 'zombie human rights' NGOs of their own.

In addition to Russia, Iran's friends and allies include the quasi-governmental Hizbollah in southern Lebanon, Assad's Syria, and the Shia government in Iraq, with a few add-ons in Bolivia, Cuba, Ecuador, Nicaragua and Venezuela.

Iran's interest in Lebanon grew after the Israeli invasion and occupation of the country's south in 1982. This was especially so since Hizbollah, with its strongholds in south Beirut and the Bekaa valley, was one of the few Shia communities to explicitly adopt Iran's own system of ultimate clerical authority, as symbolized by its own mini-Ayatollah Sheikh Hassan Nasrullah, Hizbollah's Secretary-General since 1992. More importantly, Hizbollah affords Iran a permanent retaliatory capacity against Israel, as was seen in the thirty-four-day war in 2006 when Hizbollah fought Israel to a standstill with Iranian-supplied weapons, a rare occurrence in the military relations of Arabs and Israelis. Since then, Iran has refurbished Hizbollah's arsenal with up to 55,000 rockets. Hizbollah and various murky terrorist grouplets have enabled Iran to strike at US and Israeli and 'Jewish' interests (they are not identical, of course) much further afield through terrorist bombings from Argentina to Bulgaria. But Iran also has to be careful not to outrage Sunni opinion within Lebanon that might affect Hizbollah's local position as part of the Lebanese government.

Notwithstanding the sectarian divide, Iran has cultivated Hamas and Palestine Islamic Jihad under the flag of an Islamic universalism it still professes, after deciding that the PLO was too secular in spirit, for example allowing women to fight alongside men. It also did not help that PLO Chairman Yasser Arafat supported Saddam Hussein. Iran refers to Israel as the 'Zionist entity' and seeks to destroy it, claiming it is a Western colonial implant in the region. This, of course, completely ignores the numbers of Israeli Jews with Iranian or Iraqi surnames or that some realists inside the Iranian regime do not feel the need to be 'more Palestinian than the Palestinians'. It could well be that in order to contain Iran, Trump will license an Israeli strike against Hizbollah, while simultaneously giving enhanced military aid to the Saudis to prosecute their war in Yemen beyond the $300 billion of weapons he is selling them.

Iran also supports the Alawite regime in Syria, chiefly because Hafez al-Assad was the only major Arab leader to support Iran in its war with Iraq following the rift between the two rival branches of Ba'athism. Trying to shame Iran with Assad's cruelty is water off a duck's back. Syria is essential to Iran's ability to resupply Hizbollah, and one day it might afford Iran direct egress to the Eastern Mediterranean towards which Tehran wants to build a road and rail link. That is why from as early as March 2011, the IRGC has been operating in Syria, while Hizbollah has provided Assad with a missing light infantry capability. Film footage captured by Syrian Sunni rebels reveals much about the motivation of IRGC combat units there. The IRGC's Qassem Soleimani played a key role in persuading

Russia to send combat forces to Syria when it seemed that Assad was on the verge of losing in 2015.

Iranian influence is also strong inside majority Shia Iraq, with which Iran shares a 910-mile border, but Tehran has to tread carefully with Iraqi Shia clerics at Najaf who enjoy great status inside Iran itself. An eminence like the Shia divine Sistani is no malleable puppet of Tehran's. Iran went to the aid of Shia militias who fought the Americans and British after the 2003 invasion, and though they failed to spot the rise of ISIS, they are back in force directing Shia Popular Mobilization forces battling the Sunni terror group in parallel to forces backed by Trump. By 2008 Soleimani was writing to US commander David Petraeus as an equal after the IRGC commander brokered a ceasefire in Basra between Iraqi Prime Minister Maliki and Shia insurgents who had taken over when the British messed up. The American did not reply. It may be that when Tehran helped the US to get rid of Maliki, it hoped also to downgrade Qassem Soleimani himself, a close ally of Maliki. Certainly Iran introduced a new man to Iraq in the shape of another IRGC war hero, Ali Shamkhani, an ethnic Arab from Iran's Khuzestan majority Arab province. At that point, Soleimani, who preferred the shadows, decided to launch a personal PR campaign. The slightly built IRGC commander with the grey beard and iron-grey hair became an Iranian media celebrity as he was shown directing Shia forces, and liaising with their Kurdish allies at crucial battles against ISIS. How he must have relished profiles in the *New Yorker*.[74]

Iran is adamant that Iraq should remain a unitary state lest federalism prove catching in an Iran that is so ethnically fissiparous. An independent Kurdish state would be a magnet for Iran's own Kurdish minority who languish amidst underdevelopment, while an independent Iraqi Sunni statelet would be a client of Saudi Arabia. The reduced Shia dominated rump would be of little account as an ally. Iran wants order in Iraq, but not an Iraq that can be a competitor or threat to Iran itself, let alone a springboard for US forces to attack Iran from the west.

When Iran does not get its way, it causes mischief through such clients as Muqtada al-Sadr with his Peace Brigades private army. Iran maintained benevolent neutrality in the removal of

Iraq's sectarian Prime Minister Nouri al-Maliki, and his replacement by Haider al-Abadi. Though the latter is more emollient towards the Sunni, his cabinet is actually more Shia in composition than Maliki's, though paradoxically he is cooler towards Iran than his predecessor, who spent years in Iran as an exile.

Iran was the first country to rush arms to the autonomous Kurdish region of Iraq as ISIS advanced, and it supplies 140 tons of arms to Baghdad every day as well as Ababil surveillance drones. While Iran arms and directs its Shia proxies to fight ISIS, its regular military interventions have been episodic and designed to ward off ISIS when it came close to the Iraq–Iran border. In August 2013 tanks from the Iranian regular army's 71st Mechanized Brigade and 181st Armoured Brigade intervened to help repel ISIS when it came within twenty miles of that frontier. Unlike the optional war in Syria, most Iranians regard the proximity of ISIS, whose depredations against Shia they are familiar with, as an existential issue, though equally they do not want to be involved in an all-out war inside rather than with Iraq. Finally, Iran has increased its support for the Houthi rebels in Yemen. Even before the Arab Spring, Iran arranged their training with Hizbollah in the Lebanon. But the Houthi are not Iran's obliging puppets. They seized the capital Sanaa in September 2015, against Iranian advice, and they rejected Iran's desire for a permanent naval base in Yemen. In Iranian eyes the Houthi are just a useful way to bleed Saudi Arabia of money at minimal cost to themselves since total Iranian casualties in Yemen have been a mere twenty-three.[75]

Iran is ruled by pragmatists as well as true believers and many Iranians chafe at clerical rule. At various times it has decided that discretion is the better part of valour and avoided conflicts with its fifteen neighbours. The republic's diplomats are silky operators, as the nuclear deal suggests, though Iran had to give up more than is often remarked. Compared with them, the moneyed Saudis seem like erratic clowns, and one positive result of the nuclear deal is that the clowns have to pedal harder to deal with the terrorism they inspire, lest the West turns to Iran instead. In Afghanistan, Iranian policies were roughly congruent with those of the US, since Iran has stabilized the western region around Herat after its diplomats and spies were murdered there, while boosting the Northern Alliance remnants to resist the Sunni Taliban. Iran is implacably opposed to Al Qaeda, despite harbouring some of its personnel under 'house arrest', and wants to suppress drug trafficking and warlordism as much as the Americans, not least because Iran itself has a major heroin-addiction problem afflicting two million people. Iran has contributed large amounts of money for Afghan reconstruction ($560 million in 2002 and another $100 million in 2006), money which it has actually paid. Some think that US cooperation with Iran in Afghanistan could be a template for future cooperation in Iraq.

Western sanctions led Iran to strengthen existing links with China. As in the case of India, it is a civilization Iranians admire, despite repression of Muslims in both countries. Trade increased from $4 billion in 2003 to $36 billion in 2013. Xi wants to push it up to $600 billion in ten years' time. Iran is China's third largest oil supplier. Iran would like to join the Shanghai Co-operation Council, the Sino-Russian block that opposes the West. One thrust is to defend 'civilizational diversity' and 'traditional values' against a universalizing Western liberalism that claims human rights are inalienable and universal. Another aspect of the relationship is less visible but no less effective.[76]

Iran has gained access to Chinese technology that can be used to monitor mobile communications and the internet (technology China probably acquires from Israel). China, Russia and Venezuela have also given Iran valuable advice on how to wage information warfare, one result being the controversial Press TV. Iran has also learned to combat Western criticism of Iran's human rights abuses by creating a Human Rights Council (under Mohammad Javad Larijani) that aggressively rebuts Western claims and norms.[77] Characteristically, the Chinese have maintained good relations with Iran while building a second pillar with Saudi Arabia, as the US did in the early 1970s with the Shah and Riyadh. Saudi Arabia is China's second largest oil supplier (after Angola) with bilateral trade worth about $60 billion, compared with half that amount with Iran. Although for the Chinese it is primarily a matter of business, at some point they may have to arbitrate between these rivals or intervene to protect their interests. For them it is all about oil in ways that were never true for the US and is certainly not the case now.[78]

•

But the future is far from assured. Neither major power centre in Tehran seems content with the other. Khamenei has frequently asked whether Iran needs a president at all, since it has a Supreme Leader and could shift to a parliamentary constitution, while opponents of the mullahs wonder if a more diluted trio of clerical leaders might be an improvement on the autocratic legacy of Khomeini. Though criticism of the Supreme Leader is taboo, Khamenei has stomach and prostate trouble, and minds are turning to the future.[79]

Although some informed observers, such as Israel's last ambassador to the Shah, believe that the regime will succumb to a democratic counter-revolution, its repressive powers are formidable, as can be seen from its lockdown of social media during the 2009 unrest. But waves of democratic protest are likely to recur in a country with a lively civic culture and a history of popular uprisings. Ordinary people like to remind Iran's rulers of a venerable metaphor in which those standing on the bottom of a ladder have less far to fall than those perched shakily on the highest rungs.[80]

The election in August 2013 of the 'emollient' cleric-politician Hassan Rouhani as President was positively received in the West. Born in 1948, he studied in Glasgow after Qom. He also did military service, from which clerics may claim exemption, as this eased his path to being a lawyer. This partly explains successive active defence roles in the 1980–88 war with Iraq, including arms procurement in China and the Soviet Union. He was also a player in the US Iran–Contra deal. This was followed by sixteen years on Iran's National Security Council. Since the late 1980s he has been involved with Iran's nuclear programme.[81]

Rouhani defeated all of the conservative candidates arrayed against him and appeared to enjoy the support of many young Iranians who had protested in vain in 2009. He also had the support of Supreme Leader Ali Khamenei in opening a limited space in which Iran's nuclear programme could be traded for the alleviation of sanctions. The current Israeli leadership remain convinced that Rouhani is a 'wolf in sheep's clothing', but other governments around the world take a different view. Since he has improved relations between Iran and countries that have not totally ingested the Israeli-Saudi world view, 57 per cent of Iranian voters gave Rouhani the benefit of the doubt regarding economic improvements to their lives.

In the immediate aftermath of the nuclear deal, some in the West hoped that Iran might evolve into a force for stability in this most volatile region where 20 per cent of the world's oil passes through the Straits of Hormuz. These waters narrow to twenty-one miles and maritime traffic there is intense, as one can see from internet sites that monitor the location of every ship in the world. Others feared that, having reaped the benefits of a partial unfreezing of bank assets, Iran would embark on a renewed cycle of mischief. This is to ignore the instant 'snap back' of sanctions that are enshrined in the deal and the continuation of sanctions by several US agencies that have the power to withdraw banking licences.

Experience and the idiosyncratic structure of the Islamic regime suggest that hedging bets is wise, given the not so submerged power of elements that do not wish the West well. But the 'hardliners' also realize that if the ordinary Iranian's lot does not quickly improve, then the next democratic wave could be the regime's last. In reality, now that external threats have eased, one suspects that the four elements of Iran's polity will persist in uneasy equilibrium, which is probably sufficiently stable for Westerners to develop their interests there. France's Total and a Chinese company signed a $4.8 billion gas deal with Iran in July 2017.

Three-quarters of Iranians say there has been no improvement in their lives since the nuclear deal, and conservatives have sought to exploit the resentments of the 96 per cent against the rich 'four per cent', without acknowledging Bernie Sanders's 'one per cent' trope. A scandal in which four bank bosses were found to have awarded themselves salaries and bonuses of $78,000 a month in a country where basic pay for a worker is $276 a month was not good for the reformers. Nor has it helped that the US House of Representatives blocked sales of Boeing aircraft to Iran, a country whose national carrier essentially flies death traps. Rouhani may play well among the sophisticated bourgeoisie of northern Tehran (a city that bulks very large in setting the tone), but the conservatives know how to work the provinces as well as promising to double or triple income support for the poor. A brief attempt by Ahmadindejad to revive his career was crushed by the Guardian Council which disqualified him from running in May 2017 for the clerics are not keen on lay Islamists. The favoured conservative clerical alternative Raisi does not yet have a sufficient profile to rival Rouhani, though it was his Tehran mayoral colleague Mohammad Bagher Ghalibaf, a perennial also-ran, who dropped out of the contest, not least so as not to queer Raisi's chances of succeeding Khamenei. Moreover, the regime usually allows presidents two terms to build on the international contacts they have forged. In the event, following a huge turnout of 40 million voters, Rouhani won the election in May 2017 with 58.5 per cent of the vote to Raisi's 39.8 per cent, a victory so emphatic that state television announced it almost immediately and few cried foul.[82] The election coincided with President Trump fawning in front of fifty Sunni Muslim autocrats gathered in Riyadh, who, with the exception of Tunisia, would never countenance such elections.

The advent of Trump and his core team of hardline enemies of Iran (who include Defense Secretary James Mattis) has immediately ratcheted up the rhetoric over Iranian ballistic missile tests and minor maritime skirmishes, while they included Iran among the seven majority Muslim nations with a terrorism problem whose citizens were banned from entering the US. Incredibly, Pakistan and Saudi Arabia were omitted, as was the UK, three of whose citizens have carried out attacks on the US, which is three more than people from Yemen. The Americans failed to mention that Iran and its Shia proxies are battling ISIS and the Nusra Front in parallel with the Americans themselves. Supreme Leader Khamenei immediately latched on to an incident at Dulles Airport where a five-year-old boy was held in handcuffs while his Iranian-American mother (a US citizen) was questioned, on the grounds that the boy might have been a 'security threat'. The 2009 drumbeat of war has recommenced, with the Murdoch-owned *Wall Street Journal* and London

Times in the lead in publishing thinly adapted Emirati, Israeli and Saudi propaganda against Iran, a constant theme in the *Daily Telegraph* too. Op-ed commentators in the *WSJ* explicitly wanted the hardliners to win the May 2017 election, to help repaint Iran in black rather than grey. Having expressed considerable scepticism towards the Saudis, President Trump duly made Riyadh his first port of call on his first foreign foray, where he acquiesced in demands to bolster the anti-Iranian Gulf axis while selling more of Raytheon's Paveway bombs and Penetrator missiles to rain down on the starving Yemenis. Trump may opt for regime change in Iran, if only to distinguish himself from his predecessor, whose hopes of the nuclear deal leading to liberalization were also illusory.[83]

We in the West are not obliged to take sides in these epic struggles by psychologically identifying with one or other rival power or subnational minority within them. Because one knows the Saudis are responsible for poisoning young minds the world over, this does not make Iran a beacon of beneficence. Much effort goes into capturing the US for each side's cause, in dozens of complex regional conflicts whose dynamics few in the US really understand. Likewise, despite the colonial era, Europeans owe nothing to those who are currently responsible for the entropic chaos of the region, unless one imagines those in power labour under some sort of psychological tutelage. Historic guilt is no more a reliable guide to policy than elite romanticism about 'Arabs' or 'Persians', where steelier views might be more appropriate regarding what is in our general interest.

Being officially evangelical about spreading democracy, human rights, or the resolution of conflicts that insiders cannot or will not support is a fool's errand. Instead of pursuing fantasies that bear no relation to reality on the ground, Western nations should look to their essential national interests (and those of the US and Europe or Israel do not always coincide). This may mean involvement with regimes that are hostile, rather than with so-called allies who wish us harm. We should abandon discretionary enterprises or interventionist wars of choice. Our major objectives should be to wean Western economies off hydrocarbons, to protect our societies from Islamist terror threats and to prevent the domination of a single regional power, by counterbalancing Iran and Saudi Arabia. The latter objective has been achieved with the nuclear deal with Iran, the ultimate objective is advanced by every new electric car. Drawing 'red lines' that are crossed, or talk of implementing the Right to Protect through ill-thought-out no-fly zones, are just some of the things we should avoid doing. Transformational diplomacy and vaulting humanitarian ambition bear no resemblance to the angry, broken, dysfunctional Middle East whose destiny is not our responsibility. Perhaps after our failures, others will play a more constructive role. How the civilized world has reacted to the eruption of barbarism is not consoling, as we will see.[84]

3

Islamic State (ISIS): Messages In Blood

The Islamic State of Iraq and Syria (ISIS) grew in stages in 2004, 2006 and 2013 from the decade of chaos and sectarian violence that ensued from the 2003 US-led invasion of Iraq.[1] The Arabic names for jihadi organizations shift with remarkable frequency, not least since jihadis regard name changes as significant. ISIS calls itself a caliphate, meaning it has a ruling caliph who combines secular and spiritual powers into a seamless whole. In April 2013 Abu Bakr al-Baghdadi (the caliph) explained why ISI should be known as ISIL, it being 'permissible to cancel the names of jihadist groups and replace them with ones commensurate with their (higher level of) development and nobility . . . new names that would make us forget the previous ones despite our affection for them'.[2]

The earliest iteration of what mutated into ISIS was conceived in Afghanistan before 9 September 2001, and transplanted to Iraqi Kurdistan as 'Tawhid wa'l Jihad' by its Jordanian Palestinian leader Abu Musab al-Zarqawi. A grant of $200,000 from bin Laden enabled him to establish a training camp at Abdul Mehdi near the Iranian border. Zarqawi was a Jordanian Bedouin criminal (from Zarqa) who had been radicalized in jail, the process aided by solitary confinement and torture, before spending years as a self-styled 'stranger' in bin Laden's Afghan camps. He was not a natural subordinate, nor a regretful man of violence.

Returned to Iraq, Zarqawi essayed a rudimentary Islamic State in towns like Biara, Khurmal and Tawela. These were run according to the primitive mores of the seventh century. Under cover of the much broader-based resistance to US occupation, Zarqawi moved his centre of gravity to the Sunni triangle in Anbar province, roughly bounded by Baghdad, Ramadi and

Tikrit, where Sunni resentment at being abruptly downgraded and marginalized burned most keenly. While Zarqawi struck at Western troops, and pioneered the first filmed beheading of Western hostages, TV mast repairman Nicholas Berg in 2004, his most psychopathic actions were reserved for Iraq's Shia majority. Venerable Shia mosques were devastated by huge explosions. As with every successive version of IS in Iraq and Syria, the struggle against the 'snake-like' Shia was more import-ant than core Al Qaeda's strategically sequenced war on the American and European 'far enemy' that propped up local Arab autocrats. In strategic terms this was the difference between Clausewitz and the Mahdi.[3]

Despite this obsession with the Shia, in 2004 Osama bin Laden accepted Zarqawi's homage, who in return renamed his mafia-like outfit Al Qaeda in the Land of the Two Rivers (Euphrates and Tigris) or Al Qaeda in Iraq (AQI) for short. It was an uneasy relationship, for Zarqawi's war against *tous les azimuths* could have discredited the wider cause. With his prison muscles long turned to blubber, Zarqawi died on 7 June 2006 when his safe house was demolished by two US bombs.

His two successors were Abu Omar al-Baghdadi (allegedly an officer in Saddam Hussein's General Security Directorate much reduced to repairing oil heaters by de-Ba'athification) and Abu Hamza al-Muhajir, an Egyptian jihadist. As a foreigner, the latter may have tactically played second fiddle while being in charge, though some claim that al-Baghdadi was a fictitious Iraqi cover for the Egyptian. In October 2006 they announced the Islamic State of Iraq, of which Baghdadi (if he ever existed) was the self-styled Emir and Masri its Defence Minister. This had ramified administrative agencies in Anbar province, the launch pad for their terrorist depredations, which again were mainly directed at Iraqi Shia, though also at Sunni tribal leaders who resented their reign of terror. Displacing traditional religious authorities and forcing marriages between jihadis and the daughters of sheikhs were gravely resented, along with the daily extortions.[4]

A Sunni tribal 'Awakening' against ISI was bolstered by a surge of nearly 30,000 fresh US troops. While ISI tried to reignite sec-tarian warfare through attacks on Shia, so as to reverse lost Sunni support, the US and its allies focused on assassinating ISI leaders. In April 2010 the Americans hit the jackpot when the location of Abu Omar and Masri was betrayed by a captured ISI leader and the two men blew themselves up as US commandos stormed the building. By May the group announced the appointment of a new emir, Abu Bakr al-Baghdadi, a figure so obscure that Osama bin Laden asked for a detailed report on his background.

Although members of his family also had footholds in Saddam's security agencies, Baghdadi studied Koranic recitation at the Saddam University for Islamic Studies, after Saddam sought to broaden his support with his 1993 'Faith Campaign'. Married and living in a small Baghdad flat, the young Baghdadi's only known recreation was playing football. His teammates dubbed him 'our Messi'. The defining moment of his life was ten months as a civilian detainee in Camp Bucca, a loosely supervised US holding pen for 24,000 Islamist suspects. The Americans named the camp in honour of a New York fireman, Ronald Bucca, who perished on 9/11; the inmates called it 'The Academy'. Two square miles in extent, near the Basra province border with Kuwait, Bucca was a dysfunctional operation that along with the literacy classes spawned a 'micro-jihad' behind the wire.[5] Known now as 'Maradona' on the camp playing field, Baghdadi consorted with the big boys of Iraqi jihadism but also with imprisoned Ba'athist military and security personnel who had been waging their own war of armed resistance against the Americans by way of revenge for their dramatic fall from favour. Apparently these future collaborators exchanged mobile phone numbers by writing them on the elastic of their underwear. After his release owing to lack of hard evidence, Baghdadi joined Zarqawi's AQI, rising quickly to the guiding Shura Council under al-Baghdadi and Masri who he would replace in 2010 after a 9:2 vote in its Consultative Council.[6]

Two developments gave fresh wind to ISI, despite it having been almost wiped out by 2010. First, Iraq's central government assumed a more explicitly Shia face under Nouri al-Maliki who became Prime Minister in May 2006. Having been exiled in Iran, in Sunni eyes he personified the ascendancy of the mighty Persian Shia neighbour over Iraq, an affront to all Iraqis who had died in eight years of warfare in the 1980s. While Iranian influence in Iraq is not automatic, for Iraq has powerful independent centres of the Shia faith, Maliki's ties with the revolutionary clerical regime in Tehran were authentic, deep and longstanding.

Even as the US lavished tens of billions on Iraq's security forces, Maliki contrived to neglect those military units that were not dedicated to protecting him and his regime. He and other senior politicians had 800 bodyguards apiece, even though they rarely ventured outside the lotus land of Baghdad's governmental Green Zone. An army that included tens of thousands of ghost soldiers whose pay corrupt officers embezzled, neglected training exercises. While Maliki turned an indulgent eye towards murderous Shia militias, he treated the 70–90,000 Sunni 'Sons of Iraq' (the force that developed during the Awakening) with suspicious contempt. He also refused to sign a status of forces juridical agreement with the US, which meant that he deprived himself of combat jets, helicopters and special forces when the Americans withdrew from Iraq at the close of 2011. Despite losing the 2010 national election, Maliki contrived to remain as Prime Minister, taking a dictatorial turn as he went after Sunnis he construed as Ba'athists and 'terrorists'. It helped Maliki that key Sunni politicians were surrounded by armed goons who they sometimes used to settle personal scores with torture and murder.

The recrudescence of sectarianism in Iraq – a Sunni protest camp in Hawija was strafed by government helicopters – gave a powerful stimulus to ISI recruitment. In addition to the arrival of tough Chechen veteran jihadists from the Caucasus, there was also a coalescence with former Ba'athist officers and security personnel (some flagged as the Naqshbandi Sufi network) who helped ISIS with their honed tactical skills, or proven ability to repress civilian populations. Claims that these security professionals really called the shots largely stem from jihadist rivals of ISIS and hence should be treated with scepticism, especially since it is likely that the Ba'athist hard men might themselves have become more religious, donning white turbans and growing beards, as their secular national socialism crashed and burned with Saddam.[7] In the immediate run-up to ISIS's military rampage, two key operations – 'Breaking the Walls' and

'Soldiers' Harvest' – respectively freed thousands of imprisoned jihadists and murdered soldiers and policemen.[8]

ISIS also profited from the local denouement of the Arab Spring in Syria, where democratic protests had mutated into a civil war and the failure of what for forty years had been a stable state. Four hundred thousand people have been killed, 4.5 million are refugees abroad and another 10 million Syrians are internally displaced. Already a poor country before the war, Syria is estimated to have sustained total economic loss of around $255 billion or five times its pre-war GDP. As elsewhere in the region, state failure led to a regression to older communal ethno-sectarian identities or the larger meta-state identities that were polarizing the entire region.[9]

The regime's forces, which are mainly mechanized, have been reduced by 50 per cent, making them reliant on Iranian Quds Force, Iraqi and Afghan Shia 'volunteers' and fighters from Lebanon's Hizbollah who act as the light infantry. Since September 2015 Russia has provided air cover, switching its order of battle from combat jets to attack helicopters to fake a draw down once Assad's position had been stabilized. The main opposition elements in the conflict, in descending order of importance, are:

— Radical Jihadi-Salafis such as ISIS and the Nusra Front, which in July 2016 shed its Al Qaeda badging and renamed itself Jabhat Fatah al-Sham to stress its Syrian identity.

— Liberal and pro-Western groups such as the National Coalition for Syrian Revolutionary and Opposition Forces and the Free Syrian Army. As the main instrument of hypothetical Western intervention, this has declined from its zenith of 40,000 fighters.

— Local actors, notably the 2.2 million northern Syrian Kurds and the southern Druze, the latter (700,000) traditionally supportive of Assad but now warding off both the regime and its Islamist opponents with the aid of Druze inside Israel.

— Independent opponents of the regime, mostly living in exile in Turkey, who have a patchy record of influence inside Syria.

Our focus here will be on ISIS and the Nusra Front. Israeli sources estimate that of the 30,000 ISIS total, 11,500 are operating in Syria, the majority foreign fighters, while Nusra Front has 10,000 fighters, 70 per cent of whom are Syrians.[10]

In May 2011 al-Baghdadi sent two trusted lieutenants, one of them a former Damascus supermarket shelf stacker, Ahmed Hussein al-Shara aka Abu Mohammed al-Julani, to see what they could do amidst the Islamist rebel forces fighting Assad. The latter had an interest in construing the conflict in exclusively sectarian terms so as to bolster Alawite support for his regime that was not universally evident in this highly unequal minority, when protests initially swept Syria in 2011. Julani established the Jabhat al-Nusra ash-Sham Front, based on a mere thirty-three recruits, whose funding, ferocity and willingness to deploy suicide bombers enabled it to attract fighters from other less zealous rebel groups on the strongest horse principle. In March 2013 the Nusra Front took Raqqa in northern Syria, a substantial town of 220,000 inhabitants. The success of Nusra ensured that by April Baghdadi unilaterally announced a forced merger of ISI and Nusra as Islamic State of Iraq and Syria. His protégés had outgrown his control while their rule over civilians was more indulgent of human foibles than his own. When the Nusra leaders rejected this hostile takeover and pledged allegiance to Al Qaeda's Ayman al-Zawahiri instead, Baghdadi turned on Nusra and other rebel groups, taking control of Raqqa in early 2014. By this time ISIS had several training camps for foreign jihadis inside Syria. To Al Qaeda's leaders all of this seemed like a reverse takeover or coup.[11]

ISIS dominated a long strip of territory running via al-Qaim into northern Iraq, towards its second city, Mosul, while its black banner also appeared further south in Fallujah and Ramadi, ominously close to Baghdad. Its battle tactics involved fast-moving columns and the advance use of suicide bombers to destroy the opponent's command and control centres. Well-publicized mass-murders of prisoners – or the un-Islamic burning alive of a Jordanian pilot – also enhanced the fear element, all re-amplified by the West's own fear industry in politics, the media and think tanks. In defence, ISIS proved adroit at using controlled flooding and IEDs to repel attackers. ISIS advances only halted when they came too near Kurdish Erbil and Kirkuk or Shia dominated Baghdad – or, as it happens, when they approached the Iranian border and met regular soldiers prepared to fight.

Neither Maliki nor any of the world's major intelligence agencies had detected this new development and all were surprised when in June 2014 a smaller ISIS shock force that travelled swiftly along Iraq's modern road system swept into Mosul, with the aid of subversion from agents and sympathizers within and multiple diversionary feints elsewhere. ISIS discovered that it was pushing at a half-open and rotting door. Numerically stronger regular army defenders – at least on paper – fled, leaving ISIS to harvest huge quantities of American military equipment including Humvees and tanks, which ISIS fighters used to churn up dust with celebratory 'wheelie' turns. On 4 July 2014 a black-clad Baghdadi, who is rarely seen in public, proclaimed himself caliph in the medieval Nuri Mosque in Old Mosul. The vainglory of this step eclipsed the pretensions of the late 'Emir of the Faithful' Mullah Omar of the Afghan Taliban and his guest, the similarly deceased 'Sheikh' Osama bin Laden. In the view of Al Qaeda it was presumptuous to declare a state, let alone a caliphate. It was also stupid, since the physical sinews of a state made it highly vulnerable to US assault.

•

Most terrorist organizations operate in the shadows rather than controlling an actual state. ISIS rules a very visible state, whereas Al Qaeda is perforce an underground and virtual network that regards establishing the caliphate as vulnerably premature until the US joins the former Soviet Union in history's junk yard. Speaking of which, ISIS has a battle-hardened Chechen contingent, and has taunted Russia's Vladimir Putin from the cockpits of captured Syrian air force MiG jets.

ISIS ruled a real physical place about the size of the UK, much of it scrub and desert, shaped like a sprawling octopus on maps that notionally depict it. It has a flag, an *a cappella* 'anthem' and metal coinage – at least in its online propaganda. It unified what Anglo-French colonial map makers divided. The caliphate had

6 million 'subjects', controlled by a pyramidal council structure and draconian Sharia law enforced by ISIS's conservative peasant foot soldiers and fanatic foreign recruits. Such manifestations of 'Western' decadence as cosmetics, bristle toothbrushes (Koranic era wooden twigs are mandatory), high heels, jeans and tattoos are proscribed, though not mobile phones, provided they do not have apps like 'Angry Birds'. What pedantic energy must go into banning use of the + sign in school maths classes in favour of 'one added to one, God willing, equals two'.

Unlike Al Qaeda, ISIS never depended on wealthy Gulf donors. An electronic financial trail would have made ISIS more vulnerable. Instead, ISIS controls an estimated $2 trillion of assets, and has $2 billion in revenues, though this has halved since 2014. Its revenues overwhelmingly derive from punitive taxes and fines, not only on minority communities and former soldiers but the Sunni population, and from ad hoc fuel refining mainly in Syria, with the (cheap) product trucked and sold into a complicit Turkey, where ISIS has burrowed itself into a few depressed rustbelt cities like Gaziantep and Kilis. There are also duties on trucks and roads, including an $800 levy on each truck entering Iraq from Jordan and Syria.[12]

Other lucrative sidelines included the looting and sale of antiquities after major pieces are broken down into manageable items. Until 2015 the government in Baghdad dutifully continued to pay the salaries of civil servants in areas controlled by ISIS, with the cash disbursed to shadowy intermediaries who then gave ISIS their cut.

ISIS attracted remoter clients who offer their allegiance in the hope that the Al Qaeda or ISIS magic dust will rub off on their endeavours, for the two groups are in deadly competition for adherents. Of the Al Qaeda franchises the one in Yemen (AQAP) is the most lethal, having also established a territorial presence in the Hadramaut, bin Laden's ancestral homeland. ISIS has eight formally affiliated *wilayats*, in Egyptian Sinai, Libya, Nigeria, Tunisia, Saudi Arabia, Yemen, Afghanistan and Pakistan.

While ISIS faces competition from Al Qaeda in Mali, in Nigeria ISIS has won the allegiance of the thoroughly degenerate and savage Boko Haram, which so far has killed 17,000 people and devastated parts of Nigeria, Chad, Cameroon and Niger. The ninth ISIS *wilayat*, Qawqaz, was announced in June 2015 covering the Russian Caucasus, where many Al Qaeda supporters switched to ISIS. Once combined with the estimated 2,200 Russian jihadis in Syria, half of them Chechens angry at Ramzan Kadyrov's servility to Putin, this could represent a real threat to Russia, though Putin has also deployed many loyalist Chechens to administer and pacify liberated Aleppo.

ISIS also has a 'presence' in forty countries, often through fighters who have returned to their homelands. Its slick internet operations (particularly on social media) mean that it can incite lone sympathizers in addition to embedded cells to commit acts of mayhem. Even when these are the handiwork of religiously deranged halfwits and loners, ISIS immediately claims the credit so as to appear more omnipresent than it is.[13]

Interviews with captured ISIS fighters reveal prosaic as well as spiritual reasons for joining an Islamist death cult. Around a thousand of these captives are being held in facilities in Kurdistan. Only those beyond redemption after being proven to be killers talk about the religious drive to commit murder. The rest feign prosaic motivation. An Iraqi bricklayer was attracted by the $260 a month pay, $60 more than he earned normally, not to mention $400 per childbirth and $65 a month in food subsidies. The prospect of breathing the purest air of an Islamic caliphate has drawn tens of thousands of foreign volunteers to augment the Iraqi–Syrian core of ISIS, though one should not omit either altruists and idealists seeking to help persecuted Syrians or bloodlust to exercise a reign of terror.

A 2004 Al Qaeda online tract entitled 'The Management of Savagery' grimly explains the utility of fear.[14] The streets of Mosul and Raqqa resembled something that had strayed from a scene of hell by Hieronymus Bosch. Every time one imagined ISIS has reached a bestial low, for example burning and drowning victims in cages, or throwing homosexuals from tall buildings, it ventured further into depravity, for example using young boys to behead or shoot prisoners. Since ISIS does not acknowledge any humanity outside the *umma*, and despises human rights, its adherents can murder and rape 'the Other' with impunity. In fact, the extreme violence was supposed to be transformative as the jihadist perpetrators moved to a higher psychological consciousness.[15]

The horror show is connected to cartoonish underlying beliefs. Unlike Al Qaeda, which obsessively sought elaborate Islamic theological guidance and jurisprudential justification from the likes of long-term British resident Abu Qatada, ISIS rejects such 'donkeys of knowledge' favoured by the previous generation of jihadis. It also rejects the global pretensions of the 'senile' Al Qaeda leader Ayman al-Zawahiri. The former are just scribblers and talkers, while the latter is a doddery and démodé irrelevance in his fugitive Afghan fastness.[16]

Generically, IS adherents are Jihadi-Salafists, meaning they model themselves on the Prophet Mohammed and the two generations of 'pious forefathers' who succeeded him. In that sense they resemble the Wahhabis, the militant eighteenth-century puritanical sect whose fundamentalist creed was co-opted by the Saud dynasty that still rules Saudi Arabia, an influence obvious from the fact that ISIS uses Saudi textbooks in its schools without adjusting them.[17]

Secondly, ISIS are takfiris, meaning that they decide who is an apostate or a genuine Muslim. This doctrine allegedly stems from Ibn Taymiyyah (1263–1328), who fled Egypt for Damascus after refusing to live under the laws of notionally Muslim Mongol conquerors whose syncretic laws stemmed from Genghis Khan as well as the Almighty. Apostates include the 200 million Shia, who the takfiris (and Wahhabis) regard as deviant heretics, but also any Muslims who drink or smoke or vote in elections, and especially those slow to denounce others as apostates. As for non-believers, in theory Christians are to be left alone provided they pay a discriminatory tax and accept second-class citizenship, though in practice Christians have fled, while ancient minorities like the Yazidis can be enslaved or killed since they are soulless pagans.[18]

ISIS also has a powerful apocalyptic or millenarian compulsion, fancy terms for belief that the End of Days is near. An epic battle between good and evil is coming, or rather two battles. One will be with the forces of 'Rome' meaning either

(Byzantine) Constantinople or the Latin West, where ISIS will triumph. They identified the future battlefield in northern Syria at a flyblown village called Dabiq, from which ISIS's online magazine takes its title, though it has since fallen to hostile forces. After this victory the caliphate will expand, taking Turkey. After a very long time an anti-Messiah will emerge from 'Khorasan', or Iran, for the Persian Shia are synonymous with evil. He and his armies will kill all but 5,000 of ISIS's followers, who will seek refuge in Jerusalem. At that point Jesus will reappear (the second most revered prophet in Islam) and spear the anti-Messiah, resulting in the total worldwide triumph of ISIS.[19]

•

The geopolitical complexities of the region, and especially of the civil war in Syria, explain why the international response to this threat was hesitant. Vowing not to do 'stupid shit', President Obama was reluctant to recommit forces to Iraq and, in contrast to Putin, seemed paralysed by the complexities of the Syrian conflict, though this is not necessarily a demerit when fools sought to rush in. The low price of oil impacted on Iraq's ability to recompense the autonomous Kurdish government for the wages of their Peshmerga fighters. States like Qatar, Saudi Arabia and Turkey wish to destroy the Assad regime, in the first two cases as part of their wider clash with Iran. Turkey – a member of NATO – was a reluctant and ambiguous ally (initially prohibiting the US from using Incirlik air base) because its President, Recep Erdoğan, wanted to prioritize the ouster of Assad and was conducting a parallel war against the PKK in the south-east. Fear that the PKK were assisting the Syrian Kurds in their desire to create a strip-like border state they called Rojava or Western Kurdistan meant that Erdoğan turned a blind eye to ISIS operations within plain sight of his own forces. Little was done to stop the transfer of incoming foreign fighters through Turkey to ISIS, and on one occasion Turkey's MIT intelligence service prosecuted Turkish policemen after they allegedly inadvertently witnessed one of MIT's covert arms transfers to ISIS.

From 8 August 2014 onwards a coalition that included four Arab nations (Bahrain, Saudi Arabia, Jordan and the UAE) commenced air strikes in northern Iraq and Syria. Very expensive bombs and missiles were launched from planes that cost $65,000 an hour to fly to eradicate four guys in a Ford or Toyota pickup truck, urban targets being complicated by the presence of civilian human shields. Subsequent air strikes have concentrated on oil wells that ISIS controls as well as the road tanker fleets used by smugglers. Cutting the economic sinews of terror means that ISIS had to reduce its fighters' pay levels, while increasing to the tune of $600 million the extortionate fines and taxes it imposes on a captive population it can no longer multiply through conquests.

Although President Obama was forced to increase the number of US armed advisers to about 5,000, the brunt of the fighting against ISIS is by Iraqi National Army units made 'match fit' by Western trainers; Iranian-backed Hizbollah and Afghan and Iraqi Shia militias; the KRG Peshmerga and Syrian Kurdish YPG. The Afghans serving in Iran's Fatemiyon division are refugees either seeking naturalization or evading death sentences for drug trafficking.[20]

Half of the Iraqi Shia militias (Hashad Shaabi) derive from southern Basra, where Grand Ayatollah Ali al-Sistani's fatwa against ISIS resonated among the young unemployed, even though Basra is very remote from where ISIS operates. Not only has ISIS lost its forward momentum, but even its counter-thrusts are not what they were, though as yet the casualty rate does not exceed the inward flow of foreign fighters, a tipping point surely critical to the destruction of the caliph's regime.[21]

ISIS has lost 30 per cent of the Syrian and 62 per cent of Iraqi land it conquered and some 20,000 fighters have been killed. The credit can be divided between the US Air Force and extremely brave local ground forces. As its physical territory shrinks, the prospect of ISIS establishing itself elsewhere is less acute than this seemed when ISIS was at its zenith in 2014–15. Since December 2015, no ISIS attack has involved more than a hundred fighters, according to US military sources, and many of them are desperate vehicular suicide bomber affairs, which the excavation of ditches around vulnerable points can neutralize.[22]

Mosul was gradually enveloped from three directions by

Iraqi army, Shia militia and Kurdish forces. Its liberators first cleared the eastern half of the city before taking on ISIS in the more densely built Old City around the Al-Nouri Mosque. After intense fighting that destroyed much of the city, the last of ISIS's fighters were either killed or dragged out covered in dust and sweat to an unknown fate.[23] It is also assumed that Baghdadi himself, from whom nothing has been heard for months, has been killed in an airstrike. Certainly the Russians think they got him and many of his senior associates in such a raid. The pervasive corruption of the Iraqi police and judicial system has enabled a number of ISIS prisoners to slip away quietly if their relatives bribe the right people. Meanwhile, the focus on destroying ISIS has enabled other neo-Ba'athist and jihadist groups, including Al Qaeda, to revive a resistance movement against the Iraqi state in places like Kirkuk and Hawija. Saudi Arabia and Turkey are funding Sunni groups that combat the Shia militias.[24]

The physical caliphate has been demolished village by village and town by town. It is likely to compensate for the impending loss of Raqqa by regressing to a combination of urban terrorism, especially in Baghdad, and a rural hit-and-run insurgency. Top Kurdish counter-terrorism experts think that the former Ba'athist officers will dominate ISIS 2.0, and they have an intimate grasp of the military terrain that ISIS 1.0 dominated. This is what earlier iterations of Islamic State did in the past. Much will depend on how Sunni populations liberated from ISIS are governed in future, especially if Iraq is ultimately federalized, because any Sunni statelet would be poor in oil and water and Iraq does not have a glowing record in redistributing oil revenues to the provincial parts. ISIS is a manifestation of Sunni traumatization at loss of power in Iraq, and their economic marginalization under Shia governments. Unless that changes, some variant of ISIS is likely to recur, and that is unlikely to be the case when so many Sunni are regarded as ISIS collaborators by their 'liberators'. With the Kurds actively considering a referendum on their own independence on 25 September 2017, to include the contested oil-rich Kirkuk, the demise of ISIS may represent just a stage in further conflicts.

Should the eventual denouement in Syria, as sophisticated

Israeli analysts predict, be its fragmentation into three or four rival entities (for Assad or his successors are unlikely to reimpose their dominance over the whole), with all the attendant ethno-sectarian cleansing that will entail, then even in any resulting Sunni 'jihadistan' ISIS will face stiff competition from Al Qaeda, which is thought to be relocating its leaders to Syria in anticipation of such an outcome. That leaves the diverse territorial manifestations of ISIS beyond Iraq and Syria.[25]

•

As ISIS forfeits its caliphate, it will compensate through terrorism elsewhere, easily enough incited through a dark virtual presence. Spurious online potency can be maintained by a couple of electronic geniuses in a rented room. But what of the presence ISIS has established in various regions? Although the refugee flows that ISIS has triggered undoubtedly have had a destabilizing effect, notably in Jordan and Lebanon, ISIS has not managed to take hold in either. The main burden of refugees is on labour markets with large numbers of un- or underemployed locals.

ISIS would ardently love to conquer Saudi Arabia, which has two of the holiest sites in Islam, and where 5 per cent of the population are deemed sympathetic. They have sought to exploit wider Saudi hostility to the country's oppressed Shia minority, most of whom live and work in the oil-rich Eastern Province. Plenty of discontent exists there already, and ISIS has tried to boost it, killing a Saudi border-police general in one clash and massacring Shia villagers in another. The Saudis are so worried by ISIS infiltration that they are building a 650-mile fence complex along the border with Iraq, with patrols, sensors, watchtowers and two lines of razor wire. In early June 2017 ISIS launched its first terror attack deep inside Iran when its gunmen and suicide bombers struck at the majlis and the Ayatollah Khomeini Mausoleum in Tehran in an obvious attempt to exacerbate sectarian tensions in the region.

ISIS has also intruded into Afghanistan and Pakistan, recruiting hardline Pakistani Taliban who have fled over the border to elude Pakistani troops. Its chief recruiter is the former Guantanamo detainee Mullah Abdul Rauf, and the local leader was Pakistani Hafiz Saeed Khan until he was killed in a US drone strike on 26 July 2016. His replacement is an obscure Afghan from Logar in the south though he may have been killed too by the Americans in April or May 2016. Concentrated in the province of Nangarhar, ISIS's fighting strength has been reduced from 3,000 to 1,000 according to US estimates.[26]

But ISIS faces competition in both countries from well-established and multiple extremists. The Taliban regard themselves as heirs to earlier struggles against British, Russian and Soviet imperialists, and regard ISIS as opportunistic interlopers.[27] Largely for this reason, in mid-2015, the Taliban leadership used an apparently friendly 'theological' letter to inform al-Baghdadi that the Taliban were the only game in town. The threat was veiled but unmistakable: 'Your decisions made from a distance will result in [the Islamic State] losing support of religious scholars, muja-hideen . . . and in order to defend its achievements the Islamic Emirate [the Taliban] will be forced to react.'[28] ISIS attempts to establish a presence in Pakistan have been stymied by the robust-ness of indigenous extremist groups, though it has sympathizers among well-heeled radicals in Karachi, and in the provinces bor-dering Afghanistan and Iran. In Indian Kashmir, ISIS has merely manifested itself in the form of pamphlets distributed in Srina-gar.[29] The very violent political culture of Bangladesh, especially at election times, but also affecting Buddhist, Shia and Christian minorities, is also a potential opportunity for ISIS in South Asia.[30]

Similarly, the failed state of Libya, another victim of Western good intentions, should have been ideal territory for ISIS, with its hundreds of militia groups and three rival governments. In reality, the potency of ISIS *wilayats* in Libya was vastly over-estimated with talk of 6,000 fighters and of using the 145 miles of coast they occupied as Plan B should the caliphate expire. Other apocalyptic scenarios included ISIS torching Libya's oil wells or flooding southern Europe with refugees. In reality, when rival Libyan militias temporarily desisted from slaughtering one another, they combined to devastating effect against ISIS, push-ing them out of Derna, Sabratha and Sirte. Surviving ISIS fighters have fled south into the deserts of the Sahel region.[31]

Wilayat Sinai in the lawless space that separates Hamas-controlled Gaza from Egypt is a more serious threat, at least to the thinly disguised military regime in Cairo and to Israel, to which Baghdadi directed a 'we have not forgotten about you' video missive in December 2015. Disgruntled and marginalized local Bedouin have combined with jihadists who fled Mubarak's jails after the Egyptian strongman was ousted by Brotherhood cypher Mohammed Morsi. Most of ISIS's attacks have been directed at Egyptian security personnel, though they have signalled a desire to attack Israel, if only to elicit sympathy in wider Arab opinion. Deep cooperation between Egyptian and Israeli security services make it unlikely that ISIS in Sinai will mount much of a challenge to either, known as they are for relentless counterterrorism, and nor does Hamas want this competitor on the threshold of Gaza. In August 2016 the Egyptian army announced it had killed local ISIS leader Abu Du'a al-Ansari and forty-five of his fighters in air strikes.[32]

Neither Al Qaeda nor ISIS have goals that can be negotiated, as if they were akin to violent nationalist separatists in Britain or Spain. The goal of these Islamist terror groups is the destruction not just of 'Western civilization' but of that of China, India and Russia too. Iraq has the death penalty, and uses it on captured ISIS members, but Kurdistan does not, which raises the issues of how to avoid the recrudescence of Sunni terrorism inside jails which are filling up with captured ISIS fighters. Those ISIS members who are not killed, captured or executed will seek to return to their countries of origin, or will become akin to international outlaws.*

The general mulch from which violent jihadism grows could be reduced if pressure was put on Saudi Arabia to desist from proselytizing Wahhabism through its 'clerical diplomats' and the Islamic University of Medina. That would entail forgoing lucrative arms contracts, and the jobs that depend on them. French Muslims have decided to establish their own mosque-funding facility to eliminate such external sources of trouble, while the

---

* Although Iraq might have counselled a period of silence, the conflict resolution consultant Jonathan Powell is ubiquitous in advice which he has codified into a book, *Talking to Terrorists: How to End Armed Conflicts* (London, 2015).

Italians ignore the law and deport troublesome imams so as to pre-empt the ghettoization the British, French and Germans have allowed to develop. Italian experience of the Mafia also gives them an edge in terms of surveillance that has made the Germans look feckless.[33]

It is undecided whether ISIS or Al Qaeda will display more resilience. Judging from the relief of people liberated from its misrule, ISIS lacks the silent, submerged local support that seems to accompany each fresh surge by the Afghan Taliban though intimidation also plays its part in securing this. ISIS is convinced that its past is a reliable guide to how it can survive loss of control of urban centres. It submerged in 2008 and had been forgotten almost entirely by the time it suddenly resurfaced in 2012, more dangerous than ever before. For IS propagandists, this is proof of its own invincibility. 'Were we defeated when we lost the cities in Iraq and were in the desert without any city or land?' IS spokesman Abu Mohammed al-Adnani recently asked in an incendiary speech: 'And would we be defeated, and you victorious, if you took Mosul or Sirte or Raqqa? Certainly not!'[34]

Al Qaeda's problem is the irrelevance of its core leadership to such powerful regional affiliates as Al Qaeda in the Arabian Peninsula and Al Qaeda in the Islamic Maghreb. However, such an affiliation also attracts Western attacks. This is why in July 2016 Jabhat al-Nusra both exchanged the black banners for white (to distinguish it from ISIS) and severed the link with Al Qaeda. The new, rebranded outfit claims to have the sole objective of defeating the Assad regime and replacing it with an Islamic state. An alternative view is that Al Qaeda's leader, Ayman al-Zawahiri, is a patient man who will sit out the eradication of Baghdadi's caliphate, and then emerge to have the last laugh, a view which ignores the fact that core Al Qaeda brings little to the jihad nowadays in terms of men or money. The fact that his most recent communications acknowledge the role of popular movements as well as armed vanguards (who should limit violence against civilians) suggests recognition of political realities and the damage ISIS has done to the wider cause.[35]

ISIS has an attack planning department (the *emni*) which both dispatches trained operatives to commit large-scale attacks and incites sympathizers who have never been to Iraq or Syria. The grim results are observable around the world. Many societies, including China and Russia as well as Europe, will have to deal with large numbers of returned jihadis whose combat experience and the charisma derived from it represent a significant future danger. Although some bombings in China have been the work of disaffected or deranged Han Chinese, the Beijing authorities identify terrorism exclusively with Tibetans and Uyghur religious extremists and separatists, and Beijing's response is not inhibited by civil-rights lawyers.[36] An estimated 5,000 Europeans went to fight in Syria, and about 1,200 are known to have returned. Britain has 350, France 250, Germany 270 and Belgium 118. They can reverse-engineer the local networks that got them to Syria in the first place, to become support networks for acts of domestic terrorism. They may also be interacting with refugees whose backgrounds are opaque, despite the availability of technology to establish quickly if someone is really from Aleppo or Idlib. In early 2017 the dozy German authorities finally woke up to the fact that refugees have smart phones on which may be stored photographs that could afford vital clues to their past whereabouts. About 14 per cent of 'Syrian' refugees in Germany are not 'Syrian' at all. The process of unravelling these networks has been vividly described as akin to 'shaking a bag of fleas'.

Although Trump made great play on the campaign trail of annihilating ISIS, in reality he seems to be continuing the approach of his predecessor. That means eschewing anything that smacks of nation-building while employing air power and minimal US special forces to bolster local efforts against the terror groups which represent the gravest threats.[37] That does not solve the problem of the conveyor belt which violent jihadis have established between war zones and what they regard as the home fronts, where they enjoy all the status of returning heroes with combat credibility. It might be better for humanity if as many as possible of these pious sociopaths died while in a war zone rather than returning 'home' to resume their marginal and alienated existences. That certainly seems to be the French approach, who are less squeamish about killing their co-nationals than others, and which involves French special forces supplying the Iraqis with details of people whose noms de guerre end in '*al-Fransi*'. Before he was slain in a US airstrike in August 2016, former ISIS spokesman Abu Mohammed Al Adnani urged supporters to kill innocent civilians in their homes or markets by running them over or by hitting them with a rock. The period of Ramadan seems to be the occasion for this strategy to go into overdrive. At present, several societies are grappling with lone-wolf attacks in which perpetrators seek the limelight by crying 'Allahu Akbar' at the scenes of their attempted massacres, though the most deadly attacks are the work of dedicated ISIS or Al Qaeda cells, and even the most lonesome of wolves acts on behalf of the imagined global *umma*. Since complex plots involving explosives leave a detectable logistic trail, the preferred current tactic seems to be using vehicles to mow down innocents followed, if survived, by some random shooting and stabbing. The availability of guns locally determines the modus operandi.[38]

It remains uncertain how long the affected societies will be content with candles, flowers, teddy bears and vigils and endlessly reinforcing the security infrastructure of public places, especially if relentless instances of terror impact on electoral outcomes. It is far from clear too whether adding extra layers of security, often managed by inept private sector contractors, will be effective. Passage through Israeli airports, after all, does not involve removing one's shoes, but rather rapid questions from trained personnel with intelligence backgrounds. Perhaps the public are sensible enough to see that the piss and wind of demagogues and shouty newspaper columnists offers no real alternative to the considered responses of existing governments as well as patiently relentless police and intelligence work. Since terrorist attacks are designed to garner maximum publicity, the media need to think about their own role as 'unwitting' amplifiers. Bans on backpacks on beaches or at Munich's Oktoberfest portend a dystopia in which citizens go about in their underwear (though we have had an 'underpants' bomber) under the watchful gaze of heavily armed police and troops, even on the sands of St Tropez. After a Tunisian ISIS adherent drove a truck into crowds at a Berlin Christmas market in December 2016, all 2,500 such markets will have obstacles surrounding them. Living in central London I have become used to seeing armed policemen and constantly revamped security barriers. I wrote part of this chapter watching police helicopters circling overhead outside my office windows as the Westminster Bridge attack unfolded in March 2017, then watched on TV the aftermath of the murder of pre-teen pop fans and their waiting parents in Manchester in May, only to then be kept awake throughout a night in early June 2017 by sirens blaring as emergency services rushed to the latest murderous van and knife assault at London Bridge and Borough Market. A third incident five hundred yards away turned out to be just an ordinary Saturday night stabbing. And so it goes on, to Barcelona in August.[39]

Doubtless the Western terrorism studies industry will continue to play on our collective fears of being killed, while contrarians point to the greater lethality of falls in the bath, bee stings, snake bites and road accidents, though baths and bees do not conspire to slip up or sting people. Book after book will chart the rise and fall of each faction, offering more or less plausible reasons for their depredations. The clever silly, as Tolstoy once dismissed George Bernard Shaw, will advocate 'dialogue' with these persons, though how do we 'negotiate' core values like women's or gay rights or cease giving 'offence' to those perpetually looking for it?

The hard truth is that the jihadis pose no existential threat to any stable society, be it the US, Europe, China or Russia. They are a symptom of disorders within Islam and the failure of states in the Middle East to include their citizens equitably, and of viruses abroad in the religion which seek to revert to a reimagined seventh century. They also reflect the failure of other societies to robustly assimilate Muslim migrants to their values and way of life, with a clear warning that 'jail or exit' beckons for anyone who regards us as infidel *kuffar*. Living with the effects of the failure of others has become our reality. Rather than a threat to our very being, terrorism is a chronic problem – though patience with the more platitudinous responses to it is wearing very thin.

4

The Sick Man of Europe: Erdoğan's Turkey

The 14 July 2016 attempted coup against Recep Tayyip Erdoğan failed within twelve hours of its initiation, though it may represent the moment when Turkey slid into the ambient chaos of the Middle East. Major intelligence services failed to anticipate the events. The British consulate in Istanbul was holding a party that night, and confused gunfire with fireworks. It has accelerated the de-secularization of Turkey under way since Erdoğan became Prime Minister in 2003, and the authoritarian tenor of his presidency since 2014. It has also immensely complicated Turkey's relations with the EU, already strained by the migration crisis and the leaching of internal conflicts into the 4.5 million strong diaspora in Austria, Germany and the Netherlands.

Twenty-five maroon-beret commandos flew in three Sikorsky helicopters into Marmaris, their mission to capture or kill the vacationing Erdoğan. On arrival at Grand Yazıcı Club Turban on the edge of town, the commandos discovered their bird had flown, though a gun battle ensued with the President's security team, who had whisked Erdoğan away to another hotel where he used FaceTime to speak live to the nation via CNNTurk. A studio anchor held her own phone to camera. The President sent a text message to every smart phone in the country, demanding Turks take to the streets. Then Erdoğan was flown to Istanbul, where his plane circled until it was safe to land. Hostile fighter jets had shadowed his Gulf Stream, but then vanished when two F-16s loyal to the President scared them away.

Meanwhile, Istanbul international airport was closed by rebel tanks, and a vital bridge over the Bosphorus was occupied by rebel troops, the majority frightened-looking Anatolian conscripts, for Turkish elites easily buy their sons out of compulsory military service for the lire equivalent of $5,000. In both Ankara and Istanbul troops stormed television stations, forcing the anchors to read a statement by the 'Peace at Home Council' to the effect that the military were taking over the country. Rebel helicopters fired on the headquarters of MIT, Turkish intelligence, while six F-16s from the rebel HQ at Akıncılar air base bombed the presidential palace and parliament building. It transpired that the rebel planes were refuelled by aerial tankers from the Turkish air force section of NATO's İncirlik base. All power to the base was cut, and its commander arrested.

In the darkness, loudspeakers from the country's 80,000 mosques boomed the call to prayer, with imams ordered to recite *sela* prayers – used for funerals or special occasions, but also understood as a call to arms. Huge crowds began to confront and then fight with rebel soldiers, who quickly gave up. Most of the rebels were from the air force and military police. A massive failure was the rebels' inability to retain control of the headquarters of the paramilitary Gendarmerie in Ankara, which gives orders to police in all eighty-one provinces. It was wrested back by loyalist troops after sixteen of the putschists were killed. The reckoning was already apparent as surrendering rebels were herded away, after being brutalized, by police who had remained loyal to the regime. By 4 a.m. Erdoğan was on the ground at Istanbul airport and fulminating against traitors. In the course of these events, 290 people were killed, including 104 coup supporters.[1]

Turkey has a long history of military intervention to defend the secular national ethos, including the coup in 1960, the 1971 'military memorandum', the 1980 coup, a 1993 military intervention and another 'military memorandum' in 1997. With the exception of former air force chief Akın Öztürk, the latest one did not enjoy the support of the military top brass on the National Security Council, many of whom had only recently been restored to their posts after convictions at political show trials. These convictions were ironically co-engineered by the Gülenists, an Islamic sect for high achievers we will explore below, only to be overturned because of tainted evidence. By

2013 Erdoğan and Gülen had fallen out, and Gülen fled to Pennsylvania, his presence in the US adding some American-CIA coloration to Erdoğan's version of what lay behind the coup. In reality he resembles the character of Emmanuel Goldstein in George Orwell's dystopian *Nineteen Eighty-Four*: a serviceable Trotsky-like hate figure to perpetually mobilize people behind Stalin's Big Brother.

In this case, however, the top military leadership was detained at gunpoint by the middle- and lower-level leaders of the coup. It may be that the coup was a pre-emptive move by officers who were likely to be purged at annual military appointment boards in August 2016. Claims that Erdoğan engineered a coup against himself seem improbable, not least because his long-time PR chief Erol Olcak and his sixteen-year-old son Abdullah were slain in the course of clashes between protestors and troops. It could be that Turkish intelligence had got wind of a plot and, confident they knew its extent, allowed the events of 14 July to play out, a time of year in which the low energy during Ramadan and the relentless heat was likely to paralyse any significant movement. Some suspect that Russian intelligence deliberately gave up their Turkish military 'assets' with an eye to the bigger prize of estranging Turkey and NATO. The plotters also relied too heavily on seizing control of the old media, to the neglect of social media, which ironically Erdoğan disdained as a modernistic distraction, not to speak of the medieval calls to arms from minarets too numerous to occupy.[2]

With suspicious alacrity, the authorities arrested tens of thousands of conspirators and Gülenists, or rather 'traitors and terrorists', whose Hizmet ('Service') sect for high achievers and strivers Erdoğan has long suspected of plotting his fall. According to a leaked report from Intcen, Europe's intelligence service, Turkish intelligence had been compiling lists of activist opponents for years. Judges and prosecutors were among the first to be dismissed, including members of the Council of State and the Constitutional Court. About 60,000 civil servants have been dismissed from their posts, including teachers and university deans, while journalists were arrested. A senior analyst at Turkey's second largest bank has been arrested for writing negative reports on the economic impact of the failed coup and the ensuing purge. The regime also wants to purge the central bank and the financial regulators. Indeed, Gülen was soon charged with insinuating an image of Halley's Comet onto a lire note as a secret sign to his followers, the pretext for curbing the independence of the central bank.[3]

Big businesses connected with the Gülenists such as Boydak Holdings and Koza İpek Holdings have been liquidated, or taken into receivership and their owners arrested. The democratic counter-coup, which enjoyed cross-party support in Turkey and sympathy from the international community, evolved via this purge into an Islamist counter-revolution, despite only 12–14 per cent support among Turks for making Sharia the law of the land, the lowest percentage in the region.

Having long sought an executive presidency by quasi-constitutional means, Erdoğan has almost achieved one through his declaration of a state of emergency in which he and not parliament issues laws, a development some have compared with Hitler's 1933 Enabling Law. Turkey's relations with the West are likely to be among the casualties of the counter-coup, despite European Union dependence on Turkey to check migrant flows and US reliance on Turkey in the fight against ISIS. Authoritarian commonalities have seen the repair of tense relations with Putin's Russia, for the new Tsar has much in common with the Turkish Sultan. A once-reliable NATO ally seems to have become an unstable black hole, more akin to the chaotic polities of its surrounding region.[4]

•

Modern Turkey was founded in 1923 by national hero Mustafa Kemal, known as Atatürk (Father of the Turks), following the Ottoman Empire's defeat in the First World War and the loss of all but 15 per cent of that empire in the Treaty of Sèvres in 1920. After Serbia, Ottoman Turkey sustained the conflict's highest casualties, which were especially dire in Anatolia.

Born in Salonika, Kemal became a national hero when the Entente's 1915 landing at Gallipoli was repelled. Following armed nationalist resistance to Sèvres in the Independence

War of 1921–22, some of the territorial loss was repaired in a renegotiated settlement at Lausanne. Turkey assumed its present borders.[5] This second treaty denied the Kurds a state of their own, as had been promised at Sèvres, and resulted in brutal population exchanges of ethnic Greeks and Turks. Even in its reduced form, Turkey had multiple remaining fault lines and claims on Mosul were unsatisfied. A third of the population are Alevis, or Turkish Shiites, who have suffered discrimination by the Sunni Turkish and Kurdish majority. The Kurds are the largest (ethnically Iranian) minority, followed by the 60,000 strong remnant of the Armenians, 1.5 million of whom died in 1915–16 in what everyone bar the Turks regards as a genocide.[6]

The Ottoman sultanate and caliphate, which had fused political and religious power, were abolished in respectively 1922 and 1924 (to the regret of radical Islamists ever after), and in the latter year Turkey became a republic with its capital re-located to Ankara from Istanbul.

Wide-ranging institutional reforms were adopted to create a Western-oriented, constitutionally secular state in a backward Muslim country. The alphabet and dictionaries were changed, religious schools closed, and men made to shave off beards and to exchange their orientalist fezzes for top hats and fedoras. Though Islam was described as the 'religion of the Turkish state' in the 1924 constitution, by 1928 this passage had been removed, with faith and state separated along the lines adopted by laicizing France in 1905.

Two years earlier Turkey had adopted the Gregorian calendar and Western time-keeping, thereby diminishing the significance of the sun. Civil servants were given three months to adopt Western script after official use of Arabic was prohibited. The Christian Sunday rather than Islamic Friday became the national day of rest. Friday prayers were to be delivered in Turkish rather than Arabic. Any promises to the Kurdish minority were broken. Not only was their language banned, but also in 1928 the letters Q, W and X (which are used in Kurdish but not Turkish) were removed from dictionaries. The only political party was the CHP, led by Kemal himself. The Father of the Nation's enjoyment of raki led to his early death, aged fifty-seven, in 1938, and the beginning of a cult, with a bust in every school, the vast Anitkabir mausoleum, and a minute's silence on his birthday (10 September).[7]

•

In 1946 Turkey at last acquired an opposition party. President İsmet İnönü (Atatürk's successor 1938–50) licensed a conservative Islamic Democrat Party led by such defectors from the CHP as Adnan Menderes. This did well enough in the 1950 election, especially among rural voters, for Menderes to become Prime Minister for the next decade, during which some of Atatürk's secularizing measures were reversed (for example Arabic could again be employed in sermons).

This was the 'golden age' into which Recep Erdoğan was born in February 1954. His father was a merchant marine captain of an untypically straitlaced kind, who disapproved of the young Erdoğan, a talented footballer, playing the game because of the revealing shorts. Even the boy's name was indicative of piety, since Recep is the Turkish version of the Arabic word Radschab, the seventh month, in which the Prophet ascended to heaven.[8]

As he never tires of reminding everyone, Erdoğan grew up in the poor, but pious Kasımpaşa district in European Istanbul, a cosmopolitan warren of dark streets criss-crossed with drying washing and a universe away from the luxury hotels and shops of the former Ottoman capital. He claims this area was a former *gecekondu bölgesi*, one of the urban shanty towns that grew up as the mechanization of agriculture sent many out-of-work farm labourers into the cities. From 1963 onwards Erdoğan attended an İmam-Hatip ('the preaching imam') school, one of the training establishments for clerics and Koran reciters that Atatürk had disdained. But in the interim, Erdoğan's idyllic childhood had been shaken by a military coup that ousted the thrice-elected Menderes.[9]

The new military dictator, General Alparslan Türkeş, proscribed the Democratic Party and hanged Menderes and three others. Magazine photos of Menderes in a white smock suspended from a gallows haunted Erdoğan. While power was concentrated in the hands of the new National Security Council, elections in 1961 returned the Kemalist CHP to office in a coalition led by Erdal İnönü. This included the recently founded Justice Party (AP in Turkish), the successor to the Democrat Party. The student Erdoğan took to producing plays. One, called *Ms-Com-Ya*, or 'Freemasons, Communists and Jews', was about a three-way plot to take over Turkey, a product of his admiration for the Islamist ideologue Necip Fazıl Kısakürek. Kısakürek had translated *The Protocols of the Elders of Zion* into Turkish and Erdoğan has frequently described him as 'the master'.[10]

The EEC signed an association agreement with Turkey in 1963, after the judicial murder of Menderes and despite protests from the Pope, the US President and Queen Elizabeth II. Military coups in Turkey tended to revert to democracy relatively quickly, as senior officers feared their anti-democratic juniors. The 'deep' security state remained a looming presence over civilian politicians. But the generals also allowed a new constitution, with more checks and balances, which paradoxically encouraged more political parties to enter the lists. The Justice Party leader, a hydraulic engineer called Süleyman Demiril, won the 1965 election, becoming Prime Minister for twelve years and then President for seven.

As in the earlier case of Menderes, this represented a return of the 'Black Turks', the modest plain people from the provinces who were servants in the plush homes of the ruling 'White Turks' in the military, bureaucracy, commerce, media and universities. Demiril's key slogan was 'The state is secular but not the nation'. This was not Islamic enough for a minority of AP members, who founded a Party of National Order (MNP), which attracted the teenage Erdoğan, who would name his second son Necmettin Bilal, after its founder Necmettin Erbakan, the main influence on his early life. These were Islamic chauvinists who wanted to range Turkey in an Islamic Union, from Kazakhstan to Morocco, against the 'Christian Club' of the EEC.

Demiril's rule ended amidst charges of corruption and militant student protests. In 1969 General Alparslan Türkeş, the 1960 putsch leader, had founded an extreme Turkish Nationalist Action Party (MHP), with its 'Grey Wolves' terror outfit based on the SS. In common with disturbances in Europe and the US,

Turkey experienced political murders and street violence, usually between the Grey Wolves and the left.

A memorandum from the chief of staff warning of an impending coup to prevent anarchy was enough to push Demiril into retirement in 1971, while a state of emergency was imposed on restive provinces and the Islamist MNP proscribed. The powers of the National Security Council were widened to include their own system of courts. After three years the CHP was elected under Bülent Ecevit. For the next seven years Ecevit and Demiril alternated in power, rather in the manner of the contemporaneous Wilson and Heath. By the late 1970s the political system was paralysed, as symbolized by the one hundred divisions it took in parliament to fail to elect a new Turkish president. The number of fatalities due to political violence rose from 230 in 1977 to 1,500 two years later.[11]

The 1960s and early 1970s were good years for Turkey's economy, which enjoyed an annual average growth rate of nearly 7 per cent. There were protective tariffs, much import substitution and many state economic enterprises. In 1978 the young Erdoğan married his consort Emine (the Arabic original was Amina, the Prophet's mother), but by then Turkey had descended into angry strike-ridden chaos, with 90 per cent inflation and frequent power cuts in a country that had to import all its oil. The revolution in Iran in 1979 was the final straw for army officers who feared Islamic fundamentalism could be contagious. On 12 September 1980 the generals struck for a third time. Two hundred members of parliament were arrested after their immunity was rescinded. 'All politicians are mud,' said the new supremo, General Kenan Evren. Three hundred senior academics were fired. In the first week, 11,500 people were arrested, a number which grew to 122,600 by the end of 1981. Ninety days' pre-charge detention also left much scope for torture, for which Turkey became notorious in that decade. What a pity the 1978 film *Midnight Express* (filmed in Malta but set in Istanbul) dealt with imprisoned Western drug addicts and not with what happened to real Turks.

Among the beneficiaries of the new order were the religious, since these Cold War generals hated the Communists more. A new generation of Islamists ironically owed their religious education to an otherwise reactionary regime that also introduced a 10 per cent threshold for representation in a parliamentary assembly they eventually reopened in 1983. All candidates had to be approved by the National Security Council. The party that enjoyed the least support from the generals, the Motherland Party, under another engineer by the name of Turgut Özal, won a resounding victory. Özal was a self-made businessman from a small town in a backward province who appealed to many ordinary Turks, who he described as the centre pole in the big tent. He sought to combine liberal economics, learned from Reagan and Thatcher, a conservative religious outlook and nostalgia for the Ottoman Empire.

By this time, Erdoğan was employed as a book-keeper in a sausage factory, though he continued as a political agitator, not for the National Salvation Party or MSP, which was banned, but in the new 'Welfare Party', until it paid him enough of a salary to become a professional politician. Despite being a promising marriage of modernity and religion, the Özal government plunged Turkey into desperate straits. 'People, eat lentils!' was Özal's response to a shortage of meat. Various acts of electoral jiggery-pokery were used to retain a parliamentary majority. His family were also mired in several corruption scandals, as when a son made a killing on the Istanbul stock exchange dealing in shares of firms that won government contracts. In 1989 Özal was elected President.

These years witnessed an Islamist revival that spread from the countryside into working-class areas of big cities. Secular Turks noted the increasing number of mosques, religious schools and bookshops. Flashpoints included people drinking or smoking during Ramadan, and pious students insisting on wearing headscarves although they were banned in universities. In the early 1990s Erdoğan made his first bid for public office, culminating in his election as Lord Mayor of Istanbul in 1994.

He worked hard to improve air and water quality, while planting 600,000 trees, but at the same time, alcohol disappeared from municipal canteens and scantily dressed women from advertisements. If he could have banned ballet as pornographic he would have; trying to twin Istanbul with Mecca was a provocation in a country where Sharia law is a major fear among secular Turks and the Alevis fear militant Sunnis. He took to using the four-raised-fingers *rabia* gesture, which derives from the Egyptian Muslim Brotherhood. In 1997 Erdoğan made a speech in Emine's hometown which included the words 'the minarets are our bayonets, the domes our helmets, the mosques our barracks, and the faithful our soldiers'. He was sentenced to ten months in jail and banned from political activity for life. The four months he spent in jail boosted his celebrity, and the ban did not prevent him playing a leading role in the founding of the Justice and Development Party (AKP) on 14 August 2001. The AKP's symbol, designed by Erol Olcak, was a light bulb to shine in dark corners. At the time, few picked up Erdoğan's comment that 'Democracy is like a street car – you need it until you arrive at your destination and then step off', an ominous echo of the Muslim Brotherhood belief in 'one man, one vote, one time'.[12]

On 3 November 2002 the AKP won 34.3 per cent of the popular vote, becoming the largest party in the 550-seat National Assembly. In 2007 its share rose to 46.7 per cent, and then to nearly 50 per cent in 2011. In each case 50–60 per cent of Turkey's biggest diaspora community (the 2.8 million German-Turks, half of whom had the vote at home) voted AKP. Bliss was it to be alive amidst the waving orange and white AKP banners.

The charismatic Party Chairman could not become Prime Minister as long as the court ban was in force, but when this was lifted he entered parliament and in March 2003 replaced PM Abdullah Gül, who became Foreign Minister in Erdoğan's first of three governments.

•

The AKP's extraordinary success was due to mobilizing the aspirational, industrious and pious 'Black Turk' masses (about half of whom had previously voted for right-wing parties) with a vision of a thriving Islamic democracy, though the AKP always publicly downplayed the theme of religion. Instead they were almost Calvinist in their association of making money with godliness. It helped that many necessary structural reforms had been dictated by the IMF before the AKP came to power, as a condition for a timely $8 billion bailout. The new government delivered remarkable economic growth of around 8 per cent. Many poor but industrious Turks entered the middle classes. Both the Welfare Party and its successor the AKP pitched for the support of the inhabitants of the *gecekondular* in the cities. In addition to welfare, relaxing development and building laws meant that developers (also in league with the AKP) built new residential housing, with the owners of the demolished properties (for the AKP gave them title) paying the price difference by monthly instalments. In practice, many inhabitants of the *gecekondu bölgesi* quickly sold their rights to developers of luxury complexes.[13]

Having no independent sources of energy, Turkish entrepreneurs descended on the oil- and gas-rich autonomous Kurdish region in northern Iraq, whose cities underwent a Turkish-led building boom. Although the Baghdad government regards it as illegal, Kurdish oil flows independently to the Turkish port of Ceyhan for export, bypassing Iraq's network of pipelines and the metering stations that count the flow. While learned Western commentators fancifully compared the AKP with European Christian Democrat parties, the likes of *The Economist* ('Europe's China') and Goldman Sachs ('global Top Ten by 2050') became major boosters of this Turkish economic miracle. Even the admission to the EU of Greece in 2000 and the Greek part of Cyprus in 2004, despite Nicosia having rejected the UN-sponsored Annan Plan for reunification that had been accepted by the Turks, were not seen as obstacles to future EU membership for Turkey, though some Turks suspected they were being strung along.

Everything seemed possible with this spare, closely barbered leader with rolled-up sleeves at the helm. Talk of joining the EU by 2010 led to the abolition of the death penalty, limitation on the kind of political disqualification Erdoğan himself had suffered and recognition of Kurdish as an official language, with a Kurdish channel available on TRT 6, the state TV, from 2009 onwards. The long-time Kurdish political prisoner Leyla Zana was freed in 2004. Formal EU accession talks commenced in

October 2005, though so far only one of thirty-five complex 'chapters' has been completed.

The dalliance with the EU had an important domestic political consequence in that it indirectly reduced generals who had deposed three governments to the role of grumblers in the wings. They tried to block Abdullah Gül's candidacy for the presidency in 2007, on the grounds that his wife Hayrünissa wore the headscarf, but fresh elections increased the AKP's share of the vote, and Gül eventually became head of state, the first religious conservative in Turkey's modern history to occupy the post. When the new President visited a military academy without his consort, who had been invited, the Chief of the General Staff, Mehmet Yaşar Büyükanıt, and his officials refused to salute Gül, as a representative of *irtica*, or religious reaction.

The generals were unaware that their downfall was being plotted. In 2001 an investigation into a fraudulent car sale had led to the discovery in the home of a member of Turkey's MIT intelligence agency of documents concerning an underground ultra-nationalist group called 'Ergenekon' (a mythical valley in central Asia where the Turks had once fled). This name cropped up again in 2007 when raids discovered arms caches hidden in suburban Istanbul. It reappeared on files found on the hard drive of a computer belonging to a retired officer, outlining plans for a putsch against Erdoğan, as well as the murder of Kurdish activist Leyla Zana and the distinguished novelist Orhan Pamuk.

So long as ordinary Turks prospered, there seemed no limits on what Erdoğan could achieve. The region around Istanbul became a hive of activity, although the rest of the country continues to depend on subsistence agriculture. Tourism thrived, much of it German and Russian. Under the AKP many Turks saw their lives improved, with factories churning out fridges and washing machines and Turkish businessmen flying into Africa in search of opportunities. AKP supporters were quietly seeded in the state bureaucracy, being already ubiquitous in the private sector. In February 2008 the historic ban on students wearing headscarves was abrogated, though female members of parliament, teachers and professors were still not permitted to do so. When the public prosecutor tried to attack Erdoğan, Gül and dozens of AKP politicians for this breach of laicizing clauses in the constitution, Erdoğan launched a counteroffensive, threatening to dilute the Kemalist majority on the Constitutional Court by adding a further nine judges. This changed the judges' view of the scarves issue. In his subsequent judicial reforms, Erdoğan would increase the number of judges to seventeen, with fourteen of them nominated by himself and three by parliament, in which the AKP held the majority.

There was a vaulting ambition too to Turkish foreign policy. Under Ahmet Davutoğlu, who became Foreign Minister in 2009, a British-style 'multidimensional' strategy was pursued, in which Turkey would be at the centre of overlapping spheres of influence. There were to be zero problems with any of Turkey's neighbours. Speaking in January 2013, Davutoğlu boasted that the number of diplomatic missions in Ankara had grown to 240 from 148 a decade before, because global powers

> know that now history flows through Ankara, and parties that ignore Ankara cannot understand history. The one that risks relations with Ankara will take risks in all regional policies. From now on, those who want to understand history must be present in Ankara, Istanbul and every other place in Turkey because from now on we will be more actively present in shaping of the flow of history.

The EU talks appeared to thrive, as long as European countries paid lip service to the ideal rather than the reality of admitting Turkey to the Union. But now Turkey wanted to develop its cultural ties with the oil and rug -stans, many of them Turkic-speaking, while re-establishing Turkey as a force for good in the Arab world. Unfortunately neither the emotive Erdoğan nor the 'Turkish Kissinger', Davutoğlu, in reality a professorial mouse of a fellow, had the skill to execute these manoeuvres. In the past, Turkey had been one of Israel's main allies in the region. Erdoğan's fury at Israeli treatment of Palestinians in Gaza led to bitter clashes with Shimon Peres at Davos over the Israelis' stupid decision to broadcast seating the Turkish Ambassador on a low sofa in front of the Deputy Foreign Minister perched at a high desk. The relationship further deteriorated when in May 2010 Israeli commandos boarded the 'Gaza Peace Flotilla' relief ship MV *Mavi Marmara*, which led to eight Turks dying in a firefight. Thereafter, Erdoğan referred to Israel as 'the spoiled child of the West' in his bid to put himself as leader of the democratic Islamist waves roiling the Middle East.[14]

Improved relations with Iran and Iraq nosedived over Syria, and what many took to be the 'Sunnification' of Turkish foreign policy under the AKP. As recently as 2008 the Erdoğans had enjoyed a holiday in Bodrum with the young Bashar and Asma al-Assad. The hope was that Assad would switch off his father Hafez's support for the PKK and accept the role of protégé of the more experienced Turkish statesman. But after civil disturbance erupted in Syria during the Arab Spring, Erdoğan was appalled by the violence Assad unleashed. He became Assad's most implacable foe, with Iran on the Syrian regime's side.[15]

The policy of 'zero problems with the neighbours' took a further hit when warm relations with the Islamist government of Morsi in Cairo (whom Erdoğan had feted as a kindred spirit) fell victim to the democratic coup, leaving their (and the Palestinians') desire to isolate Israel in ruins. Relations with Russia initially improved as Putin became the first Russian leader to visit Turkey since Nikolai Podgorny in 1972, but declined as Erdoğan backed the marginalized Crimean Tatars, and then in 2015 his air force shot down a Russian fighter which entered Turkish air space for a couple of minutes.

Since AKP statutes forbade anyone having a fourth term as prime minister, Erdoğan's ambitions turned to the succession to President Gül, whose term of office ended in 2014. In 2007 Erdoğan had already ensured that the President was directly elected, for five-year terms. In the chaotic aftermath of the Arab Spring he could plausibly claim that the continuity of an American- or French-style executive presidency would be better than Turkey's historic alternation of fractious coalition governments and military coups. But then beer, trees, sex and social media intervened.

The AKP had always been sympathetic to pious and crass developers who made big money from rapid modernization. Turkey's construction industry is worth 17 per cent of its GDP.

The regime's favourite sound was the soft plop of poured concrete and the clanking of excavators. It does not care about environmental impact, let alone the destruction of historic sites. Erdoğan is building an airport six times the size of Heathrow outside Istanbul, and a huge canal connecting the Black Sea to the Sea of Marmara so as to relieve pressure on the Bosphorus. The new Marmaray rail tunnel (13.6km long) linked European and Asiatic Istanbul under the Bosphorus, while above the sea, with an eight-lane road and two rail lines, Yavuz Sultan Selim Bridge was the tallest such structure ever built. Alevis did not fail to notice the commemoration of the Sultan known as 'the Grim' who had massacred 70,000 of their co-religionists in the sixteenth century.[16]

The vulturine beaks of these developers turned to Taksim Gezi Park near Taksim Square, one of the few places with grass and shade on central Istanbul's European side. This green oasis was to be erased in favour of a retro Ottoman barracks, a mosque and a shopping mall – a revealing example of the AKP's priorities. The project coincided with Erdoğan's desire to ban sales of alcohol between 10 p.m. and 6 a.m. It did not help that he personally thought anyone enjoying a beer was a dangerous alcoholic, and that he claimed the republic's liberal alcohol laws had been pioneered by two 'boozers', meaning Atatürk and İnönü.

Education had always been a key priority for the AKP. The education budget has mushroomed from 7.5 billion lire in 2002 to 34 billion in 2011, the largest item of state expenditure. Compulsory schooling has increased from eight to twelve years, textbooks are free and, since 2008, every province has its own university, though teaching Darwin has quietly disappeared. In 2003 the administration launched a joint programme with UNICEF (called 'Come on, girls, let's go to school!') to close the gender gap in primary education, and near-parity is working through to the secondary and higher educational levels. The goal of raising future 'pious generations' was reflected in the decision to give equal (or privileged) status to the İmam-Hatip religious schools like the one Erdoğan himself had attended.

An entire generation of young Turks flooded into Gezi Park

to protest the creeping authoritarianism and Islamization that impinged on their lives, like the stentorian announcements that notoriously stopped a couple kissing on a metro platform. Mixed private student accommodation seemed to give Erdoğan nightmares: 'Nobody knows what takes place in those houses. Very intricate things. Anything can happen. Then, parents cry out, saying, "Where is the state?" These steps are being taken in order to show that the state is there. As a conservative, democratic government, we need to intervene.'[17]

This followed AKP opposition to women having caesarean sections and abortions unless they already had three children. At the same time, prohibitions on religious marriage ceremonies without prior legally binding civil marriage, which stipulated jail terms of between two and six years for offenders, were lifted, opening the way for temporary (*mutah*) marriages and polygamy in the view of feminist and secular critics.[18] Worse, in the provinces the AKP provided newlyweds with books about how to have sex (pleasurably but quietly, lest a baby be born mute or with a stutter) and encouraging men to beat their wives on the grounds that this would increase the wife's sexual desires, once she had served the husband placatory coffee.[19]

Although the economic prosperity that Erdoğan had brought about was responsible for a generation that wanted to enjoy its freedoms and leisure, he frothed with fury at these 'bums', 'layabouts' and 'terrorists', eight of whom died in the resulting police riots. While AKP business cronies had bought up much of the corporate media, they did not control Facebook and Twitter, the contemporary version of the old Arabic *fizahs* who ran from house to house with cries of 'death to the Christians or Jews' to set mobs in motion. These technologies had a dark side, unapparent to media boosters of the role of social media in the Arab Spring. As Erdoğan contemplated deploying the army, help was at hand to fulfil his imaginings that 'traitors' were plotting his downfall, a theme given contemporary salience by the deteriorating fortunes of his fellow Islamist Morsi in Egypt.

AKP rule always depended upon the party being seen to be 'whiter than milk'. Turkey is not a conspicuously corrupt country, though the legal system leaves much to be desired and the police are brutal towards anyone without clout. In the global corruption index Turkey ranks 54th out of 174 – better than Italy (72nd) and Greece (94th), sniffy Europeans should remember. This image was tarnished when, in late 2014, the sons of three cabinet ministers were arrested in two waves of judicial corruption probes, forcing their fathers to resign. Prominent members of the Turkish business elite were also detained. The main accused were construction tycoons (a sector where bribery tends to be the norm) and bankers involved with converting illicit Iranian oil revenues into gold bullion through the state-owned Halk Bankası, or Halkbank. So much black money was piling up that these white-collar criminals were storing it in towers of shoeboxes. The investigations touched Erdoğan's son Bilal, with mysterious tapes appearing to show father and son allegedly conspiring to hide illegal money before the police arrived at his home.

Erdoğan responded to this corruption scandal by blaming it on a conspiracy to depose him, and by purging and transferring 5,000 of the investigating detectives and prosecutors involved. He claimed they were agents of sinister 'foreign' powers, meaning Israel and the US. Many of the policemen, and even police support staff like janitors and tea-makers, were transferred to traffic control in provincial cities, places which Turkish wits claim are the current epicentres of the conspiratorial 'parallel state'. At the same time this most touchy of leaders used the country's libel and defamation laws promiscuously to pursue his critics. They included twenty-eight-year-old designer Merve Büyüksaraç, a former Miss Turkey, who received a fourteen-month suspended jail sentence for posting on her Instagram account a satirical poem about corruption that may or may not have been directed against Bilal Erdoğan. Since 2014, Erdoğan has brought 2,000 such actions.[20]

Erdoğan claims that these senior officials are members of the Gülenist movement. Some claim it is an Islamic version of the Roman Catholic 'entryist' society Opus Dei, which similarly focuses on recruiting high achievers in many fields. It has no formal membership or organization and is not a political party, but it runs a thousand elite charter or free schools inside and beyond Turkey which produce high-performance individuals dedicated to *hizmet* (service), which is how the movement describes itself. The stellar students are offered special sessions in so-called Houses of Light. It claims that while the AKP represents 'political' Islam, it is solely focused on 'piety'. Its adherents do not drink alcohol or smoke, and they are obliged to give 10 per cent or more of their income/wealth to Gülenist educational projects in Turkey and abroad. Major donors are remarkably reticent about what they hope to achieve with their philanthropy, beyond providing educational scholarships in Turkey and the Third World.[21]

Unlike the AKP, the Gülenists are pro-Western, and pro-Israel, which is not a popular stance in Turkey, and advocate interfaith dialogue. They are keen opponents of the Kurdish PKK – and by extension of Erdoğan's peace initiatives – which has checked the expansion of their boarding schools in Turkey's south-east. Their exiled guru (a former imam), or master teacher (*hocaefendi* in Turkish), Fethullah Gülen, resides in a villa complex in rural Pennsylvania. While he claims to be merely a peaceful cleric, helping people to improve themselves, the AKP has him on tape saying that his followers should infiltrate key state or private institutions, doing nothing to rock the boat until they are assured of assuming total power.[22]

The Gülenists were responsible for one major service to Erdoğan before they fell out.

They helped him reckon with the 'deep state' embodied by the military, which, as a bonus, would also demonstrate to the EU that Turkey's long-term problem with coups was finished for ever. The EU initially welcomed this judicial reckoning with the 'deep state', but then began to wonder why it included judges, professors and opposition journalists among the military accused.

Two successive waves of mass trials, 'Sledgehammer' and 'Ergenekon' – named after the alleged nationalist plots – resulted in the conviction of the top brass, though some of them committed suicide before they had their day in court. They were accused of conspiring to foment chaos and disorder through bomb attacks on mosques and faking Greek attacks on Turkish aircraft, so as to bring down the AKP government as they restored public order with the aid of covert arms dumps. The accused included former chief of staff Kenan Evren and Engin Alan, the officer who with the aid of the CIA had captured PKK leader Abdullah Öcalan in 1999 travelling to Kenya on a Greek Cypriot passport.[23]

A society prone to conspiracy theories consumed lurid testimony from secret witnesses and evidence from illegal wiretaps which improbably linked the extreme right and left in a single vast conspiracy against Erdoğan and the AKP. In 2013 some 300 senior officers were convicted and imprisoned for long terms, including life for several generals and admirals, though most were released after the digital evidence was revealed as tainted.

Ironically, the modern Turkish leader who came closest to rapprochement with Turkey's Kurds is now waging a semi-civil war in eastern Turkey. Good relations with Iraq's KRG, where the Turkish military periodically intervened to hit the PKK in their Qandil Mountains refuges, emboldened Erdoğan to bury the hatchet with the 15 million Turkish Kurds. About 40,000 people had died in a war of terrorist attrition and military brutality that had raged since 1984. Under Erdoğan, Turkey's MIT intelligence officers held secret talks with the imprisoned Öcalan which established a road map to disengagement that would culminate in his release from the island prison of İmralı.

Of course, Erdoğan had an ulterior agenda, which was that ethnic Kurd political support would be necessary for the two-thirds majority he needed to grant himself an executive presidency, an office which, since the clock goes back to zero, he could look forward to occupying until 2024. He was going to do so in some style. Deciding that the old Çankaya Palace was poky, Erdoğan devoted €500 million to the new 200,000m² Ak-Saray ('White Palace') edifice, replete with 1,150 rooms and a 5,000m² mosque. That it arose in a nature conservation area named after Atatürk was waved aside. Ceremonial guards in pseudo-Ottoman costume are the latest adornment adopted by a man his critics have called a sultan.

Erdoğan fought the June 2015 general election on an aggressively Islamist platform. Straws in the wind included launching a new Islamic bank, to make Istanbul the hub for this form of interest-free finance, and an unsuccessful attempt to criminalize adultery. To Erdoğan's fury, the sudden success of a new pro-Kurdish liberal party, the HDP, in the June 2015 elections stymied his ambitions for an executive presidency. Its popular leader, the human rights lawyer Selahattin Demirtaş, attracted all those who feared a further extension of Erdoğan's enormous powers. One of the eighty-two HDP's new MPs was Öcalan's niece.[24]

Turkish Kurds had been incensed by the President's duplicitous response to the advent of ISIS hard by the Turkish–Syrian border. Erdoğan had done nothing to prevent ISIS using decayed industrial towns like Gaziantep and Kilis to funnel through foreign jihadist supporters of ISIS. Smugglers sold fuel on behalf of ISIS inside Turkey with impunity. But he was absolutely determined to prevent the Syrian Kurdish PYD from establishing a statelet that might coalesce with Kurds elsewhere. This was called 'Rojava' (Western Kurdistan), consisting of the 600 kilometre strip of predominantly Kurdish cantons along Turkey's southern border with Syria. This would bring closer the nightmare of the region's 25–30 million ethnic Kurds coalescing, and the dismemberment of the Turkish republic. That is why Turkish army tanks parked passively as Syrian Kurdish fighters battled to take back the town of Kobane from its ISIS occupiers. He refused, too, to allow Iraqi Kurdish Peshmerga fighters, let alone the PKK, to come to the aid of those fighting ISIS.

Instead of resuming attempts to make peace with the Kurds, for which he was rumoured to be in line for the Nobel Peace Prize, Erdoğan deliberately increased the tension, calculating that in a fresh election Turkish patriots would rally to him, including the military, which wanted the PKK wiped out. It helped that ISIS carried out three major bomb attacks, in Diyarbakir, Suruç and Ankara, the first aimed at the Kurds, though these attacks also led to a precipitate decline in Western tourist numbers.

After Erdoğan nullified the peace process on 24 July 2015, the depressing cycle of tit-for-tat killings by the PKK and the army resumed. Several predominantly Kurdish cities in eastern Turkey were put under martial law, while HDP offices and party rallies in the rest of Turkey were subjected to AKP-instigated mob violence. On 1 November 2015 the AKP won almost 50 per cent of the vote, and 316 seats in the Assembly, tantalizingly short of the 330 majority Erdoğan needed to change the constitution. The HDP vote declined as Erdoğan succeeded in painting them as bourgeois confederates of the camouflage gear-clad PKK. That the HDP now advocates Kurdish autonomy is a measure of Erdoğan's failure to resolve the Kurdish issue.

Although the EU depicts itself as a beacon of liberal virtue, criticism of Erdoğan's repression of a free press and social media was suddenly muted and a controversial report on Turkish progress to European standards was postponed until after the AKP had won the November elections.[25]

At great cost, Turkey had taken 2.7 million refugees, half from the war in Syria, the rest from Iraq, Afghanistan, Iran and Pakistan. About 15 per cent of them are housed in camps, the majority in towns and villages. Only about one in five of the Syrian refugees want to leave Turkey, which is culturally and geographically nearer a homeland they want to return to if and when peace is restored.[26]

When Chancellor Merkel's declaration of open house to Syrian refugees resulted in a rush of humanity through the Balkans and across the narrow waters to the Greek Dodecanese islands, Erdoğan offered to staunch the flow through a one-for-one exchange of repatriated illegal migrants for up to 72,000 legitimate refugees in camps in Turkey. Under this March 2016 deal, a substantial EU payment of €6 billion would ensure Turkish coastguards and police enforced their own laws and that the southern border with Syria was closed. The deal was done after various Balkan states began fencing and policing their borders, while the Visegrad Group states refused to take EU-mandated refugee quotas.

As if to absolve itself from charges of kowtowing to Turkey, the German Bundestag – which has eleven ethnic Turkish members – passed a cross-party resolution condemning the Armenian genocide over a century ago. After recalling the Turkish Ambassador to Berlin, Erdoğan accused the German-Turkish parliamentarians of lacking 'Turkish blood' and suggested they undergo tests. The leader of the German Greens, Cem Özdemir, has had his police security bolstered after receiving assassination threats from Turkey, where the official media has been poking around in the home village of his parents.[27]

While nobody wants the EU deal with Turkey to fail, no one wants it to fully succeed either if this entails visa-free travel for Turks in the Schengen Area or Turkish admission to the EU. The deal highlights a fundamental clash between Europe's interests and values, a clash Erdoğan deliberately fuelled when in March 2017 he picked rows with the Dutch and Germans when they sought to stop most of the Turkish cabinet attending rallies to win the diaspora vote. Buried in the small print was the stipulation 'The EU reiterates that it expects Turkey to respect the highest standards when it comes to democracy, rule of law, and respect for fundamental freedoms, including freedom of expression.' Even supposing that at some future date talks on all thirty-four outstanding EU accession chapters were concluded, the resulting agreement would have to be ratified by all member states. This seems highly improbable in the current climate of raging populism and conditions in Turkey. Meanwhile, relaxed visa requirements are almost sure to boost the number of Turkish illegals living in Europe, which, with Turkish internal religious and political animosities playing out on German streets, will in turn stoke hostility to Turkish EU accession. Ties with Nato are also fraying. Because of alleged ties between Germany's Die Linke and the PKK (which is proscribed in Germany), Turkey banned all German politicians from visiting their air force at Incirlik air base, resulting in Berlin relocating this force to Jordan. This is before one imagines such black swans as a major clash with Turkey's large Kurdish minority, which could generate its own refugee exodus.

Parallel PKK and ISIS terrorist attacks have also wrecked Turkey's tourism industry, which, while constituting 6 per cent of GDP, provides 8 per cent of employment. Of these tourists, 5.5 million were Germans and 4.5 million Russians in 2015, though numbers are down 40 per cent in June 2016. Russians were deterred from visiting Turkey by Putin's fiat, while Turkish fruit (a substitute for Russian counter-sanctioned EU imports) was suddenly subject to Russia's fearsome phytosanitary inspectors.

In late March 2017 Erdoğan made ominous general threats to Europeans travelling anywhere.[28]

If the aftermath of the failed coup on 14 July has damaged Turkish relations with the US, EU and NATO, nothing so minor as the downing of a Russian fighter jet (one of whose pilots was murdered by Turkmen) has dissuaded President Putin from repairing relations with Ankara. With Poland objecting to the expanded Russo-German Nord Stream 2 gas pipeline, Russia's need for an alternative Turkish Stream in the south becomes more important, for it matters little how and where Moscow bypasses Ukraine as long as it does so, and strips Kiev of transit revenues. The rapprochement even survived the assassination of Russia's Ambassador to Ankara in December 2016. The fact that the bumptious and cocky Erdoğan is a supplicant to the bumptious and cocky Putin is obvious.[29] If he is to swim deeper into the authoritarian camp, Erdoğan may also have to eat humble pie with China, since his pan-Turkic sympathy for Uyghurs in what he calls Eastern Turkestan (aka Xinjiang) angers Beijing, which otherwise has allotted Turkey a key role in its grandiose Silk Road strategy to link China with Europe. Too many ISIS Uyghur sympathizers seem to have Turkish passports. The main suspect in the New Year's Eve Raina nightclub shootings in Istanbul is alleged to be a Uyghur.

Despite its domestic disorders, Turkey is aggressively harrying the PKK and its Syrian Kurdish analogue, while making irredentist moves about Mosul in northern Iraq. Erdoğan and Putin concluded the 2016 Moscow Agreement, in which in return for ceasing to call for the departure of Assad, Erdoğan was given a free hand to meddle along his southern borders with Iraq and Syria. Suddenly by 2017 there were 4,000 Turkish soldiers with tanks fighting ISIS in al-Bab, whose capture would conveniently frustrate Syrian Kurdish attempts to join up their border cantons. Erdoğan is especially concerned about the disposition of a post-ISIS and predominantly Sunni Mosul, which was torn from the Turks by the British and gifted to Iraq.[30]

To that end, there has been much official revisiting of the 1920 National Pact, the manifesto of the resistance movement to Entente dictation, just as crude maps shown on Turkish TV include places with Turkish minorities in other people's countries. The Iraqis are not happy that Erbil and Kirkuk appear in a Turkey that has grown bigger on paper. Erdoğan imagines that he can get a better deal than Atatürk. There has also been another transformation.[31]

As Erdoğan ventures his changes to a presidential constitution in 2017, Atatürk is becoming an attractive model, even for an Islamist president. Erdoğan is often called *baskomutan* (commander-in-chief), not to mention *ata* (father) or *reis* (the chief) as was his secular predecessor. There is now an 'Erdoğan March' similar to the 'Atatürk March'. Ironically, the man who pushed Turkey in a secular Western direction is being co-opted by an Islamist authoritarian who is making Turkey more like the rest of the Middle East.[32]

Turkish relations with the EU and the US will be contingent on how far they cooperate in repressing the 'Gülenist' opposition, which will not be much, given claims of Turkey's resort to torture and possibly a revived death penalty, especially if demands for extradition also extend to fleeing military conspirators. There is also a real risk of internal Turkish strife being replayed on the streets of European capitals which have large Turkish and Kurdish diasporas. The US may find that cooperation against ISIS is entirely contingent on cooperating with Erdoğan against externally based domestic foes. A case in point is the Syrian Kurdish YPG (a subset of the Syrian Defence Force) who are the chosen instrument of the US in combating ISIS. Turkey has continued to bomb these fighters, even when the bombs fall very close to the Kurds US special forces advisers.

From being the darling of Goldman Sachs, Turkey has become the Sick Man of Europe again. Investment and tourism have fallen away. Its government will in future face a secular Kemalist underground, as well as ISIS and the PKK, and a much more restive indigenous Kurdish population. Vast public rallies, with the red and white flags waving, cannot mask the fact that Turkey has not just survived a one-night crisis, but has undergone a seismic shift in its domestic affairs and international position. Turkey's destabilizing impact on the region and shifting of alliances are one worry, with poor relations with the

Saudis after Turkey opted to support its Qatari ally in resisting the Saudi-sponsored blockade. Another is Erdoğan's abandonment of the rule of law – with claims from expropriation to torture. Erdoğan may well have his executive presidency after he won the referendum vote in April 2017, but the price may mean no more talk of accession to the EU (especially with their British boosters gone), and possibly Turkey leaving NATO too, which would be a major strategic accomplishment for the Russians.

5

Failed Nation? Russia Under Putin

The Russian President, Vladimir Putin, shares Erdoğan's authoritarianism, hostility to the West, irredentism and touchiness. Both men have also exploited the religion, or at least religiosity, of their peoples. But Russia has its unique history and it is also a nuclear superpower. It deserves respect, though what for remains elusive. Many of Russia's postures can be explained by the equivalent of phantom limb syndrome, where one imagines a leg itches despite it having been amputated. Russians, and their leaders, feel twitches from a Soviet empire that no longer exists, though their experience of decolonization was much more abrupt and traumatic than that of other European powers.

In 2016 mass data leaks from a big Panamanian law firm, Mossack Fonseca, exposed colossal international resort to offshore banking so as to evade tax. Minimizing the local fallout from these revelations was important for President Putin. Though his official salary is $133,763 (and 63¢), with only a small apartment he owns and another property rented, persistent rumours of his fortune range from $40–200 billion. His daughter Katerina and her banker husband are also worth $2 billion, with a £2.4 million mansion overlooking Biarritz, chump change in these circles.

Imagine Kremlin strategic communications advisers listing possible responses to Western reports on the Panama scandal.[1] How the responses evolved can be roughly charted. First, dispatch a press spokesman to say the Panama documents contain nothing new, while hinting that 'dark forces'/ 'a hostile attack' (optional choices) may be behind the vast information dump. It helps that Russian state-controlled TV and a press whose oligarch owners can be raided by the police at will could hardly mention the subject. Putin himself initiated the rumour that investment bank Goldman Sachs owns the German paper which released the Panama Papers, even though two days later this rumour was officially discounted by his press spokesman Dmitri Peskov, and Goldman Sachs does not own the *Guardian* or *Le Monde*.

Next, do not toss any sacrificial victims to the crocodiles of the press since they will come back for more. The cellist Sergei Roldugin is godfather to Putin's other daughter, Maria Putina. He is personally worth $345 million and allegedly controls $2 billion in offshore accounts. There was not just an innocent, but a *noble* explanation. Roldugin had used the money to purchase rare musical instruments abroad, including a $12 million Stradivarius cello, with much smaller sums to recruit professors for his estimable music school in St Petersburg, ensconced in a House of Music which Putin gave him after the cellist had languished unhappily for nineteen years in a minor orchestra. Showing his (well-hidden) human side, Putin announced: 'I am proud that I have such friends,' ignoring inconvenient facts like the total value of all musical instruments (guitars, pianos, saxophones etc.) imported into Russia in 2015 was a mere $50 million.[2]

Next encourage this special friend to speak for himself. Roldugin gave a TV reporter a tour of the House of Music, plaintively saying that he 'had to beg all over the place because the instruments were so expensive'. That was why patriotic oligarchs (unnamed) donated so much to help otherwise disadvantaged Russian youngsters with musical talent. This may be the first time in recorded history that the subject of offshore accounts has reduced TV audiences to tears. Then claim that sometimes offshore accounts are positively *useful* to patriots. One account which cost Roldugin $1 to open (!) could then borrow hundreds of millions (!) from state telecoms provider Rostelekom.

Anything to do with espionage plays well with Russians, who share this juvenile obsession with Britons. So the Russians claimed that the Panama scandal was *really* an FSB undercover operation designed to protect Russia's cable TV companies from a sinister plot by US intelligence agencies to acquire them through surrogates based in Panama. FSB front companies saved the day by buying the cable companies themselves, before handing them over to Rostelekom. This 'Petersburg punch in the teeth' (that being a favourite image of Stalin's too) was profoundly patriotic.

Boring little people like journalists were still sceptical and persevered with their wicked allegations. Patriotic activists (unnamed) asked the state prosecutors to investigate the newspaper *Novaya gazeta*, which carried the Panama revelations. Has the paper paid all the taxes due on its foreign holdings? Just pose the insinuating question rather than answering it, a tactic common to all 'fake news' that Trump is also exploiting.

Emboldened by how this was playing, the Russians moved harder on the attack. Who was crying 'stop thief' the loudest? Attention was turned to dissident blogger Alexei Navalny, then under house arrest, and the Anglo-American hedge fund tycoon Bill Browder, who has been waging an international campaign on behalf of his murdered Russian lawyer, Sergei Magnitsky. Of course, Russia claimed, these two are MI6 agents, codenamed 'Freedom' and 'Solomon'. Who will notice that the documents 'proving' these claims are riddled with grammatical errors that only Russians make?

We are not done with Browder, a small thorn in Putin's foot somewhere in London's Soho. He is not to everyone's taste. He has published a book, *Red Notice*, about the Magnitsky saga. When we meet after a long interval at his Hermitage Capital offices, Bill mentions his book will become a film.[3] Hermitage made big money in Russia in the 1990s and paid large tax bills too. After a police raid Browder discovered that company seals were missing, and that dummy companies with fabricated liabilities had claimed $230 million in tax rebates through court judgments in the provinces. The proceeds disappeared to offshore accounts held by the policemen and judges involved in stealing the $230 million from the Russian taxpayer. The loot was converted into fancy cars and luxury property in Europe (notably the London *souk*) and Russia, far beyond the means of anyone earning a civil servant's known salary. Leaked papers suggest that Sergei Roldugin received $800,000 from one of the bogus firms through which these illicit funds flowed. In 2013 the Russian authorities put both Browder and the long-dead Magnitsky on trial for embezzlement. Browder was sentenced to ten years in prison in absentia.

The film he plans to make is worrying the Kremlin so the counterpunch has to go in hard before Browder's screenplay is even finished. Find an obliging Russian film director (Andrei Nekrasov) with a record of criticizing the regime, notably a 2007 documentary about Litvinenko, featuring murdered journalist Anna Politkovskaya. 'I'm the anti-Putin hero, not Europe. Their talk of Russia is free of charge blah, blah, blah. I put my life on the line fighting Putin,' he said, mentioning a documentary he made about the FSB blowing up Moscow apartment blocks to facilitate a second war in Chechnya. Persuading French Arte and German ZDF to fund the film, with Norwegian and Finnish broadcasters chipping in, so as to void the charge of the film being state propaganda.

The film is called *The Magnitsky Act – Behind the Scenes*. It accuses Browder of constructing an elaborate alibi (it claims Magnitsky died of a heart attack rather than from a beating in prison) to avoid Hermitage being held to account for its own tax violations in Russian courts. A Finnish MEP named Heidi Hautala helped organize a screening of the film in the European Parliament. Five Russian TV stations attended the premiere. She invited Nekrasov and Browder, but also two of the men Browder says were involved in embezzling Russian taxpayers' money, Andrey Pavlov and Pavel Karpov, who are on US blacklists. Their names are also among thirty-two on EU lists, but the EU declines to enforce travel bans. Of course, the moment ZDF cancelled the screening of the film on legal and technical grounds, the Russians and their PR circus (as usual orchestrated by some smooth British chancer) crowed about there being no free speech in the EU.[4] This is how an amoral state can indeed dodge any bullet, in ways that make Western 'spin' look tame by comparison.

•

The fact that Russia is governed by former intelligence officers (though its Prime Minister, Dmitri Medvedev, is a lawyer) does not automatically make it any more liable to make epic foreign policy mistakes, for we have witnessed many of those committed by Western liberal democracies governed by civilian politicians, some of them trained lawyers too. Amusingly, this subject rarely figures in the profession's grave admonitions about legal ethics.[5]

Russia's obsession with espionage and security is in the blood, and what began with the ubiquitous Tsarist Okhrana continued in more ruthless form in the *organy* (agencies) of the Communist era, the NKVD and its successors the OGPU and the KGB. These men had something of a caste or medieval order about them, a spirit brilliantly reimagined in a contemporary setting by the novelist Vladimir Sorokin. The quest for security was a global as well as a national mission.[6]

In many parts of the former Soviet Union's empire the downfall of Communist regimes in 1989–90 led to a reckoning with their security services. This was not the case in Russia itself, where many of the half-million former KGB officials bitterly resented the 1991 collapse of the system they and their predecessors served as the 'sword and shield' of the Communist Party. So did many ordinary Russians, who liked or loved aspects of the old order.

In Putin, a lieutenant colonel in the KGB until August 1991, these circles found their ideal spokesman, whose powers over the intelligence machine rival those of party leaders – but more so. Under Soviet rule, the KGB was subordinate to the elderly Politburo. The latter were never in it for the money. Their successors frequently are, which enormously boosts the power of their patron-in-chief, who can take as well as give. Collective leadership has been replaced by the personal rule of a man who incarnates not just the ethos of the security establishment and its dubious associates but the hopes and fears of many Russians.

The son of a minor policeman, whose parents suffered grievously in the siege of Leningrad (his elder brother was killed), and who, as a KGB operative based in Dresden, was later to see his country and its satrapies disintegrate around him, Putin remains a symbol of everything Russian that is morose, resentful, paranoid and revanchist-minded. After seven years, partly spent fighting official corruption in St Petersburg, albeit effortlessly combined with membership of a dacha property association in which murderous gangsters figured, in 1998 Putin 'stepped into the same river twice' – as he put it – when Yeltsin appointed him Director of the FSB.

A year later Putin's highly popular eagerness to 'bash the hell out of' insurgent Chechens saw his appointment as Prime Minister, and then his election as President after Yeltsin's resignation. Almost his first act was to give the Yeltsin clan general immunity from prosecution.[7] From 2000 to 2008 Putin was Russia's President, then after a decent interval as Prime Minister (2008–12), he was elected President again in 2012 for a period that ends in 2018. If he stands for re-election, as he is entitled to do, then he could be president until 2024, eclipsing Brezhnev and Stalin.[8]

Under Putin the *siloviki* – the Russian term for the quasi-chivalric order with security service backgrounds – have risen to commanding heights. They have infiltrated not only the state apparatus and state-owned enterprises such as oil and gas companies, but also the media and the private sector. They are the main beneficiaries of assets grasped back from greedy and overweening oligarchs in a process cynically called 'velvet reprivatization' by Igor Sechin, one of the key players in this story.[9] The best-known examples of the type are Alexander Bortnikov, head of the FSB; Vladimir Kolokoltsev, Chief of Police and head of 80,000 interior troops; Defence Minister Sergei Shoigu; Chief of Presidential Staff (until 2016) Sergei Ivanov; and Sechin, head of the oil major Rosneft and a former KGB officer who served in Mozambique.[10]

That last posting suggests these men were hardly the cream of the KGB, which, generally speaking, had a better grasp of the Soviet Union's problems than anyone else.* Putin himself spent his 'spying' career with seven or eight colleagues in provincial Dresden rather than at the vast KGB headquarters at Berlin-Karlshorst where hundreds of agents worked.[11] It was while in Dresden that Putin experienced the collapse of Soviet Communism, receiving the ominous response 'Moscow is silent' when he called for reinforcements to defend his HQ as a crowd stormed

---

* I owe this insight to Sir John Scarlett delivered at a private lunch. As a former Soviet specialist and head of MI6 he has reason to know.

the Stasi building opposite. This experience scarred him in a manner reminiscent of Yuri Andropov, Ambassador to revolutionary Hungary in 1956, who would go on to head the KGB and in 1982–84 the Soviet Union.[12]

Experts say that the number of Kremlin officials from such security backgrounds has risen steadily, from 25 per cent in 2003, to 42 per cent in 2007 and an incredible 77 per cent if 'unofficial' agents are included. As Putin grows more confident, he is replacing them at the centre and in regional governorships with others in their forties who are little more than yes-men. The main beneficiary of this 'rejuvenation' process was Ivanov's forty-four-year-old deputy, Anton Vaino, who replaced Ivanov when he was moved from defence to nature reserves, ecology and transport.[13]

This is not to claim that there are no rivalries and turf wars within this elite group, for example between the internal Federal Security Service (FSB) and external Foreign Intelligence Service (SVR), or between these civilian agencies and the military Main Intelligence Directorate (GRU). But unlike in the former Soviet Union, where faction fights largely involved matters of principle, contemporary Russia has been compared to the incessant vying for power and spoils at a Renaissance court, these being objects in themselves rather than by-products of ideological goals.[14]

An analogous set-up involving FBI, BVS or MI5 officers from the boondocks with policemen thrown in would appal the average American or European, but in Russia the alleged efficiency and undoubted ruthlessness of these security bureaucrats make them relatively popular as they combat the country's enemies: overmighty oligarchs (not a few of them Jewish) and the alleged attempts by the US and the EU to degrade and demote Russia as a great power by fomenting 'colour' revolutions, notably in Georgia and Ukraine, which the Kremlin regards as its 'zone of privileged interests'.

Unlike the old KGB, however, the FSB is not in the business of mass purges. Serving FSB personnel (and alumni) pride themselves on being 'non-ideological' technicians of power, chiefly because, unlike Soviet leaders, they have no hostility to capitalism, and see themselves as libertarian advocates of such things as flat taxes (13 per cent in Russia, though this may rise to 20 per cent once the 2018 presidential elections are over). The regime is mercurial and postmodern in its ability to cynically or ironically synthesize old and new elements (as one can see in the recourse to eighteenth-century Tsarist symbols in eastern Ukraine's 'Novorossiya'). In reality the *siloviki* are consistently authoritarian, nepotistic, nihilistic and contemptuous of the rule of law on which any rules-based free market relies. They have been known to hound those who elude their grasp with 'lawfare' waged in Western courts with the aid of Mutual Legal Assistance Treaties and Interpol Red Notices.

Attempts by the FSB to declare the Russian online property database a state secret (so as to prevent embarrassing disclosures affecting their own ranks, such as the separate cold storage structure for his wife's fur coats at the vast estate of Russian Railways boss Viktor Yakunin) are symptomatic of the 'securitization' of even the most prosaic areas of life.

That they and their associates regard the civil and criminal law as tools to achieve their own ends means that Western democracies can no longer deal with Russia as if it shared common norms and values, which for a period after the fall of communism it attempted. However absurd it may seem, this has enabled some of the world's most rapacious businessmen to make the legitimate claim that they are victims.[15] In a final twist, in September 2016 it was reported that plans are afoot to reassemble all the various domestic and external security agencies in a single Ministry of State Security (MGB), the name Stalin gave the Soviet spy apparatus until it was renamed KGB after his death. Like a re-forming aged rock group, the band is back, their hearts beating a bit quicker at the thought of all the secrets they know.[16]

·

Russia's 1993 constitution guaranteed Russians the right to freely leave and return, and judging by central London many leapt at the chance to depart for good. A strikingly large number of the offspring of Russia's ruling elites, like the daughters of Putin's press secretary Dmitri Peskov, live in considerable comfort in London or Paris. But millions more enjoyed holidays abroad, spending $54 billion in 2015 on tourism before numbers fell by a third.

This came about partly by force of circumstances – the collapsing rouble, the terror threat in Egypt, Turkey and Thailand – but there are increasing indications that the Russian government is not displeased with curbs on foreign travel. Like freedom of expression, established after the fall of Communism, freedom of movement goes against the grain of Putinism, and the Kremlin can be expected to welcome any means of constraining it.

This began in 2010, when FSB employees became the first to fall under the travel ban, after a major defection and revelations about sleeper cells in the UK and US.

Then there was a Federal Bailiffs Service ban on citizens who owed the government money, or who had been taken to court for outstanding debt (back taxes, bank loans, alimony, fines, mortgage payments). The FBS database covers 1.4 million delinquent citizens.

The Ukrainian crisis was the excuse to ban some 4 million more people from visiting 114 countries with which the US has extradition treaties, members of the Interior and Defence ministries, the Prison Service and the Drug Control Service as well as firemen and employees of the Prosecutor General's Office. The Syrian war has also led to Soviet-type controls on pilgrimages to Mecca. The Federal Tourism Agency, Rostourism, has encouraged employers to buy Crimean holiday vouchers for their employees. Outbound tourism has been collapsing at the rate of 22 per cent a year and travel agents have gone bankrupt.

In practice, travel and holidays abroad will increasingly become a rich man's prerogative, and in Russia rich men are mostly in hock to the Kremlin. Even they are not immune, however, since they have been warned to repatriate their ill-gotten assets from such notorious pirate lairs as London, Nicosia and Panama.[17]

As in the past, grounding the masses is also a means of preventing ideological contamination. Comical as they seem, official health warnings against travel to Britain (ridden with tuberculosis brought in from Africa), to America (bubonic plague), or elsewhere in Western Europe (diseases imported by Syrian refugees) are a symptom of a developing national psyche, and many a paranoid Russian will take this outlandish advice seriously. True, many more Russians have begun travelling to Lithuania, though this will be of little comfort to a country whose forces are engaged in exercises simulating an unconventional attack from the east in order to ward off such a thing. The Kremlin is thinking of restricting travel to the EU because of the terror threat; some claim exit visas are only a matter of time.

Keen to ensure that such holiday money as they have is spent at home, the government is likely to increase the subsidies it has already given to the construction of facilities in places like Sochi and the Crimea, where the goal is a gambling mecca like Macau or Vegas. The problem is the dearth of tranquil sunny climes. Warm but terrorist-ridden spots such as Chechnya, Ingushetia or the long stretch of Caspian seafront in Dagestan are not recommended for the holidaymaker's peace of mind.

As the Russian economy flounders, the rouble sinks, a recovery in the oil price recedes, sanctions continue and import substitution grows, autarchy and proud self-isolation will be the watchwords. In the past state propaganda sold the splendours of Soviet tourism and *Sovetskoe shampanskoe* (Soviet champagne) to a locked-in people.

One Russian does get to feel the sun whenever he chooses. Russia's President often visits financially struggling Greece, the last time including an excursion to the secluded, male-only Orthodox sanctuary in Macedonia, Mount Athos, whose jewel is St Panteleimon, a vast Eastern Orthodox monastery. Patriarch Kirill of Moscow, head of Russia's Orthodox Church, accompanied him.

Putin discussed energy cooperation and Russian investments in Greece during a meeting with radical Prime Minister Alexis Tsipras, who had turned to Russia (in vain) at the height of the country's tortuous 2015 negotiations with the EU and IMF over austerity, debt relief and bailouts. He got nothing but warm words.

•

In a further reversion to Soviet proclivities the Kremlin has revived Soviet-style front organizations in which foreign stooges say nice things about Moscow. The media wing of this operation – *RT*, or *Russia Today*, with its 2,500 staff and $300 million budget – is the most visible vehicle. But there are also the supplements Moscow intrudes into otherwise conservative Western newspapers desperate for revenue, and more opaque channels of influence. The Russians have also encouraged links between conservative evangelical Christians such as Franklyn Graham or the National Rifle Association and their own God-fearing gun-toting folk.[18]

The Moscow-based Russian Anti-Global Movement, led by a young Russian called Alexander Ionov, is a throwback to the anti-imperialist conclaves of yore, under the guise of promoting a world in which major powers have an equal voice. Its second meeting in September 2015 was aimed at establishing 'an international working group to coordinate the global struggle of fighters for independence'.[19]

The group supports separatist movements with links to Moscow. Participants at the conference are not named, allegedly for security reasons, but appear to have included representatives of Puerto Rico, Catalonia, Western Sahara and Sinn Fein, along with pro-Russian MEPs from the French Front National and its violent Hungarian equivalent, the overtly fascist Jobbik party. The most recent meeting included representatives from California and Texas, though the 'King of Hawaii' appeared only by video link. The Californian exponent of a referendum on Calexit from the US actually lives with his Russian wife in Yekaterinburg, though he has just opened a Californian embassy in the Russian capital. His separatist views are aimed primarily at Russians, who would be daft to imagine that many Californians share them. All commingled happily with delegates from Novorossiya, as Eastern Ukraine has been rebaptized to reflect Russian eighteenth-century reality. Various websites, such as one purporting to be run by emigrants from the West, proclaim their purpose as being to counter Western anti-Russian propaganda.[20]

The movement's promiscuous mixture – Irish leftists, the French far right, Hungarian neo-fascists and separatists from Texas – reflects its non-ideological nature and cynical intent. All the Kremlin wants is to stir up troubles for the West by promoting nationalist passions and resentments. Its money comes primarily from an obscure charitable fund set up by Putin some years ago to support serving soldiers and for 'military-patriotic projects'.

The movement's ethos is crudely anti-American, anti-EU and in favour of the destabilization of countries like Spain, Ireland, the UK and Poland. The Kremlin has already invented a 'Latgalian' separatist movement in eastern Latvia where people speak a Latvian dialect as well as Russian. Latvian security services have failed to find the originators of an online 'Latgalian People's Republic' equivalent to the one in Ukrainian Donetsk.

The Kremlin must be pleased with its work over the past year or two, since it has now doubled the movement's funding. As a handy tool for black propaganda and subversion, and maybe a useful vehicle to channel covert cash to foreign separatist movements, it can probably count on sub rosa funding itself.

In Moscow's eyes the new movement and others like it will be seen as payback for 'subversive' Western efforts to promote democracy in Russia through NGOs and the like. Promotion of any form of separatism in Russia itself brings a five-year jail sentence. Further proof of Russia's selective tactics, should it be needed, lies in the absence from its membership of the two most active and prominent separatist movements in China and Russia itself – the Chechens, and China's East Turkestan independence movement, the Muslim Uyghurs. Beijing, however, is likely to have private reservations about the promotion of separatist movements round the world by its Russian friend, as its frequent invocation of the principle of sovereignty and half-hearted support for Moscow's military backing for its East Ukrainian clients suggest.

Putin's closest European ally was the politician tycoon Silvio Berlusconi, a man who knew how to combine power and money, though Putin has since taken both the Lega Nord and Five Star Movement under his eagle wings through cooperation agreements with his own party, United Russia. The Greek Marxist Alexis Tsipras nestles there too. Putin regards Britain as a US puppet and a peripheral irrelevance, save for the number of oligarchs who reside in London and the Home Counties, on whom he keeps a beady eye. He is disappointed in President Hollande's

France, though a President Marine Le Pen was thought promising. Putin was also the man of the moment for the rival conservative candidates François Fillon and Nicolas Sarkozy.[21] But getting such admirers into high office may not be what is afoot. Their disruptive effect is all that is required. Without the clear ideological divide of the Cold War, Russia has had to define itself by what it is not. The rise of the populist right throughout Europe helps Russia accentuate Europe's instability while Islamist terror attacks confirm Europe's weakness. Thriving LGBT cultures help too, as epitomized for Putin by Conchita Wurst, the bearded Austrian drag artiste who won the 2014 Eurovision Song Contest, though the Russian President professed himself liberal in questions of sexual morality. Russia it is claimed represents a rock of social conservative stability by comparison.[22]

Moscow's attention especially focuses on Germany, where there has always been a persistent strain of Russophilia on the rebound from a Western civilization such people despise, while German big business, from Deutsche Bahn to Siemens via BMW and Daimler, is notoriously accommodating of Moscow. How could it not be, since 6,000 German firms have business in Russia? Such sympathies run across the German political spectrum from the likes of former Social Democrat Chancellor Gerhard Schröder, who joined the board of Gazprom with indecent haste adding Rosneft in August 2017, to the Putin enthusiasts of the populist Alternativ für Deutschland who would like a reversion to the alliances of Bismarckian times. This is why in the summer of 2016 a Russian-funded Institute for Dialogue Between Civilizations was moved from peripheral Vienna to the German capital under the direction of a former general in the KGB, naturally a close associate of Putin.[23]

Putin would like to shatter the European Union, so that he can deal with sovereign states, bidding for his favour, while deepening a rift between Europe and the US too. He does not need to exert himself too much since elections on both sides of the Atlantic might yield populist nationalists who prefer him to each other and he has Trump in the White House, who cannot bring himself to speak the EU's name. But even in those parts of Europe where there are deep cultural and religious affinities with Russia (such as Bulgaria, Greece and Serbia) or a 'common' authoritarianism such as Hungary or Poland under their current leaders, one can hardly claim that Putin is in the ascendant. Most Greeks want to remain in the EU, and most Serbs want to join it. Neither they nor Bulgaria are keen to adopt Putinism. Poland is a robust democracy. The more Russia asserts its unique identity, the less likely it is that anyone wishes to adopt it, let alone its authoritarian market system. For the revival of pride in Russia as a distinctive *civilization* is also part of a claim that the West has abdicated the right to defend a 'Western' civilization whose content has been voided by Euro-American liberalism. 'Gayropa' is never coming to conservative Russia.

•

Russia is a resource-rich country. Russia contains just over a quarter of the world's proven reserves of natural gas. European demand for gas may have declined along with its price, because of coal and renewables, but for Russia gas is also a geopolitical weapon.

The EU's priorities are different, judging from its 2017 'State of Energy Union' report. The EU, it says, is on course to meet 2020 emission reduction, efficiency and renewables targets. But the picture for security of supply is mixed. Several new LNG terminals are live, there are more gas interconnectors to switch flows, and work has commenced on parts of the Southern Gas Corridor to bring gas from the Caspian region (including Iran) to Europe.

But there was no mention of Nord Stream 2. Although the EU's dependence on Gazprom is a major strategic worry, this Russo-German project undermines it. It will raise Gazprom's share of the German domestic energy market to 60 per cent, and focus 80 per cent of Russian gas exports to Europe on a single (dual) pipeline system under the Baltic. It reflects a kind of German *Ostpolitik* (pursuing special relations with Moscow), and it has been bitterly opposed by a number of Germany's EU partners.

The Poles were so incensed that the Anti-Trust Office in Warsaw forced Austrian OMV, French Engie, German Uniper and Wintershall, and Anglo-Dutch Shell to pull out of their joint partnership with Gazprom, forcing Gazprom to find the €8 billion the two Nord Stream pipelines will cost. This will not be easy, since Russia is excluded from Western capital markets because of banking sanctions, and because Gazprom's own market value has shrunk from €350 billion (2008) to about €50 billion, making it an unattractive borrower.

Nonetheless, the Russians are coming. Obviously their political aim is to deny Ukraine about €2 billion a year in transit revenues, which will be difficult for Kiev to replace. But something else may be afoot. There is no reason why Russia should not build a pipeline from its Kaliningrad enclave to Germany. But instead it is very keen on a small harbour town called Karlshamm in southern Sweden, especially after neighbouring Norway prohibited the Russians from installing themselves on the strategically important island of Gotland.

The Russians have inflated the number of Russian ships that already call at Karlshamm, while claiming the pipeline work would create more jobs. The Swedish authorities leapt at this, and Norway turned a blind eye. Like Finland, Sweden does not belong to NATO. Were anyone thinking of isolating the Baltic states, having a presence building pipelines would be one way to do it, especially as the Russian navy will be protecting the pipe-laying vessels. There is another strategic agenda. The amount of gas Russia will supply to Germany is enough for German needs, but not enough to be systematically reverse-flowed to anywhere that Moscow might cut off from gas, should Putin feel that they need to experience the cold.

Meanwhile, Putin has also been tantalizing Balkan states with the dream of an analogous South Stream. One version involved a pipeline moving gas under the Black Sea to Bulgaria and then to Serbia, Hungary and Austria. This was dropped in December 2014, but not before a rival EU Nabucco scheme was also abandoned, largely because Putin had suborned some states (Austria, Bulgaria and Italy) into his own project.

Putin's next gambit was a Turkish Stream, with gas going across the Black Sea to Turkey and on to Greece, and from there up into the Balkans. Alexis Tsipras eagerly signed up, seeing the prospect of massive transit fees to help his ailing economy, but that scheme never came to anything either, especially after the Turks shot down a Russian fighter jet in November 2015. Recently, however, the Russians have revived a modest Turkey–Greece–Italy scheme, as well as a Turkish Stream after Erdoğan buried the hatchet with Putin. Doubtless he will find a way to stop the shifty Cypriots from making Cyprus a hub for eastern Mediterranean natural gas from Egypt, Israel and others that exclude Turkey.

Putin is playing on the national egotisms of Germans, Greeks and Italians (thereby dividing nation-states from the EU), but at the same time using schemes that may never be realized to undermine the commercial viability of rival EU projects. Although Iran is a Russian ally, Putin does not actually want gas from the giant South Pars field to reach Europe, as the Europeans clearly hope from their support for the 2015 JCPOA nuclear deal.[24]

•

Russia is the largest country in the world, its vast extent spanning nine time zones. Yet it is only the world's ninth most populous country (146 million). Between 65 and 75 per cent of Russians are Orthodox Christians and 14 per cent are Muslims. Given recent Soviet history, it is surprising that only 7 per cent of Russians declare themselves as atheists.

This is even more surprising, given that religion is one key to Russian self-understanding as a nation. The rise of Moscow on the ruins of the Viking-led Kievan Rus (the first state to figure in this region) depended on the atrophy of the Mongol Golden Horde – the most westerly Mongol khanate – and the conquest of Constantinople by the Ottoman Turks in 1453. As elsewhere, nervous clerics worried about their huge landed estates were instrumental in fuelling the pretensions of a monarch. In the sixteenth century a Russian monk wrote to Tsar Ivan IV – Ivan the Terrible – saying, 'Two Romes have fallen, but the third stands, and there will never be a fourth.'[25]

The grandiose image conjured of Moscow as the third Rome symbolizes more powerfully than anything else Russia's global pretensions and its frequently tragic history. Russians were not alone in seeing themselves as a chosen people, but the monk's aspirations for his country were badly out of sync with the facts of the time. The Orthodox Church itself was a profoundly backward, obscurantist institution, in the service of the most extreme form of serfdom. Unlike other forms of slavery, which involved war captives, serfdom was 'voluntary' as starving people relinquished their freedom to escape crushing exactions and taxes. Unlike in Western Europe, serfdom did not decline and disappear at the end of the Middle Ages: in Russia the buying and selling of men and women continued until it was finally abolished by Tsar Alexander II in 1861.

Ivan the Terrible was hardly a model monarch himself, and his successors, notably Alexander II's father Nicholas I, continued to rule with iron fists. Except for the Westernized members of the aristocracy, the country's contacts with the more advanced nations of Europe were small.

The image of Russia the monk projected turned out to be prophetic, in a negative sense. For all its backwardness the country was never able to free itself of a conviction of its spiritual superiority over other peoples, a nation with a world-historical destiny as a saviour of mankind. Hence in part its twentieth-century aspirations to be the leader of global Communism, a creed by which humankind would be redeemed by Marxist-Leninist theology as developed in Moscow.

Yet for all their self-delusions the Russians proved themselves a people with heroic qualities and remarkable powers of endurance. As Frederick the Great realized after the Battle of Zorndorf in 1758: 'It is easier to kill these Russians than to defeat them.' Their resilience and capacity for suffering were to show themselves time and again, from the defeat of the Napoleonic invasion at the beginning of the nineteenth century to their ferocious resistance to Hitler's polyglot legions in the middle of the twentieth. In that sense they did indeed help save the world, or at least Europe, from the Nazi yoke, encouraging the view that Russia is an indispensable power with a right to be heard in every international crisis, even if it rarely provides solutions. One Russian response to US and EU sanctions after the annexation of Crimea and stealthy invasion of Ukraine has been a stoical shrug of the shoulders.

Socially, however, stagnation has been the norm. Held back by its antiquated system – its landed aristocracy were legendary for their indolence, and serfs are not inspired by the work ethic – economically the Russians were late developers compared with Western Europeans. Only at the end of the nineteenth century did industrialization finally get under way, causing tensions in its own right.

The Russians' famed powers of endurance were needed as the rule of Lenin and Stalin replaced the despotism of the tsars after the Bolshevik Revolution of 1917. Civil war, purges and famines brought about by collectivization blighted the lives of a generation. And although the forced pace of industrialization under Stalin's Five Year Plans produced results, the Gulag and the Moscow show trials of 1937 were the price of progress. And it was during the Communist era that the Russian obsession with security and espionage reached its peak.

The Soviet economy consisted of vast enterprises, some producing a single product, others too many, with glass, rubber and steel going in one end and a truck coming out of the other. Sole producers made 96 per cent of diesel locomotives, 100 per cent of air conditioners and 66 per cent of all the batteries produced in the Soviet Union. These factories doubled up as comprehensive welfare agencies for their employees, providing education, housing, cultural and health services. What they did was subject to central planners. Inefficiency was normal. The giant Stalinist steel plant at Magnitogorsk employed 60,000 workers to produce 16 million tons of steel (roughly the same output as Canada or the UK), whereas the USX plant at Gary in Indiana, which Stalin sought to copy in the Urals, produced 8 million tons using 7,000 workers.[26]

Privatizing state owned industry in the 1990s proved nightmarish, partly because committed reformers (privatizers) led by Yegor Gaidar and Anatoly Chubais in the executive were up against a Duma dominated by Communists, with an uncommitted 'marsh' of deputies in the middle who could be swayed either way. About 30 per cent of assets were retained in state hands, such as aerospace, defence, forests, roads and so on. The main privatization method involved giving ordinary people, including minors, vouchers which they could swap for shares. This opened enormous scope for enterprising individuals to buy the vouchers for bread and bottles of vodka, and gradually to aggregate them until these new oligarchs had huge holdings. Gazprom was acquired for $250 million despite its real value being $40 billion and with reserves of gas amounting to hundreds of billions. In some industries, such as aluminium, around a hundred people were murdered, since gangsters were involved, before metal trader Oleg Deripaska and oil magnate Roman Abramovich emerged on top. Because ownership depended on fickle political favour, oligarchs tended to asset-strip the firms, moving the proceeds abroad to various pirate havens like London's Mayfair, where something like Chelsea FC or a newspaper or two could be acquired for pocket change. A cash-strapped Russian government also took loans from oligarch bankers in return for massively discounted shares in huge enterprises – another reason why Russia has such glaring and endemic social inequalities.[27]

Historically, the need to secure the frontiers of the world's largest, sprawling nation drove territorial expansion. Russia's huge land empire in Siberia came about within 150 years, partly on the back of a variant of the Californian gold rush (although rare furs such as marten and sable were the lure). Like Australia, these vast regions became a dumping ground for undesirables, or a refuge for people who fled onerous Tsarist rule. Imperial control was notional in such vast spaces. But this was an all-points-of-the-compass expansion, with the new cities of St Petersburg, Odessa and later Vladivostok as its jewels.

The Treaty of Nystad (with Sweden in 1721) ceded Russia control of the eastern Baltic littoral; that of Kuchuk Kainardji (with the Turks in 1774) opened the Straits and gave Russia vague protective powers over all Ottoman Christians, while Russia also planted itself on the Black Sea coast. The treaties of Gulistan (1813) and Turkmanchai (1828) with Persia saw Russia move into the Caucasus and Transcaucasus, the area between the Black and Caspian seas. This brought Armenians and Georgians into the empire, though the wild men of Chechnya or Dagestan proved reluctant subjects and remain so today. In 1783 Russia took the Crimea; in 1795 Russia joined Austria and Prussia in the partition of Poland, with Warsaw coming under Tsarist control.[28]

Expansion into central Asia led to the clash with imperial Britain in Afghanistan and India known as the Great Game. The weakness of the Qing dynasty in China resulted in the 'unequal treaties' of Aigun (1858), Peking (1860) and Tarbagatai (1864), under which China lost 1.5 million square kilometres of territory in what became the Russian Far East. Contestation of Manchuria duly resulted in crushing defeat at the hands of an imperial but modernized Japan in 1904–5.[29]

In some respects, the collapse of Communism liberated the Russian nation from having to make polite obeisance to the charming folkways of the other peoples in the Soviet Union, especially as the criminal underworld of Moscow and other big cities was riddled with such obvious foreigners whose presence was resented. Loss of empire is a traumatic thing when it extends over decades. It deranges when it happens almost overnight. First came security concerns about what was dubbed the 'near abroad', though many of Russia's neighbours wished they were less near and more abroad, as an American official put it. This rapidly translated into doctrines of legitimate spheres of influence. Next came irredentist and revanchist fantasies and 'philosophical' justifications of a kind of 'Eurasian' manifest destiny based on culture, history and language.

But one relationship could not be altered by dreams and wishful thinking, namely with Russia's giant Asian neighbour China. As it ingratiates itself with Beijing and accustoms itself to its new role as junior partner, Moscow is rightly concerned with the danger of Chinese economic clout replacing its own in the sparsely populated Primorye region around Vladivostok. In west and central Asia, Russia is doing what it can to recreate the Soviet sphere in the guise of a Eurasian Economic Union, with political overtones. So far only Russia, Kazakhstan, Belarus, Armenia and Kyrgyzstan are signed up, and some of them are zealous of their sovereign independence. The big prize was to be

Ukraine, but the EU-orientated overthrow of Moscow's man in Kiev and the subsequent war put paid to that. At the time of writing Putin has had to settle for another frozen conflict there, like those in Georgian Abkhazia, South Ossetia and Moldovan Transnistria. It is based on two eastern oblasts, Donetsk and Luhansk, controlled by Putin's eastern Ukrainian russophone clients under the supervision of the FSB and GRU. These conflicts have cost the Kremlin an estimated $18 billion per year, with $4 billion more spent on Crimea.[30]

Linked to this backward-looking mindset is a tendency to favour strong leaders over genuine democracy, a preference we are seeing again under Putin. Every year he receives over a million petitions from ordinary people asking this Tsar manqué to right some local wrong perpetrated by wicked local 'boyars', meaning officials he has himself appointed. Trying to impress Putin with a hot air balloon or tractor adorned with the President's face is not a winning formula, and should the petitioners try to organize into groups they might be arrested.[31]

Historically speaking, the freeing of the serfs is relatively recent, the habits of subordination instilled by Communism die hard, and remnants of servile thinking and deference towards power continue to be the norm. This is apparent in the 450-seat State Duma, where, despite the presence of parties which claim to be the opposition, only a lone deputy, thirty-five-year-old Dmitri Gudkov, had the temerity to ask for a minute's silence after the liberal politician and critic Boris Nemtsov was murdered on a bridge next to the Kremlin in February 2015, and the Speaker refused the request. Gudkov lost his seat in the September 2016 elections in which fourteen parties competed on what was not a level field. Though the turnout was low, United Russia, the Communists and fascist 'Liberal Democrats' won a large majority, even without using such tactics as 'carousel' voting in which busloads of stooges tour polling stations. It helped that municipal employees tore down opposition posters, and that the only independent pollster, Levada, was closed down two weeks before the election.

Billionaires often suffer from the delusion that politicians are their cyphers and puppets, especially when the former acquire media empires. In his memoir, *Beyond Business*, Lord Browne, the former CEO of BP, recalls dealing with one of them, the exiled former billionaire Mikhail Khodorkovsky: 'He began to talk about getting people elected to the Duma, about how he could make sure oil companies did not pay much tax, and about how he had many influential people under his control. For me, he seemed too powerful. It is easy to say this with hindsight, but there was something untoward about his approach.' Western glossy magazines regularly profile this British-based wire-puller extraordinaire as Russia's coming man. His vivid backstory includes a decade in a labour camp after he crossed Putin, whose associates stole his company Yukos. Putin is not unassailable, but Khodorkovsky's past and exiled present rules him out as an alternative.[32]

All this helped to strengthen Putin's hand against the threat of a 'colour revolution'. The first (Rose) occurred in Georgia in 2003, though the Kremlin was not displeased by the defenestration of former Soviet Foreign Minister Eduard Shevardnadze, who they blamed for the collapse of the Soviet Union. They detected an ominous pattern when the Orange revolution occurred in Ukraine in 2005. The presidential election to replace Leonid Kuchma was rigged in favour of the pro-Russian Prime Minister, Viktor Yanukovych. After widespread protests, though not in the russophone East, where there were separatist rumblings, the opposition candidate Viktor Yushchenko won. He was a survivor of dioxin poisoning that left his face disfigured. Putin thought that the West had covertly rigged this surprise, blaming US Senator Richard Lugar, who was in Kiev as an observer.

The 'orange plague' spread. After the opposition candidate in Abkhazia (a breakaway region of Georgia) beat the head of the local KGB, Putin strangled the economy by banning imports of mandarin oranges. Next came the Pink (or Tulip) revolution in Kyrgyzstan, which sent President Askar Akayev scuttling into exile in Russia. The series only stopped when the Uzbek autocrat Islam Karimov had troops shoot down 'Cotton Revolution' protestors. A 'Denim Revolution' the following year in Belarus also failed. Russia's leaders were convinced the West would seek to foment a similar colours revolution in Russia too.[33]

Like the Chinese or Iranians, the Russians are suspicious of Western agendas hidden within supposedly universal values, agendas which conspicuously leave the repressive autocracies of, for example, Bahrain or Saudi Arabia untouched.

Putin intends to contain what he regards as Western subversion. He is fully aware of how the CIA and other agencies subsidized West European centrist parties and trade unions in the Cold War to check Communist infiltration and subversion, and he and many other leaders around the world suspect that the West is doing much the same by subsidizing NGOs, civic activists and human-rights lawyers who promote Western-style democracy.

It would be remarkable if such agencies were not doing the same today, though it is extremely difficult to discover the facts of the matter – other than that about $1 billion is spread around at least thirty countries for these purposes. One of the few studies of the subject says, 'The motives of US government agencies that fund (but do not specifically direct) many of the democracy groups are similarly complicated, ranging from the principled to the instrumental, depending on the country in question and the officials in charge.' To Russian eyes the clincher was that former CIA Director James Woolsey went on to chair Freedom House, whose mission is 'the expansion of freedom and democracy around the world'.

In Russia now it takes two months to establish an NGO, whereas one can start a business there in five days. To that end, too, Russia's new July 2012 treason law expanded the definition of treason from 'espionage, disclosure of state secrets, or any other assistance' to '*financial, technical, advisory,* or other assistance' harmful to Russia's security, especially '*its constitutional order, sovereignty, and territorial and state integrity*'. After fifty-five groups were investigated, twenty of them were obliged to register as 'foreign agents'.[34]

American claims to be promoting universal values were hard to swallow, as President Trump freely acknowledged in his 'killers' interview, when he dismissed criticism of Putin by saying that the US had killed many people too. Most people are aware of the decennial backdrop of a US-led war on terror that included assassination, illegal rendition and torture, though Russia is hardly in a position to criticize any of these things. The pattern of Western-engineered revolutions seemed to resume in the Arab Spring in 2011. The final straw for Putin was the ousting and murder of Libya's Gaddafi in late 2011, after the then President, Dmitri Medvedev, had acquiesced in the imposition of a no-fly zone to prevent a massacre in Benghazi. Prime Minister Putin made his disagreement public: 'They [NATO] talked about a no-fly zone. So why are Gaddafi's palaces being bombed every night? They say they don't want to kill him, so why are they bombing him? What are they trying to do? Scare the mice?' It did not help that Senator John McCain commented that Putin himself should be 'nervous' about Gaddafi's ghastly fate.

The flourishing of the economy following Putin's early years in power, based largely on an upsurge in gas and oil prices, is history. Western sanctions and Russian counter-sanctions (mainly on agricultural goods) together with falling crude oil prices resulted in 2015 in Russia entering recession, as the economy shrank by 3.7 per cent. Between 2013 and 2015, exports fell by 40 per cent and in 2015 the average salary fell by 10 per cent (as did Russian consumption) while public sector wages were frozen and pensions were indexed at 4 per cent despite 13 per cent inflation. Twenty million Russians live below the poverty line of $180 a month. In some parts of the Russian Federation benefits payments ceased and there are 50,000 homeless in St Petersburg alone, dependent on mobile soup kitchens. Russia also has an exceptionally high divorce rate (fifty-six per hundred marriages), negligible welfare provision, and 400,000 children in orphanages and maybe even more homeless children.[35]

Yet some optimists, and many informed Western investors, do not foresee a collapse. An economy based on raw materials and oil and gas always has customers, share indices are up and there has been a certain amount of import substitution, although it has cost $50 billion. Oil production has risen consistently since prohibited Western technology came into play only in remote regions where exploration is still at the geological survey stage. Since 2011 Russia has been undertaking a $700 billion defence modernization effort while increasing defence spending to 4 per cent of GDP. Although the loss of Ukrainian shipyards has hit naval output and Western sanctions have affected advanced aviation electronics, Russia seems to have acquired the clout for its global assertiveness while hoping to sell its cheap but uncheerful armaments on the back of well-publicized wars.[36]

None of which masks the fundamental problems in Russia's economy. These include overdependence on hydrocarbons; a worker-to-pensioner ratio that will be 2:1 by 2030 (it is currently 2.5:1); no rule of law; capital flight; and too great an emphasis on big companies with links to the political elite and not enough on competition and small and medium-sized enterprises, such as the famous German Mittelstand. These firms account for 40 per cent of the EU economy; the equivalent Russian sector is only 15 per cent. Russia earns less in export revenues than Belgium.

It is worth dwelling on Russia's demographic problems since Russia's leaders regard these as a major strategic problem, and could make them behave even more erratically in future. UN projections claim that Russia's current population of 144 million will decline to between 70 and 100 million by 2050, a third non-Russian, though this may be unduly alarmist. Natural population increase stopped between 1990 and 2013, though in the last few years the birth rate has gradually risen in a population where females are 53.4 per cent of the total. In 2010, average male life expectancy rose from a shockingly low fifty-nine to sixty-three, and it is seventy-four for women. Thirteen thousand villages have no people. Some 34,000 villages are inhabited by fewer than ten people, most of them old women.

Put another way, according to Rosstat, Russia's official statistical agency, since 1992 12.5 million more Russians have been buried than born, meaning three funerals for every two live deliveries of babies.[37] Life in the countryside and decayed single-industry towns of the deep Russian *glubinka* (the sticks or boondocks) remains bleak, and the lot of pensioners is not enviable, despite boosts to their income by Putin (along with those of the armed forces and police) so as to establish a voting claque for his United Russia Party. There is immigration from the FSU countries, but many of them are Muslims of whom Russia has 20 million already, and there is a terrorist threat too from Chechnya, Bashkortostan and Tatarstan.[38]

Underlying all this, and a key to Putin's psyche, are feelings of envy and resentment towards Western powers, chiefly the United States (for the EU is too flabby to respect), which Moscow sees as determined to deny Russia its respected place in the world. The humiliation of the collapse of Communism, and with it the country's claim to superpower status, cannot be underrated, though this mood may lighten with Donald Trump in the White House since he is humiliating the US by the hour.

While 75 per cent of Russia's huge land mass is in Asia, only 22 per cent of its population live there, anxiously eyeing a neighbour that is fifteen times more populous, whatever mutual admiration society Putin currently enjoys with President Xi Jinping. Despite much Russian talk of a turn to the East, the reality has never lived up to its billing in either diplomacy or economic relations. Although China and Russia share limited anti-American commonalities regarding human rights and liberal interventionism, the Chinese rightly suspect that Moscow has an instrumental view of China, as a power to be cultivated whenever Russia is on the rebound from relations with the US and Europe, with which China wishes to maintain good relations to facilitate its peaceful rise.

As Beijing's wealth and influence in the world grow and those of Russia decline, older Russian anxieties about the 'Yellow Peril' have been supplanted by resentment at being treated as a commodities 'resource cow' by the Chinese, as if Russia were in Africa or Latin America and not Eurasia.[39] When it comes to commercial practice, moreover, the Chinese remain unsentimental, as shown in the May 2014 gas mega-deal in which a needy Moscow found itself screwed on prices by a China that can also diversify its energy sources in non-Russian central Asia or with LNG from Australia, Qatar, Indonesia and Malaysia, not to mention whatever hydrocarbon riches lie under the South China Sea. Russian attempts to diversify relations away from a Sinocentric focus to India, Japan, South Korea and Vietnam have been fitful, apart from arms sales, for Russia can hardly admit to a desire to contain a 'brother' whose embrace has been compared to that of a boa constrictor around a rabbit.[40]

Hemmed in east and west by China and the EU, with scant

hope that its breakout into Syria in October 2015 will do much for the country or its people, and with a wounded economy, Putin is looking far from the brilliant statesman and strategist his admirers on the right and left affect to see. Sooner or later ordinary Russians may face the choice between the chauvinistic propaganda on TV and their empty refrigerators.

Europe and the US, whose handling of the Russians has been less than deft, may take comfort from the cost their policies are helping to impose on the Kremlin for its forward policy in Europe. The danger, however, is of driving a bankrupt Putin to new extremes of aggressiveness. At the most recent count, Russia has 1,796 nuclear warheads and 508 missiles, while the US has 1,367 warheads and 681 missiles. Both are upgrading relatively old systems. The Russians make much of this threat since their demographics would not sustain a mass conscript army, and only parts of their forces are truly modernized, the sole diesel-belching *Admiral Kuznetsov* aircraft carrier being a case in point. Tactical nuclear 'de-escalation' of conflicts, Putin has stated, is the new doctrinal norm.

With no collective leadership, the President locked into a vengeful mentality and increasingly reliant on ultra-nationalists within the security and military establishment, we could be nearing a point of domestic economic crisis where Putin seeks to rally his people by some new adventure, possibly in the Baltic states. This would be to brave a collision with a twenty-eight-member NATO, though admittedly one whose lumbering ambassadorial North Atlantic Council and diminished defence budgets compound the problem of knowing when subversion becomes war. We have seen the relish with which the Kremlin has embarked on its Syrian game, though with body bags coming home, the risk of getting sucked in, and the rising threat of domestic terror, Putin's Syrian adventure is unlikely to be popular for long.

•

Outsiders are partly right to view the over-represented KGB/FSB contingent in Russia's ruling elite as merely thugs with attitude. President Obama compared Vladimir Putin to the sullen delinquent lounging at the back of any classroom, though the state assassination of journalists, renegade spooks and opposition politicians is more suggestive of Capone's Chicago than a 'problematic' inner-city school. Thanks to the work of journalists such as Peter Pomerantsev, outsiders also grasp that Russia's state-controlled media have mastered blending truth and falsehood, 'exceeding the power of force of weapons in their effectiveness', as Chief of the General Staff Valerii Gerasimov boasted in 2013.[41]

In the West, the postmodernist capture of university academics does not matter much, since they are a solipsistic irrelevance, but in Russia their common disregard for truth has captured a government. The ruling elite have ideas, for otherwise their amoral cynicism and postmodern irony would not resonate so deeply among the Russian population, which is succumbing as direct memory fades to the nostalgia epitomized by the museums dedicated to the Soviet era. These emphasize the imperial military might, welfare egalitarianism and scientific achievements rather than the repression and shortages. But there has also been a rediscovery of ideas that were once dissident, marginal or subterranean in the Soviet Union. These seeped into the Kremlin's pipework as dry Marxist-Leninism ceased to work and the search was on for a more potent alternative. This is not to suggest that these ideas directly inspire actions such as the invasion of northern Georgia or eastern Ukraine, but they are certainly useful as post-hoc justifications for what has been done.[42]

Rather in the way that Germany's turbulent Weimar Republic witnessed many 'barefoot prophets' and crazy 'St John the Baptists' before the 'Messiah' arrived in 1933, Russia's more recent Weimar years (particularly the truly desperate 1990s) saw the rise to prominence of several ideological crazies who could explain the economic havoc and the loss of imperial greatness which were tangible enough. One aspect of this was the liberation of Russian nationalism from the constraints of a polyglot Soviet Union. But if Russia's rulers were to seek to restore even the inner core of empire they needed something less ethnically exclusive, which is why 'Eurasianism' was useful in a state that still has 185 officially recognized ethnicities.

Russian nationalism has always involved rejecting European

and North American norms, as one can see from Nikolai Dani- levsky's *Russia and Europe* (1871). This was given a more imperial twist by Konstantin Leontiev, who admired the Byzan- tine and Ottoman empires for integrating different peoples and religions and preparing their souls for the afterlife. Eurasianism was a product of Russia's late-nineteenth-century Silver Age. It became modish among some White Russian émigrés who rejected pan-Slavism as being too obsessed with common lin- guistic roots. Instead they favoured the shared civilization of the Mongol-dominated steppe. Discover your inner Mongol was the summary, for they spoke of group consciousness rather than dry philological affinities. The aim was to capture the Bolshevik revolution they had fled from, by investing it with grandiose trans-temporal content. The symbolist poet Alexander Blok conveyed the resentful gist of this rejection of universalizing 'Romano-German' civilization: 'You are millions. We are hordes and hordes and hordes. Try and take us on! Yes, we are Scyth- ians! Yes, we are Asians – With slanted and greedy eyes!'

This flirtation was not welcome. For much of the Soviet period, the handful of people who espoused these views were either shot or confined to the Gulag. However, from Brezhnev onwards, some members of the Soviet elite took an interest in the nationalist Russian right to counter the liberal-minded dissident intelligentsia. While Marxist-Leninism expired in an economy where a banana or an orange was a rarity, indulgence towards nationalists was first extended to the neo-fascists of Pamyat. In 1987 they held the Soviet Union's first unlicensed demonstration, with Vladimir Zhirinovsky's Liberal Democratic Party, a creation of KGB chief Vladimir Kryuchkov, going on to win 6.2 million votes in 1991.[43]

China's 'Century of Humiliation' lasted from 1842 to 1949; Russia's was condensed into the 1990s, though with faint echoes of centuries of domination by the Mongols. Throughout the 1990s Russia was alternately criticized and patronized by the West as its GDP fell below that of Portugal. It has since recovered to match Italy's. The downward spiral of the Yeltsin years, with a President too pickled to stand upright and grasping oligarchs raiding the nation's assets, intensified the search for an ideology to counter the privatizing liberal reformers sheltered by the drunken President, such as Yegor Gaidar and Anatoly Chubais.

It was not an edifying epoch, as former plastic toy duck manufacturers allegedly made trains of oil vanish, or poor people who had been given shares in national assets worth the price of a bottle of vodka sold them to roving aggregators for a bottle and a half, enabling some of the most rapacious klepto-crats on the planet to own oil refineries, mines and steelworks. Many people – gangsters among them – had to be blown up or shot to facilitate 'mergers and acquisitions' in such industries as aluminium. The flashy new elite celebrated its own wealth in astronomically expensive nightclubs and restaurants, debouch-ing from armoured SUVs amidst rings of bodyguards. Private jets and yachts whisked them off to the playgrounds of the international rich, in the Alps, Mayfair or the Riviera. In Britain they could even own national newspapers. An entire service sector, from expensive watches and designer gowns to homes and yachts, grovelled to serve them.[44]

In this hour of national humiliation at the hands of the 'Coca-colonialists', the military and security factions alighted on the deep intellectual demi-monde, where protest took the form of dressing up in SS uniforms while espousing Orthodox Chris-tianity. It was a mutiny against the Soviet version of political correctness, whose keystone is the Great Patriotic War against Nazi Germany. Eduard Limonov, a bisexual playboy originally from Kharkov, returned from a life of sexual excess in New York to help found a National Bolshevik Party with Alexander Dugin, a kind of impresario who physically resembles Dostoevsky.

A guitar-strumming beatnik, with more than a casual inter-est in Nazi occultism, Dugin found himself lecturing at the Russian General Staff Academy on geopolitics along with his French neo-fascist guru, Alain de Benoist, the leading light of the Parisian *nouvelle droit*. He contributed the key insight 'the nation-state is exhausted, and the future belongs to large spaces ... strategically unified and ethnically differentiated'. It has been well said that 'Dugin made a huge impression on people who never read books'. He and others are a kind of avant-garde, tantalizing people with fringe fantasies. Anything else seems earthed by comparison. That is the danger, and it also applies to former Trump adviser Stephen Bannon, who also dabbles in similar reading, like the Italian Nazi Julius Evola.

Putin himself professes to read Ivan Ilyin, a conservative Russian philosopher and admirer of Mussolini, Hitler, Franco and Salazar, who suspected the dark wirepullers in the West (the Jews of course) of trying to dismember Russia and called for a 'national dictatorship'. In 2014 Putin told all regional governors to read Ilyin's *Our Mission* over the Christmas break. It was a call for strong authoritarian leadership and Orthodox religious renewal as antidotes to chaos and Western-backed disintegration.[45]

Such ideas hold appeal not only for a Russian ruling elite that needed the smells and bells of Orthodox religiosity and anti-Westernism as a surrogate for Communism. Putin also has a personal confessor, Bishop Tikhon Shevkunov of the Sretensky monastery. A kind of religiosity became widespread in a country where 65–75 per cent of people call themselves Orthodox Christians. But Putin's appeal, as evidenced by the results of a 1999 opinion poll, is obviously bound up with his brisk persona. Above all, he is not a drunken clown.

The erstwhile hooligan beatniks and the neo-fascist intellectuals are now TV talk-show seers, entertaining or boring audiences with their wild provocations. The Liberal Democrats of Zhirinovsky have joined the Communist Party as the systemic 'opposition' to the ruling United Russia. On 18 April 2016 Putin awarded Zhirinovsky Russia's highest civil decoration, the 'Service to the Fatherland Order', Class II. 'Gladiator' football hooligans from Spartak Moscow have been reconfigured as the intimidating political militia called 'Nashi', the brainchild of Putin's aide Vladislav Surkov. Putin has his chaplain-cum-godfather Father Tikhon to dispense the incense along with the clerical chauvinism. He also has the fealty of Alexander 'the Surgeon' Zaldostanov, a former doctor who leads the Night Wolves biker gang. Any Russian colours revolutionaries will have to face them as well as OMON riot police, who have been subsumed under a new national guard run by another of Putin's judo partners, Viktor Zolotov, a former steelworker who headed Putin's security detail. It will have the power to shoot down

Maidan 2.0 style protestors. The President can say with authority: 'Eurasian integration is a chance for the entire post-Soviet space to become an independent centre for global development, rather than remaining on the outskirts of Europe and Asia.'[46]

·

Another aspect of containment, Russian style, is to force the West to acknowledge Russian spheres of influence. This includes the 'frozen conflict' zones Putin has engineered, including the separatist one he has created in eastern Ukraine in addition to the irreversible annexation of Crimea. The modus operandi tells us a lot. Military experts noticed that among the russophone rebels in the Donbass there were 'Tier One' special forces or Spetsnaz, simply judging from their martial demeanour and the high quality of their arms (Pecheneg machine guns), gloves and boots. They lacked any identifying symbols, especially the black and orange ribbons that other Russian troops – allegedly taking a soldiering vacation – wore on their sleeves in commemoration of the Order of St George medal ribbons Catherine the Great created in 1769 for those who carved out Novorossiya in the Ukraine. Fashionable among Russian nationalists, critics call them the 'Colorado ribbon' since they resemble the vivid beetle.

Such troops hailed from the Main Intelligence Directorate (GRU), the Federal Security Service (FSB), the Foreign Intelligence Service (SVR) and the 45th Special Purpose Regiment of the Airborne Division. These formations include specialists in SIGINT and spying as well as special forces as we usually understand them. Since 2013 the GRU contingent has been under a separate Special Forces Command. Since 2014 Russia has also had a new Russian National Centre for the Management of Defence to iron out glitches that occurred in similar earlier operations in Chechnya and Georgia. There are probably about 12,000 GRU Spetsnaz organized in seven brigades of 1,500 with four more marine detachments attached to each of four fleets, maybe 2,000 men in total. The FSB Spetsnaz consist of two units, Alpha and Vympel, totalling 300–500 men, whose tasks include counter-terrorism and protecting nuclear installations. The 45th adds extra muscle, rather as the UK Special Forces include units that back up the SAS or SBS as US Rangers do for the Seals and Delta Force. The SVR has a 300-strong Spetsnaz force which protects Russian embassies abroad, but which can be assigned other roles.[47]

In 2008 Putin warned NATO that if ever Ukraine joined the alliance, he would take Crimea, where Russia had held a lease on a naval base at Sevastopol since 1991. Russia was entitled to station 20,000 troops there too. When the Ukrainian people rejected Yanukovych's attempt to steamroller them into Putin's beloved Eurasian Economic Union, rather than an association with the EU, he was kicked out, much to Putin's fury.

Masterminded by Defence Minister Sergey Shoigu, it took nineteen days for Russia to take over and annex the Crimea, apparently without a shot being fired. Paratroopers and Spetsnaz were flown in, it being easy to infiltrate them into existing Russian bases. After seizing the centres of power, army veterans of wars in Chechnya and Afghanistan arrived too, to act as 'local' demonstrators calling for Crimea's return to the Motherland, which it did following a referendum in March 2014.

Small detachments of a dozen or so Spetsnaz next appeared in the restive Donbass oblasts of Donetsk and Luhansk, which wanted to break free from the disintegrating authority of Kiev, especially as claims were made that Right Sector fascists were in the ascendant there. Generally speaking they avoided combat, in favour of providing intelligence and training for the local rebels, the more crazed of whom they told to 'fuck off'. It helped that several of the rebel leaders appeared to be volunteer agitators who had come from urban Russia and who had backgrounds in earlier frozen conflicts. Sabotage also came within the Spetsnaz remit, as was seen when a GRU agent blew himself up while trying to destroy trainloads of aviation fuel at Osnova railway station in September 2014. The FSB Spetsnaz contingent was much more focused on herding the spitting rebel cats along a particular political path, coercing difficult individuals who were legion in such circles. The political aim was to control the rebel east so as to be able to exert permanent leverage on the Western-backed government in the rest of Ukraine. Another frozen conflict is expensive, apparently costing Russia $185 million a month in cash, as well as free gas and electricity. Russia's leaders seem to imagine that it and the parallel conflict in Syria can be intensified or calmed down in order to extract concessions in one or the other.

These 'green men' have led to much anxiety in the West about Russia's adroitness in 'hybrid warfare'. Whether it is *warfare* is dubious, since hardly a shot seems to be fired, and the term has also been used in ways that are meaningless, as when *Die Welt* announced that Russia was using 'hybrid warfare' to undermine Chancellor Angela Merkel. They meant that the Russians had manufactured demonstrations by ethnic German Russians after a child – dubbed 'our Lisa' – was allegedly raped by foreign migrants (untrue), while the Kremlin also seemed to be courting Merkel's CSU coalition partner Horst Seehofer, who cut up rough about the cost of migrants to Bavaria, which he governs. But that is not warfare either.[48]

What Russia has learned is how to use the Western right to free expression in an asymmetric fashion, much as one does in jiu-jitsu. They can synchronize social media, broadcasting and telecommunications in ways that twenty-eight free societies cannot, the basic problem for all NATO strategic communications specialists. Flooding (mainly right-wing tabloid) Western newspaper comment boxes with the pro-Putin musings of Russian online trolls gathered in several known and unknown troll factories is not warfare, especially since so many Western readers seem to agree with them. Killing jihadis is one major shared enthusiasm. Hijacking the Twitter feed of a Swedish TV station to broadcast Russian propaganda is clearly a case of state-directed disinformation.

The ubiquity of social media, and the foolishness of those who post details of their lives, was evident too when US soldiers rotated into the Baltic states and Poland found such media flooded with claims that named US officers seconded to Kiev were child-rapists. Protestors in Kiev's Maidan Square received intimidating SMS messages reading 'Dear subscriber, you are registered as a participant in a mass disturbance.'

The predominantly Russian composition of the population in Crimea and Donbass lent themselves to campaigns that relied heavily on information – with the occasional cyber-attack – and manipulation of pre-existing political trends on the ground. Common borders with Ukraine also helped. Russian-supported rebel operations in the Donbass took place against a menacing backdrop of huge military manoeuvres on the Russian side designed to intimidate Ukrainian forces with threats of envelopment. What was new about all of this was the concerted use of non-military power, including social media, state broadcasting and public diplomacy, to muddy the moral waters into a relativistic miasma. This enabled Russia to claim it was thwarting sinister attempts by NATO and the EU to extend their sway over Ukraine, and then into Russia itself, building upon the subversive role of NGOs and manufactured dissidence. They had hacked phone calls by US envoy Victoria Newland to prove it.

But ultimately, when it comes to real war, Russia is also spending prodigious sums not on 'hybrid warfare' but on conventional full-spectrum assets to deter any Western attack or future action that might fatally damage Russia's ability to act as a sovereign power deserving global respect. Maybe, conceivably, Russia could invent separatist movements in Latvia and Kazakhstan, or use the separatist enclave of Transnistria to make trouble in Romania.

Russia's armed forces are actually modest for a country of such vast size. The total military manpower is 900,000 but the deployable land forces are roughly 300,000, which is considerably less than the 400,000 that Pakistan or Turkey can each field. Russia uses auxiliaries and proxy forces (occasionally supplemented by the Spetsnaz units referred to above), but with the main weight of its army kept in reserve as an intimidating presence. They moved around Ukraine's borders chiefly to keep Ukrainian forces tied up. Russia uses relatively cheap and agile forces to change diplomatic and political realities, as it has done in Syria vis-à-vis Turkey and the US. Not having to deal with public opinion (or political opposition) that Moscow cannot manage, Russia's leaders can calibrate their interventions, adapt the mix of forces involved and get in and out with speed should anything go wrong. Unlike the US military, the Russians know how to withdraw too, so they do not get bogged down when control becomes ownership and ownership degenerates into a quagmire, a process likened to turning water into tar. Meanwhile, the US is stuck with its big military, and a Weinberger–Powell Doctrine that there is no alternative to overwhelming force, a view which resembles an over-equipped gardener with every tool who gardens only when it is a pleasant seventy-five degrees outside.[49]

But in the Baltic states, not to mention Poland, they would be messing with governments that are in control, and with states that belong to NATO, whose members are obliged to defend them. That would entail, however, the latter deciding at what point multifarious malign activities had crossed the threshold of war. Above all, dealing with this involves a strategic assessment of Russia's objectives. Does it want to recreate something less ambitious than the old Soviet Union? Or does it seek to protect Russia with a series of peripheral frozen conflicts that can be inflamed or cooled at will? Assessing Russia's overall strategic intentions counts for much more than how to deal with a tactic whose applicability seems limited.

Misperception of one's enemies is commonplace and hard to shake off, rather like trying to see past a mirage to the reality. A fearfully credulous West invests every Russian move with sinister significance, especially since Russian bombers are now ostentatiously patrolling north European and Scandinavian airspace, while in one case a fighter buzzed a US destroyer operating in the Baltic as part of a NATO exercise.[50]

Up on the roof of the world Russia is bent, people claim, on taking over the Arctic, or rather the mineral riches beneath the ice caps. Certainly, Moscow has established small military bases – for example one housing 150 soldiers on Alexandra Island – where troops can briefly venture into the −47°C cold to ride around on reindeer sleighs toting machine guns. Its bombers have also launched cruise missiles in the region.[51]

This should not be confused with the separate legal claim Russia is pursuing to the seabed (but not the ice and water above) under a continental shelf that extends 200 miles beneath the North Pole. Should we care? International oil majors have already ceased prospecting there as they adjust to lower revenues, so how will technologically backward Russia afford or manage this? Moreover, taking Norway as an example, Oslo is more interested in the underutilized 'blue economy' (fishing) and possible shipping traffic than in oil prospecting.

Moscow has also made much of the commercial possibilities of the Northern Sea Route to move goods from the Far East to Europe. It theoretically shaves 3,400 nautical miles and up to fifteen days off the 11,000-mile, forty-five-day voyage through the Malaccan and Bab-el-Mandeb straits and the Suez Canal. But there are hardly any ports up there, and the ones that exist can only handle half a million tons of cargo a year, or nothing next to the 186 million tons processed by a single mid-sized Chinese port like Xiamen. Even nuclear-powered icebreakers, of which there is one costing $100,000 per day to operate, can only plough a twenty-five-metre-wide channel through the ice – far too narrow for Panamax tankers or Suezmax container ships. Since the northern route is also 35–60 per cent more costly than the southern, there are few takers, and tonnages have fallen from 1.26 million in 2012 to 39,600 in 2015. Nor have the Russians had much luck in exploring for oil and natural gas in this harsh environment, especially since oil prices have sunk from over $100 per barrel to $50 while there is also a glut of natural gas. Who cares what alarmists claim Russia is trying to do when all the economic facts point elsewhere?[52]

•

On Putin's sixty-third birthday screens around the world were dominated by footage of Russia launching cruise missiles at Syrian rebels from ships in the Caspian Sea, even though Russia has a large fleet just off the Syrian coast. Most of us are happy to launch a firework, but not Russia's leader.

Twenty-six long-range Kalibr-NK cruise missiles struck eleven targets in Syria after flying 950 miles at a height of about 150 feet. Early risers in Iran and northern Iraq saw them scoot past. The US made much of claims, in a sour grapes way, that four of these missiles went astray, killing four sheep.

US Tomahawk cruise missiles do not have a flawless strike rate either. In 1991 the US launched 294 Tomahawks from ships, of which 282 were successfully on target. Nine failed to launch and six hit the sea. Six more were shot down.

TV images deceive. At maximum, Russia has 2,000 troops and fifty aircraft in Syria, though the numbers were reduced when the order of battle shifted to attack helicopters. The US has 35,000 troops in the Middle East and hundreds of advanced aircraft, plus two imposing fleets of eleven ships each clustered around a pair of aircraft carriers in the Gulf and Med.

Be that as it may, there is one obvious reason why the Russian navy has been keen to show these cruise missiles being launched. Commerce. Western media have effectively done the free advertising too.

The striking thing is the modest size of the Russian vessels involved: one 1,900-ton frigate and three 950-ton corvettes, each of which can launch eight cruise missiles. These are minnows compared with the destroyers and guided missile cruisers the US Navy used to launch its Tomahawks in 1991, 2003 and 2011 in Libya, for we should not forget who seems to like firing missiles most.

Since there was no tactical reason to fire these missiles, the obvious inference was that the Russians are showcasing ships that more modestly endowed navies can afford, as well as the Kalibr missiles, whose detachable warhead is rumoured to hit Mach 2.9 as it plunges down on the target.

This would be of a piece with other items of advanced weaponry Russia has deployed to Syria, including ground-to-air missile systems and sophisticated radar-jamming devices that can block aircraft communications a hundred miles away.

Many potential Middle Eastern customers for Russian weapons have visited Moscow. Now they can see these items under operational conditions, as they could watch drones coordinating highly accurate artillery fire in eastern Ukraine. The price of oil and gas may have fallen, but something could be recouped from weapons sales.

.

On 5 May 2016 Sergei Roldugin, who we last encountered patriotically buying antique musical instruments, appeared with his cello at a concert amidst the newly liberated ancient ruins of Palmyra in Syria, performing a solo from the quadrille by Rodion Shchedrin, the highlight of a concert by the orchestra of St Petersburg's Mariinsky Theatre conducted by Valery Gergiev, Putin's chief musical stooge. Bach and Prokofiev resonated from ruined columns that turned ochre in the sunset. A video link from his residence in Sochi beamed in Putin, who congratulated the musicians on their bravery.[53]

Bombing can't win wars, we are told, but if you bomb often and ruthlessly enough, as Russia has in northern Syria, it may seem possible to impose peace on your terms.

Since the beginning of the campaign in September 2015 the Kremlin promised it would be in and out in months. Partly this was to soothe the West and Sunni Arabs, partly cost, partly fear of an Afghan-type 'quagmire'. Syria was never as popular a war as Ukraine, and by quitting in time, in Russian eyes at least, the Kremlin could claim a 'heroic victory' against terrorists at minimal cost. Especially since Russia has also deployed private security consultants from a Hong Kong-registered firm called Slavonic Corps Limited run by a forty-six-year-old ex-GRU lieutenant colonel called Dmitri Utkin, cover moniker 'Wagner', who has been active in eastern Ukraine too, ensuring rebel separatists toe the line. Conveniently their training base in a village called Morkino is also home to a training base for a brigade of GRU Spetsnaz. These men get €3,200 a month, and their families €40,000 if they are killed. Among the couple of dozen who have died in Syria (official Russian losses are six men) was Major Sergei Shchupov (fifty-one), a former paratrooper who served in Afghanistan before joining OMON, and who was quietly buried in March 2016 in a small town near Moscow. He died near Damascus.[54]

Losses in Syria explain why Russia ostentatiously removed some combat aircraft in 2016, though in fact it was merely re-arranging the order of battle. Putin had already made it clear that he has the means and the will to send his planes back in, to kill more innocents, should the non-terrorist rebels give any trouble. Russia has put in place the infrastructure it needs for a permanent base at Tartus and for planes at Hmeimim. All Russian personnel in Syria now have legal immunity from Syrian courts.

The only loss to the Kremlin could be a big one – the slowing of the hugely divisive refugee crisis that its indiscriminate onslaught was causing for the EU – though another could be triggered by encouraging a clash between Iraq and Turkey. And we can be sure that the new peace-loving Putin was looking for a quick pay-off over Ukrainian sanctions, where Cyprus, Greece, France, Hungary, Italy and Slovakia were soft within the EU camp. In fact, the EU extended the sanctions in July 2016, without making them automatically renewable.

If Putin's tactic works – and the idea of a settlement followed by elections run by either an Assad or a post-Assad regime boggles the mind – the benefits to Russia of massive intervention, compared to the costs, will remain a moot point.

The costs we can see, and they are not over: subsidies to a broken Syria that will take a decade to mend, if it ever does in its present form, while a new airfield, expanded port and other military facilities will go on drinking up roubles in lean times, along with the stalled Ukrainian offensive. The Syrian campaign has cost Moscow an estimated $2.5 million per day, on top of the $18 billion spent subsidizing unrecognized regimes in frozen conflicts, not to mention the $4 billion Crimea has cost to annex.

In the end the Syrian gains to Moscow will be largely of prestige. Not only has the US been obliged to deal with Russia, but to deal with it on Russian terms, by being forced to choose between Assad and the jihadis. Part of what is happening now is to play games with the West, designed to show that the Kremlin has the initiative in the Middle East, or at least that it can act as a negative wild card. If that makes Putin feel good, bully for him. He has also caught the attention of every power in the Middle East at a time when the loyalties of more modest powers have become much more fickle. It may be that this decision will also help Riyadh find a quid for Russia's quo should major oil producers one day opt for coordinated production cuts to drive the price back up.

But it will do little for the Russian economy or the average Russian, any more than the on–off conflict Putin is conducting in Ukraine, or the brutalist activism of his foreign policy in general. There could be more deals with the West, but distrust of

Putin will not go away. In addition the Kremlin can look forward to endless trouble with its Syrian clients.

For the moment there is no lack of admiring talk by those ready to be impressed by a strong man imposing peace while the US dithers: Putin, the man of the Syrian match, who forced an end to the war. Leaving aside what happens next, this overlooks the fact that by sustaining the rabid regime over five long years, then sending his planes to bombard civilians and their cities when the regime failed, responsibility for the death and disaster was largely his in the first place. Getting out in time may look smart, but doesn't make it smart to have got yourself in. A strategic genius Putin is not.

•

Many Westerners have difficulty understanding Russia's relations with Ukraine, let alone with China. Relations with Russia's southern neighbours are even more complex, but we need to consider them. These relations include those with Iran and Turkey, which have immediate bearings on, among others, Armenia, Azerbaijan, the north and south Caucasus and Georgia, and hence on such major issues as Europe's quest for energy alternatives to Gazprom. Russia is also a significant player in Greece and Cyprus. It has also begun to play havoc with Western alliance networks in the Middle East by reinserting itself as the indispensable great power. There is no criticism in this region of Russia's actions in Ukraine, not even from Israel, the democracy the US underwrites with $38 billion in decennial arms funding, which has been uncharacteristically reticent about Russian incursions in Crimea and Ukraine. You don't hear a peep about that either from the likes of Jordan and Saudi Arabia.

As Russians like to remind Turks, from 1568 onwards the Ottomans and Russians fought twelve wars, the majority lost by the Turks. Historically, Orthodox Russia's relations with Turkey were clouded by Ottoman treatment of Christians in the Balkans and Levant, and Turkey's ability to inhibit Russian access through the Bosphorus into the Mediterranean. The Russians (and Soviets) were also staunch supporters of the Kurds. During the Cold War, Turkey swung firmly into the Western camp, having been neutral until almost the end of the Second World War, joining NATO in 1952. Under Shah Reza Pahlavi, Iran was also a staunch Western ally, unsurprising given Soviet wartime occupation of northern Iran (though, as it happened, Stalin eventually withdrew), a line that was reversed after the 1979 Islamic Revolution.[55]

Nowadays, Russia and Iran are close, not least in resisting what they regard as Western undermining of absolute state sovereignty through colours revolutions and/or reckless military interventions in Afghanistan, Iraq and Libya that have created total chaos.

This was reinforced during Putin's visit to Tehran in November 2015, which included ninety minutes with Supreme Leader Ali Khamenei, a meeting billed as one between 'titans' in the Iranian media. There was good news from the Syrian battlefields to celebrate since, with Russian air support, Iranian-backed Hizbollah troops took some key towns and villages in the vicinity of Homs from ISIS before the visit. Russia is going ahead with the sale of S-400 anti-aircraft missile batteries to Iran, and plans for enhanced cooperation in the civil nuclear field beyond the reactor at Bushehr. Another plus in the relationship is that Iran does not meddle in the Caucasus. In fact, the Putin government has been soliciting Iranian help in converting Sunni Muslims to the relatively harmless Shia version of Islam on the grounds that this diminishes terrorism.

In the longer term, Iranian–Russian interests may not be so congruent since Iran wishes to capitalize from EU anxieties about Gazprom by exporting gas to the West from the huge Iranian Pars field via Azerbaijan, now that a pipeline through its ally Syria has become a pipedream.

Iran is also more wedded to the Syrian Assad regime than Russia since it needs southern Syria as a supply route and logistical base for Hizbollah, should it ever have to distract Israel. Moscow is less invested in Assad; it just can't think of a suitable replacement Alawite to guarantee its slender bridgehead in the Levant, not to mention the 44,000 Russian expats who settled in Syria, some of them ex-KGB officers with Syrian spouses.

Like the EU, Turkey chafes under its energy dependence on

Gazprom. Turkey's natural gas is 99 per cent imported, roughly 60 per cent from Russia and 20 per cent from Iran. To that end it has sought alternatives in Iraqi Kurdistan, as well as deepening ties with Georgia and Azerbaijan, which cut across the north–south Russia–Armenia–Iran axis.[56]

Since Turkish–Armenian relations are freighted with historical suspicions, Ankara has sought to cement relations with Azerbaijan, through a strategic partnership in 2010 and a major gas pipeline deal called TANAP in 2012, designed to bring Caspian Sea gas across Turkey to Europe.

Ankara has more generally encouraged the pro-Western orientations of Azerbaijan and Georgia, while aggravating Russia by playing host to about 100,000 exiled Chechens since the wars of the 1990s (some of whose leaders the SVR has quietly assassinated). By contrast, Iran remained silent about Russia's military incursions into Chechnya. Moscow immediately responded by backing the Kurdish PKK, of course.

Attend any high-level foreign policy event devoted to the Middle East in London or Washington and before long some well-meaning innocent will pipe up: 'What about the Kurds?' The Kurds have long been the objects of naive 'what a plucky little people' enthusiasm in the West, where the corruption and nepotism of Erbil are unknown or muted because of the relative freedoms enjoyed in Iraqi Kurdistan by women.

Much less is known about the Russian version of this syndrome, probably because it has nothing to do with sentimentality, but much to do with hard geopolitical calculation.

Russia has been the Kurds' longest-standing great power patron. Empress Catherine the Great commissioned the first publication of a Kurdish grammar in 1787, interest in the Kurdish tribes being connected with Russia's many wars with Qajar Persia and Ottoman Turkey. With St Petersburg the world centre for Kurdish studies, Tsarist Russia was well placed to incite Kurdish uprisings in Turkey, while in 1923 the new Bolshevik regime established a Red Kurdistan between Soviet Armenia and Soviet Azerbaijan which was intended as a beacon for Kurds everywhere.

Although this project was wound up in 1930, Stalin returned

to it when in 1941 he established a regional Kurdish administration at Mahabad in the part of northern Iran he divvied up with Churchill. Transformed into the 'Mahabad Republic' in December 1945, this lasted a year until Truman's backing enabled Reza Shah to crush it. The leader of the ill-fated republic's army fled to the Soviet Union with 2,000 men. He was Mullah Mustafa Barzani, father of the autonomous KRG's current President.

Soviet clandestine services were especially interested in the Kurds after Turkey joined NATO in 1951. They recruited Kurds studying at the world revolutionary Patrice Lumumba University in Moscow, and used the Bulgarian intelligence service to arm Kurdish rebels in south-eastern Turkey. In 1978 they alighted upon a newly spawned national liberation movement, the Kurdish Workers Party or PKK, led by Abdullah Öcalan, one of a number of Marxist sects the Soviets armed and trained (in Lebanon), and which in 1984 went to war with the Turkish state. Forty thousand people have died in that conflict, which has flared up again. Soviet support was channelled through Moscow's local client, President Hafez al-Assad of Syria, where the KGB had a major presence. Despite the collapse of the Soviet Union, the new regime in Moscow continued to patronize the Kurds, with a cultural complex at Yaroslavl, with its own Kurdish-language Roj satellite TV.

One major use for the Kurds in Moscow's eyes was to counter Turkey's support for Chechen militants in the Caucasus. The Chechen threat to Russia is far less existential than that of the Kurds to Turkey, and was ultimately solved (after two vicious wars in the 1990s, one lost, the second won) by boosting Ramzan Kadyrov as President Putin's chief client and by showering money on reconstruction. Once ruined by Russian shelling, Grozny is modern-shiny today, with a mosque in which 10,000 can worship. A plus point has been that this thuggish Chechen henchman is always available to do Putin's more sinister bidding, with reports that he provided a pair of migrant Chechen stooges to mask who had actually pulled the trigger following the assassination of Boris Nemtsov.

Russia is supplying arms and intelligence to the Kurds, both to the PKK inside eastern Turkey and in northern Iraq (their headquarters are in the KRG's Qandil Mountains) and also to the PYD inside Syria. Russian support for President Assad means that the latter has not ruled against a separate Syrian Kurdish statelet (Rojava or Western Kurdistan), though Moscow has to be careful how far it supports the Kurds since it needs Iran and Hizbollah to fight for Assad. One problem here is that the PKK (and PYD) are allies of the Iranian Kurdish insurgents, who the meddlesome Saudis are inciting against Tehran.

But this is minor compared with the dilemma Moscow has created for the US. Washington has also been arming and training the PYD, the most effective Sunni force fighting ISIS, though this is putting huge strain on US relations with Turkey, which is barely fighting ISIS at all. When Brett McGurk, Obama's chief point man on the Middle East, visited the PYD in Syria, President Erdoğan angrily asked 'whether the US was on Turkey's side or that of the PKK'. The Americans could reasonably respond that they have the same doubts about Turkey vis-à-vis ISIS.

Russia has used the Kurds to drive a wedge between the US and Turkey, just as by merely showing up in Syria in force, Moscow has all the region's minor potentates scurrying to pay homage in the Kremlin, Netanyahu being keen to continue bombing Hizbollah arms convoys without clashing with the Russian air force or having IDF war planes downed by S-400 missile systems deployed in Syria.

Ankara also backed Georgian President Mikhail Saakashvili's rash attempts to use his Western-trained forces (including the red-bearded sergeant who commanded ISIS in northern Syria until he was killed in a US strike in 2016) to retrieve Abkhazia and South Ossetia from pro-Russian separatists, which resulted in Russia's annihilation of them, and Saakashvili's appointment as mayor of Ukrainian Odessa (as a deliberate Ukrainian provocation against Moscow). In late 2016 he resigned after falling out with the corrupt regime in Kiev.

Iran is opposed to Turkey's bid to become a major energy hub for Azeri gas (what is beneath the Caspian Sea is disputed between Azerbaijan and Iran) because it would downgrade its own future gas sales to Europe. It also sees a pro-Western, and largely secular, Azerbaijan as a potential launch pad for any

Western/Israeli strikes, as well as a source of subversion among her own 12.8 million ethnic Azeris (about 16 per cent of Iran's population). Saddam Hussein will not be the last to play upon Iran's fissiparous ethnic composition as he did in the long war against Tehran. That is why Iranian agents and mullahs are covertly active in Azerbaijan, and why their secret agents have essayed terror attacks there too.

While Iran goes from strength to strength as a regional actor, not much remains of Erdoğan and former PM Ahmet Davutoğlu's hubristic neo-Ottoman foreign policy ambitions. Russian–Turkish relations plunged into the freezer after the Turks shot down a Russian jet that ventured across their air space for a couple of minutes. But since the failed coup against Erdoğan in July 2016, relations have improved, to the point where some Americans fear that Turkey may drift out of the NATO camp and are making alternative plans based on Cyprus, Israel and Jordan, all underpinned by natural gas discoveries in the eastern Mediterranean. It seems that Putin and Erdoğan have also struck a deal. Although this will not please his AKP base, Erdoğan will mute calls for Syria's Assad to go, while Putin will encourage Turkish irredentism in northern Iraq around Mosul. This would complicate Turkey's relations with Iraq and with the US.

As for Russian diplomacy, no wonder Putin's customary stern look cracks into a Botox-paralysed laugh, now that he has the whole Middle East paying court to him, from Israel's Netanyahu and Egypt's President Sisi to kings Salman of Saudi Arabia and Abdullah II of Jordan as they hedge against the unpredictable occupant of the White House. Decades of diplomacy designed to keep the Soviets out of the Middle East are crumbling before our eyes.

Although the British and Americans regard the 'Jords' as ultra-reliable allies, King Abdullah has visited Russia sixteen times since 1999, hosts an intelligence-sharing facility with the Russians in Amman and may join the Russian-brokered Syrian peace talks in Astana. The King would have to seal off Syrian rebel access via his borders, which is what Putin presumably seeks, with a leading role in a major campaign against ISIS as the reward. Abdullah is ideally placed to convey Putin's views to

Trump. Egypt and Jordan also support the regime of General Khalifa Haftar in Tobruk in eastern Libya, who refuses to accept the Western- and UN-sponsored government in Tripoli. The Russians are cultivating Haftar, as an anti-Islamist strongman who could put the Libyan Humpty back together again after the British, French and Americans broke it in 2011. It will not have escaped Putin's notice that Europe has morbid terrors of refugee flows from Libya, which he might be able to influence at will via his new Libyan friend. Putin can also take comfort from the legions of foreign admirers who post on any online newspaper story about Russian operations in Syria. He's the man, they say, though whether he is much of a strategist as opposed to a tactician seems questionable.[57]

•

When politicians start talking philosophy, something is up, and people would do well to lend an ear. According to a new report by a Kremlin commission on nationalities, unlike lesser folk, Russia is not just a country but a 'civilization'. The idea goes back to Danilevsky, who compared civilizations to flowers that flourish one by one before withering away. Russia's turn was coming, Danilevsky prophesied darkly.

Crises of identity tend to be expressed in bullish talk, and according to President Putin's state of the nation address on 12 December 2012, Russia's time had arrived (the subtext being, of course, that America's day in the sun is passing). And as a 'unique' civilization Russia doesn't need alien forms of democracy foisted on it from outside. This and other digs at the West reveal the conservative and nationalistic substance beneath the highfalutin talk. Metropolitan Russian liberals will scoff, but among large numbers of Russians, and not just officials, such stuff goes down well.

After fifteen years of neglect, in May 2014 Putin announced Russia's 'own pivot to Asia', largely in response to Western sanctions over the annexation of Crimea and invasion of Ukraine. A big Russian trade mission to Shanghai delivered many memoranda of friendship and understanding, which conspicuously failed to be realized in trade figures that fell by 28.6 per cent the following year. Over 90 per cent of Russia's foreign direct investment comes from Europe and the US. Chinese trade with the US is ten times greater than Russian trade with China. Chinese banks are also reluctant to lend to Russian firms, and those that do offer terms which the Russians call 'highway robbery'. Rather than playing a Chinese card against Europe, Russia is being played by China, and is becoming Beijing's junior partner. The current Russian relationship with China is effectively one of asymmetric dependency, though Xi is very careful to treat Putin with inordinate respect to mask this stark fact. Behind the scenes, the Chinese regard Russia as a declining power with nowhere to go.

Relations between the two authoritarian giants are deep and multiple, and largely based on what they do not like in the modern world: US hegemony, human rights, democracy-promotion and chaotic wars of intervention. Its institutional foundations include the 2014 Strategic Partnership, joint membership of the Shanghai Cooperation Council, and the ongoing fusion of the Eurasian Economic Union (Armenia, Belarus, Kazakhstan and Kyrgyzstan) with China's Silk Roads. The two actively collaborate in counter-terrorism and in policing the internet. They have very similar curbs on foreign-linked NGOs.

As Putin knows, only fools put all their eggs in one basket. To that end, Russia has also cultivated relations with Japan, South Korea and Vietnam. Russian plans to open naval ties with Hanoi particularly irked Beijing, but they will be concerned too about Russian attempts to develop relations with Seoul and Tokyo. The Russians want Japanese investment in the empty Russian Far East to show that they are not international pariahs.

But there are limits to how far Putin would go with Prime Minister Shinzo Abe, though the two did share a hot tub when they met in late 2016. With an election in 2018, Putin scotched any thoughts of formally ending the Second World War by relinquishing the four Kuril islands (Kunashiri, Etorofu, Shikotan and Habomai) in a peace treaty with the Japanese (who call them the Northern Territories, by the way). Seventy-eight per cent of Russians oppose any peace treaty that hands even two of the Kurils back to Japan. Abe's hopes of dividing China and

Russia duly came to naught. Some claimed that President Trump was playing the same game by making friendly noises to Putin and needling China, over Taiwan, before he even assumed office. Nothing will come of that gambit either.

Another sign of Russia's underlying insecurity is its desperate efforts to replant its flag in the Far East, where Russian, Chinese, Japanese and South and North Korean economies intersect. Putin makes little secret of the fact that if the Russians don't reverse the westward migration of their own population, others will dominate the region. The demographic realities are stark: 6.2 million Russians live in the vast Far East region north of Kamchatka and Magadan, whereas 109 million Chinese live in adjacent Heilongjiang, Jilin and Liaoning provinces across the Amur River. This is why Putin has approved a new law granting settlers a modest hectare plot of land gratis, after they have productively cultivated it for five years. About 140 million hectares of land will be available for settlement, though, as critics warn, few will come, for names like Magadan are historically redolent of remote Soviet Gulags. The land cannot be sold to foreigners, of course.

These daunting demographic imbalances are not restricted to the Far East. This unique Russian civilization whose time has come needs people, and the urgency of boosting a declining population was another theme of Putin's state of the nation address in 2015. He claimed that the policy of paying cash and benefits to mothers of a second child was helping matters. He'd also like all mothers to have three babies. What he didn't say was that Muslims, who already make up 14 per cent of the population, and are giving him trouble in the southern Caucasus and elsewhere, will be numerically boosted too. Putin is already worried about Islamic cultural separatism, evident in the number of women wearing headscarves and veils in Chechnya.

One can't have a unique culture that is horribly corrupt, so Putin dealt with that as well, in his inimitable way. Instead of confronting the problem in his own circle of cronies, he linked it to the West, by calling for restrictions on Russians having foreign bank accounts. As with his proposal to force international NGOs in Russia to register as 'foreign agents', the implication was that economically as well as politically the West is the ultimate source of corruption. A glance at how much it costs Russia to build new roads ($237 million per kilometre) compared with the US ($6 million) shows either that Russian construction companies are hopeless (the roads are ranked the 111th worst in the world) or that roads are diverted in bizarre ways to suit major vested interests.[58]

It would be a good thing for Western investors as well as Russians if the President were to tackle bribery and the rest energetically, but the signs are mixed. His government hit back at the US over its refusal of visas to named Russian officials connected to the Magnitsky affair by prohibiting American meat imports on bogus phytosanitary grounds. Every year an estimated $80 billion leaves Russia by way of capital flight because of the atrocious legal framework. Much money leaves illegally too, judging by the arrest of Colonel Dmitry Zakharchenko, head of an anti-graft section of the Ministry of the Interior after $131 million in cash was discovered in a steel cabinet in his sister's home, and a further $337 million in Swiss bank accounts controlled by his father, who had no apparent source of income.[59] According to Transparency International, the situation has improved, with Russia ten places up between 2014 and 2015. So it is now only the 133rd most corrupt country out of 174. Just above Syria but on a par with Mozambique.

•

Western conservatives may admire Putin's ability to murder his critics and opponents, or to talk tough about Islamists, but most Westerners would not wish to live under such a corrupted system. Forget the Islamists, about whom we all talk too much anyway. Imagine being beaten up by his bodyguards if you inadvertently bumped an oligarch's car and were then laughed at by the police – if they came at all? What if your home stood in the way of a powerful person's land grab, as in the acclaimed 2014 film *Leviathan*? Where would legal redress come from? Would we really want opposition politicians or over thirty critical journalists murdered by persons unknown, or the news permanently editorialized by the government or its tame media oligarchs?

If this decayed, resentful nation is a threat, then how best to deal with it? Since Putin regards natural gas supplies as a strategic weapon (he can sketch pipeline systems like advancing tank columns), energy diversification and renewables will diminish European dependence on Russian gas, though not by making us dependent on Iran, Turkey or a dodgy polity like Cyprus. Energy is the only real weapon in Putin's hands, for the patrolling bombers and exercising soldiers are a bluff in a world with nuclear weapons. US military power remains greater than anything Russia could deal with, and the rest of NATO is no pushover. Surely it would be wise to develop communication systems to avoid any incident escalating into a war? Dealing with information war is not insurmountable. While the West cannot and should not direct its own media, the latter can unmask what Russia does, specifically the effects on ordinary people of a state of lawlessness or the colossal sums which corrupt Russians salt away in foreign banks, notably in London.

Could Russia be more intelligently and sensitively handled? Yes, but not by cack-handed infiltration of experts on democracy and free markets in a rerun of the early 1990s, let alone through pastiche versions of *Encounter* and its analogues. The era of Orwell and Robert Conquest is over, and even Alexander Solzhenitsyn (who knew a thing or two about the Soviets) made his peace with Putin, who in 2007 awarded the eighty-eight-year-old writer the State Prize of the Russian Federation. How Solzhenitsyn would have approved of the extinguishing of the artificial state of Ukraine. Putin, he said, had brought the 'slow and gradual restoration of Russia'.

Putin is more dangerous than the post-Stalin collective bureaucratic regime since he is more than primus inter pares, but he is also not the Bond villain of Western fantasy. How this regime ends will probably be more complicated than how it came into existence. With an eye on elections in 2018, Putin is pitching for six more years (having extended presidential terms from four to six years in 2012) to complete his 'mission'. There are few signs of the mission succeeding in an economy that has failed to diversify or in small towns where life is grim. Still, Russians are stoic people, and Russia is more liberal and richer than it has ever been, under the latest incarnation of what is called the power vertical. Earlier glimpses of an alternative, whether in February 1917 or in 1991, are just that – transient – and one should not forget that it was Boris Yeltsin who altered the constitution that made Putin possible.

It must also be understood that Russia shares the experience of loss of empire, and the neuroses of de-colonization, but all condensed into a few short years. Showing Russia respect costs nothing.[60] Because of Russia's size it straddles many overlapping geopolitical 'sets' and Russian foreign service and international relations experts are outstanding. This could be positive were Russia's capable diplomats to engage in a genuinely multilateral way with a world that is no longer unipolar. Mephistopheles' '*Ich bin der Geist der stets verneint*', 'I am the spirit that always denies', is not a strategy. Very little is likely to change under Putin, whose instinct is always to go on the attack, though he showed 'Putin the Magnanimous' when Obama retaliated for cyber interference in the 2016 election. As the Russian economy deteriorates, perhaps powerful men will decide that a less confrontational leader is called for. It is difficult to believe that a cowed opposition has much fight or traction, and one-off protests by truck drivers and the like are unlikely to escalate. A modus vivendi with a regime and a society in resentful decay is all we can hope for.[61]

6

China: A Country for Old Men

China has successfully coupled authoritarianism and modernity in ways that perplex some in the West, who imagine that economic progress and commerce must ineluctably lead to Western-style democracy. China's Communist Party, whose membership is greater than the population of Germany, could survive the demise of its current strongman, the sixty-three-year-old President Xi Jinping, a leader different in style from his two predecessors Jiang Zemin and Hu Jintao. He has already amassed ten different titles, and is probably the most powerful 'core' leader China has had since Mao Zedong died in 1976. In 2017, and halfway through his tenure, he is likely to formalize his array of powers, perhaps also relaxing the retirement at sixty-eight rule for members of the Politburo, the key organ that ensures party control of China's state apparatus and society.

Xi is physically imposing at nearly six feet tall, with the assured bearing of a 'red princeling', the group whose revolutionary pedigree, training and connections make them born to rule in China, though his life has also included an enforced sojourn among the peasantry when his father fell out of favour. He has a vision (or 'Dream') for his country, based on 're-moralizing' both the Party and Chinese society; securing the international respect due to what is already by some indicators the world's largest economy; controlled reforms to escalate China up the value chain; and ramifying links with the outside world, as exemplified by schemes to link China via central Asia and the Middle East to Europe, which rely on $4 trillion of foreign exchange reserves to export China's overcapacity in construction, nuclear power and heavy engineering.

Those who confidently predict the (Chinese) system's collapse may be disappointed at its resilience, or the high satisfaction levels when Chinese people are polled, for, like Putin, President Xi enjoys 80 per cent positive ratings because of his aggressive campaigns against Party corruption and his muscular foreign policy. To adapt a Churchillian aphorism, Communist rule is better than any conceivable alternative, especially as these seem increasingly dysfunctional. Unlike Russia, China does not meddle in Western politics, beyond the usual spreading of money around Washington that many other countries indulge in. It just watches the West succumb to self-generated problems, from government gridlock to the rise of clowns and showmen, though there is still respect for Germany as a kind of (highly civilized) European China, and Beijing has the measure of many other 'partners'.[1]

The 2016 US presidential election encouraged much crowing in China about what the Xinhua news agency called 'an entertaining drama that illustrates the malfunction of the self-proclaimed world standard of democracy'. A video produced by a company close to the Communist Party (CCP) entitled 'How to Make Leaders' contrasted a meritocratic system in which potential leaders are repeatedly stress-tested at successive levels with the US, where the mere ability to accumulate huge campaign funds ultimately counts. There was much Chinese amusement too about the rise of a braggart real-estate tycoon from reality TV stardom to winner in the race for the White House, though 'Emperor Trump' is popular among Chinese 'netizens' as the kind of mercantilist nationalist they want their own leaders to emulate. Although political content on the Chinese internet is rigorously controlled, there is surprisingly little 'PC' thought management so that Trump's more intemperate utterances, regarding Muslims for example, often resonate with an audience that freely expresses its own prejudices. But ultimately this is a high-level relationship that does not concern the man in the street in Shanghai. All of Trump's big talk about punishing China for its trade surplus evaporated after the first encounter between President Xi and his host at the Mar-a-Lago complex in 2017, especially since Xi helpfully took ten minutes to explain the complexities of dealing with North Korea.[2]

Hopes of the CCP evolving into Singapore's authoritarian

People's Action Party – as Deng Xiaoping and Lee Kuan Yew once mused – ignore the problems of scaling up what works in a tightly controlled city-state of 5 million people to a complex society of nearly 1.4 billion people in thirty-three provinces (some much bigger than the biggest European states) in a vast country. The notion put about by law professor He Weifang that the Communist Party will evolve into some version of European social democracy is also improbable. This political tendency is in deep secular decline in its European heartlands as its electorate fragments and turns to left and right populist alternatives. Why copy what has palpably failed?[3]

As the world's second largest economy, China already occupies a global role that 'democratic' India, which does not emerge well from any life-metrics comparison, is unlikely to match. Leaving aside India's outdoor defecation, absentee teachers and 300 million illiterates, China's almost 3,000-strong National People's Congress may have more billionaires than the US Congress, and its share of crooks, but India's Lok Saba parliament has 162 members (out of 543) facing criminal charges, including seventy-six charged with murder, rape or kidnapping rather than graft.[4] But if we shift the view, it is also true that China's economic growth is unremarkable compared with South Korea, which at a very early stage developed a welfare state, based on corporations and voluntary agencies, which China is only belatedly adopting.[5]

Being very large, China does not have to do much to make its neighbours anxious, especially as it routinely trades on how such-and-such an action will offend the 'feelings' of 1.4 billion Chinese. One expert has astutely compared China to a very fat man, called Mr China, getting into a crowded elevator that has already adjusted to the presence of an equally corpulent Mr America.[6] Beijing is also good at presenting its neighbours with stark binary choices. When Seoul installed a US-supplied Terminal High Altitude Area Defense (THAAD) missile system to protect South Korea from a nuclear-armed madman in Pyongyang, a system moreover whose radars could peer into China's ICBM launch sites, then Beijing threatened to disrupt Seoul's most important external trading relationship.[7]

China's global postures are closely bound up with domestic insecurity and fear of Western-engineered 'colours revolutions' in which human-rights lawyers and NGOs with Western 'dirty hands' behind them are the thin end of the wedge. China is very active in containing such influences, exporting its experience and knowhow to the like-minded. There is a relationship between the Communist Party's ability to satisfy rising domestic expectations that may no longer be exclusively material and China's no less keen desire to exercise the power such a huge country warrants within an international system originally designed by the US and its allies in their interests.

Should the first goal falter, not so much in terms of delivering stratospheric growth statistics, but in breathable air, clean politics, the rule of law and a functioning health and welfare system for nearly 1.4 billion people, then the temptation might be to compensate with aggressive national self-assertion, testing US commitments to China's Asian neighbours who do not relish relapsing into an imperial-era tribute system. For sure, China's leaders also know that a war by accident or design in Asia-Pacific would surely jeopardize both prosperity and Party rule, with collateral effects on the entire global economy, for about $5 trillion of trade passes through the seas where such a war would be fought.[8] Far better, surely, to lock others into a mutually profitable relationship with China through the 'One Belt, One Road' strategy, or '*yi dai yi lu*' as it sounds better in Mandarin.

·

Claims by the regime that Chinese civilization is 5,000 years old began after President Jiang Zemin visited Egypt in May 1996. Piqued by the Pyramids, he and the leadership decided to add an extra thousand years to the existing national story. The so-called Yellow Emperor has as much historical reality as Romulus and Remus or King Arthur. There was nothing smooth, either, about the succession of Han, Jin, Tang, Song, Yuan, Ming and Qing dynasties, any more than was the case with Franks, Carolingians, Saxons, Capetians, Normans and Plantagenets. Foreign interlopers like the Mongols and Manchus were part of a story in which imperial power sometimes disintegrated.[9]

The last century and a half looms largest in the historical memory of a people who, being 93 per cent ethnic Han (the word refers to an early dynasty), do not have substantial minorities to contest the dominant view of history as, for example, African-Americans, Jews and Latinos do in the US. The Chinese are all history's victims in the official and public versions, regardless of how powerful China is. The Chinese can also smell Western hypocrisy. Talk of copyright theft and the like sounds hollow from nations that stole the secrets of ceramics, gunpowder and tea cultivation from China.

The 'Century of Shame and Humiliation', as the Chinese call a century of Western interference, can be more swiftly rehearsed than it would be in China, where nativist and patriotic resentments burn as brightly as elsewhere. Internal stagnation and corruption under the late Qing dynasty (1644–1912), who, ironically, were Manchu outsiders themselves, facilitated reversals at the hands of European nineteenth-century colonizers, notably in the Opium Wars (1839–42 and 1856–60), and the imposition by Britain and others of 'unequal treaties' which made such coastal ports as Shanghai legally extraterritorial.

Defeat by a modernized imperial Japan in 1895 followed defeat by the West; then came the downfall of the Qing dynasty in 1912 and the degeneration of a brief attempt at republican democracy into a warlord system. During this period the Japanese successively occupied Taiwan (1895), the Korean Peninsula (1910), Manchuria (1931–3) and finally, from 1937, much of coastal China, in a war (Nationalist) China fought alone until December 1941. Before it was over this had cost China 15 million dead with such ghastly Japanese atrocities as the Nanjing Massacre. A further 100 million people became refugees. These horrors were followed by famine and civil war between the forces of Mao Zedong and Chiang Kai-shek's nationalist Kuomintang (KMT) until the Communist victory in 1949. In Party mythology this subsumed the victory over Japan four years earlier into a single Communist triumph over nationalism, imperialism and fascism.[10]

The price paid for the stability that followed, and for such advances in health and education as the revolution brought, was colossal. Some 70 million people are estimated to have died

during Mao's dictatorship, more than half from starvation in the
Great Leap Forward of 1958–62, the worst man-made disaster
in history. The rest perished from endless purges and the severity
of life in China's *laogai* (reform through labour) penal system,
and finally during the Cultural Revolution (1966–76), in which
ideological 'redness' displaced competence and expertise in all
areas. By the time of Mao's death in 1976, average per capita
GDP was $163, or a little more than that of Bangladesh ($140).

Those who survived twenty-seven years of radical socialist
laboratory experimentation had suffered the most absolute suppression of personal freedoms outside North Korea. At the end of
Mao's life, some 80 per cent of Chinese still lived in the countryside, where communes were the norm, with the urban population
organized in work units that in their totalizing control resembled
life on a military base, though services were rudimentary (rations
consisted of four eggs, a hundred grams of sugar, and 250 grams
of pork per month albeit bulked out with rice). Under Mao's
disastrous Third Line strategy, industry was dispersed across the
vast interior to minimize the effects of a US nuclear attack.
Although Mao famously met Henry Kissinger and then Richard
Nixon (in 1972) to outflank the Soviet 'revisionists', this was only
after the self-isolating Cultural Revolution in which China's sole
overseas ambassador was Huang Hua in Cairo.[11]

The ghost of Mao, the tall, mercurial, romantic poet turned
murderous Great Helmsman, still haunts China, increasingly so
as the lived nightmare recedes and myth takes over. But the
contemporary People's Republic owes more to the diminutive
pragmatist Deng Xiaoping, and the neglected Hua Guofeng
(who had been initially selected as the new chairman, only to
be ungratefully edged aside by Deng in 1980). Deng would be
adept at claiming credit for everything that went well, and blaming others for whatever failed.

Between 1978 and 1992 Deng, a former military commissar
and self-styled simple soldier, was China's paramount leader,
though paradoxically he was never formally head of government, state or party but simply Chairman of the Central Military
Commission. During those decades, Deng began the transformation of China into an urban society, with 200 million new

urban dwellers during his time in power, followed by a further half-billion more migrants by 2015. China also acquired a common national culture, based not just on the Mandarin lingua franca, but shared tastes in everything from films and TV to food, and a much stronger sense of itself.[12]

•

Deng had been recalled from 'rustication' in the provinces after being adjudged a 'capitalist roader' during the Cultural Revolution. His son Deng Pufang was paralysed for life after Red Guards threw him from a window. This was the beginning of Deng's gradual political rehabilitation. Two years after Mao's death, Deng – who saw himself as an impresario-cum-general manager for other talents rather than possessor of Heaven's Mandate or the divine right to rule – launched China's current crypto-capitalist policy at the 1978 Third Plenum. If Mao was the revolutionary leader, Deng was the transformative one.

Deng travelled widely to the developing 'little dragons' of Japan, Singapore and South Korea as well as to Europe and eventually as leader to the US in 1979, where he grasped the extent of China's backwardness. At a Tokyo press conference Deng admitted, 'We are very poor. We are very backward. We have to recognize that. We have a lot to do, a long way to go and a lot to learn.' He also studied the role of the state, banks and foreign investors in the transformation of these neighbouring economies. A heterogeneous array of foreign economists, from Eastern and Western Europe and the US, were brought in to advertise their intellectual wares. The Mongol Khans had likewise amused themselves with competing holy men from the world's great religions.[13]

It undoubtedly helped that the Communist system was not distracted by any Western-style separation of powers, or a legal order that could inhibit development, scant consolation for those in labour camps or whose house was torn down by spiv developers. Worse, the latter were encouraged by local authorities whose own future promotions depended on putting in as much infrastructure, industry and housing as possible. Deng was sufficiently relaxed about the probability of corruption in a system where Party bureaucrats and businessmen became an indeterminate blur to remark: 'When you open the door, flies will get in.' Though perhaps he could not foresee the current infestation.

Deng was fully aware of the dangers of being seen as China's Nikita Khrushchev, who had denounced Stalin while the tyrant's admirers and clients were ubiquitous. Deng beached Mao's legacy under the 'interim' formula '70 per cent good and 30 per cent bad', admittedly an unsatisfactory accounting for the deaths of tens of millions of people. He used homely sayings from Sichuan about the colour of cats being irrelevant to whether they catch mice to explain fundamental changes in economic and social policy affecting the lives of hundreds of millions. Copious use of the bland foreign word 'management' made it possible radically to reorder how goods were produced so long as the leadership of the Party was never questioned, one of four 'basic principles' adopted by the CCP.

Four key factors facilitated policies that were not Deng's alone.

The first was a prolonged demographic 'sweet spot' between 1975 and 2010, during which the dependency ratio, that is the number of under-fifteens and over-sixty-fives, fell from eighty to thirty-five per hundred working-age people. This partly reflected China's 1963–73 baby boom in which the population rose from 680 to 880 million. Although it took time to counter this trend, the one-child policy that was in effect between 1980 and 2015 is cancelling out the advantages of those three and a half decades, so much so that by 2050 there will be two workers per retired pensioner.[14]

A decision not to invest in war was also important. Following the twenty-nine-day People's Liberation Army invasion of Vietnam in 1979, Deng focused on the domestic economy rather than spending huge sums on a bloated PLA that desperately needed both modernization and reduction. It helped that the Soviets were mired in Afghanistan, for in Beijing's eyes Moscow was a bigger threat than Washington, and that Deng believed in good relations with the US. The PLA headcount was cut from 7 to 6 million. Whereas Chinese defence spending had been 4.6 per cent of GNP in 1979, by 1991 it was 1.4 per cent, with facilities and manpower redirected to civilian economic expansion.[15]

Thirdly, the sheer size of China, with its thirty-three provinces, five of which are also autonomous regions, meant that reforms could be piloted on what to anyone else would be a national scale to test whether they worked, before they were made national in a country the size of the US. For Deng's other simple formula was of cautiously feeling for stones to ford a stream. These provinces range from the region of Tibet (3 million people) via the average (45 million, or the population of Spain) to Guangdong with 104 million. There are also four directly administered conurbations: Beijing, Chongqing, Shanghai and Tianjin, and about 3,000 counties which include 50,000 townships. Finally, China has 700,000 village administrative units, though some of these are within or part of the creeping urban sprawl.[16]

It helped that one province was opposite Hong Kong, one of the most enterprising societies on Earth, with a good port, and one where mainland wealth would be 'round-tripped' so that, although originating inside China, it could be recorded as foreign direct investment. The latter also played a far more important role in China than in Japan or South Korea. The provinces of Guangdong, opposite Hong Kong, and Fujian, became laboratories for four Special Economic Zones in which the entrepreneurial skill of the Hong Kong Cantonese diaspora was combined with a limitless pool of local and migratory cheap rural labour.[17]

The modest market town of Shenzhen, which in 1980 had a population of only 30,000, has been transformed into a metropolis of almost 12 million, whose economy is regarded as more dynamic and innovative nowadays than that of Hong Kong. Locals gradually lost their rustic air and began to dress like the rich islanders. Initially sceptical, the Guangdong provincial Party secretary, Xi Zhongxun, became an enthusiast. Xi is better known today as the revered father of Xi Jinping, China's current President. Cast into the darkness in 1962, the elder Xi was not fully rehabilitated until 1978, while his son spent seven years being 're-educated' in the countryside, including a period living in a flea-ridden cave while shovelling coal or as a mechanic repairing agricultural vehicles.[18] During the sixteen years Xi spent working his way up the hierarchy to Governor of Fujian, the province benefited from improved relations with Taiwan which brought much inward investment and the transfer of assembly plants like Foxconn.[19]

Shenzhen also illustrates something else about modern China: the distinction between town and country is notional. Only 2 million of the 12 million inhabitants possess urban identity cards. Half of the remaining 10 million migrants live in urban villages. Forget clichés about London or New York being a series of charming 'villages' like Chelsea or Greenwich. Shenzhen has incorporated real rural villages, such as Baishizhou, whose 2,700 original inhabitants sold off their outlying fields for development, but since they retained their core household plots, now make a very nice living renting out rooms in jerry-built tenements to 150,000 migrants from all over China. The village is run by a collective government, which in practice is dominated by its wealthiest citizens The many migrants have few rights, as do their children, since their registration or *hukou* is in their home rural village even though they were born in the cities.[20]

There were parallel changes in the deep countryside, where it had not been uncommon for people to starve to death on a yuan income equivalent of US $39 per year. Since even the most dogmatic Maoist found it hard to argue in favour of starvation, collectivized agriculture (based on communes, brigades and work teams) was abolished in favour of household production units, beginning in Anhui province, though all rural land remained (and remains) in public ownership. Farmers only have limited rights of usufruct, usually extending to forty years. Surveying and registration of land is patchy, and titles are nonexistent or insecure.

However, the introduction of family farming led to an enormous growth in productivity, and the doubling of rural incomes between 1979 and 1984 as peasants cultivated cash crops as well as grains. Farmers had money to spend on equipment and fertilizers, and their savings could be ploughed into industrial development by state banks. New 'township and village enterprises', including barbers, repair shops and restaurants, were a transitional phase in the transfer of excess rural labour to the full-blown urban industrial economy. Though the rural economy initially benefited most from Deng's reforms, after 1989 the emphasis switched to the cities, with the countryside lapsing into relative stagnation. The reasons for this shift were essentially political.

Deng's industrial strategy involved a shift from heavy industry to light, which utilized China's superabundance of low-cost labour. Both generated the foreign exchange and foreign direct investment needed to buy capital equipment. In 1980, following Deng's tour of the US, China was awarded Most Favoured Nation status by the US, minus any equivalent to the Jackson–Vanik Amendment (on Jewish emigration from the Soviet Union) which complicated US–Russian relations. Deng quipped to Carter that 'if you want me to release 10 million Chinese to come to the US, I'd be glad to do so'. By 1981 China was exporting more to the US than the reverse, and this has remained the pattern until the present. Parallel investment in the infrastructure and urbanization gave the economy a massive boost, as the urban population rose from 172 million in 1979 to 731 million in 2013. Industrial energy costs were also stable. It also helped that 'break bulk' shipping was replaced by the steel intermodal container which could be stacked on dedicated ships, and that Taiwan became one of the hubs for the burgeoning electronics industry. This enabled China itself to become a giant assembly plant for computers and mobile phones as the suppliers of Apple and the like moved there.

Heavy and strategic industries including coal, oil and steel were dominated by state-owned enterprises (SOEs), where revolving doors with the Party ensured continued control of the overall economy, though from 2001 onwards private businessmen could join the CCP too. While the glitz of Shanghai may seem a testament to the wonders of private-sector capitalism, in fact 80 per cent of its economy is publicly owned, including many of the skyscrapers with luminous billboards. Ninety-two of the giant SOEs are on the Forbes 500 list of the world's biggest corporations by revenue. SOEs still control 35 per cent of China's GDP, with 60 per cent in private hands and 5 per cent owned by foreigners. Ironically, between 1993 and 2010, bankers from Goldman Sachs and Morgan Stanley, notably Henry 'Hank' Paulson who would become US Treasury Secretary, helped bail out and rationalize these huge concerns with floats worth $653 billion on domestic and international markets. Effectively the survival of the SOEs meant the survival of the Party since they were its main source of revenues.[21] Most of the 10 million private-sector businesses are what are called SMEs, or small and medium enterprises. How to prune the number of SOEs without creating mass unemployment, is the biggest conundrum facing Beijing, though it has managed to introduce competition within each sector and some of them such as CNPC and Sinopec are major players in the global oil industry.[22]

Had Deng retired in the late 1980s, before the overheated economy had to be reined in with a dose of austerity, his reputation would be unsullied. But he insisted on remaining in power, not just to oversee his economic miracle but to insulate China from the popular revolutions that were rocking the Eastern Bloc and ultimately the Soviet Union itself. Such protests crept nearer, against Ferdinand and Imelda Marcos in the Philippines in 1986, the year in which the authoritarian Kuomintang regime allowed Taiwan's first opposition party since 1949.

Deft footwork by Shanghai mayor Jiang Zemin (who would succeed Deng) ensured that sporadic student protests in 1986, against political tutelage, corruption and nepotism, petered out without state violence. Although Deng and the late Zhou Enlai had been the honoured focus of student protests in 1976 which had cost Deng his job, ironically in 1989 his was the iron fist when student protests in Tiananmen Square escalated out of control in front of the world's media, who were covering Mikhail Gorbachev's historic visit after thirty years of Sino-Soviet estrangement. This very public humiliation in front of the Russian leader Deng regarded as 'an idiot' – others called him a 'traitor like Trotsky', which was less flattering – doubtless tilted the scales towards repression, though not before the gentler Premier Zhao Ziyang had resigned in tears.

More serious than student hunger strikers calling for 'democracy' to a credulous media for whom the terms 'chaos' and 'turmoil' (*dong hun luan*) had no resonance, was the fact that ordinary Beijing citizens blocked the paths of 50,000 PLA troops entering the capital to disperse the students. Many more followed, ready to use live ammunition on those who obstructed them, as well as on the students, some low hundreds of whom died on 4 June 1989 while many more ordinary people were gunned down on approach roads. Warning shots deterred Western cameramen there. Arguably, the Orwellian erasure of these events from public consciousness, especially among the young, is dangerous since they have no recall of how the armed Party can react when its back is against the wall. No one should have any illusions about the very hard face of the CCP if it senses a threat to its survival.[23]

Before he died in 1997, Deng identified the Russian-trained industrial engineer Jiang Zemin as his immediate successor, and since Jiang was in his early seventies, the fifty-four-year-old hydroelectric engineer Hu Jintao as the favourite for taking over from 2002 to 2012, albeit in a much more collective framework.

As 'core' leader, Jiang continued Deng's economic reforms, the biggest decision being to privatize urban housing stock, along the lines of Margaret Thatcher's earlier 'right to buy' council housing. Anyone who bought much-discounted and undervalued homes made a killing as values adjusted to a new market, especially if a husband and wife could each buy from their SOE landlords, or inherited a second home from their parents. Attempts to impose a modest property tax to help local government and to curb speculation have failed. With prices surging as much as 30 per cent a year in some cities, owners do not even bother to let apartments since there are no mortgage or tax costs. Such a tax would also entail public disclosure, which would expose how much wealth officials have themselves. No such favours were extended to rural Chinese, though they benefited from limited health, welfare and pension provision. If any one policy stabilized Communist rule in China, this was it.[24]

Jiang relaxed notions of public ownership to include shareholders, and identified a thousand of the 370,000 SOEs that would be developed as national champions to compete with companies such as General Electric and Siemens, with admittedly limited success.[25] China has yet to develop major international brands to rival Apple or BMW, though it has a huge domestic market for Lenovo computers, after acquiring IBM, and the car maker Geely, which is the parent company of Swedish Volvo. It can build ships but not advanced passenger aircraft, and without a more innovative economy it will not develop an iPhone equivalent either, even if Chinese workers assemble them.

There are obviously limits to how much infrastructure a country can build, and in China some of it was built swiftly – and shoddily. Until experts from Boeing and United Airlines were imported to reform the country's civil aviation system in the late 1990s, Chinese Aviation Airline Company or CAAC was known as China Airlines Always Crashes. China's container ports handle more shipping than the next six busiest countries combined, and it adds as many new power plants each year as Great Britain operates in total, or roughly one a week. In around 2000, Jiang sought to extend the prosperity of the eastern coast to the vast regions of the West through a form of twinning relationship between for example Shanghai and Xinjiang. Expertise in infrastructure is also for export, partly to find something for these experts to do, but in Africa and Latin America.

Jiang sought to reverse the moral and spiritual desuetude caused by both the Cultural Revolution, which had erased such 'bourgeois' habits as good manners, while insulating China from the worst cultural depredations of a West he otherwise admired sufficiently to insist his entire family speak English during a New Year's feast. On his visits to the West, Jiang made full use of his polyglot smatterings in public debates and press conferences, while charming his hosts with eager renditions of Elvis Presley or 'O Sole Mio'.

He exercised more restraint than many Chinese people expected when in 1999 five US 'smart' J-Dam bombs hit the Chinese Embassy in Belgrade and in 2001 when a slow-moving US spy plane was hit by a fast PLA F-8, killing the incautious pilot, Wang Wei, who specialized in close intimidation. Following 9/11, China assisted the US by moving some of the joint communications intercept stations set up by the CIA and MSS in the 1980s under Operation Chestnut to monitor the Soviets to near Afghanistan to listen to Al Qaeda and Taliban conversations. Although China reluctantly conceded more freedom to the media in the wake of the 2002 SARS epidemic and the loss of a submarine in 2003, it remains a tightly controlled society, though not one in control of the powerful forces that decades of double-digit growth unleashed. In a break with Deng and Jiang, Hu Jintao has really vanished in retirement. Celebrity speeches and lucrative memoirs (options for every Western pip-squeak politician) are not available to the men who ruled China.[26]

•

In China from 2011 onwards, the budget for internal national security exceeded defence expenditure ($83.5 versus $81.2 billion per year). There are 25 million personnel in the country's Ministry of Public Security forces. Whenever the Party requires more eyes on the ground, for example during the Shanghai Expo in 2010 or the G20 in 2016, it can rely on 'volunteer vigilantes'. In Beijing there will be 1.3 million of them when the Party holds its 19th National Congress. This and the other main intelligence agency, the Ministry of State Security – which do not correspond to the CIA and FBI – spend 80 per cent of their time monitoring the domestic population rather than spying abroad, though PLA intelligence has extensive cyber operations resembling the National Security Agency in the US and its hacking unit '91638' is said to be formidably capable, having tapped into the twenty-one million digital files in the federal Office of Personnel Management and the email accounts of Obama and McCain in 2007.[27]

Domestic order is maintained by 800,000 policemen, who are gradually being armed after a long period when they carried no guns, and a paramilitary People's Armed Police which is one and a half million strong. They guard the borders and official buildings. But one consequence of an overwhelming concern with political crimes is that other varieties flourish, with so much money involved that the police themselves can be co-opted. One notorious case involved the tri-state city area known as Hailufeng of which Lufeng was the most notorious. This was home turf to a gang which cooked methamphetamine, China being the biggest cultivator of *Ephedra sinica*, the key precursor. In addition to China's 1.4 million synthetic-drug addicts, the gang was exporting meth to Hong Kong and the Philippines in consignments weighing tons. They also corrupted not only the Lufeng police, but those in Shanwei, the prefectural capital. It took a raid involving three thousand police officers in late 2013 to bring 182 gang members to justice.[28] The regime also disposes of small armies of informants and plainclothes thugs who seem to appear and disappear when intimidation is called for. There are parallel legal systems for the Party and civil society, as well as for the military, maritime and transport issues. Court proceedings before tribunals of three judges are usually swift, as the result has been decided in advance. China executes more people than the rest of the world combined, though nowadays by lethal injection rather than a bullet families have to pay for. At 117 per 100,000 Chinese incarceration rates are lower than in the UK (148), Russia (615) and the US (737), though no one knows exactly how many delinquent drug addicts, prostitutes and the like are being 're-educated' in what are no longer called 'labour camps'. It is also not unknown for those who seek to petition the central leadership in Beijing about a local abuse to find themselves being abducted and held in 'black prisons' by thugs working for the local potentates they are complaining about. But artificial intelligence and big data can do far more than any thugs. The absence of privacy laws means that every form of data can be accessed by the security services, from bank accounts via online activity to travel habits. This is being combined with facial recognition technology linked to all 170 million surveillance cameras. When linked with a 'social credit' data bank, it will be possible not only to follow everyone's movements, but also to reward and punish, for example rescinding freedom to travel.[29]

But at the same time, opinion is more freely expressed than one might imagine. The ruling elite have an enormous range of expertise in thousands of think tanks and university institutes that study not just China but other political cultures. President Xi has also created his own sources of informed analysis, bringing in foreign experts to rectify deficiencies in the (global) regional reporting of his own intelligence services. If he puts a tick on a report, these experts get a bonus. North Korea fascinates the Chinese as a negative example of what to avoid, not least because China would face a refugee crisis, and possibly US troops on its borders, if the Kim regime were to collapse. Systems in which the ruling party has enjoyed great longevity (India, Japan, Mexico and Taiwan among them) are one focus, but so too are those in which an authoritarian party rests on consent, notably Singapore's People's Action Party.

The collapse of Eastern European Communism, and then of the Soviet Union, caused China's rulers palpitations even if domestic censorship prevented the public from seeing the revolution live. The corpses of such staunch allies as Nicolae Ceauşescu, sprawled in the snow, concentrated minds. The CCP's own experts spent more than a decade analysing what had gone wrong, with a 2006 eight-disc DVD set *Consider Danger in Times of Peace: Historical Lessons from the Fall of the CPSU (Communist Party of the Soviet Union)* condensing lessons learned for mandatory secret viewing for the Party at central, provincial and municipal levels. Collapse of central Communist rule in China would also unleash regional frictions, perhaps centred on the Beijing, Guangdong and Shanghai conurbations.[30]

The waves of 'colour' revolutions in Georgia, Ukraine, Moldova and Kyrgyzstan between 2003 and 2009 and the 'Arab Spring' from January 2011 onwards have preoccupied other Chinese experts since many of the Middle East's autocracies were solid Chinese allies and the MENA region is vital to oil and gas supplies. The ability to block internet searches of the word 'jasmine' (the synonym for Tunisia's revolution in 2011) shows how far the Chinese authorities would go in a nation of flower lovers and where jasmine is a favourite tea.

The contribution of corruption as well as official arbitrariness in causing Arab social disorders that coalesced into political form is one lesson perhaps overlearned by China's present leaders. Corruption is a complex thing, and not every aspect of it is bad. In a country as vast, dynamic and prosperous as China, corruption does not play the same catastrophic role as in Africa's resource kleptocracies, where the wealth of nations is syphoned off by a 'tribe' that even has a name – the 'WaBenzi', after the Mercedes car.

For a start, how else did China's reforming leaders persuade an ideologically egalitarian party to buy into the rise of a capitalist economic system, other than by letting the comrades take slices of the pie for themselves? Was it so bad if some arbitraged a two-tier pricing system, if the result was to have a single price system? Even smuggling, which was endemic in southern China, had its positive side since it forced the regime to abandon import tariffs of 100 per cent or more, and therefore lowered the price of consumer goods. Anyone too brazen would go to a labour camp or be shot in the back of the head.[31]

Yet how corruption has come to be such a serious concern is worth dwelling on. It is partly a delayed manifestation of the decision in 1984 to decentralize control of the Party nomenklatura to the provincial level, so that powerful local Party bosses assumed control of many appointments and promotions. This was not necessarily corrupting so long as control of assets remained relatively frozen. But in the 1990s this was followed by the decentralization of control over such assets as land, mines and SOEs, whose ownership remained notionally public, but whose use could be alienated. This provided enormous scope for collusive corruption involving Party officials, businessmen and organized crime, without the governance mechanisms or private-investor oversight that exist in a market economy. A system based on provinces competing to raise GDP, and hence revenue returns to the centre, upon which top level careers depended, also resulted in a lot of blind eyes being turned.[32]

Corruption is politically dangerous in so far as it engenders envy and division within the ruling elites, as well as between the elites and people. Chinese could just about swallow the corruption of a senior official who had worked his way up, but his spoiled son who drunkenly crashed his Ferrari with two half-naked daughters of the elite on board was another matter. As with every major campaign in China, the anti-corruption drive is competitive. This means a preoccupation with numbers and targets. This had led to people being beaten with cables and burned with cigarettes to make them confess to bribing officials. Threats to families are also commonplace. The bribe-giver is then coached to give the correct testimony, with the threat 'if you don't get your words right, you either die or get disabled', as a brave pig farmer in Taizhou reported after he was jailed for two years for recanting his confession of bribing four officials with supermarket holiday gift cards.[33]

This is particularly so when growth stalls and the retreating tide leaves the system's flaws as visible as the carcass of a beached whale, as we have seen, for example, in Brazil or South Africa. But again, a caveat is in order. Enough Chinese have done well out of a system which has no personal income taxes (only businesses pay tax and VAT) and no capital gains tax either on house price rises for them not to resent colossal inequalities as measured by Corrado Gini's famous coefficient.* Even if there were to be a house-price crash, strict borrowing rules make the negative-equity traps of the West highly unlikely, and Chinese banks are paragons of virtue compared with their Western equivalents. Desperate poverty has been eliminated as a health and social security system spreads across the country. Since all children have to attend school until fifteen, child labour exploitation, endemic in India, is virtually nonexistent.[34]

Attempts to eradicate corruption are perilous, in the sense of increasing insecurity and rivalry among the elite, for there is a great deal of collateral damage being done to the client and family networks of the hundreds of thousands directly under Xi's imperious gaze. Moreover, even were the Communist system to collapse, the ensuing democratic institutions would be so weak and open to demagogues that, as in Russia or Ukraine, the most corrupt elements would doubtless emerge with even more influence than they enjoyed under the old system. Of course, this also presupposes an opposition *movement*.

Some experts on China highlight the '200,000' (2010) instances of 'social disorder' which occur every year as evidence for the extreme fragility of the system, should these local events coalesce into political movements. But defining 'manifestations of public disorder' is a problem and they never coalesce into a political form either. Only incidents involving more than a hundred people are counted, by a police apparatus always keen to advertise its zeal.

David Bandurski has written a brilliant account of how the urban-village rich sell off very valuable 'urban-rural' land to developers, often without their fellow core villagers even knowing about it. The contracts allow the developers to do what they like, and they and the city bosses have *Chengguan* goon squads, or

---

* The Gini Coefficient says that 0 equals perfect equality and 1 where all wealth is controlled by one person. Most countries score between 0.3 (developed) and 0.6 (undeveloped and unequal). China is on 0.49, by some metrics. The UK is 0.35, the US 0.39.

'urban management officers', to enforce their will on the often elderly protestors rather than fly tippers and vagrants. Intimidation starts with the power cables to a house or business being cut. Next dead rats are thrown through the windows. The odd beating occurs. It ends with threats to chop off feet and hands. If protestors persist, next the police riot squads arrive though they have been banned from facilitating evictions. Inevitably, even those who invest in the resulting shopping malls are not safe either since these often lack the required building permissions and trading licences. This does not matter provided they pay protection money to the criminal gangs who are part of the developments.[35]

There is a world of difference between a hundred angry people shouting for a few hours about late pay or greedy developers and the 30,000 who reportedly protested at Wuhan in Ghizhou province in June 2008 after the police covered up the alleged murder of Li Shufen, a sixteen-year-old girl, by men connected with local officials. The police station, cars and 160 office buildings were burned down. The fact that China's labour force is rapidly ageing, and that there are labour shortages, means that wages are increasing (to the point where it is cheaper to employ someone in Mexico), even in a system with one trade union that usually represents management.

China will also navigate any shift to production in which humans and robots cooperate. Labour unrest is not going to destabilize China. Nor will the urban middle class – a quarter of the population – since they have been the main beneficiaries of rising house prices, the expansion of travel and tertiary education and the delights of consumerism.[36] It is also worth uncoupling the middle class from claims to automatic virtue. Not all middle-class people are nice human-rights lawyers and academics. As Jonathan Watts astutely observes: 'China's political system now exhibits the worst elements of dictatorship and democracy: power lies neither at the top nor the bottom, *but within a middle class* of developers, polluters and local officials whom it is difficult to hold to account.'[37]

Such large-scale protests are the exception rather than the rule, even in a system where a controlled media, no independent judiciary and scant respect for a range of rights almost guarantees injustices. Sceptics say that the increased rate of petitions protesting local abuses and injustices to central government indicates that there is no automatic link between such protests and criticism of the political system that might really undermine the Communist regime if it took an interregional and political form. Although the regime has a very hard face, it also has a special department called the Bureau to Guard Domestic Security within the MPS which specializes in taking celebrity dissidents out of town for 'tea' when there is an important occasion.[38]

The Party also allows a controlled space where Han Chinese can protest about harm to such public goods as air and water. That is no more challenging to the system than the groups that protest fracking in rural Sussex or Pennsylvania threaten those in power in Britain or the US. Boosters of the internet claim that 640 million Chinese internet users include people who have found ways round the Great Firewall (unwittingly with government-supplied virtual private network technologies which have now been banned) not to mention the 2 *million* engaged in monitoring the World Wide Web. But then the political impacts of the internet have never lived up to their billing, and social media were actually much more marginal to the Arab Spring than their enthusiasts claim. In China, social media are also a way of venting rabid opinions that would be seen as highly un-PC or downright racist in the West. Besides even in the West, the likes of Twitter very much feel like declining businesses that teenagers are bored with, even in societies where the secret agencies may not be watching or quietly analysing the data people so naively volunteer.[39]

•

Like all national liberation and revolutionary parties in the developing world, the CCP lives off a treasure of inherited political capital that diminishes as time passes and society changes, especially one that professes egalitarianism but has such vivid inequalities. Not just 'Marxist-Leninist-Mao Zedong Thought' but also the business-school platitudes that the leadership use as a kind of esoteric jargon and which have no deep emotional purchase in a society that has long reconciled itself to people being rich beyond the dreams of avarice. Since the leadership are personally haunted by their and their parents' grim experiences of the Cultural Revolution, the mass mobilization of hysterical (and murderous) enthusiasms is all but ruled out to achieve the Party's goals. Bo Xilai, the disgraced charismatic boss of the city of Chongqing, played around with a kitsch Maoist nostalgia before his sudden downfall (which came after his wife poisoned a British business adviser-cum-lackey who reputedly drove around in a Jaguar with the number plate 007).

Although China has eight licensed parties, including the Kuomintang, only one counts. The Communist Party leadership consists of a 370-strong Central Committee, selected by 3,000 delegates who meet every five years as the National People's Congress. The latter also has a Standing Committee of around 200 which meets for a week every couple of months and which acts as a legislature. Real power is located in the Party's twenty-five-strong Political Bureau (Politburo), and especially in its seven-man Standing Committee. Military power resides in the eleven-man Central Military Commission which controls the PLA and its various districts.

At the apex is Xi Jinping, state President, Party General Secretary and Chair of the Central Military Commission.[40] Leadership is supposed to be collective, with an orderly changing of the top guards every decade and a mandatory retirement age of sixty-eight. The heir apparent to the party leader is supposed to heave into view after five years, though significantly these 'customs' are being dismissed as 'folklore', suggesting they may be changed. Currently, there are rumours that in order to disqualify the sixty-one-year-old Prime Minister Li Keqiang, President Xi may delay designating a younger successor, or raise the retirement age to allow his sixty-nine-year-old friend Wang Qishan to rise to the top. Such acts of legerdemain may cause internal ructions.[41] One man to watch is Li Zhanshu, director of the Central Committee General Office, which services the top leadership. Li has known Xi since 1983 when they served in neighbouring counties in Hebei Province. Without connections to the top leadership, Li was posted to such rustbelt provinces as Heilongjiang or China's poorest province Guizhou, before Xi needed an old friend and promoted Li to the Politiburo in 2012. His experience of China's poor interior also complemented Xi's stints on the rich coast. In addition to his running the General Office, Li has been entrusted with missions to Putin and was seen on the periphery of summits between Xi and Obama and Trump. In the run-up to the 19th Party Congress Xi has been accelerating the promotion of several loyalists, some of whom, like Cai Qi, have skipped over membership of the Central Committee.[42]

At 87.7 million members, the CCP includes one in sixteen Chinese, including anyone and everyone who counts. The Party's presence is everywhere, ranging from the equivalent of eager local community activists in the West to emperor-like rulers of huge provinces who greet visitors from mini-thrones. Walmart's Chinese operation thought it politic to have a Party branch. The Communist Youth League includes a further 88 million fourteen- to twenty-eight-year-olds, a powerful vested interest in its own right, and one that is associated with former President Hu Jintao. Other identifiable factions are the so-called 'Shanghai Gang' who, like former President Jiang Zemin, cut their teeth in that wealthy city, and the 'Zhejiang Clique', the eastern province where President Xi was Governor and Party Secretary between 2002 and 2007. There is also a more amorphous group of 'red princelings' whose parents, like Xi's, were senior Party, state or military luminaries.[43]

China has been a meritocracy for millennia. When in 1793 a British mission proudly displayed a Joshua Reynolds portrait of the Duke of Bedford as a boy, a child destined for the House of Lords, the Chinese hosts 'laughed heartily at the idea of a man being born a legislator, when it required so many years of close application to enable one of their countrymen to pass his examination for the very lowest order of state officers'. No wonder the British did not detect the calculated insult in their ambassador being escorted by a mere salt-tax collector, as the elderly emperor specified in hand-penned marginal notes.

Joining the Party is competitive and protracted, akin to entrance to an elite university such as Harvard, MIT or Stanford, crossed with an intelligence service. As someone with a suspect father, Xi Jinping had to apply ten times for Party membership.[44] Forty per cent of applicants are students nowadays, with quotas reflecting the university's ranking in league tables.

The candidate and his or her background and acquaintance are thoroughly vetted, which may explain why employers like to recruit Party members since they do not have to vet them themselves. Both activism and self-criticism are important, though this does not seem to exclude the many who see Party membership as a route to riches.[45] Although the families of the leadership are off bounds to the media in China, Western investigators such as Bloomberg have revealed the immense wealth of the families of many Party leaders.

The Communist Party leadership is based on a lengthy apprenticeship system, the foothills of a slow climb to the 1.2km² Zhongnanhai compound where Party and state leaders are based inside Beijing's Forbidden City. The current President had to spend twenty-five years working his way up through provincial roles before joining the Politburo. The state apparatus is run by a twenty-five-member State Council, though typically this has an inner executive council led by the premier, four vice-premiers and state councillors with supra-ministerial briefs. There are twenty-five ministries, whose command structure is replicated down to the provinces through governors, though they have Party officials by their side. While an increasing proportion of government revenue is in central hands, 80 per cent is spent by provincial officials.

In Zhongnanhai, government or state offices are clustered around the northern gate, while Party offices are in its south. Visitors are surprised by the beauty and calm within after the bustle outside. Merit must accompany revolutionary pedigree, which is still important though increasingly remote. One senior official acidly remarked that 'Hu Jintao, Wen Jiabao, your fathers were selling shoelaces [actually tea] while our fathers were dying for this revolution.' Hu and Wen were privately disdained as *huoji*, or hired help, by some red princelings. But leadership also requires the ability to forcefully communicate a message without sounding like a speaking weight machine reading out a briefing paper. The system favours laconic characters like Deng or Xi over the constant febrile gush that Western politicians have to emit for a 24/7 media circus and an increasingly bored and indifferent public. It helps that Xi has a telegenic and vivacious folk singer spouse (Peng Liyuan), a ranking PLA officer known to half a billion Chinese TV viewers from her appearances on the CCTV New Year Gala show. In addition to possessing simple tastes, Xi does not drink much, smoke or spit (Deng's most disconcerting habit), and he can kill someone stone dead with a withering glance, for example when he barely looked at Japanese Prime Minister Shinzo Abe on their first encounter. His concern with image extends to banning any comparisons with Winnie the Pooh, who some Chinese unwisely think he resembles. Xi's closest advisers, most of them former academics he has known for a long time, have spells at Harvard and Stanford on their CVs, the destinations of choice for the children of the leading cadres.

The ruling system also rests on patronage and reciprocal favours extending over decades. There is a very fine line between patronage based on merit and what is called *yongrenweiqin* or 'hiring officials based on favoritism' especially when competence is subjected to matters of loyalty to the ruling faction. Every leader tries to stack the deck in his own interests.[46] Although Deng formally retired in 1992, he played a major role not just in choosing and directing his immediate successor, Jiang Zemin, but also by bringing on a fourth generation of leaders such as Hu Jintao whose legitimacy stemmed from meritocratic capabilities rather than revolutionary pedigree. They would also serve for limited terms of ten years, a break with the gerontocracy that Deng alone was exempt from. Even at the age of eighty-seven, Deng famously embarked on his 1992 southern sojourn, basking in the economic miracles of Guangdong and Shenzen, but also meeting senior PLA commanders in Zhuhai in a not so veiled warning to Jiang's more conservative colleagues not to obstruct rapid growth or the development of greater Shanghai. The hint was taken up at the 14th Party Congress, in 1992, where the term 'planned market economy' was replaced by 'socialist market economy', while 'Deng Xiaoping Theory' was canonized alongside an increasingly sere 'Thought of Mao Zedong'. At that point, Deng could really retire, receiving a simple send-off, as a soldier, when he died in 1997.

His successor, Jiang Zemin, similarly retained a great deal of power after his formal retirement in late 2002. He remained Chairman of the Central Military Commission, for Hu was deemed to be weak in this area, and as 'chief representative' he arbitrated any Politburo disputes and had to be consulted on any major decisions. In 2007 he identified the fifth-generation leader Xi Jinping. His succession in 2012 was made more dramatic by the downfall of Bo Xilai and rumours that Jiang had expired in 2011. Jiang and the 'Gang of Old Men' helped narrow down the runners and riders at their annual retreat at the seaside resort of Beidaihe before the last cut was revealed at the 18th Party Congress, where the top team under Xi Jinping presented themselves.

The patronage of old men is only one of the many high cards winners need to hold in this system, for any voter choice in an inner-Party electorate the size of a big village (say 3,000 people) has been 'discussed' long before votes are cast to get someone onto the Central Committee. An extremely subtle analysis of the current leaders conveniently lists what each man brings by way of connections, experience and abilities. The fact that there are seven rather than nine of them indicates a desire to streamline decision making as important reforms are essayed. The nominal titles do not necessarily reflect an individual's power:

— President Xi Jinping: Family, military, business, provincial, elite support

— Premier Li Keqiang: Family, provincial, business, some elite support

— Secretary Central Discipline Committee Wang Qishan: Family (inherited), provincial (brief), business (central and intellectual), elite support

— Vice-Premier Zhang Gaoli: Provincial, elite support, business

— Chairman of the Standing Committee of the National People's Congress Zhang Dejiang: Provincial, elite support, business

— Chairman of the Chinese People's Political Consultative Conference Yu Zhengsheng: Family, provincial, business, elite

— Secretary of the Secretariat and Chairman of the Commission for Building Spiritual Civilization Liu Yunshan: Business (intellectual, central), some elite support

The sharp-eyed will notice that Xi Jinping holds the highest cards, with close connections to the PLA as well as experience governing booming provinces. After graduating, through gritted teeth, in chemistry at Quinhua University, Xi became a (uniformed) *mishu* or private secretary to a general-cum-diplomat in the Central Military Commission. Xi's mother arranged this appointment, while Xi's father reciprocally fixed up a journalism job for the general's daughter. One might call this precautionary nepotism, since 'If our sons succeed us, at least they won't turn against us.'[47] That very senior people admired Xi's father as a straight bat (see above) did not harm him, nor the minor courtesies Xi is careful to pay to his elders and betters. In his first post in Hebei province he donated his official car for the use of the veteran cadre office, while easing their access to medical services, and his first act when posted from Zhejiang to Shanghai in 2007 was to refuse an official villa, insisting it be given to veteran cadres as a retirement home.[48]

Of the others, it has not damaged witch-finder general Wang Qishan to be a very well-read historian or Liu Yunshan a Party journalist in a Party dominated by business and economics graduates, or that the spook older brother of Yu Zhengsheng had defected to the US in 1985 exposing China's spy network. His work as head of the China Foundation for Disabled Persons brought the patronage of Deng Pufang and his father. Although running a thriving province with a population equal to that of Europe's biggest countries helps, managing natural or man-made disasters (or unrest) in much poorer or peripheral regions, some with ethno-religious complications, also attracts positive notice.[49]

Xi unveiled an ambitious series of economic reforms at the third plenary of the 18th Party Congress in 2013. They consist of 340 policy initiatives, from ending the one-child policy via land reform to supply-side restructuring of the economy towards consumption and services, not to mention the ongoing urbanization of China. In 2011–13, China used 50 per cent more concrete than the US consumed in the entire twentieth century. The aim is to have 60 per cent of people living in urban centres by 2020, 70 per cent by 2030 and nearly 80 per cent by 2050. This means that whereas in 2016 54 per cent or 731 million

Chinese lived in cities, by 2030 the number will be a billion.[50] Even if this is achieved through partial amnesties for the 100 million people living illegally in cities without *hukou* residence permits, it will entail enormous expansion of education, housing, health, pensions and welfare provision.

While Western societies grapple with the urban cultural effects of 'diversity', China has a similar problem with its own people in the sense that, as in Victorian Britain, the poor are another 'race'. The smart and rich in the biggest cities like Shanghai have ensured they will not have to rub shoulders with the rural unwashed in teeming slums, by insisting migrants are redirected to cities of a million or so inhabitants.[51] This has also indirectly contributed to a worrying housing-price bubble, to which the government response has been to make house purchase more difficult. One manifestation of this is people risking buying homes on land designated for 'dual use' commercial development, only to find that developers have only one use in mind.[52] Pensions and welfare are another potential problem in a rapidly ageing population where many people retire at fifty-five. With 400 million Chinese aged over sixty anticipated by 2030, the unfunded pensions gap is projected to rise to $128 trillion by 2050, by which time the median age will be forty-nine, or nine years more than the US demographic equivalent. The big fear in China is that unlike Japan or Germany it might get old *before* it gets rich, with a rise in such diseases as diabetes and dementia associated with an ageing population.[53]

The overarching strategic goal is to shift the economy's gravity from zombie-like SOEs in coal, heavy machinery, shipbuilding and steel to education, entertainment, green technologies and improved health care. Redressing some of the environmental havoc of decades of crash industrialization (and promiscuous use of chemical fertilizers in farming) is obviously part of it, though this is being done retrospectively as it was in the developed world.

China wants to move up the value chain too and to create global Chinese brands to rival Audi or Apple. Paradoxically the Great Firewall, which cuts China off from the American-dominated web, has led to the creation of a few e-commerce champions like Alibaba, but these do not have the global reach of an Amazon or Google. SOEs benefit from opaque low-interest loans and discounts on land, electricity and water. Their executives are selected by the Party's personnel office, and there is much political pressure to maintain workers' jobs in loss-making plants, though we should note that between 1995 and 2005, 30 million workers in SOEs were laid off, while more went into early retirement, all without political ill effects.[54] There has been significant consolidation among SOEs in the belief that scale will ensure survival, an example being the merger of China Shipping Group and China Ocean Shipping Group (COSCO) to create the world's largest container-shipping line.[55]

Issuing hundreds of policy directives does not guarantee speedy implementation in a system where there are powerful provincial and municipal fiefdoms which control huge revenues in their own right. That requires some stick, which comes from Wang Qishan, head of the Central Commission for Discipline Inspection, who has held a Sword of Damocles over underperforming or corrupt SOE bosses. Described as 'the handle on President Xi's knife', Wang has said in a leaked video that 'the anti-corruption campaign is not like a gust of wind or something that passes in a few days. There is a beginning, but no end to this.' In his attempt to combat foot-dragging, President Xi has short-circuited the State Council in favour of eleven dedicated Party 'leading groups', such as the one for economic and financial affairs, which bash heads together and override state ministries and regulators. In internal Zhongnanhai terms this is a case of the Party south taking over the state north.[56]

President Xi's anti-corruption campaign announced four years ago has endured much longer than those of either Jiang Zemin or Hu Jintao (whose corresponding drives proved episodic). It is being used to strike down enemies and rivals and to reform sclerotic institutions so as to also maximize the power of Xi and the Party. It is not just the economic loss, though the People's Bank of China estimates that $125 billion was lost to corruption between 1990 and 2010.[57] As a leader who speaks about moral issues more than most, Xi has always stressed that corruption will undermine the legitimacy of the Communist Party. He seeks a China in which 'nobody dares be corrupt'.

His multipronged campaign of 'killing tigers [people at vice-ministerial level and above] and swatting flies [more humdrum cadres]' has led to 414,000 officials being investigated and disciplined by the CCDI, while 201,600 have been prosecuted in Party courts. Even a quarter of the funds of the sports and social welfare national lottery (the only legal form of gambling in mainland China) had been diverted into hotels and office blocks or simply embezzled, the National Audit Office found.[58]

To keep the comrades on the straight and narrow, official guidelines tell them how many cars they are entitled to, the permitted size and value of their houses, who can have secretaries and security personnel, and that instead of banquets with endless toasts they should settle for 'four dishes and one soup' all to be consumed within an hour. That is why official banquets seem to end so abruptly, after all the toasts. They must report major changes in their lives, including divorce or remarriage, foreign travel, big purchases and investments. Since 2016 imports of luxury cars like Ferraris and Rolls Royces have been subject to an extra 10 per cent duty to curb conspicuous consumption. Corrupt officials who have fled abroad are not safe either from the 'Skynet' international legal initiative, which has brought back a thousand economic fugitives from sixty-eight countries. In a society where every citizen has a mobile phone camera, officials are being circumspect about watches and jewellery, or ostentatious banqueting. The casinos of Macau and luxury goods stores in Hong Kong have noted a marked fall in custom since Xi's drive began.[59] While in the past the Chinese authorities banned any media references to corruption, nowadays they encourage the dramatization of the heroic forces investigating it. A fifty-five-episode series called *In the Name of the People* has been seen online by 1.7 million viewers. It uses real-life case studies to follow a team of anti-corruption investigators as they cope with counting mountains of corruptly acquired cash, no small feat in a country where the highest denomination bank note, the Rmb100, is worth only $16.[60]

A further effect of this drive has been an increase in the number of Communist bureaucrats committing suicide. The number of 'abnormal deaths' has risen to 120 since Xi Jinping

became President, from sixty-eight under his predecessor Hu
Jintao between 2003 and 2012. While some can be attributed
to such causes as alcoholism or depression, the majority seem
connected with the appearance of anti-corruption investigators
from the Central Committee for Disciplinary Inspection.

Suspects can be held incommunicado in a secret location
until such time as they are handed over to public prosecutors.
But if the person dies while under suspicion, or in detention,
then the case will be closed, which spares families not only
shame but also the prospect of handing back shared illicit gains.
In China, corruption is a family affair. Indeed membership of the
Party is often seen as an intergenerational meal ticket, one of
the reasons candidacy is intensely competitive.

Yet all this zeal surely only tackles the manifestations of corruption, rather than such systemic causes as ambiguous ownership
rights, poor auditing and taxation, few investigative media, and
toothless courts. Moreover, incessant vigilance seems to have
impacted on the implementation of wider reforms, as every official watches his or her back, while many of China's richest and
brightest have decided to move themselves or their offspring
abroad. As in Russia, that is a sure sign that something is wrong,
though students do return to what are often high-paying jobs.

Xi's anti-corruption drive also has ulterior agendas though
both men were surely corrupt. Most obviously Xi struck down
the bumptious Bo Xilai, but also the more senior former head of
security and Politburo Standing Committee member Zhou Yong-
kang, who was jailed for life in 2015. In order to eradicate the
enduring 'spirit' of Bo Xilai, Sun Zhengcai, his successor in
Chongqing and the youngest member of the Politburo, was suddenly purged in July 2017. The campaign has reached into the
supporters of Jiang Zemin and Hu Jintao, and struck forcefully
at the most powerful bastion of quasi-independent power: the
People's Liberation Army. Xi closely identifies with the armed
forces, appearing at the new joint command centre in military
battledress rather than a civilian suit. Over two hundred officers
above the rank of lieutenant colonel, including thirty-seven major
generals, have been punished since 2013 for corruption. Speaking
to officers at the HQ of 16th Army Group in the summer of 2015,

Xi dwelled on the case of General Xu Caihou, Vice Chairman of the Central Military Commission and a Politburo member in whose home more than a tonne of cash and precious stones were found, the fruits of selling promotions to his juniors. Xu died of cancer before he could be tried but his co-conspirator General Guo Boxiong is serving thirty years in prison.[61]

The military anti-corruption campaign is partly a reminder of who is the boss (President Hu was publicly slighted by the PLA on a couple of occasions) but also a tool to restructure the armed forces. As in the US, ground forces are being edged aside by the navy and air force and the strategic rocket division, which under Xi has become an independent command. That means a 300,000 cut in headcount, especially those in green uniforms, reducing the number of regional commands from seven to five and refashioning departments dealing with armaments, logistics, political work and the general staff, who are now joined by eleven new agencies all subordinate to Xi.[62] If the new balance of force structures should worry China's maritime neighbours, so should how a chastened PLA might seek to restore its domestic power base through a more confrontational response to external 'provocations'. Should the political leadership balk at a confrontation with Japan or Vietnam, which would be massively unpopular among the Chinese public, then the ensuing backlash could suit the PLA very well.

China today is sometimes described as a cynical country in which nothing but money and individual self-interest matter, based on the underlying deal 'you allow us to make money and we allow you to rule'. Yet this idiosyncratic Leninist-capitalist model has endured more than three decades, and hundreds of millions of Chinese have seen their living standards soar as a result, with horizons lifting from a radio, fridge and TV, to a bicycle, car, apartment, foreign holidays and a few shares on the stock exchange, long after Westerners took such things for granted. Nor do even older Westerners have living memories of mass starvation. The average at birth age of mortality in China is now 76, which is higher than that in seven of ten countries in Eastern Europe.

The Communist Party problem is how to explain what its rule is for, once one excludes the maintenance of social order, impressive economic advancement and the respect of foreign powers. From time to time it proclaims such cloudy goals as 'the harmonious society' (Hu Jintao) or the American-style 'China Dream' (President Xi) in which national and individual goals become one, though each time the results have fallen short of the aspiration. Xi published a book of classical aphorisms in 2016, in which neither Marx nor Mao warrant a mention. Instead, the emphasis is on Chinese traditions in order to restore internal and external moral boundaries under the perennial ruling Party. China will not 'evolve' into a democracy, though it will acquire more welfare aspects, but nor will it become a 'fascist' state as some alarmists hysterically predict. Its leaders are pragmatists experienced in cautious experimentation, and well aware how to avoid what they see unfolding abroad. One suspects Chinese leaders are as perplexed at the erratic antics of Trump as any world leaders, but how they react matters more than most. It should be noted too that anxieties about the US taking an authoritarian or fascist turn are far more frequent in Western circles than anything one might read about contemporary China.

The reign of materialism is also belied by a rich film culture, made by such directors as Lou Ye, Zhang Yimou, Tian Zhuangzhuang and Jia Zhangke, as well as many Taiwanese, and fine novelists like Chan Koonchung and Yan Lianke, but also by labour activists and civil-rights lawyers and NGOs who resist China's daily injustices. You have to be obsessive about civil rights to learn all the laws you need to quote to the police when they arrest you. The very notion of civil society is anathema to Xi's leadership as it subverts the Party's social foundations and vision of what China is. Without it, however, any sudden transition to 'democracy' would probably be an unmitigated disaster, as it has been in other authoritarian systems with no record of civil society and in which the most amoral and corrupt elements rise to the top amidst the chaos. Look at Russia, or the increasingly oligopolistic crew that now govern the US.

The risks facing China's leaders are multiple and there have been signs of panic, as when SOEs were obliged to buy shares, putting a floor under a collapsing stock market. For the increasing financialization of the Chinese economy means that even the most cautious reforms are instantly picked over by China's own markets, whose overreactions duly incline politicians and central bankers to soften their own policies.[63] Resistance from vested interests and bureaucratic foot-dragging continue to slow reforms due for completion by 2020, and real growth could be lower than the official 6.9 per cent announced in late 2015. If the housing bubble bursts, living standards fall and unemployment spreads because former SOE workers cannot be repositioned, Xi's hitherto unassailable and unparalleled position could become fragile. On the other hand, with its high savings rates and lack of dependence on fickle foreign investment, a huge internal market and a population that will recover from the defunct one-child policy, China could plausibly negotiate the transition to an economy based on domestic consumption, though with very bumpy intervals as the SOEs shed labour.[64]

The Fourth Industrial Revolution has implications for China as for everywhere else. Another major worry for China is that, as its workers' wages rise, manufacturing will be relocated to the likes of India, Mexico and Vietnam. The Taiwanese electronics giant Foxconn, which makes components for Apple and Galaxy smartphones, employs a million people in China but plans to replace most of them with robots. If at the same time the Fourth Industrial Revolution results in production being re-shored by developed economies (because AI and robots will eliminate these countries high wage costs) then China will be in an unfortunate place, the middle-income trap which China's leaders fear most of all. To that end, it is investing massively in industrial robotics, while purchasing German robotics companies such as KUKA, so that even if 'Made in Britain' or 'Made in Germany' replaces 'Made in China', at least they will be employing Chinese-built industrial robots. Experts predict that, in ten years, China's robots will match those of Germany and Japan, the leaders in the field.[65]

Yet it would be a mistake to allow current political and economic problems to detract from the big picture. We are witnessing the rebirth of one of the world's great civilizations, a people whose prodigious talents were violently submerged from 1949 to the 1980s by one of history's most vicious dictatorships. Nothing symbolizes the country's new dynamic as starkly as the phenomenal Silk Road Economic Belt and the twenty-first-century Maritime Silk Road projects. Awesome reminders of the country's global future, they will finally break with its isolationist past by opening the country directly to Europe, central Asia and the Middle East and beyond. The Chinese are allegedly 'colonizing' sub-Saharan Africa, with the connivance of rulers like Mohammed VI of Morocco. His kingdom is China's special friend in Africa. China is to build Africa's tallest skyscraper in Rabat. There are Chinese banks in Casablanca and Moroccan banks in Shanghai, and the Chinese are building a $10 billion industrial city outside Tangier to avail themselves of Gibraltar's gateway to the European Union. They are a less welcome presence in Casablanca's mercantile Derb Omar district, whose locals say they are unable to compete with these entrepreneurs from the East.[66]

China is also turning commodity rich nations like Australia or Brazil into the equivalent of the mints with a hole in the middle. China wants to capitalize on any damage the erratic US President does to American soft power, meaning how the image of America is diffused throughout the world through films, TV, sport and products as well as more formal public diplomacy. Trump's alienation of Mexicans is felt across Latin America more widely, forcing conservative and populist regimes together and giving the latter a fresh wind at a time when experts see them slowing. Since Trump's election, the fortunes of Mexican populist López Obrador have significantly improved in response to Trump's threats to NAFTA and the mistreatment of legal and illegal Mexican migrants by US authorities behaving like 'little Hitlers'.[67] It may be Trump, rather than the ghost of Chávez, who unites Latin and Central America, and the Caribbean states, whose moribund CELAC community has become more united since his election. Many Latin American states will turn towards China as a more reliable alternative to the US, where many outsiders cannot calculate who exactly is in charge. Finally, Chinese entrepreneurs are buying up venerable German *Mittelstand* firms from uninterested heirs who face increased inheritance taxes, and building nuclear infrastructure in Britain to advertise their global expertise in this sector.[68]

•

The legendary Silk Road beguiles many adventurous tourists, the name being vaguely reassuring as a symbol of cultures intermingling long ago. Yet the historic Silk Road never touched Belarus or the Czech Republic, let alone Germany or the United Kingdom which now has a rail-freight link to China. Today's land-based Silk Road has already resulted in freight trains from China trundling into German and Iranian depots, though when it is completed sixty countries will be participants. It also means small armies of Chinese engineers and construction crews, oil and gas flowing out from the -stans, and Chinese purchases of agricultural land. In Kazakhstan in 2016 this led, once the price of oil had fallen, to cries of 'Down with the Chinese, Kazakhstan for the Kazakhs!'

China wants to protect its ramifying economic assets and Chinese citizens working in what are sometimes very dangerous places. For example, in 2011 it took China a week to evacuate 35,000 nationals from Libya as the British and French intervention plunged that country into anarchy. Similarly, in 2015 a Chinese warship removed 600 citizens (and two hundred foreigners) from Yemen.[69] China is also a major maritime power, responsible for one-fifth of the world's container traffic and building 40 per cent of the world's commercial tonnage. The maritime Silk Belt consists of a so-called 'string of pearls' (though there is no strategic plan bearing that name), a chain of bases, ports and airfields from the South China Sea, through the Singapore–Malacca Straits, across the Indian Ocean to the Red Sea and Suez Canal. These include dual-use ports in South Asia (Colombo and Hambantota in Sri Lanka, Gwadar in Pakistan, Sittwe in Burma, Port Victoria in the Seychelles and now Djibouti) with such add-ons as the container docks at Piraeus in Greece, leases on ports in Ashdod and Haifa in Israel, a port in Panama and a lease on Australia's Port Darwin. While the former have an obvious strategic significance in protecting China's main maritime trade route, the latter are probably as much about making money as the tourist resorts Chinese companies have built on the tiny Maldives. Like the terrestrial Silk Road, these colossal projects also enable China to export the manpower and knowhow accrued through decades of infrastructural improvement at home that has reached saturation point and overcapacity.[70]

Nothing is for nothing and Chinese loans have many strings attached. Gwadar and Hambantota are ports used by Chinese submarines and the former is defended by Chinese warships. Loans are a way of drawing the likes of Burma, Cambodia, Laos and Thailand into China's orbit as the ASEAN nations endeavour to contain their powerful neighbour. If a country cannot pay on the loans, or if, like Sri Lanka in 2015, it elected a government that takes another view of alliances, then China either reschedules the terms or, more usually, insists on yet more mega-projects while taking a raised ownership stake in the existing ones. For example, it owns 80 per cent of the port at Hambantota, and has a 75 per cent stake in a major dam in Nepal.[71]

The Western world pays lip service to the idea that an economically omnipresent and powerful China should join the Western-themed global clubs, but then does not like it when China tries to modify the rules or, worse, sets up rival institutions. This may change since, judging from Xi's speech at the Davos World Economic Forum in early 2017, China now has a leader who sounds more presidential (in the historic US sense) than the blustering Donald Trump. Apart from quoting Charles Dickens, Xi gave a reasoned analysis of the pitfalls of globalization while committing China to free trade and international institutions, in the same week that Trump's hard-edged inaugural address rejected both.[72]

In Beijing's view, the West would like China to remain a regional power, a kind of giant curiosity on the margins. Yet it is surely reassuring that, rather than simply deploying its enormous financial power, China increasingly chooses to work through such agencies as the BRICS' New Development Bank or the more ambitious Asia Infrastructure Investment Bank, multinational entities where Beijing does not call all the shots. At the same time, the West (or rather the US, since Europe has no dogs in this fight) has relied on China to keep its friends North Korea and Pakistan on a tight leash, to co-manage Afghanistan after ISAF forces have departed, and to craft the successful nuclear deal with Iran. Like it or not, China may have to assume a greater role in the Middle East, though if it has any sense, it won't.

China's primary foreign policy concerns are with itself, as if the US were preoccupied with Texas or the UK with Scotland, a part rather than the whole. China borders fourteen nations by land, ranging from forty-seven miles with Afghanistan to over 2,500 miles with India, and has (disputed) maritime borders with six others. Most of its land border disputes (with the exception of that with India in Aksai Chin and Arunachal Pradesh) have been settled reasonably, with China trading off territory, but, as we shall see below, several maritime disputes have escalated. The border with Burma is another source of trouble since both narcotics and wild-life 'products' used in traditional Chinese medicine flow into Yunnan from the lawless areas on the Burmese side along with stray bombs and bullets when the Burmese military exerts itself.

Beijing's most pressing concerns, other than internal stability, stem from its own volatile peripheries, landlocked Xinjiang and Tibet, and the islands of Hong Kong and Taiwan. In Xinjiang and Tibet restiveness is bound up with ethno-religious resistance to what some regard as quasi-Han occupation. Tibet has witnessed uprisings and immolations (147 between 2009 and 2015) and has become the darling of Hollywood's Zen Buddhism set who seem otherwise incurious about monkish feudalism. But of the two, Xinjiang is the more existential since it constitutes a sixth of China's total area and is rich in oil and natural gas. Development of the 'Wild West' is crucial to China's future development, and to the land Silk Road Economic Belt to link China with Eurasia.

After trying economic carrots, Beijing has resorted to sticks such as operation Strike Hard to suppress Uyghur militants who over time have exchanged pan-Turkic and Marxist affiliations for radical Islam. The threat of separatism grew as Tajiks, Turkmens, Kazakhs and Uzbeks sloughed off the Soviet Union, one of the reasons China (and Russia) founded the Shanghai Five (plus Kazakhstan, Kyrgyzstan and Tajikistan) in 1996, which has since become the Shanghai Cooperation Organization. Uyghur Islamic militancy flourished in anti-Soviet jihadist training camps in Afghanistan, and then relocated operations to

Pakistan's Federally Administered Tribal Areas after the US struck at the Afghan Taliban and Al Qaeda. Since communal riots in Urumqi in July 2009, which left 197 Han dead, there have been sporadic Uyghur militant bomb and knife attacks in Xinjiang but also in Beijing and Kunming. Only in China could the authorities, fearful of vehicular bombs, take the drastic step of putting GPS monitoring devices in every vehicle, from bull-dozers and trucks to taxis, in a vast prefecture in Xinjiang province so as to better track the movements of a handful of violent separatists. Those who do not have the devices will not be able to fill up at petrol stations. The prefecture has 1.5 million inhabitants, in an area twice the size of the United Kingdom. The police are also collecting DNA samples from all Uighurs for a new $10 billion DNA storage facility.[73]

Though Pakistan is the closest China has to an ally, because of its use in perpetually distracting India, Chinese workers in Pakistan are liable to kidnap or murder, not just by militant Islamists but by Baloch separatists who resent Chinese involve-ment in major infrastructure projects such as the port at Gwadar. In 2007 vice-and-virtue vigilantes from Islamabad's Red Mosque abducted seven Chinese women from a massage parlour in one of the plusher neighbourhoods, imprisoning them in a madrassa a stone's throw from centres of government. With patriotic Chinese posting their leaders calcium tablets to help them grow backbones, Beijing told Islamabad to act, while insinuating that Uyghurs had had a hand in the kidnapping. Although the Chin-ese women were released in burqas, after typically murky negotiations, the Pakistani army besieged the mosque and killed 103 militants. Gunmen murdered three Chinese engineers in an auto-rickshaw factory in Peshawar the following day.[74]

In Hong Kong and Taiwan there is no ethno-religious prob-lem, though on both islands (7 million and 23 million inhabitants, respectively) most people do not describe themselves exclusively as 'Chinese' either. Hong Kong is supposed to be governed under the 'One China, Two Systems' deal reached with the outgoing British, at least for the time being, though the deal was struck at a time when Hong Kong eclipsed mainland cities like Shenzen, which is no longer the case. In 1997 Hong Kong's economy was

18 per cent of China's GDP, but nowadays it is 3 per cent, and heavily reliant on banking and property too rather than innovative start-ups. Beijing has also adopted this formula for another 'renegade' province, which calls itself the Republic of China, aka Taiwan. Pressure from Beijing on both islands is relentless.

China has been successful, usually by deploying its economic clout, in isolating what is the world's twenty-third largest economy. The ROC is a diplomatic orphan, with only Paraguay recognizing Taipei in the whole of Latin America, though six central American and five Caribbean countries still do, for what good that does. As the 2014 'umbrella revolution' illustrated, young Hong Kongers are alert to Beijing's jiggery-pokery with 'elections' to the Legislative Council or Legco. Some want universal suffrage rather than the quaint corporatist arrangements in which people elect architects, physicians and so on. They also have good reason to be worried by Beijing's brazen abduction and intimidation of five publishers allegedly engaged in smuggling sensational political biographies about China's leaders onto the mainland, not to mention how the dissident Nobel laureate Liu Xiaobo vanished down an electronic black hole before and after his death in July 2017.[75] The youthful protestors have since formed their own political parties which will make Legco sessions more lively, tempting fate if they press for independence.

In 2014, too, young Taiwanese, this time bearing sunflowers, occupied the legislature to protest against the ruling Kuomintang's attempt to pass a services liberalization agreement with mainland China without adequate parliamentary scrutiny. This seemed yet further evidence of how Beijing was seeking to bring about reunification through economic dependency. Despite 200,000 anxious Taiwanese flying home from the mainland to vote for the KMT, the opposition candidate Tsai Ing-wen and the Democratic Progressive Party won the January 2016 election on a platform that seeks greater distance from the PRC and closer ties with India, South-East Asia and the US. Donald Trump briefly dallied with the thought of abandoning the 'One China' policy, but then after a frosty silence from President Xi, decided to stick with the established US line.[76]

•

Wider Chinese foreign policy in its own Asia–Pacific region is rooted in a sense of historic entitlement and victimization. Historically, China's emperors possessed *tian xia* or the Mandate of Heaven to rule their neighbours through tributary arrangements until meddlesome foreigners upset this natural order of things. Two of the neighbours were troublesome. Though being culturally derivative of China, both Japan and what we call Vietnam were populated by warrior peoples who subverted or contested Heaven's Mandate. A rapidly modernized Japan defeated China in 1895, and then conquered vast tracts of it between 1937 and 1945, killing fifteen million Chinese people in the process. The less well-known example of Vietnam was a case of 'mini-me' despite the outward signs of submission to China's rulers. For Vietnam won the struggle for mastery it waged with Siam (Thailand) to dominate the 'child-like' peoples of what became Cambodia and Laos, creating its own smaller scale Heaven's Mandate.[77]

Present-day conflicts in this huge region mainly revolve around maritime disputes in seas China's neighbours suspect Beijing of trying to turn into a Chinese lake. The problem arises from something called the Nine-Dash-Line, first devised with help from the US Navy, which loops around seas far from China's own lawful maritime zones in the manner of a droopy cow's tongue. It first appeared on Chinese maps in 1947 when the Nationalists were still in power, though from 2009 it also appeared inside the covers of all Chinese passports. It forms the basis for Chinese claims to 90 per cent of the coastal waters of Brunei, Malaysia, the Philippines and Vietnam. Parallel claims are also made to a cluster of islands in the seas between China and Japan, known as the Diaoyutai to the former and Senkakus to the latter, which the US had used for target practice. Since Japan annexed these uninhabited islands in 1895, Tokyo does not regard them as subject to any post-Second World War settlements.

These disputes have escalated in recent decades. They involve big fishing trawlers, vast oil rigs like Haiyeng Shiyou 981, and a much enlarged Chinese coastguard whose ships use water cannon to make their point. So do what some suspect are militarized fishermen, known as the 'little blue men' after the colour of their overalls. These clashes have sometimes been violent. In 1988 Chinese marines machine-gunned Vietnamese troops who were bravely standing up to their knees in the waters covering Johnson's Reef to assert their country's claim. Since 1999, equally courageous Filipino marines have garrisoned a rusting 100-metre-long hulk (a former tank transporter) called *BRP Sierra Madre* which was deliberately run aground on the Second Thomas Shoal of the Spratly Islands. Huddled in one habitable area of the orange wreck, they spend their time singing Karaoke songs, while hoping that their resupply vessels can thwart China's prowling coastguards. Moreover, as a commissioned Philippines naval ship (albeit one propped up with concrete blocks and listing to one side) Manila could theoretically invoke its US alliance were it to be stormed by something other than the weather.[78] Though these are the most fraught disputes, there are others even further afield. Indonesia has been drawn into these conflicts after aggressive Chinese patrolling of the southerly Natuna Islands, 2,500 kilometres from the coast of southern China. So far Malaysia, which needs Chinese help with its debts, has kept quiet after large Chinese fishing fleets appeared in its waters.[79]

While China accepts the UN Convention on the Law of the Sea (UNCLOS), which it signed and ratified in 1996, regarding foreign jurisdictions, it rejects this in its own neighbourhood, demanding that ships declare their presence in what China defines as its territorial waters. These include the new features China has built within its self-defined Exclusive Economic Zone. China rejects the right of Hague adjudicators to rule on this, or to argue that only land which is continuously inhabited and self-sustaining can be considered part of an EEZ. China simply reverted the dispute to its own Supreme Court in Beijing, while continuing to seek bilateral resolution of multiple maritime disputes.[80]

One reason why these disputes have intensified is the discovery of oil and gas reserves. Though the estimates vary, the East and South China seas have considerable offshore gas and oil reserves (maybe 60–100 million to 125 billion barrels of oil and between 25–56 billion and 14 trillion cubic metres of gas, respectively), all attractive if the alternatives are suppliers in the Middle East (Saudi Arabia and Iran) and Africa, notably Angola which supplies 13 per cent of Chinese imports. The Chinese state oil conglomerate CNOOC has invested heavily in deep-water mobile rigs like the HYSY-981, with a deck the size of a football pitch, which can operate in 3,000 metres of water and drill 12,000 metres below the seabed. Wherever this rig has appeared, trouble follows.

But these disputes are also about fishing. Apart from consuming a third of the world's seafood produce, China is a major fish processor, exporting to Europe, Japan, North America and Korea. China's inshore waters have been overfished and are polluted by sewage, run-off fertilizers and heavy metals. At the same time, state subsidies to fishermen are so generous, notably through allocating fuel simply according to the vessel's horse-power, that they can afford ever bigger trawlers whose builders are also subsidized. Where they venture, in huge flotillas, so do Chinese coastguard and navy escorts. The Administration of Fishery and Fishing Harbours Supervision may be part of the Ministry of Agriculture, but it also has 2,287 patrol vessels including a couple in the 2,500–4,000-ton range. The China Maritime Surveillance Agency also has its own fleet and planes, which double as navy reserve units. The Maritime Safety Administration of the Ministry of Transport and the Maritime Police, part of the People's Armed Police, have more ships. Judging by recent provocations, it is not at all clear that such forces would willingly avoid lethal incidents far out to sea or that they are under stringent central control. One major flashpoint is the islands in the Diaoyu/Senkaku group, like, Ishigaki, where large Chinese fishing fleets with coastguard escorts are a frequent presence. If the fishermen landed on the islands, then the Japanese would repel them with coastguards they have also been bolstering in recent years. Then there are the new 'features' in the South China Seas.[81]

China's creation of artificial islands on rocks and reefs in the Spratly Islands tells us something about both its future ambitions in its Asian neighbourhood and its scant regard for international law.

The foundations of a coral reef were torn up and killed by Chinese fishermen hunting giant clams. Geologists arrived who did heavy dynamic penetration tests with pile drivers. Ocean-going dredgers, supplied by the German-Dutch firm Vospa, equipped with a discotheque-like ball armed with teeth and connected to pipes used cut-and-suction to bring up gravel and sediment which was projected through the air into a ring of gravel so that sand replaced water. The filler materials were compacted with rollers and paved over, but not before the installation of underground water and fuel tanks. A lighthouse and a 3,000 metre-long runway followed, and then hardened aircraft hangars and high-frequency radar. Surface to air missiles and J-11B fighters follow. Fiery Cross even has a hospital, which, like the three lighthouses that have appeared in the Spratlys (one is 180 feet tall), is designed to advertise China's devotion to public common goods even as they restrict freedom of the seas. Although since 1989 China has been subject to a Western arms embargo, German firms like MTH-Friedrichshafen supply the silent diesel engines that enable Chinese submarines to stalk US carriers at alarming proximity.

Commencing in late 2013, it took about eighteen months to complete each artificial island. Since the cost of a simple break-water is anything between $400 and $200,000 per linear metre, the cost of these platforms must run into billions of dollars at a time when China's defence budget is an estimated $140–145 billion a year.

There are other costs, mainly ecological, as there have been as the mainland itself rapidly industrialized. The South China Seas contain 10 per cent of the world's fisheries resources. These reefs are important pit stops for mackerel and tuna that feed on smaller food fish sustained by micro-organisms living on the coral. Kill the coral and say goodbye to the bigger commercial fish. Fuel discharges and the like do not help either, along with plumes of sand and debris when the construction fails under marine stresses. If the intention is to provide fish protein for the huge urban populations of coastal China this is not a smart way of doing it in the long term.

China is not the only nation to convert semi-submerged

rocks and reefs into islands. Vietnam occupies about twenty-seven such features in the Spratlys, though Hanoi has only installed the odd concrete bunker. The Philippines has nine and Taiwan one, though none is militarized save for Filipino troops on board the *Sierra Madre*. The US itself also increased Johnston Atoll from nineteen hectares to 241, using it in the 1960s and 1970s to test nuclear bombs and to store Agent Orange.

But why this is being done is as important as how. Nationalism partly explains the desire to bring back under Beijing's control every feature within the Nine-Dash Line. Evidence of dual civil and military use of these new 'features' is also part of China's 'A2/AD strategy', or anti-access/area denial. Scarborough Shoal is only 140 miles as the crow flies from Manila, and it sits across routes used by the US Navy to reach bases in Japan and South Korea, not to mention access to Taiwan. These clashes are ones Beijing carefully calibrates, though there is always the risk of commanders at sea losing the plot. Observers have noted a certain seasonality to the tensions. They rise between March and June, and then abate from July to September when typhoons incline Beijing to negotiations, in the run-up to regional summits in October and November. This cycle is also known as *fang shou*, or squeezing and relaxing, like a python, in Beijing diplomatic circles. Being very large, when China throws its weight around, others respond in kind. Defence spending in South-East Asia has dramatically increased from $14.4 billion in 2000 to $40 billion in 2016.* While it seems inconceivable that great powers might go to war over reefs that are underwater for part of the time, one should not underestimate public opinion. Chinese economic growth has contributed

---

* Originally the Kuomintang map had eleven dash lines, but these were reduced to nine after China and Vietnam agreed their boundaries on the Gulf of Tonkin. The 1982 UN Convention on the Law of the Sea (UNCLOS) allows states sovereignty over a maximum of 12 nautical miles (22.22 km) over their territorial sea and jurisdiction over a further Economic Exclusion Zone up to 200 nautical miles (370.4 km) provided no other state faces it at a distance of less than 400 nautical miles. In that case, boundaries must be agreed. See Didier Cormorand, 'For a Fistful of Rocks', *Le Monde diplomatique*, July 2016, pp. 8–9, for the legal issues.

to chauvinism and national hubris. Moreover, should there be any serious domestic upheaval it might suit China's rulers to demonstrate their might, though that might not satisfy enraged Chinese netizens. Europe's patriotic leagues similarly contributed to heightened tensions before the July–August crisis of 1914, and it is not inconceivable that this could happen again half a world away.

Worrying though these clashes over artificial islands are, there is one consolation. The region is plagued by cyclones and typhoons. Winds of 115 mph and seas nineteen feet high are not uncommon. Even if coral atolls protect artificial islands, these are being constantly eroded by wave motion that upsets the erosion/growth cycle of the coral, and sea levels are also rising.

•

Its recent assertiveness has partially compromised China's self-proclaimed 'peaceful rise'. This implies that China's foreign policy is just, morally unimpeachable and principled (much the same claim as is routinely made by the US, of course). Any objections to what China does are not only wrong but also morally compromised. This stance may be counter-productive since it encourages countries with a history of mutual animosity, such as Japan and South Korea, to bury their hatchets so as to collectively thwart China. All with the connivance of a US which is not going to be easily extruded from primacy in the Western Pacific, even though it has affected a legalistic neutrality in the various maritime disputes. Beijing's assertiveness can also result in changes of policy in ways that do not favour China. In 1991 the Philippines government cancelled US leases on Subic Bay (used by the navy) and Clark Air Base. One reason was that US personnel regarded the Philippines as a giant whorehouse. Instead of capitalizing on this estrangement, Chinese provocations resulted from 2012 onwards in Manila inviting the Americans to return, though the maverick and murderous President Rodrigo Duterte is busily reversing this after Beijing laid on a lavish reception in late 2016.

If a large Chinese PLA Navy fleet appeared in the Gulf of Mexico or a Russian fleet off Cape Cod, these would rightly be regarded as 'provocations', yet the US expects China to simply acquiesce in US fleets operating in its maritime neighbourhood. Of course, Americans would respond that India does not claim the Indian Ocean or Mexico the Gulf of Mexico. The US is remarkably anxious at even the most minimal assertions of Chinese power or when such close allies (Britain, Israel and Saudi Arabia among them) join the AIIB or make their supplications in Beijing. China is feared even when its intentions are plainly defensive or part of internationally approved actions against such scourges as piracy. Though China has no overseas bases, the US press sounded very jittery when the PLA Navy began building a modest logistic facility at Obock in Djibouti, where the US military has a much larger footprint at Camp Lemonnier to strike at jihadists in and around the Horn of Africa. This former French Foreign Legion outpost is one of 662 overseas bases the Pentagon maintains in thirty-eight countries.*

As with any serious country, China ruminates deeply about its interactions with the world and external image, though about 85 per cent of the time of China's rulers is absorbed by purely domestic affairs. Every day they have to deal with some crisis: earthquakes, floods, food safety scandals, pollution, train derailments, or 'incidents' that the security services regard as serious threats to internal stability. Some call this the autism of great powers, for Russia and the US are similar in both this inward focus and obliviousness to the sensitivities of neighbours.

The main vehicle for the assertion of China's view of the world is the Shanghai Cooperation Organization, which was established in 2001. It includes China, Russia and the four Central Asian -stans, though Iran and Turkey are keen to join it. The aim is to combat the universal pretensions of Western liberalism, by asserting absolute state sovereignty. Inconveniences like Taiwan, Tibet

---

* China's generally applauded participation in anti-piracy operations off Somalia was one reason for the Obock base, the other being the $4 billion it is spending on a railway to link Djibouti with a landlocked Ethiopia, where Chinese shoe manufacturing firms have significant interests. Such anxieties also extend to Chinese private and state firms' involvement in sensitive nuclear or telecommunications industries in Australia, Britain or the US, and to huge Chinese land acquisitions and mines in respectively Latin America and Australia.

and Ukraine are airbrushed out by insisting they are not independent states at all. The SCO slyly uses Western concepts against the West, notably by insisting on 'civilizational diversity' and 'traditional values'. In the last case they do not mean the charming folkways of Inuit. The SCO has also adopted some of the means used in the West's own 'global war on terror' (GWOT) to get their hands on people suspected of 'terrorism'. Non-members like Cambodia, Malaysia, Nepal and Thailand all extradite people accused of terrorism. A nice touch was to clothe repatriated Uyghurs chained to Chinese policemen in hoods and Guantanamo-style jumpsuits when they were flown back to China.[82]

China's discourse on the outside world extends beyond the universities and think tanks to a nationalistic and sometimes xenophobic public that makes its sensitivity to slights clear online and sometimes on the streets. This can of itself result in a breakdown of public order. In 2012 Honda, Mazda, Panasonic and Toyota plants were attacked, along with Japanese-owned convenience stores, after a maritime clash, which then led to rioters burning police cars too as they intervened.[83] Should the government show lack of resolve in external disputes, then there is a risk that it could be held to account by a public opinion it can enrage almost like turning on a tap, for the regime has mobilized a small army of bloggers. These are the 'Angry Youth' or *Fen Qing*, whose ranks are swelling in China. Many of them have studied in the West, cooled on its way of life, and then joined the 80 per cent of Chinese students who elect to go home to a country they are justifiably proud of. Calcium tablets will be the least of it. It is often overlooked that these angry nationalists have a democratic history to draw on going back to the May Fourth movement in 1919, which combined nationalism with demands for reform, and therein lies a danger for the regime. Recent anti-Japanese protestors in Guangzhou carried placards saying, 'Turn fury into power. Desire political reform.' Much of their ire was directed at a state-controlled media that does not report honestly until a line is declared, but it could easily detonate against other areas of life in Communist China.[84]

Lazy historical analogies play their usual unhelpful role, just as they do in the Western world, where every second-rate dictator becomes another Hitler or Stalin. But China also has its own version of lazy thinking. It would be surprising if a venerable imperial tradition of hierarchy and tribute, as well as the ritual etiquette of handling barbarians, did not play a more or less conscious role in Chinese thought, along with much-revered strategic thinkers, most obviously Sun Tzu, whose 'wisdom' has limited applicability to the contemporary world except in the minds of businessmen who pick up his book at airports. They would be better advised to study Alain Peyrefitte's vivid account of how imperial China responded to Lord Macartney's culture and trade mission in 1793.[85]

Again, much of this may involve the regime's domestic image. Why else do Chinese rulers encourage a constant stream of leaders from minor Third World states to visit Beijing, or host such talking shops as the G20 summits except to impress on China's own people that their rulers are the masters of the universe?[86]

After the Mao era, China's foreign policy was clear enough. Perplexingly, there is no evidence that Deng Xiaoping ever said that China should practise *tao guang yang hui*, or 'hide your light and rise in obscurity', and not seek leadership, but 'do some things'. But after his successor Jiang Zemin used these words in 1998 this became official policy, and convenient to attribute retroactively to Deng nine years earlier.[*][87] From 2009 onwards this approach went into abeyance, perhaps because of a triumphalist response to the 2007–8 Western financial crisis and the mood of self-doubt that swept the US in the wake of Afghanistan and Iraq. It was time to leverage membership of international organizations, and actively promote China's values through a version of 'soft power'.

Although the top Chinese leadership determines foreign policy (the Foreign Ministry – like foreign ministries everywhere – is comparatively weightless) there is an enormous range of elite opinion about its goals and tone, ranging from aggressive

---

* Though Deng did say in 1992: 'We will only become a big political power if we keep a low profile and work hard for some years, and then we will have more weight in international affairs.'

nativism – amusingly from a claque called the 'Neo-Comms' – to an emphasis on multilateralism and soft power. Discussion in such circles seems relatively uninhibited, judging by very frank views on whether to let the Kim regime in Pyongyang fail, or at least whether China could welch on its treaty agreements, though when Deng Yuwen, the author of this suggestion, rashly published it in the *Financial Times,* he found himself teaching at the University of Nottingham rather than at the Central Party School in Beijing thereafter.[88] While China has considerable leverage over Pyongyang (90 per cent of North Korean trade is with China), it does not want to deal with a major refugee crisis, or to see US forces reappear on the Yalu River. That is why China always prefers negotiations and mild rebukes whenever that weird despotic regime undertakes a new nuclear provocation so as to extort more food aid. At the same time, Beijing has suppressed reporting of anything that might further damage views of North Korea among China's population, for example instances of North Korean soldiers crossing the border to rob and murder Chinese villagers for food. Many Chinese 'netizens' refer to 'Fatty Kim the Third', but if they knew that hungry North Korean troops were robbing their co-nationals, they might demand their own government respond robustly.[89]

Constant themes of China's foreign policy include 'anti-hegemonialism', meaning opposition to a world dominated by the US and its values, and a pervasive realism that requires China to amass hard power in an unpredictable and volatile world, even if this brings about hostile strategic permutations that a more benign rise would deflate. China categorically rejects evangelical human-rights moralism and liberal 'humanitarian' intervention too, though its participation in UN peacekeeping missions is accelerating. In 1999 this same creed resulted in five American precision bombs 'accidentally' destroying the Chinese Embassy in Belgrade and killing three Chinese reporters. Russia's annexation of Crimea and support for separatists in Ukraine put Beijing in a quandary, for it has separatists in Xinjiang, which was clumsily resolved by blaming the whole Ukrainian crisis on US support for colours revolutions it is seeking to foment in and around both Russia and China.[90]

Then there are disagreements about whether to focus on the major powers, the US, Russia and the German-dominated EU; Asia-Pacific; or the commodity-rich global South? There are also selective and idealistic multilateralists, who regard global engagement as either a useful tactic or an absolute goal, with China assuming responsibilities commensurate with its scale. Others, who correspond to American 'isolationists', regard all talk of 'responsibilities' as a cunning snare set by the US to mire China in the overseas miasmas that dragged down first the Soviets in Afghanistan and then the US in Iraq and Afghanistan. In the latter case though, the Chinese are uncertain whether, unlike Russia, the US is declining at all.

In the 1950s under Nehru, there was much hope on India's side of *Hindi-Chini bhai bhai*, or Indians and Chinese are brothers. The Chinese thought Nehru insufferably pretentious, while he felt he was treated like a supplicant at the court of Genghis Khan. But as India moved from non-alignment into the Soviet camp, while providing sanctuary to the Tibetan Dalai Lama, China and Pakistan moved closer together. It did not help that China and India share a vast border in the Himalayas that virtually invites disputes. China's crushing defeat of India in the brief 1962 war over Aksai Chin and Arunachal Pradesh sealed the deal. While from Beijing's point of view the advantage of the relationship with Islamabad was obvious, namely to keep India permanently distracted on its Western frontier, up to and including helping Islamabad develop a nuclear weapon to neutralize India's populous mass and strategic depth, China has never lived up to Pakistan's dreams of a security umbrella in repeat wars it lost against its neighbour. It is enough if the relationship prevents India from playing the larger role New Delhi, and the US, would like it to assume. Instead it is always dragged back to a hyphenated relationship with its troublesome neighbour. China is also determined to ensure that India never becomes a strategic rival. It regularly blocks New Delhi's claims to a permanent seat on the UN Security Council, and its application to join the Nuclear Suppliers Group which prevents the proliferation of nuclear weapons. Although India's volatile Prime Minister Narendra Modi talks the talk, he rarely walks the walk, with many of his populist gestures amounting to little, while India's fundamental problems, from caste to sanitation, go unaddressed beneath the flimflam about high-tech hub Bangalore and Bollywood.[91]

At the same time, Beijing invariably joins the US in curbing Pakistani military adventurism, as it did following the 'hybrid' incursion by Pakistani troops dressed as Kashmiri mujahedeen at Kargil in 1999. Since Nawaz Sharif was in Beijing, China's leaders were in hourly contact with the Clinton administration, which took over his management after he flew to Washington, until the crisis had de-escalated. Ideally China would like to keep India and Pakistan in a state of managed mutual mistrust, while it profits from economic ties with both.[92] Ironically, having found it useful for first the Soviet Union and then the US to be mired in Afghanistan (and in the latter case Pakistan), Beijing now finds itself being sucked into the space the US is vacating, if only to secure one of the major axes of China's future economic development. It is involved in multilateral attempts to manage Afghanistan after any US withdrawal, and it worries about the creeping Islamization of Pakistan's armed forces and intelligence services. This has led to far from theoretical discussions about how China would react if the US decided to send troops to secure Pakistan's nuclear weapons, having demonstrated its reach into Pakistan on 2 May 2011 at Abbottabad:

> Would we accept [this]? No. Are we as worried as the US about the security of Pakistan's nuclear weapons? No. Nuclear weapons are all they have, it's the single thing we're sure they'll protect. But China is willing to help Pakistan defend a Pakistani bomb. We won't help them protect an Islamic bomb. If it's under the control of a mullah, then everything changes. It's not unconditional.[93]

Any consideration of China's global stance must take into account hard military power, regularly on show in vast military parades. One in September 2015 to commemorate the end of the Second World War included tanks, missile launchers and 12,000 troops, though President Xi was careful to pledge that China 'would never seek hegemony or expansion. It will never inflict past suffering on any other nation.' He also announced a 300,000 reduction in troop numbers, a 13 per cent cut in the 2.3 million PLA total, that since 1997 has been reduced by 1 million. The brunt of the cuts have fallen on the army, whose numbers have been reduced to below one million for the first time in the PLA's history.[94] Whether decelerating growth will sustain the strikingly increased defence spending of recent years remains to be seen.

At present China spends between 1.3 and 2.1 per cent of GDP on defence (depending on what nominally civilian elements are counted) or roughly $216 billion, compared with 3.1 per cent of GDP by the US (or roughly $600 billion). For every dollar China spends on defence, the US spends $2.77, or the equivalent of the next seven largest military budgets combined. As it happens, prior to his first meeting with Trump, President Xi reduced the annual rate of increase in military spending from the double digits normal until 2016 to around 7 per cent, with most of this going on destroyers, frigates and submarines.[95] Much of the PLAN southern fleet is based at a twenty-five-square-kilometre complex called Yulin Naval Base on Hainan Island in southern China. Under construction since 2000, this consists of a man-made harbour wall in Yalong Bay, with hardened pens for China's nuclear submarines under a mountain. The base is also home to surface ships and is heavily defended with missile systems. The Northern Fleet has a similar base at Jianggezhuang.[96]

Perhaps to reassure the world, though the US was not reassured, China is bidding to take over the UN Department of Peacekeeping Operations, which France has headed for nearly two decades. China has a good case since it is the second-largest funder of peacekeeping operations, paying 10 per cent of the $8 billion budget, and deploys more blue helmets (2,639 at present) than the other four permanent Security Council members combined. They are currently deployed in the Democratic Republic of Congo, Darfur, Lebanon, Liberia, Mali and South Sudan. The only condition was that embedded UN human rights officials would disappear in an economy drive.[97] China has also been active in bending the UN Human Rights Council (UNHRC) to its will by shaping its agenda, excluding NGOs and insisting that the issue of human rights is kept out of interstate diplomacy.[98]

It is not so much mere numbers as the rapid modernization of PLA forces that worries China's neighbours and the US, even though China has not fought a modern war, and its men and their equipment remain untested in battle. Nevertheless, China has enough advanced military hardware to deter the US and its allies from rash actions, for 'provocation' is usually a two-way street. It should also be recalled that US alliances in Asia-Pacific are much less tight than those in Europe; that they involve vast areas of ocean; and that Japan is a complicating factor because of its imperialist depredations in the Second World War, as Shinzo Abe discovered after being photographed giving the thumbs-up in a fighter cockpit whose identification number (731) was the same as that of a wartime unit that killed Chinese and Korean prisoners with experimental bacteriological weapons.[99]

The last war China fought, against Vietnam in 1979, proved an involuntary wake-up call. In its brief duration it resembled the incursion into India twelve years earlier, but the Vietnamese were not Indians, and in fact did not bother to send their crack units to fight the Chinese. The invasion was intended to punish Vietnam for trying to topple the Pol Pot Khmer Rouge regime, and to prevent the Soviets from developing a second front in South Asia with the aid of Hanoi. A major invasion by 100,000 PLA troops across the Vietnamese northern border exposed multiple weaknesses, such as soldiers wearing sandals and signals sent by flag, as was the case in Korea nearly three decades earlier. Twenty-five thousand Chinese troops died fighting Vietnamese forces that were better armed and motivated. Scant attention is drawn to their graves just over the Chinese border.

The 1991 Gulf War showed the high-tech might of the American war machine at its most devastating, especially as the US was fighting so far away. Then, in 1995, the US interposed two carrier groups in the Taiwan Straits after Beijing had fired missiles into the sea to send a warning to Taipei. In 1999 the US sent long-range stealth bombers to hit Serb opponents, with the pilots famously back for baseball or bath-time with the kiddies, a demonstration repeated in Iraq and Afghanistan in 2001–3.

Ensuing US counter-insurgency campaigns there underlined the willingness of the American public to tolerate high numbers of casualties, though this mood changed. All of which has inclined the PLA to modernize and professionalize its forces, notably by reducing the army by half since 1985, but also, under Xi, rationalizing its command structures. There are five major theatre commands, with four covering the four points of the compass, and a fifth central command defending Beijing and providing a reserve to the other four.[100]

The main beneficiary has been the navy, or PLAN, which is in transition from a 'green-water' or littoral force to an ocean-going 'blue-water' fleet though it lacks the global capacity of the US Navy. China has about 300 warships (some of them very advanced) to the US's 289, with ten more submarines than the American navy by 2020. The fact that 90 per cent of China's imports and exports (including 40 per cent of its crude oil) travel by sea, largely through the Malacca Straits which narrow to 1.7 miles, explains why such a fleet is needed. So does the first island chain, consisting of Taiwan, Japan and the Philippines, which are within striking distance of China's coast. Some suspect that one reason for the island-building is to create the equivalent of the Malacca Straits in the South China Sea, bounded by Hainan and Woody Island in the west and the new artificial islands in the east, which are transforming an international waterway into a choke point with Chinese bases, radars, aircraft and ships to police it. But as yet, China's maritime military strength is insufficient for truly global projection of power. It does not yet possess a blue-water navy.

A decommissioned Soviet carrier, the *Riga*, purchased as the *Varyag* from independent Ukraine and renamed the *Liaoning*, is the jewel of the PLAN fleet, though more carriers will be built in China. One is undergoing sea trials and five more are planned, though it seems odd that China is investing in such power-projection vessels whose vulnerabilities its own latest missiles are designed to explore. Problems with planes landing and taking off from the existing carrier indicate the gap between aspirations and reality, for the *Liaoning* is not fit for global operations. In addition to the carrier, the PLAN has acquired twenty-two modern destroyers since 2000, two dozen frigates, four amphibious landing platforms, an amphibious helicopter assault ship, dozens of fast catamaran-hulled missile attack craft, and twenty-six diesel-electric and five nuclear-powered submarines. There are also few doubts about the potency of China's arsenal of supersonic missiles, or the agility of their most modern (Russian-supplied) combat aircraft, and capabilities in cyberspace and outer space. China has an active anti-satellite warfare programme. In 2007 the PLA shot down a low-orbiting meteorological satellite with a ballistic missile, a warning to the one opponent that relies so heavily on space-based assets. Parenthetically one should add that China is estimated to have 260 nuclear warheads (for comparative purposes the Israeli range is 100–200) though it can deliver multiple warheads to separate targets, which is a significant advance.

A series of acronyms disguise how China and the US might square up to each other. The PLA seeks A2/AD, or anti-access/area denial, which is designed to push US forces far away from China's first and second island chains, whether by using aircraft, mines, missiles or submarines to make the loss of a carrier possible. Ideally, the US would be forced to fight China from as far away as Guam. The US Navy subscribed, from 2009 onwards, to ASB, or Air-Sea Battle, which means the ability to retain freedom of action and operational access wherever it wants. In 2015 this was changed to the less provocative JAM-GC (pronounced jam, gee, cee) or Joint Concept for Access and Maneuver in the Global Commons, which stresses the partnerships with local allies and potential foes of China.

Yet there remain reasons to suppose that the worst may not happen despite the prognostications of academic alarmists whose cogitations are like a wet dream for the US Navy. With modern China, more than any other country, it is important to see its problems in historical perspective. What is striking is not the reduction in growth rates to a new 6 per cent norm that far exceeds anything achieved in the West, this or that corruption scandal, nor its inevitable impatience to exert itself internationally, so much as the fact that China has come so far so fast, and that its potential remains enormous. Just because aggregate data on China's economic numbers is imposing is no reason for anxiety, any more than was the case when the US economy sailed past those of Britain, France or Germany. Or for that matter that during the thousand years before the Industrial Revolution took off around 1800, when China was the world's largest economy too.

The fact remains that the average Chinese citizen would be happy with the average per capita GDP of a Greek, since it is two and a half times that of his or her own. Average annual disposable income for an urban Chinese is $4,000 and only $1,300 for the half of the population who still live in the Chinese countryside, 70 million of whom still eke out a livelihood on an annual income of Rmb 2,300, or $335. Moving millions of them each year to jerry-built apartment blocks in towns has not proved a success since their only skill is to grow and sell vegetables. Even the most squalid village is preferable to 'drinking the north-west wind', the Chinese expression for living on thin air.[101] Even if and when China becomes the world's largest economy, its people will still be one-quarter as wealthy as the average Westerner. Developed democracies have nothing to fear from an authoritarian capitalist model that does not travel well, and whose daily arbitrariness and injustices even fervent Western 'Panda-huggers' would not tolerate for five minutes.

Instead of imagining that China is imperial Germany 2.0, a wise response would be to abandon hypocritical moralism about human rights and accommodate China's desire for respect. Constantly depicting China as an often unspecified threat is dangerously irresponsible, as in response it may become one. For sure China has powerful armed forces, but the one-child policy has also made the Chinese very wary of sending 'the' son or daughter to die in combat. Since the US has made such a hash of many of its armed evangelical efforts to spread democracy, and has a President who has called for torture, why not see whether China can offer other, or even better, solutions? So far, Chinese mediation of major conflicts has had modest results, but that might not always remain the case in future. With Trump and Putin around, Xi seems like the only responsible adult in the room. Many in Europe think so already, and Washington should not bank on their support in any clash with China that Trump rather than Xi is likely to provoke. To the new US President we duly turn.

7

The USA: The Noisy Nation

In the seventy years since 1945, and under twelve US presidents, there was a consensus that America would furnish some of the services that individuals around the world expect from their national governments. This meant free trade as the underpinning of the global economic order, and alliance systems that defended Europe and East Asia with a US shield.[1] At no point were the American people explicitly asked whether they wanted to pay for this global government, let alone send their sons and daughters to die for it. Needy allies, enormous arms lobbies and other vested interests ensured, however, that they would.

Even when their Soviet strategic adversary imploded in 1991, inertia meant that America's global mission was redefined, rather than abandoned. In that year, the Soviet Union lost half of its population to fourteen independent successor states, leaving Russia economically shattered and with only 150 million people. The US and many of its allies, meanwhile, reaped a short-term peace dividend. Even after a 10 per cent defence cut, the US still had 1.4 million military personnel and a core defence spend of $400 billion, which under Bush Junior rose to $500 billion, with another $200 billion for fighting wars on top, making $700 billion at the height of the war in Iraq.

In 1991, 200,000 US troops remained deployed in Western Europe and north-east Asia, and US military spending continued to dwarf that of any possible combination of other powers, friendly or hostile.[2]

In the same year the US relinquished control of one of its most vital geo-strategic assets, though hardly anyone outside Central America noticed. Fearing that local nationalists might seize the huge zone straddling the Panama Canal, in 1977 Presidents Jimmy Carter and Omar Torrijos had signed a treaty which agreed to transfer sovereignty over the waterway and protection zone to Panama on 31 December 1999. The zone included Fort Sherman, the main American jungle warfare training base, a spy centre (Galeta Island), two air bases, a naval base, the HQ of Southern Command (Quarry Heights) and Fort Kobbe, home to the 193rd Infantry Brigade. All of this vanished in 2000. Two giant ports and a container terminal were sold to Hong Kong and Taiwanese operators.[3]

But there was a wider indirect consequence of the collapse of the Soviet Union (though not of communism in China) that attracts less notice than it should. The sole remaining superpower could act with relative impunity. No equivalent power stood behind any smaller country that the US might fight. This looming presence had made US involvement in Korea and Vietnam very costly. In both wars, Americans encountered local forces bolstered by Chinese troops and Soviet weapons, and in the last case the US lost to the plucky Vietnamese, ushering in a national mood of self-doubt.

Such bouts are recurrent in a country that is bipolar in the psychiatric sense, though it is not alone in that. There were earlier neurotic reactions to Sputnik in 1957, after Vietnam in the 1970s, and when Honda, Mitsubishi, Sony and Toyota seemed to carry the day in the 1980s. The most recent bout was in 2012, when China became the world's largest trading nation, with a $4 trillion cumulative trade surplus with America. Today, after the Great Recession and the Clinton–Bush–Obama wars of intervention, the US is in a similar mood. The continuities are more striking than those who claim that under George W. Bush the US became a rogue state would acknowledge. Similar fears are rife under the Trump presidency. But first we need to explore how US foreign policy is made and what the options include.

Although there are important checks on executive-branch authority, the person Americans elect as president has considerable powers regarding America's place in the world and they have the power to go to war before Congress declares it. All modern US presidents have had foreign policies that mix and match many diplomatic, military and strategic postures, from accommodation and engagement, via containment to armed intervention. Fewer presidents have retrenched from overseas commitments, though Dwight D. Eisenhower and Richard Nixon both did. Even the toughest are also not averse to scuttling away if they run into trouble. Content with firing a few huge shells from an old Second World War battleship, Ronald Reagan withdrew from Lebanon in February 1984 after 241 US servicemen (and 58 French paratroops) had been blown up in Beirut four months earlier.*

Presidents invariably shift the emphasis between policy options, usually with a keen eye on their own domestic political base as well as their legacy, meaning their bid for historic greatness. In a significant departure from the past emphasis on big-picture defence and containment, a younger generation of leaders were tantalized by the meliorist visions of what can be called a human-rights lobby (in the sense it is an interest group like any other, though it is considered bad form to say so). The parallel cultural attention given to the Holocaust – though the Allies had conspicuously not intervened even as they defeated Hitler – contributed to a 'never again' mood.[4]

This human-rights caucus dismissed traditional statecraft's insistence on absolute state sovereignty (as embodied in Article 2 of the UN Charter) as an outmoded fetish dating back to the Treaty of Westphalia. Some asked what was the point of America's enormous military power after the Soviet Union had disintegrated. President Clinton's UN Ambassador and later Secretary of State, Madeleine Albright, had the temerity to ask Chief of Staff Colin Powell: 'What's the point of having this superb military you're always talking about if we can't use it?'[5] Although the public did not share her evangelical zeal, it would not object to humanitarian interventions, provided the cost in American blood and treasure was minimal and there was no blowback on the homeland. An ongoing 'Military Revolution' with its emphasis on connectivity, speed and accuracy seemed to make that technically possible. Generals fretted about use it or lose it.

---

* I vividly recall Admiral Pennington, commander of the USS *New Jersey*, explaining over dinner one night in Virginia how the ship fired shells the size of a VW Beetle.

Clinton undertook successive humanitarian interventions in Somalia, Haiti, Bosnia and Kosovo, though the results invariably fell short of the grand ambitions. These were limited-liability operations, designed to demonstrate that the Democrats were not cowards, but also casualty averse so as to appease Republicans in Congress and a career military that did not like inconclusive messy little wars either.[6]

His more reckless successor, George W. Bush, became absorbed after 9/11 by transforming Afghanistan and Iraq into caricature democracies and pursuing terrorists around the globe as if he were the international sheriff. Cumulatively, these two Presidents put an end to any peace dividend, ushering in decades of indeterminate wars for ill-defined ends, which heightened suspicions of US motives. Eventually the American public would weary of the costs – especially as they coincided with the Great Recession and the job-destroying effects of globalization.

Under Clinton, Bush and, from January 2009, Barack Obama there was another change that warrants notice. Unlike in the Cold War, where the main theatres were Europe and Asia-Pacific, the strategic focus progressively shifted to the Greater Middle East, if one includes Afghanistan and Pakistan, technically in South Asia. This was partly because the region contained two-thirds of the world's most easily accessible oil reserves, vital not just to the US, though hydraulic fracking is changing that, but particularly to China, Japan and Europe. The multiple hatreds, rivalries and instabilities of the region also generated Islamist terrorism and the risk of rampant nuclear proliferation in countries with no record of restraint or the command and control systems that had prevented the US and USSR from destroying the northern hemisphere.

In this region the US had two allies – Israel and Turkey – though at various times Egypt, Iran and Iraq had governments sympathetic to the US. Saudi Arabia was a kind of loyal 'frenemy', responsible for global propagation of the sectarian dogmas on which Islamist terrorism thrived. Arguably, too many successive US administrations obsessed about a chimerical Arab–Israeli peace process as the magic key to inducing a durable change in the relationship between ordinary Arabs and their governments, while neglecting a host of other Middle Eastern conflicts and the sectarianism and tribalism bubbling beneath the region's gimcrack autocratic surface. When in 2011 the so-called Arab Spring threatened to promise an alternative future, it was rapidly extinguished. Deep darkness characterizes the region today and for the foreseeable future, with the real prospect of sectarian conflict and states disintegrating into statelets, some of which may be controlled by jihadists.

•

In 2008 the US elected a new leader who, like Eisenhower in 1952, said 'Enough' to promiscuous intervention, even though Eisenhower was no stranger to black ops and subversion. Barack Obama's overriding goal was to implement a liberal progressive and genuinely transformative domestic agenda, from which overseas military entanglements were an unwelcome distraction. The manner in which the escalation of troops in Vietnam in the 1960s derailed Lyndon Johnson's Great Society reforms was a stark reminder of the perils of overseas quagmires. Obama made clear the connection between domestic reform and foreign adventurism in a speech delivered as an Illinois state senator opposing the prospect of war with Iraq:

> What I am opposed to is the attempt by political hacks like Karl Rove (Bush's deputy chief of staff) to distract us from a rise in the uninsured, a rise in the poverty rate, a drop in the median income – to distract us from corporate scandals and a stock market that has just gone through the worst month since the Great Depression. That's what I'm opposed to.[7]

Obama was also the first Asia-Pacific African-American President, with time spent in Hawaii and Indonesia and family ties to Kenya. He was an outsider looking in. A highly articulate, cerebral figure, Obama believed his cosmopolitan odyssey uniquely equipped him to understand the cultural nuances of the vast Muslim world, even though Indonesia is atypical, while his relative youth meant he could transcend outmoded Cold War thinking.

Obama had a clear idea of what was not going to influence

him. He did not rate his three predecessors as much as he admired Ronald Reagan, whose overseas interventions were minimal. Obama was sceptical of an almost routinized resort to military force and, unlike Secretary of State Hillary Clinton, he was not a fan of ambitious politicized generals like David Petraeus.* But he also could and did disregard the urgings of some of the more zealous human-rights activists around him. He had to tell Samantha Power, the excitable Irish-American journalist and author of *A Problem from Hell: America and the Age of Genocide*, who joined his national security team, that he 'had read her book'.

Obama and his young inner circle were also bored by portentous lessons from an older generation that had been shaped by the Vietnam War, notably Ambassador Richard Holbrooke, who Obama kept at arm's length after a brief stint as special advisor on the Af–Pak issue.[8] Instead, the closest Obama had to a foreign policy guru was Brent Scowcroft, the 'realist' former Air Force general and National Security Advisor to Ford and Bush Senior. Obama also had the 'grim Irishmen', John Brennan, Denis McDonough and Tom Donilon, all hard as nails with no scruples about terrorists and who counterbalanced the 'planetary humanists' congregated around Hillary Clinton, though she was no softie either.

As a former member of the Senate Foreign Relations Committee, Obama was alive to the limitations of the Washington foreign policy Establishment. He believed, rightly, that it was permeated with fully bought Arab and Israeli lobbies and think tanks who wanted the simple-minded American giant to use his muscle in their local interests, something many ordinary Americans resent too. On the positive side he had a keen appreciation of transformational technologies, from hydraulic fracturing to social media, and realized where the hunger for human betterment was at its strongest (Africa, Asia-Pacific and Latin America) and at its weakest (the Middle East).[†]

---

* I had lunch in London with Petraeus (by then working for private equity group KKR) in 2014 with half a dozen others (all neocons), who seemed to think they were in the presence of George Marshall or Eisenhower.
† As Obama made clear in Jeffrey Goldberg's 'The Obama Doctrine', *Atlantic*

One does not have to be among Obama's critics to detect a degree of hubris, but he would not be alone in that. The rhetoric was too full of 'arcs of history' bending this way or that, and too much Martin Luther King and Reinhold Niebuhr, whose thoughts were from another age. A final problem was that what was undoubtedly 'transformational' in a US domestic context (the election of the first African-American President) did not mean he had the gift of 'transformation' in the wider world. He first offered accommodation and engagement, as if powerful words and emollient gestures could change the world, as his critics were quick to point out.

•

Severally, this meant a reset in relations with Russia and deeper cooperation with China; an open hand towards a hostile Iran and North Korea; an end to George W. Bush's war in Iraq and the darker shadows of the 'war on terror' such as rendition and torture; and a form of outreach to the peoples of the Muslim *umma* starting with promises of a more even-handed approach to the Israeli–Palestinian conflict than his predecessors had managed with the exception of the team of George Bush Senior and James Baker III.

But these diplomatic gambits had an overriding domestic agenda. Accommodation and retrenchment would not only promote global peace, giving the US as global policeman a well-earned respite, but also facilitate Obama's domestic reforms, notably the health-care provision epitomized by his Affordable Health Care for America Act. There were other important initiatives that often spoke meaningfully to the gender and identity constituencies that had enthusiastically supported him, perhaps less so to an unemployed car or steel worker in Michigan. For,

Monthly, April 2016, 'For Obama, Asia represents the future. Africa and Latin America, in his view, deserve far more US attention than they receive. Europe, about which he is unromantic, is a source of global stability that requires, to his occasional annoyance, American hand-holding. And the Middle East is a region to be avoided – one that, thanks to America's energy revolution, will soon be of negligible relevance to the US economy.'

like it or not, at some point in his presidency a visceral alienation grew between the parts of America that espoused different values. Within the conceited and self-referential bubble of the traditional mainstream media, metropolitan America lost sight of what many ordinary Americans felt or thought about epochal transformations, though they were also in plain sight on the streets of Boston, Chicago, New York and Los Angeles.

All foreign policy has to negotiate a fundamental economic and political context. Under Obama US defence spending fell from 4.9 per cent of GDP to 3.62 per cent, though this reflected wider federal budget cuts that a Republican House of Representatives insisted on as the national debt soared in the wake of the 2008 financial crisis that their own mania for deregulation had partly caused. It was also highly significant that for the first time in a Republican Party that under Eisenhower, Nixon, Ford, Reagan and George H. W. Bush had adhered to a consensual conservative internationalism, insurgent Tea Party fiscal hawks began to rival the GOP's traditional defence hawks.[9]

In effect, the 2011 Budget Control Act mandated $1 trillion of federal budget cuts, half of which were to come from the Pentagon's core $500 billion annual budget (live wars are separately funded), spread over ten years, but which would double to $1 trillion of defence cuts if a process of automatic 'sequestration' (meaning major cuts which took no account of each side's political pet causes) began, in the event of no agreed budget settlement.

This had implications for war-fighting strategy. The 2012 Defense Strategic Guidance abandoned the notion that the US should be capable of fighting major wars in two regions simultaneously, and that any conflict should be both swift and light-footed. Instead of a 50/50 split of navy vessels between the Atlantic and Pacific, in future the ratio would be 40/60 in favour of the Pacific, while large cuts were imposed on an army that had become over-invested in the theology of COIN or counter-insurgency warfare. Obama himself shifted the emphasis from soldiers play-acting as visiting anthropologists to predatory special-forces raids and fixed-wing and drone strikes. He dropped a lot of bombs too. In 2016, his final year in office, some 26,171 bombs fell in seven countries, including 24,287 in Iraq and Syria.[10] Unfortunately,

Obama did not visit the doctrine of offshore-balancing, under which US allies would be forced to defend themselves with the US hovering over the horizon to make critical interventions. Instead, the US still has many forward military assets in Europe and Asia-Pacific, and in 2017 has a new President who seethes about being ripped off by rich allies that refuse to pay for their own defence, a view Obama wholly shared, even though Trump does not understand the entire basis of NATO funding.

Since the early 1970s, the Democrats have suffered from seeming weak on national security, though in reality the Congressional party contains many hawks and some neocons remain registered Democrats. Obama was no retread of the hapless Jimmy Carter.

Obama's desire to curb military expenditure was combined with a greatly enhanced campaign of targeted assassination against Islamist terrorists, notably the killing of Osama bin Laden in May 2011 and incessant drone strikes in Pakistan and Afghanistan, with Libya, Somalia and Yemen added on. In the targeted-killing stakes, Bush was very much an amateur compared to Obama. Part of the thinking was a by-product of the human-rights industry's objections to extrajudicial rendition and extra-territorial detention: 'Once they're dead [the terrorists] then Human Rights Watch or Amnesty International doesn't bring a habeas corpus case against them [for illegal detention]'.[11]

Obama simultaneously drew a line under Bush's messy large-scale wars. His more delusional critics think he should have seen through the various 'surges', perhaps in ignorance of the fact that all such surges were geared to US electoral cycles, and that each of them merely signalled to America's opponents that Washington was not in Afghanistan or Iraq for the long haul. Republican historians were not above rewriting the history of the Vietnam War to make the 'if only we had sustained a late surge' argument. After calling time in Iraq in 2011, Obama withdrew the majority of US forces from Afghanistan a year later, though at the time of writing there are still 8,448 US troops in Afghanistan and another 5,262 in Iraq.[12]

Al Qaeda's regional affiliates were far from finished. The Taliban returned to fight another day, and few predicted the danger of Islamic State. A dogmatic refusal to subject US personnel to

Iraqi courts if they ran down a pedestrian or raped a girl meant that no helicopters or combat planes were in Iraq to neutralize ISIS's rampage. The President repeatedly claimed that his intelligence services missed the rise of ISIS. This was incorrect.

Testifying before the annual House and Senate intelligence committees' threat hearings in January and February 2013, General Michael Flynn, the recently fired director of the Defense Intelligence Agency, said the group would likely make a land grab before the end of the year. ISIS 'probably will attempt to take territory in Iraq and Syria to exhibit its strength in 2014'. Of course, the prediction was not hard to make. By then, Flynn noted, ISIS had taken the cities of Ramadi and Fallujah, and had demonstrated an 'ability to concurrently maintain multiple safe havens in Syria'.

The ability of ISIS to hold that territory will depend on its 'resources [and] local support, as well as the responses of [Iraqi security forces] and other opposition groups in Syria', Flynn added. He noted that while many Sunnis likely opposed ISIS, 'some Sunni tribes and insurgent groups appear willing to work tactically with [ISIS] as they share common anti-government goals'.

In November 2016 the maverick Flynn became Trump's National Security Advisor, only to be forced to resign in February 2017 after misleading Vice-President Pence about his contacts with the Russians.[13]

Obama initially dismissed ISIS as the 'jayvee team' of jihadism, meaning 'junior varsity' or high-school league, but went on to compare it with the Joker, the criminal mastermind who orchestrated all the gangs of Gotham City to cause mayhem in the 2008 Batman movie *The Dark Knight*.*

One of the demerits of Obama's critics – especially if they are British – is that they often know nothing about the regions where Obama's policies were most effective (though ignorance has never prevented anyone writing an op-ed column).† These

---

* 'These are men who had the city divided up. They were thugs, but there was a kind of order. Everyone had his turf. And then the Joker comes in and lights the whole city on fire. ISIL is the Joker. It has the capacity to set the whole region on fire. That's why we had to fight it.' Goldberg, 'The Obama Doctrine'.
† The British Foreign Secretary at time of writing, the clownish Boris John-

include Cuba and Colombia in the Caribbean and Latin America, or Burma, India, Indonesia, Malaysia and Vietnam in
Asia-Pacific and South Asia. India is now a US partner, after
years as a pink pro-Soviet non-aligned client, the generals have
grudgingly relinquished power in Burma, and after five decades
of war in which 220,000 people died, FARC have swopped guns
for the ballot in Colombia. US naval vessels also happily dock
in Cam Ranh Bay in Communist Vietnam, for the Asia-Pacific
'pivot' was more like a South-East Asia one, though it is the
Russians who are upgrading the facility.

•

Although the US remains the mightiest military power on the
planet, it faces two regional great-power competitors with the
strength to give the US a bloody nose before any conflict on
their doorsteps, which they or the Americans might provoke,
escalated into a nuclear exchange in which the US would lose
whole cities too.[14]

After the 2008 financial crisis, the US found it hard to have
a conflictual relationship with the power that owned $1 trillion
of US Treasuries. On the main stage, relations with Beijing,
Obama followed his predecessors in downplaying talk of human
rights in favour of securing Chinese international economic
cooperation and climatic meliorism. An American economist, C.
Fred Bergsten, coined the term 'G2' in 2005 to symbolize the
most important relationship on the planet.[15] Obama's relations
with Hu Jintao were not easy, and he hoped to build a better
relationship with President Xi. How to peacefully integrate a

---

son, made much of Obama's part-Kenyan ancestry, while the angry ex-metals
trader and former UKIP leader Nigel Farage described the President as a
'loathsome creature', an epithet many think is more apt a description of its
guffawing coiner. Both men illustrate the 'Anglospheric' delusion that Americans are just like 'us', though in Johnson's case he was a US citizen too until
he renounced it. Their country's insecurity was reflected in anxiety about
Obama relocating one of two busts of Churchill in the White House and his
inept intervention in the UK referendum on Europe. They would have had
apoplexy if they'd heard Obama say that pseudo-Churchillian rhetoric
had got Bush into a lot more trouble.

rising China's enormous economic might into the world order is the biggest task of any US President. Obama was less successful in persuading China to rein in, let alone depose, the insane regime in Pyongyang, which continued its idiosyncratic juggling of financial extortion and nuclear blackmail. But then he also did not regard North Korea as a top-tier threat, not least because the totalitarian Pyongyang 'hermit kingdom' has zero external appeal in its region, and no discernible allies except China, which cannot find a way of making Kim Jong-un disappear without major costs to itself.

Faced with China's forward naval policy in the East and South China Seas, Obama and Clinton launched the 'pivot' to Asia-Pacific. The White House rapidly rebranded it as 'strategic assurance'. This meant limited deployments of US Marines to Australia and Singapore, and a larger repositioning of naval assets, with serious attempts to mobilize an alliance network to contain China without being seen to do so, since cooperation with China in the management of the world economy is very much in US interests. Because of sheer geographical distance – between Australia, India, Indonesia, Vietnam, South Korea and Japan for example – this regional cooperation was much harder to effect than had been the case with the contiguous states in NATO. There were also virulent historic animosities, most involving the wartime role of imperial Japan, which the nationalist Abe government exacerbated rather than disowned, even as it sloughed off constitutional restraints on its forces actively assisting allies.

The President's policies towards Russia were more erratic, as if he resented even having to think about this country of 'merely regional' significance that happened to span nine time zones, a rare moment when emotion got the better of him. An ostentatious 'reset' of relations with the modern-seeming President Dmitri Medvedev in 2009 was ineptly handled. The transliteration of 'reset' into Cyrillic read 'overload' to Sergei Lavrov on the plastic device with a button that Hillary Clinton presented to the Russian Foreign Minister. The Russian word for 'reset' is the English 'reset'.

It made scant difference in Moscow that Obama decided to uncouple human rights concerns from security issues, since Hillary Clinton ratcheted them back up again. Owing to

Obama's longstanding interest in preventing nuclear proliferation, the New START agreement (2010/11–2021) limited nuclear
arsenals to 1,550 warheads and 700 intercontinental ballistic
missiles and heavy bombers on each side. But the combination of
Russian determination to assert itself in its self-styled 'Near
Abroad'– in Belarus, Georgia and Ukraine – and the ill-concealed
contempt of many leading Americans for Russia's economic
decay proved fatal to the relationship. Few of Obama's critics
recall that Russian intervention in Georgia in 2008 was at a time
when Bush had 100,000 troops in Iraq, though no one said at the
time that Bush was overly cautious for not waging war on behalf
of the bumptious Mikheil Saakashvili.

Once Putin was back in the saddle for his third presidential
term in 2012, the relationship rapidly deteriorated. He bitterly
resented that Medvedev had been duped into accepting regime
change in Libya the previous year. Cack-handed and murky EU
and US meddling in Ukraine before and after the ousting of
Russia's client Viktor Yanukovych in February 2014 resulted in
the hybrid response we have already examined. It may not be
bon ton to say so, but Ukraine is not a vital US interest, and the
Europeans were only making gestures regarding a corrupt klep-
tocracy that, as Dutch voters proved in 2016, few Europeans
actually want in the EU.*

Although Obama is a super-cool fellow, he was not good at
concealing withering contempt for leaders whose motives he could
not fathom if they departed from objective self-interest. He clearly
loathed the cocky Netanyahu almost from the word go, especially
after the latter lectured Obama in front of cameras in his own
Oval Office. As Bill Clinton said after a similar verbal battering,
Netanyahu seemed to forget who was the superpower and who
the midget. Netanyahu's speech to a joint session of Congress in
March 2015, in an attempt to stymie the deal with Iran, was
another low point in the Israeli's brazen attempts to dissolve a
bipartisan American approach to Middle East foreign policy.

Revenge is a dish best served cold. In the dying days of his

---

* In a 2016 referendum Dutch voters categorically rejected even the limited
association agreement that the EU negotiated with Ukraine.

administration, and after giving Israel a new ten-year, $38 billion defence package, Obama refused to exercise the US veto as a unanimous UN Security Council Resolution 2334 condemned Israeli settlement building in East Jerusalem and on the West Bank as an obstacle to a two-state solution that in reality has become hopeless. The resolution effectively absolved the Palestinian side from any responsibility for this being moribund. Claims that the US was saving Israel (and Netanyahu himself) from captivity by the Israeli far right seemed disingenuous. Already the lunatic fringe around President Trump seem to be arguing that Egypt should take Gaza, while Jordan should absorb whatever cantons are left to the Palestinians by the Israeli settlers, many fresh off the planes from Russia or the US. This is the view of the personal bankruptcy lawyer and friend of the settlers David Friedman, Trump's ambassador, although so far Trump has refrained from shifting his embassy from Tel Aviv to Jerusalem.[16]

Obama's open comparison of the steely Vladimir Putin to a truculent teenager was ill advised, especially since he also described him as always scrupulously polite and punctual. So far, EU and US sanctions have had a limited impact on the Russian economy, certainly not enough to budge Putin on Ukraine. In fact, the Russian leader doubled down by sending Russian forces into Syria, where Obama had announced and then not enforced red lines on President Assad's use of chemical munitions.

Whereas some thought Obama compromised US 'credibility' by issuing and then not acting on a threat, others point to doubts in the CIA about whether Assad had used sarin gas, while Chief of Staff Martin Dempsey warned that 70,000 US personnel would be required to take Assad's air defences down. The President himself believed the US was being lured into a trap of escalating involvement in Syria. In the event, Putin and Lavrov organized the removal of Assad's chemical munitions, that result being one of the few times that Israeli PM Netanyahu congratulated Obama (and the Russians) for introducing 'the one ray of light in a very dark region', for the Israelis fear a post-Assad fractured Syria (one canton being a 'jihadistan') more than they fear Assad. Although this may come as a shock to neocons critical of Obama, it was the Israelis who brokered the deal with the Russians (they have excellent relations with Putin) to remove these munitions.[17]

In effect, Obama has bequeathed his successor a series of negatives on Russia, derived from the old Cold War playbook he was so keen to reject. Expelling GRU assets in the US was a perfect way of putting Donald Trump in a bind. Either the new President would be Putin's friend, or he would have to observe Obama's last-minute executive order in punishing Russian interference in Western elections, a policy the vast majority of Republicans endorse. In the event, Trump's presidency is mired in an open-ended scandal about relations with Russian diplomats before and after he and his team entered the White House. Trump is likely to soon discover the truth of the old fable about the frog and the scorpion. 'It's in my nature,' Putin will explain after he's stung Trump. We will see how Trump survives the first double-cross he will undoubtedly experience, though how Putin deals with a friendly US (his regime is based on Western hostility) will be more fascinating to witness.

•

Only in one area did cooperation with the Russians survive the confrontation between Obama and Putin. Russia continued to be an active participant in the 5+1 nuclear negotiations with Iran, possibly the most significant element in Obama's foreign policy legacy. An opening gambit to repair thirty years of hostility since the 1979–80 US Embassy hostage crisis was rebuffed by Iran's leaders who a year into Obama's first term reinstalled President Ahmadinejad in fraudulent elections.

While desultory talks continued to halt Iran's attempts to acquire the wherewithal to build a nuclear weapon, Obama ratcheted up sanctions in conjunction with the EU and UN. Like President Bush, he realized that the Israelis would seek to force the US into completing whatever bombing Israel might undertake. It was fortuitous that the vainglorious Ahmadinejad allowed cameras to film him touring Natanz, where the personnel, computers and centrifuges were all on view. While Israeli proxies assassinated Iranian scientists and engineers, the CIA and NSA (plus Israel's Unit 8200 cyberwarfare experts) jointly developed malware (Operation Olympic Games) to disrupt Iran's scientific endeavours.

Despite the urgings to bomb Iran from elements of the Israeli government and their American lobby, Obama kept his nerve and allowed sanctions to do their worst. It helped that since 9/11, the US Treasury had developed sophisticated ways of tracking electronic payments, and that the US can fine errant British, French and Turkish banks large sums of money for helping Iran evade sanctions.

The election in June 2013 of President Hassan Rouhani signalled that Iran was under sufficient economic pressure to negotiate seriously. Oman hosted secret initial talks, for like Qatar it hedges its bets with Tehran. After moving to Geneva and Vienna, formal negotiations involving Wendy Sherman and John Kerry, Lavrov and Foreign Minister Zarif yielded the 2015 deal that retards Iran's nuclear programme for fifteen years while removing some of its crucial elements altogether. Very senior Israeli intelligence personnel regard that as a victory, especially if they are in retirement. The greatest living former US Secretary of State, James Baker III, thought that the deal was a good one, since 'no military solution could work in his assessment: an American strike would only generate more support among Iranians for the fundamentalist government, and an Israeli strike would neither be as effective nor carry American support'.[18] Obama hoped that this would be his Nixon-in-China moment. Given the nature of the Iranian regime, it seems highly improbable that any deeper rapprochement will ensue, though if the Machiavellian aim is actually to introduce a balance of terror in the region, Obama's policy may be more successful than it seems. Keeping the duplicitous Saudis and their Gulf hirelings in check seems eminently sensible, though the British government and arms companies who need Gulf money would not agree. Nor would Trump, who has concluded what may be the world's biggest arms deal with the Saudis.

Time and again, Obama was sucked back into a region that many thought cost more trouble than it was worth, especially as domestic hydraulic fracturing greatly reduced US consumption of imported oil and natural gas on his watch. The US is now a net gas exporter, while tight oil production has reduced import dependency from 65 per cent to 40 per cent in a development that is in its technological infancy. The Saudis, who Obama rightly never trusted, tried and failed to bankrupt the US shale industry by increasing oil production, though as of December 2016 they have thought better of this strategy.

But sentiment sometimes got the better of a realist President whose 'no drama Obama' manner was compared to the *Star Trek*'s Mr Spock. During the 2011 Arab Spring, Obama succumbed to the heady, bliss-to-be-alive mood among excitable CNN, ITN and BBC reporters as they mistook events on central public squares for the mood of entire countries. This proved to be disastrously wrong-headed. It was also deeply hypocritical, since Obama did not move a muscle in support of pro-democracy protestors in tiny Bahrain, home to the US Fifth Fleet and a client of the Saudis.

As the stirring events in Tunisia spread to Egypt, Obama dropped the longstanding US-backed autocrat Hosni Mubarak. He then stood back as the highly organized Muslim Brotherhood, rather than young pro-democracy protestors on Cairo's Tahrir Square, capitalized on the temporary fright that overcame the Egyptian military. The President miscalculated that the Brotherhood's Freedom and Justice Party had undergone the same evolution as its Turkish Justice and Development Party 'prototype' under Erdoğan, though in 2016 that proved illusory in Turkey too.

No sooner had the US tried to accommodate the Islamist regime of President Morsi than it was overthrown in a 'democratic coup' and replaced by the thinly disguised military regime of former general and President Abdul Fatah al-Sisi. The alacrity with which Obama dropped Mubarak shocked many Arab allies in the region, while underlining the constancy of Vladimir Putin, who could point to his loyalty to Syria's embattled President Assad by way of proof. After a brief hiatus in which the US refused to supply advanced weapons to the new regime in Cairo, relations were gradually restored, though not before Moscow had joined Washington as a must-visit venue for all the region's leaders.

Only if Obama had mentally written off the entire Middle East as not being worth the bones of a single US Marine could that stance be justified. The truth is that he had. The region was regressing to primary loyalties to clan, tribe and religious sect under regimes whose oil wealth made democratic accountability otiose. When people got the vote, they often elected the Brotherhood or its surrogates like Hamas in Gaza, proving it was likely to be a case of 'one man, one vote, one time'. It is worth hearing this damning verdict on the Middle East from the man himself, in which Obama contrasts these regressive societies with bigger parts of the world where future hope lies:

'You have countries [in the Middle East] that are failing to provide prosperity and opportunity for their people. You've got a violent, extremist ideology, or ideologies, that are turbocharged through social media. You've got countries that have very few civic traditions, so that as autocratic regimes start fraying, the only organizing principles are sectarian . . . Contrast that with Southeast Asia, which still has huge problems – enormous poverty, corruption – but is filled with striving, ambitious, energetic people who are every single day scratching and clawing to build businesses and get education and find jobs and build infrastructure. The contrast is pretty stark.' In Asia, as well as in Latin America and Africa, Obama says, he sees young people yearning for self-improvement, modernity, education, and material wealth. 'They are not thinking about how to kill Americans.'[19]

But instead of sticking with the logical consequences of what this stance entailed, Obama was susceptible to the passionate moral outrage of his inner circle. At home these included Secretary of State Clinton, UN Ambassador Susan Rice and the ubiquitous Samantha Power. It was also hard to dissuade the British and French when they stepped up to the plate and assumed the lead role in preventing Libya's Colonel Gaddafi from killing his opponents in Benghazi. The principle of R2P was to be vindicated, despite the experience of Iraq, and a general ignorance about the complexities of Libya. After US cruise missiles obliterated Gaddafi's air defences, the British, French and Italians spent eight months bombing the regime's forces, thereby clearing the way for total anarchy and the entrance of

ISIS into Libya. Urged to act by the peacock action-man philosopher Bernhard-Henri Lévy, Cameron and Sarkozy had no plans
for Libya's future either beyond photo ops and seemed remarkably insouciant as the country plunged into chaos. An estimated
seven to ten times more Libyans died in the aftermath of Western military intervention than even theoretically Gaddafi might
have slaughtered in Benghazi.[20]

With three rival governments and thousands of heavily
armed militias, the country descended into the chaos it remains
in today: a source of men and arms for jihadists throughout the
Sahel states and an open door for sub-Saharan African migrants
to Italy. Along with migrants through the Aegean, this contributed to a populist nationalist political resurgence in Europe.
There was an ominous coda involving the US. On 11 September
2012 fighters from the Ansar al-Sharia group attacked a US compound in Benghazi and murdered US Ambassador Christopher
Stevens and three of his American bodyguards. Disgracefully, the
Obama administration initially claimed that a demonstration
about a ranting anti-Muslim video in the US had got out of hand.
One might legitimately ask what the point of intervening in
Libya had been, other than to demonstrate the ongoing relevance
of a legal principle that failed to protect Ambassador Stevens.

While the Arab Spring was still in its expansionary phase,
Obama also called for President Bashar al-Assad to depart, after
Assad responded to peaceful protests with armed force and mass
arrests. This was a turnaround from the general hope that many
Western governments had invested in Bashar, the London-trained
ophthalmologist who by accident had succeeded his father
Hafez. Such hobbies as assembling a large collection of the suggestive postcards working women leave in London telephone
kiosks had to go by the wayside as the young doctor underwent
a crash course in ruling Syria. Bashar proved as adept at 'Hama
Rules' (the city where Hafez killed thousands) as his father.
Again, TV reports which should be required to carry the equivalent of a health warning for urging the public and politicians
to 'do something' clouded any strategic perspective.

The rapidly multiplying complexities of the Syrian civil war,
which involved Sunni and Shia, Iran, Lebanon, the Gulf Arabs,

Turkey and eventually Russia, militated against any direct US involvement, though limited arms and training were afforded by the CIA to identifiable 'moderate' Syrian rebels. These were a diminishing band since more radical elements like Jabhat al-Nusra grew stronger through their suicidal prowess on the urban battlefields. Leaving what remained of the 'moderate' rebels in the lurch, Obama focused on the fight back against ISIS, a fight that eventually meant the return of low thousands of US troops to advise the Iraqis and Kurds. Syria is not a top-tier US strategic concern, but by making it a Russian one the US can relax and watch as Putin's (and Iran's and Hizbollah's) far more modest resources are drained in a conflict which they cannot resolve either even though they have co-opted Turkey to their team.* This view had already been aired by Denis McDonough in June 2013 when only Iran and Hizbollah were in play.[21]

•

Like most men of my age, as a child in the 1960s I read comic books in which Second World War commandos like Captain Hurricane in the *Valiant* figured prominently. I see similar images still, except they are the graphics quality newspapers use to illustrate special forces' acts of derring-do in dusty places. Shadowy figures enter villages with guns that flash yellow and orange, all that is missing are bubbles reading 'Take that, Anwar!' or 'SPPPPLAAAAT!!!!' when a drone hits its target, which are indeed called 'bug splats' by their operators.

Nowadays I am a confirmed defence sceptic and a fiscal hawk, sceptical about generals and spies and with a strong aversion to mawkish sentimentality about the military too. My respect for diplomats has significantly risen. Every military excursion should be carefully planned and costed, with precise information on which parallel civilian budgetary items – say education and health – are going to be cut to pay for it, while

* One doubts Iranians are 'smiling', as some British commentators have claimed without any supporting evidence, since the IRGC have lost at least a thousand men in the conflict as well as the lives of their Shia militia allies. Maybe that is why the Americans are not rushing to remove them from Syria.

shoving the costs onto future generations. There should also be a full explanation of how such excursions are going to make any of us safer, including every contingency that could go wrong, for the burden of proof does not rest with those of us who oppose most interventions. This is not some radical pipedream but a reversion to the post-Vietnam doctrine associated with General Creighton Abrahams and Reagan's Defense Secretary Caspar Weinberger, after whom it is named.[22]

It is often wrongly assumed that military people are badly paid, but this is not true of the US. As the US Congressional Budget Office revealed, once one factors in education and health benefits (which include 7 million family members) the average total compensation of all 2.2 million service persons is $115,500 a year. Retention or re-enlistment bonuses for experienced NCOs or specialists like bomb disposal experts, navy divers and fire controlmen are in the $45,000 to $150,000 range, the latter for special forces. This largesse also reflects the fact that these people can earn far more working for private military contractors DynCorp and KBR Inc.

While compensation is the really big cost, there are others. Weapons platforms, for example. Donald Trump has already rightly said he would 'take a look' at the spiralling costs of the F-35 Joint Strike Fighter. He should perhaps also take a look at the Lockheed Martin F-22 Raptor.

The F-22 was designed in the 1980s to fight an enemy that disappeared in the 1990s. The F-22 is a fifth-generation air-superiority stealth fighter, which can cruise at supersonic Mach 1.5 speed without using afterburners. It is armed with air-to-air and air-to-ground missiles and can carry 'smart' JDAM bombs too. So far, the Pentagon has spent $65.3 billion on acquiring 187 Raptors, costing on average $349 million per plane, though the through-life costs (maintenance and integrating new technologies) rise to $670 million apiece. Each aircraft costs $68,000 per hour to fly.

As the production costs spiral, the number of planes purchased sinks. Meanwhile, much older aircraft have to be kept flying, at great expense, to cover a range of missions a much smaller number of F-22s cannot perform, such as shooting up a Toyota truck in

Iraq which a slow A-10 Warthog with a seven-barrelled Gatling-type cannon in the nose can do much more effectively.

Many Congressmen had a stake in the F-22. They include representatives from Georgia, where the airframe is assembled, and Texas, where the tail and wings are built by Boeing, and Connecticut, where the engines are made by Pratt & Whitney, but there are also a thousand subcontractors involved, in forty-one states. Production of the JSF has also been artfully spread around the country for similar reasons.

Production of the Raptor was halted in 2008, before any had flown in combat and only a year after the first squadrons were declared fully operational. There had been some teething difficulties, like pilots suffering from hypoxia after problems with the oxygen supply. The F-22 was banned from Afghanistan and Iraq with a kind of leaves-on-the-rails excuse. If it flew low it was vulnerable to random small-arms fire; if it bombed from high altitude it would cause collateral casualties.

Finally, in 2015, F-22s did see limited action. A couple of these planes simply had to make an appearance for Syrian jets bombing Kurdish fighters to scarper, and then in 2016 a pair of Raptors actually bombed an ISIS command-and-control facility. The most advanced fighter aircraft in the world was more than a match for a terrorist organization whose most sophisticated air weapon is a hobby drone anyone can buy via Amazon.[23]

One major problem for the Raptor is that China and Russia do not possess fighters worthy of its attentions, though they are catching up with the J-16 and Su-PAK FA T-50, Russia's first stealth jet. While the Raptor can pick off these opponents over the horizon, it would be vulnerable to swarming should China and Russia have more basic cheaper planes to throw away once the Raptor ran out of missiles. The Chinese and Russians have also invested heavily in multilayered anti-aircraft radars and missiles, the former operating at multiple frequencies, which can detect 'stealth' aircraft like the Raptor if caught by low-frequency radar, especially if the F-22s have non-stealthy drop-off fuel tanks attached that enlarge its profile. Despite the fact that the Raptor's computer systems and avionics are now out of date, hope springs eternal among big defence contractors. Although altering the design of existing stealth aircraft is virtually impossible, the latest idea is to upgrade such planes with high-energy lasers, though any kind of airborne testing will not be until at least 2021, and so far no one has succeeded in miniaturizing such weapons to put them on board a combat fighter. This tale of ill-conceived programmes and profligacy could be repeated for the F-35 JSF, the V-22 Osprey tilt rotor helicopter, submarines and littoral combat ships and the USS *Ronald Reagan*, which was contracted at about $2 billion but came in costing $4.3 billion. It could be applied to British or German procurement too. It's comic in ways that beefy Captain Hurricane never was.[24]

•

Sometimes one gets the impression that the US has more professional foreign policy experts than voters interested in foreign affairs. That would be unfair to most of the Americans I have met, including while living in three very different US states. The percentage of Americans who want to 'stay out of world affairs' is now at the highest since 1974, though a majority still believe in international engagement, but nowadays a greater proportion of these anti-interventionists are Republicans than Democrats by a 64–60 per cent margin. Interestingly, a growing number of Americans (59 per cent) think the US should work within the UN structure to deal with international problems. This makes a nonsense of those neocons like the choleric former ambassador John Bolton, who would like to slice several floors off the UN headquarters in New York. President Trump seems not to have made his mind up about the UN, whether to reform or relinquish it. Reluctance to use non-defensive, optional, military force is up too. Seven in ten Americans think the wars in Iraq and Afghanistan were not worth the cost. Only 17 per cent would send US troops to Syria and only 30 per cent intervene in Ukraine in the event of a Russian invasion. Less than one in five regard democracy promotion as a 'very important goal'.[25]

Over the course of the Obama presidency three streams of strategic thought on the Republican side became clear, as the party's old establishment complacently presumed that their voters were content to be led like sheep in this area if no other.

This breakdown of consensus was aided by the fact that in the US system there is no equivalent to the British leader of the opposition. Donald Trump will have to decide which of these tendencies wins, though in all likelihood they will simply vie for his (limited) attention, with none of them emerging completely victorious. All imagine their man has won, which explains why they are busy projecting onto Trump (who is too busy to have ever read a book) what they want him to be.

If he is true to his word in 'Making America Great Again', a large part of his considerable entrepreneurial energy will be devoted to domestic reconstruction. Voices he should listen to, like Richard Haass, think domestic repair is the precondition for America to act effectively on the global stage. If Trump has any sense, he may leave the tricky stuff to others. Foreign and national security strategy is not for amateurs, Tweeters or the easily bored. A very bad development came when Trump lopped 29 per cent off the budget of the State Department with the acquiescence of Secretary Tillerson.[26]

The first grouping, conservative anti-interventionists, seek to eschew foreign wars, cut military spending, reduce alliance obligations and radically prune US overseas commitments. They see war as an excuse for the stealthy expansion of government and taxation, as indeed it always has been throughout history. It is wrong to say they are 'isolationists' since they believe in diplomatic and economic engagement with America's competitors, friends and foes alike. In the pre-war period many in this camp wished to turn away from a fractious Europe to what they imagined would soon be a democratic and Christian China, a magnet for so many US Protestant missionaries, under a victorious and Methodist Chiang Kai-shek.[27] Their adherents included the boy Gore Vidal, the Yale student Gerald Ford, the architect Frank Lloyd Wright and Walt Disney. Nor is it correct to say that they were anti-Semites, though support from the pro-Nazi aviator Charles Lindbergh was the kiss of death after he blamed the British, the Jews and Roosevelt for dragging the US into war shortly before Pearl Harbor and Hitler's declaration of war. China also fell to Mao eight years later.[28]

The fact that they got these big calls wrong does not invali-

date their criticisms of foreign entanglements, criticisms that
have venerable origins in the likes of John Quincy Adams refusing to go forth to slay monsters as well as George Washington's
farewell address. This is Republican Senator Robert Taft months
before American entry into war in 1941:

> [Interventionists] seem to contemplate an Anglo-American
> alliance to perpetually rule the world. Frankly, the American
> people don't want to rule the world, and we are not
> equipped to do it. Such imperialism is wholly foreign to our
> ideals of democracy and freedom ... We may think we are
> better than other peoples, more equipped to rule, but will
> they think so?[29]

There was a moral as well as a pragmatic realism about such a
stance, and one entirely rooted in America's unique story.[30]

Big in the German, Scandinavian and Irish-American Midwest-
ern heartlands before the Second World War, this tendency was all
but wiped out after General Dwight Eisenhower beat Taft to the
Republican nomination in the 1952 presidential election. The
course was set fair for decades of Republican internationalism and
big defence spending to support it, even though Eisenhower himself reminded people in 1953 of the lost domestic civil opportunity
costs of big defence items like destroyers and bombers, and warned
in January 1961 as he left office of a ramifying 'military-industrial
and congressional complex' as the initial draft averred.[31]

In recent years, anti-interventionists have effected a major
comeback, whether in their libertarian or 'palaeoconservative'
guises, though neither Pat Buchanan nor father-and-son senat-
orial team Ron and Rand Paul were successfully nominated
as GOP candidate. Ron Paul had some of Bernie Sanders' truth-
telling grandfather appeal to the young; his son Rand, a Kentucky
physician turned Senator, is an effective operator and a man of
deep conviction. Disgracefully, Senator John McCain, a man who
seems to want to bomb the whole world, used the McCarthyite
Red-baiting charge that his Republican *colleague* Senator Paul
was 'working for Vladimir Putin' when Paul opposed admitting
Montenegro to NATO.[32] This resurgence of Republican anti-
interventionism is a reaction to more than a decade of costly wars

of choice for uncertain goals supported by the likes of McCain. These drained the US Treasury rather than the swamps in which terrorism thrived. It is also rooted in deep concern for how liberty is being constrained by an over-mighty executive and unaccountable intelligence agencies who with the connivance of technology giants spy on electronic communications. Some worry that an all-professional military, hatched in academies for warriors, is contributing to *militarism*, not least as so many former generals seem to be meddling in politics or TV punditry for the more raucous networks like the ghastly Fox News channel.[33]

Anti-interventionists have acquired an institutional presence, in Washington's Cato Institute and, from 2002, in the excellent *American Conservative* magazine (which even the *Guardian* now identifies as 'interesting', though some of us discovered that years ago). The equally interesting 'Nixonian realist' *National Interest* also often publishes articles broadly sympathetic to radical strategic retrenchment and is refreshingly sceptical about alliances with the Gulf Arabs. There are also a number of leading intellectuals, like (Colonel) Andrew Bacevich and Daniel Larison, who have criticized the entire interventionist project and the rise of US militarism with an astuteness that is often far sharper than the 'it's all about oil' clichés of the American or European left. Revealingly, this view is virtually debarred from 'quality' British newspapers, with the exception of Matthew Parris, even though many British readers agree with him, in favour of neocons who never miss a dirty trick to cement their dominance.

Supposing, too, that trade in physical goods is becoming obsolescent? Should more production go local because of technological advances, for example through 3D printing or 'hydroponic agriculture', then the need for a huge military to secure supply and arterial transport routes will be diminished, with no need for an expeditionary land army at all.[34]

President Trump's scepticism about America's freeloading allies and profligate defence spending is indebted to this anti-interventionist stream. Since relatively few Americans could be persuaded that Hillary Clinton was a hawkish warmonger tantalized by the top brass, or Obama an international assassin, it is probably just as well that Rand Paul was knocked out of the 2016 Republican contest which Trump won, though as a powerfully placed Senator, Paul will make the new administration answer for anything it gets wrong.

As evidenced by the mass refusal of the Republican foreign policy establishment to serve Trump, many remain conservative internationalists, but of a more hawkish cast of mind than Democrat multilateralist idealists. They believe in America's international leadership, but differ on whether to achieve this through or despite multilateral organizations like the UN. These Republicans are sceptical about the promotion of democracy, foreign aid, human rights and such threats as climate change. They favour large-scale defence spending to support a US forward presence in Europe, Asia-Pacific and the Middle East, arguing that withdrawal would lead to chaos and the massive costs of returning again. This is a major bloc of opinion inside the Republican Party, and until recently it was assumed most Republican voters were in sympathy with this camp. By dint of their expertise alone, Trump will have difficulty not including some of this group in his administration. Their views are therefore likely to count.

This brings us to the camp most congruent with Trump's own temperament and outlook. These are conservative Jacksonian nationalists, who admire the seventh US President Andrew 'Old Hickory' Jackson for combining a Jeffersonian scepticism about futile foreign involvements with a robust defence of American national interests. They believe in Teddy Roosevelt's big stick and far fewer carrots, have no interest in foreign aid, human rights, multilateral organizations, democracy-promotion and nation-building. They regard all US allies as free riders on 'Uncle Sucker'. Unlike Jackson himself, they have little regard for questions of 'honour', taking an entirely transactional view of international relations.[35]

Jacksonians regard the US as a nation-state and not as a congeries of Enlightenment ideals which the rest of the world admires. They regard their own elites as kleptocrats and traitors, who are in league with immigrants and needy minorities, with political correctness as a shield that stops anyone airing such a view of what is afoot. As self-styled core Americans they have a right to jobs and guns, with perhaps the National Rifle Association as the only true embodiment of Jacksonianism in American public life. They have a live-and-let-live approach to other countries, but if you pick a fight, they will be as ferocious as their Scots-Irish 'hillbilly' ancestors, the main fighting and dying class of person. There is also more than a whiff of white identity politics. Some of the main political players hail from the Roman Catholic right, which may account for the odour of anti-Semitism evident in the energized alternative-right Breitbart online crowd, though they also admire Israel. Since Trump is a strong supporter of the Netanyahu Likud government, which should not be confused with Israel, let alone a largely liberal and Democrat-supporting US Jewish community, some Jews seem prepared to downplay such striking facts as one of his advisers wearing a wartime Hungarian fascist symbol in his buttonhole.[36] But then in July 2017 Netanyahu himself ignored nasty anti-Semitic posters that had proliferated in Hungary at the government's instigation on the bizarre grounds that their wire-pulling 'hate figure', George Soros, was also an 'enemy' of Israel for supporting NGOs sympathetic to the Palestinians. Establishing a French version of Breitbart seemed to be about ensuring Marine Le Pen became next President of France, an event surely fraught with peril for Jews as well as Muslims in France. Above all, many of these nationalists feel, for this is an instinct rather than an ideology, that their white identity is threatened by changing American demography and globalization. They are not alone in that since their French equivalents fear *le grand remplacement* and the Germans what the Nazis called *Umvolkung*, in other words, waking up and seeing more black and brown faces. They are not sympathetic to free trade, Islam or Hispanic immigration, being ignorant, as they are, that the Spanish were in North and South America before Anglo-Saxons.[37]

Effectively these are hard-line national security hawks and believers in untrammelled American sovereignty. Unlike the internationalists they are sceptical towards globalization and free trade. Their support is strongest among white working-class Americans, in the Midwest, Greater Appalachia, the South and parts of the Californian/Florida Sunbelt, and among many Tea Party supporters. These views are often shared by members of the US armed forces, who want to operate as 'warriors' with a clear mandate to win wars, rather than according to the vagaries of political calculation. Having openly gay people in the armed forces is not, it is fair to say, their big priority. The intelligence agencies are cooler towards this line since they know a thing or two about foreign countries. Under Trump both the CIA and FBI are under suspicion as a kind of enemy within and not just because of their dogged investigations of his links with Russia.

Conceivably the strong military they want might never be used, since they are also hostile to futile interventions, especially in the Middle East, where they see no friends beyond Israel. Although these nationalist views have been articulated by the likes of Michele Bachmann, Ted Cruz, Rick Perry and Sarah Palin, it took an outside and outsized media celebrity, Donald Trump, to reap the full benefits of the angry, insurgent mood of this constituency, which unlike the other two has little or no organizational or intellectual base. Social media and internet news services have provided an electronic amplifier or echo chamber in which such people can psych themselves into a rage, a means of argumentation that is also easily infiltrated by the 'alternative right' (aka 'alt-right') and overt neo-Nazis, anti-Semites and racists. The revolting Fox News has numerous over-paid Irish-American thugs who bawl out much the same message in return for salaries of up to $26 million a year. The impress of the modern postmodern academy, which these people otherwise despise, enables them to claim that they are being 'ironic' when they endorse 'post-truth' euphemisms for brazen lies and like Trump attack the respectable press for propagating 'fake news'.

•

Commentators were divided on whether in November 2016 the US had elected Lady Gaga, Silvio Berlusconi or Mussolini. The performance-artist analogy is obvious about a president who said: 'I play to people's fantasies.' The Berlusconi comparison is more apposite, including the alleged Mafia connections, media intimidation, dodgy lawyers and rampant sexism. Trump heads a vast organization with casinos, hotels, TV production, modelling, and Trump-licensed products, like the $10,800 gold-and-diamond bracelet Ivanka Trump flashed as a CBS interview was shown. The fact that the eighty-year-old Italian is having a comeback from reputational ruination should caution against treating Trump (or indeed Berlusconi himself) as a right-on comedian's joke. Italian journalists say that they know how to deal with someone like Trump after their years of covering Berlusconi.[38] Conflicts of interest are rife in the Trump administration, and they start at the very top. Will visiting foreign delegations stay at the Trump Hotel on Pennsylvania Avenue? Can the Department of Justice fine Deutsche Bank, the President's own largest creditor? What about the Chinese bank which leases a floor in New York's Trump Tower? Or the Iranian-linked bank in Azerbaijan which bailed out one of his projects in Baku?

Trump is surely a modern manifestation of a populism that has venerable roots in the US. Populism there has historically included those who wanted to curb the power of robber-baron elites. It was strong among early trades unionists like the Knights of Labor, as well as farmers in the Midwest and South who were charged ruinous interest rates by banks and then ripped off by railway monopolies charging extortionate freight rates amidst an agricultural depression. Some populists espoused a kind of raucous civic nationalism of the little folk or, secondly, a more racial nativism that regarded immigrants as the tools of the same powerful vested interests. The first type was exemplified by the Populist or People's Party, whose platforms were subsequently hijacked by the Democrat nominee William Jennings Bryan in the 1890s. The second strain was represented by the anti-immigrant Know-Nothing Party in the 1860s, or the Workingmen's Party of California (1877) which identified an insidious alliance of powerful interests (railway barons) and the Chinese immigrant labour they imported to crush militant railway unions. One result was the self-explanatory 1882 Chinese Exclusion Act.[39] Some have claimed that *The Wonderful Wizard of Oz*, published in 1900, was a populist fable, about bimetallism (Dorothy's shoes are silver in the book) and with the East and West witches being the banks and railway barons. The twentieth century saw episodic populist political eruptions. The Louisiana Governor Huey Long pressured Roosevelt to go further with income redistribution, though FDR did not cap wealth, and later Governor George Wallace of Alabama combined a social conscience with segregation. The cost of running for high office meant that subsequent populists were like billionaire Ross Perot (1992) or insiders turned outsiders like Pat Buchanan (1996). Both were John the Baptists preparing the way for Trump in 2016.[40]

The often-made comparison of Trump with Benito Mussolini owes much to theories derived from Theodore Adorno, and then rewarmed in 1960 by the American sociologist Seymour Martin Lipset, about how 'authoritarian personalities' are drawn to communism and fascism, for liberals are never like that.[41] The analogy with fascism is based on the Mussolini/Trump fusion (or 'triangulated') form of politics, an ability to bully and manipulate the hostile media, and the intense bonding of a charismatic leader with his followers. Of course, Bill Clinton and Tony Blair tried to triangulate ideology too, and, though not a journalist like Mussolini, Blair and his crony Peter Mandelson had Alastair Campbell for the bullying. As for charisma, well, Mussolini shares that with Ronald Reagan, Bill Clinton and Barack Obama. Finally, Bernie Sanders was not murdered (the fate of Giacomo Matteotti in 1924) and rich Californian farmers did not hire thugs to pour castor oil down the throats of Mexican field workers.

So no, Trump is not Mussolini and talk of fascism is melodramatic and unimaginative. Unlike many of his supporters he is not even anti-liberal, and being anti-liberal is not the same as being anti-democratic. Most contemporary 'populists' want democracy to work better on behalf of ordinary people, rather than elites who manipulate it, not to abolish it in favour of totalitarian leader-worship. The times we live in are not like the 1930s, and our institutions are much more robust than they were in Germany, Italy and other states that succumbed to fascism. Lest that sound too Panglossian, a major war, of course, could change all that in the loser nations.[42]

But let's put the historical analogies, the jokes and the snobbish outrage of high-class liberal wordsmiths to one side. Donald Trump is very much a product of our times, whose rage became a running dialogue with enough voters angry about globalization. He won in 2016 by fusing anti-interventionism, protectionism and hostility to immigration. Few commentators noticed how massively globalization had shaken the kaleidoscope of history to Trump's advantage, despite his own dismal record of bankruptcies, stiffing small contractors and exploiting undocumented immigrant labour, like the mystery Polish wrecking crew who hammered down New York's Bonwit Teller department store amidst clouds of asbestos dust, only to find their wages withheld by the subcontractors.[43]

The disruptive effects of the Great Recession were visible in both political parties, especially since 55 per cent of Americans wrongly thought that America was still in recession even though it was not in November 2016. Blue-collar whites and a not inconsiderable number of Hispanics – who aren't all Mexican – voted for Trump, whose supporters were clearly not just feral red-neck 'deplorables'.

This gaffe, describing half of Trump's 62 million voters, was delivered by Hillary Clinton at an LGBT fundraiser in New York's Cipriani Hotel with Barbra Streisand as the entertainment where the candidate over-relaxed among the likeminded.[44] As Mitt Romney discovered in 2012, and Clinton herself did on election day, it is not a good idea to insult the electorate. Calling Trump supporters 'racists' sits oddly with the fact that in 2008 and 2012 Barack Obama won in Ohio, Pennsylvania, Michigan and Wisconsin, often in deindustrialized and heavily white working-class counties.[45]

But being crudely insulted by wealthy Democrats was only part of a story that also includes progressive websites with advice on 'How to talk to your uncle at Thanksgiving dinner'.[46] Thanks to a lot of instant anthropology, we know quite a bit about Trump's supporters, even though we should object that plenty of the 'metropolitan liberal elite' also have tough back stories, however inbred and nepotistic that elite has become, monopolizing even those areas of popular culture that briefly afforded the working class a chance of mobility.

Globalization wrought havoc on blue-collar America. Between 2001 and 2013, 65,000 factories closed and five million jobs disappeared, bringing misery to many millions more dependants. China's factory workforce grew by 14.1 million over the same period, churning out the cheaper clothing, furniture, shoes and toys which Americans consumed. A large number of working-class Americans know that they were superfluous to requirements, since between 1965 and 2015 the percentage of such males outside the workforce rose from 10 per cent to 22 per cent. They are not unemployed and they do not have wives and children; they have ceased to work, opting to spend their days and nights sleeping or watching screens filled with reality TV or pornography (a fine distinction) for hours every day. Their ranks include many of the 20 million convicted felons, of whom over 5 million have been in prison, for the US uses community supervision and fines a lot too, and prisoners are released. At present one in six of the 25–54 male age cohort fall into the men-without-work demographic. Some experts (such as Larry Summers) estimate that by 2050 it will be a third of them as the technological change described so well by Tyler Cowen renders them completely superfluous. The political class has no idea what to do about this impending problem.[47]

In the decayed steel town of Youngstown in Ohio, the 1930–60 population of 170,000 sank to 60,000 after the mills closed. The alternatives to the blast furnaces were jobs that people had to calibrate with non-cash benefits, and extra-legal ducking and diving, so as to avoid the fate of the poor whites in the town's trailer park. The parallel demise of the Mafia meant that black gangs took over crime in the decayed town centre too.[48] These people's dignity was on the line, and in many cases their lives too. Mortality rates for middle-aged whites increased from 1999 onwards, the only demographic for whom this was true: cirrhosis of the liver (+50 per cent since 1999), suicide (+78 per cent) and alcohol or drug poisoning (+323 per cent). The US has undergone a horrific rise in deaths from opioids like Carfentinal (used to tranquillize elephants), Fentanyl and Oxycontin, which are mixed with heroin to achieve greater highs from which there is no return. According to the US National Center for Health Statistics, for the first time since 1993 life expectancy in the general population declined, as a result of Alzheimer's, diabetes, heart disease and strokes, though smoking-related cancers fell.[49]

•

It took Team Clinton eighty-five attempts to come up with the anodyne slogan 'Stronger Together', which did not have the resonance of 'Make America Great Again' (a phrase originally used by Ronald Reagan). The Democrats also outspent Trump three to one in order to lose. Trump knew how to suck media attention to himself, while President Putin ensured that Clinton got the wrong kind of publicity through well-timed leaks. The former FBI Director James Comey (he was sacked in May 2017) obliged too by stopping and then restarting investigations into Clinton's use of email. But we can make too much of foreign manipulation or the entirely separate FBI investigation into Hillary's emails. Clinton lost, or rather won the popular vote by 2 million but decisively lost in the Electoral College.

Clinton failed to assemble the usual Democrat coalition, as Obama succeeded in doing when he fought off Mitt Romney in 2012. Six million people who had voted for Obama in 2012 voted for Trump rather than Clinton four years later. Her attempts to mobilize a multicultural army tanked because in the upper Midwest Electoral College states that mattered, the opponents of multiculturalism were able to counter-mobilize more effectively than in the past. They resented Clinton as a celebrity dynast from an entitled elite that graduates, marries, inherits and interns its way into the good life, while holding those they cannot patronize in contempt. Democrat explanations for those who were not on message were revealing and tortuous. If Trump voters were black (8 per cent) or Hispanic (27 per cent), they must be misogynist. If they were white, they must be racist rather than men and women voting about stagnant wages or being dumped on the wrong side of the radiant future Clinton's Silicon Valley friends envisage, which threatens to be a techno pastiche of the Soviet version circa 1920. How many people actually want their fridge to tell them it is time to order the milk or light bulbs that work on voice command?[50]

A few key statistics sum up what happened in 2016. African-Americans voted 88:8 for Clinton over Trump, but 93:6 for Obama versus Romney. Hispanics voted 65:29 for Clinton versus Trump, but 71:27 for Obama over Romney. Asian-Americans voted 65:29 for Clinton versus Trump, but 71:27 for

Obama versus Romney. Millennials voted 55:37 for Clinton versus Trump, but 60:37 for Obama against Romney. As Bernie Sanders said, the line 'I'm a woman! Vote for me!' did not work with women under fifty, and nor did it for just under half of Sanders's supporters who said they would not nominate Clinton. Clinton gained only one point (54:42) among women, who were 52 per cent of the electorate, whereas Obama scored 55:44 among women in his battle with Romney. Education played a part here. White women favoured Trump by 53:43, a figure which rose to 67:28 if such women lacked a college degree, though Trump only lost narrowly among that degree-holding demographic too (51:45).[51]

•

In the end, working- and middle-class Americans voted for a billionaire with weird hair and a foul tongue, because billionaires are not part of their universe, except on TV or in magazines like *Lifestyles of the Rich and Famous*. Though Trump was born with a silver shovel in his little mouth, it is important that he grew up in the outer New York borough of Queens, where he assumed the rough manner of the locals, learning his trade in a city collapsing around the inhabitants' heads from his millionaire father who was so mean he would pick up individual nails to hand back to the careless carpenters.[52]

Many Americans detest New York and its brusque, rapid-fire inhabitants, but they overlooked Trump's provenance as the quintessential New York wheeler-dealer. Possibly his most winning line on the campaign trail was: 'I've been greedy. I'm a businessman . . . take, take, take. Now I'm going to be greedy for the United States,' which was greeted with wild cheers. They will not be the first people to be deluded that the talents it requires to turn round a business – basically shedding extraneous costs – can simply be generalized into government.[53]

By contrast, as Joan Williams has sharply written, the working and middle classes have experience aplenty of professionals: physicians are quacks, lawyers are shysters, journalists are liars and professors are phonies. Not forgetting teachers who object to fried chicken wings rather than a banana in your kid's lunch box. Seeing a very rich man dismissing a bossy privileged woman – schoolmarm to the nation in a pants suit – as 'crooked Hillary' was priceless. 'Lock her up!' they roared. They laughed at 'lying Ted' (Cruz), 'Little Marco' (Rubio) and 'low energy Jeb' (Bush) too, for these were like pygmies next to the larger-than-life Donald.[54]

Many Trump supporters were also fed up with decades of enforced deference towards minority groups policed by despotic political correctness, and which rewarded the tribunes of the victim groups with cultural and political power. In an epidemic of very timely police shootings of black suspects, these people empathized with the black and white working-class police making split-second judgements on the streets, rather than with the rent-a-mob Black Lives Matter that gathered in memory of the victims. They did not like being told what to feel either, by the likes of Christiane Amanpour of CNN about Syrian refugees – the US equivalent of Lindsey Hilsum on Channel 4 or Orla Guerin and Fergal Keane on the BBC. 'I'm a good person,' one Trump supporter explained to Berkeley sociologist Arlie Hochschild, 'and I *don't* feel sorry for them.' Suddenly not having to manage one's emotional and verbal responses was liberating, and Trump was the liberator in chief, with his off-colour remarks about menstruation and grabbing women 'by the pussy' as revealed on an old tape. When he boasted of not paying taxes, he was on the home stretch

Trump's supporters see themselves as victims too, a minority without the powerful attributes of the alternative organized ones for blacks and gays, save on such focused issues as abortion and guns. They feel left behind, left out and very precarious in their small towns and on the dark land. Their self-pity was well described in J. D. Vance's *Hillbilly Elegy*:

> We talk about the value of hard work but tell ourselves that the reason we are not working is some perceived unfairness: Obama shut down the coal mines, or all the jobs went to the Chinese. These are the lies we tell ourselves to solve the cognitive dissonance – the broken connection between the world we see and the values we preach.[55]

In rural Wisconsin, researchers found much resentment against city dwellers in Madison and Milwaukee, who did not seem to work as hard as farmers and loggers who were being denied their fair share of what their taxes paid for, including the vibrantly progressive University of Wisconsin at Madison. This was *despite* the fact that any new high-tech jobs are likely to be spun off from its technology faculty. Sometimes this animus had racial undertones too, with Obama allegedly benefiting 'his' people through affirmative action programmes. A final unremarked tendency has been the quiet exodus of professional people like bankers and lawyers from small towns to big cities, with a corresponding diminution of precisely those classes who generally support a Masonic or Rotary Club type civic consciousness. America's political crisis is one involving not just manufacturing but also shifts in where professionals choose to ply their trades.[56]

In her fine book *Strangers in Their Own Land*, Arlie Hochschild gets to the guts of how the neglected classes feel, by asking us to imagine a long line of people ascending a hill, over whose brow lies the American Dream. You are in the middle. You are white, male, middle-aged, Christian, and may have a college degree, though it wasn't from MIT or Stanford. Right at the back are blacks, who you don't dislike or know, but you don't want to look back there too much. The line is no longer moving forwards as it did in your parents' and grandparents' days and it is hot standing in the sun. It is going backwards. Your income is static, when it is not falling, and only if you have a job, which technological change and immigration have brought into question. Your children might be replaced by Mexicans and robots (though in reality more Mexicans are going home, where work in car-assembly or white-goods plants is plentiful, than are arriving). Something as essential as a new car is beyond your reach, partly thanks to emissions and safety features that have pushed up the cost, and the pious middle class disapprove of your older gas-guzzler too.

Then there are the line-cutters or queue-jumpers. African-American beneficiaries of affirmative action, women, migrants and public-sector workers who don't seem to work much – except to make your life difficult – and who have fat pensions.

And then you start to think how this came about. With the Internet separating Einstein from complete madness with one click of a mouse, one might alight on any absurd explanation for what was *really* going on. How did Barack and Michelle Obama get so far in life? Why are they waving to the line-cutters? Is he even an American? Is he a Christian? Didn't he remove his watch during Ramadan? He's the president of all the line-cutters rather than you. Since the mainstream media won't entertain much of this (except Fox News, of course) you rely on more marginal sources to tell the truth, which usually involves some elite conspiracy to do you down.[57]

These folks are also despised and they know it. Since post-modernism displaced Marxism, there are few remaining licensed prejudices in the developed world other than against 'chavs' and 'white trash', where the usual pious hypersensitivity goes out of the window. I can recall the faux commiserations when I moved from a visiting chair in New Jersey to one in southern Virginia, though no one offered new white sheets to sport under the fiery Southern Cross. Ironically, of course, my new southern colleagues were entirely card-carrying Democrats of an old-fashioned kind.[58]

This worldview predominates in universities and colleges. The gerontocratic oligarchy which runs them – most American humanities academics do not get tenure until they are over forty and then cling on until they fade out in the professorial Alzheimer's club – could easily be dismissed as a branch of the Blue elite that flies over the Red states and the separate nations that reside in them.* That Blue elite lives longer too, than those in Louisiana, Mississippi and Tennessee, where life expectancy is more akin to Nicaragua, not least because of dismal industrial pollution.[59]

Religion played its part too, even though Trump is tone deaf to it and can cite nothing from the Bible he claims to read each day, which sits oddly with his parallel boast that he has never read a book. Only the staunchly Republican Mormons of Arizona and Utah were sufficiently repelled by Trump's crude comments about women to substantially reduce the vote that

---

* I owe my insights into the Alzheimer's clubs to an emeritus surgeon friend who established the one at Yale.

they gave Bush and Romney in earlier contests. Fifteen million Southern Baptists (the largest Protestant denomination) ignored a leadership which, in their eyes, had gone soft on social issues to win upper-middle-class backing, to support Trump.

America's largest Christian denomination underwent a political sea change after October 2016, when Clinton led Trump by 57 per cent to 33 per cent among Roman Catholics. Whereas Catholics had voted for Obama by margins of 9 per cent in 2008 and 2 per cent in 2012, in 2016 52 per cent of them backed the nominally Presbyterian Trump and 45 per cent the Methodist Clinton after Trump came out in the third presidential debate strongly against abortion. As Pope Francis subsequently noted, a worrying number of American Catholics were also susceptible to Steve Bannon's brand of 'apocalyptic geopolitics' that had more usually appealed to Evangelicals. Even American Hindus rallied to Trump, impressed by his detestation of Islam, and before he said that (Muslim) Pakistanis were 'great people'.[60]

The ultimate, flawed, insider Democrat challenger Hillary failed to bridge the gap between the Party's ascendant left wing under Bernie Sanders and her husband Bill's own moderate followers. Lack of trust in Clinton herself was important, with 68 per cent of voters polled saying she was untrustworthy.[61] She was so convinced of her own virtue that she could not grasp that the remorseless money-grabbing left a bad smell. Her redemptive platitudes seemed a poor cover for the pay-to-play greed she and her husband practised via their Foundation after he left the White House. Emiratis and Saudis don't give money for the fun of it but to buy face time on the clock.

Nomination of outsiders is nothing new in US politics – think, for example, of Republican Barry Goldwater in 1964 and George McGovern in 1972 for the Democrats – but these were also Senators who would not capsize the boat entirely and, besides, they lost the elections. Was something more systemic at fault, a general corruption of the political ecosystem?

Some argue that the end of the Cold War lowered people's perceptions of what was at stake, so that they could afford to be more critical of their leaders. Whatever the reason, Presidents Clinton, Bush, Obama and now Trump have had their legitimacy questioned, though only in Obama's case did this outrageously extend to where he was born. A rackety voting system (2000) and the Electoral College/popular vote counting did not help to erase ambiguity either. Each of these presidents was viewed in quasi-demonic terms by their opponents, with discourse led by shouters in Fox News and partisan websites where every crazy view could pass back and forth among the online commentators like noise in an echo chamber.[62]

For years the US political system has been increasingly dysfunctional at the federal level. Where once there was considerable overlap between liberal Republicans and conservative Democrats, now the blue and red colour bands were distinct with no purple patch in the middle. While the role of big money is nothing new in the US, nowadays it is anonymous and corporate. Hugely powerful vested interests and their lobby groups can push or veto what they like or dislike, in a system where every Congressman comes up for re-election every two years and needs their money for campaigns.

After 2010 the insurgent Republican Tea Party did not help smooth government either, especially after Republicans in Congress felt obliged to pander to it. It does not have a single philosophy, but support for tax-paying 'makers' over entitled 'takers' is a good summation, with bankers and speculators lumped in the class of parasites. 'You are not entitled to what I have earned,' read one bumper sticker. Seventy per cent of Tea Party supporters disapproved of 'compromise' per se, and a similar percentage had a bad opinion of the Republican leadership in Congress. Instead, the Tea Party favoured the downright nasty (Ted Cruz) or backwoods ignoramuses like Sarah Palin, who had her admirers in the UK too.* Since 2015, this tendency within the Republican Party has organized itself as the Freedom Caucus, which may have three dozen or so members in Congress.

Small wonder that in trying to appease these insurgents, the Republicans ceased to do deals with like-minded Democrats in what were no longer smoke-filled rooms, as in this moralizing atmosphere all the customary methods that greased the cogs of

---

* Notably neocon Melanie Phillips in *Standpoint* magazine.

the business of government were abandoned. The traditional system of party discipline, of professional 'pols' and party managers house-training insurgents and mavericks, from when they were selected to their steady ascent of the committee system, went into desuetude. The Establishment was no longer safe. The Tea Party's Dave Brat ousted House Majority Leader Eric Cantor in June 2014 for tempering his stance while in office, and then in late 2015 they took the scalp of House Speaker John Boehner too with the new Freedom Caucus to the fore. In 2013 they were prepared to see the US go over the cliff and default on its sovereign debt rather than raise the government's debt ceiling.[63]

Government dysfunction fed the anger of voters, and enabled committed extremists to hijack primaries. Once elected, their ideologue candidates created more governmental dysfunction, which enabled someone as thoroughly despised by his own colleagues as Ted Cruz to then make a bid for the presidency. Even this nasty piece of work failed, after he was 'monstered' by Trump as 'Lying Ted'. For one result of an increased number of 'politiphobes' (i.e. voters and non-voters who think all politicians are lying and venal) was to maximize the contrasting appeal of 'ENSIDs' or 'empathetic, non-self-interested decision-makers'. This was ideal for self-made candidates with no political track record to tear apart, no fixed party allegiance, but with the celebrity and money to gain notoriety and to pay the colossal costs of running for the highest office. The independent Ross Perot was a harbinger of this trend in 1992 and 1996, but he did not have the sulphurous allure of Donald Trump, reality TV star.[64]

Many Trump supporters liked him *because* both parties hated him in equal measure. It was surely telling that both George H. W. Bush and his son 'W' said they would not vote for Trump, deploring his threat to abolish NAFTA. After creating his 'movement', Trump captured the hostile Republican GOP, which resembled a very dilapidated mansion, occupied by dysfunctional families. Effectively Trump added the GOP to his huge property portfolio with a hostile takeover. Relations between the GOP Establishment and Trump were lousy. He is against free trade and supports Social Security and Medicare. But just as the Republicans hoped they were improving their image among minorities, not least with immigration reform, along came Trump fulminating about Mexican rapists and accusing the 'Mexican' judge Gonzalo Curiel (born in Indiana) of being biased in a case involving Trump University which the nominee quickly settled. But he is on trend, in an international sense, with his vow to build an awesome wall, even if Texan geography and ranchers' rights preclude it.[65]

Trump was like Prince Uncharming kissing a dormant princess, though she was a he with an unshaven face and a baseball cap bearing the legend 'Make America Great'. The off-colour remarks and indulgence of wild conspiracy theories merely lent a loud voice to what his supporters would have liked to say, and what they believed about how the world really works. There was no taboo he would not breach. Consider the sheer audacity of his dismissal of the hawkish octogenarian Senator John McCain as a 'loser' because this war hero had been captured and tortured by the Vietnamese. That takes nerve in a country that is easily mawkish about veterans, and from a man who, like many sons of privilege, found mystery ailments to avoid the draft.

During the nomination debates Trump's hapless Republican rivals stood on stage with one hand tied behind their backs, while he drew viewers into his own bubble, mixing abuse with regular 'awesomes', 'beautifuls', 'fantastics' and 'huges' from his limited repertory of superlatives. This inhibition was because of his rivals' fear of alienating a party base that no longer believes in their mantra of trickle-down economics, and which is angry about the export of manufacturing jobs and colossal income inequalities. Like many populists, Trump had a licence to say irresponsible and untrue things, partly because as they shuddered in faux horror the elite were sure he could never get into office, where he has continued to speak in his accustomed fashion, even to an audience of perplexed Boy Scouts and their shocked parents. Of course, things are not as bleak as this suggests, not least because Texas remains as the 'Americans' America', a new frontier based on no taxes and minimal services, where jobs are plentiful, including those created by fracking. As an outsider Trump also enjoyed a 'huge' advantage against opponents who themselves had gridlocked the system to the brink of US default on its debts. The 'Master Builder' would make America work again, though he merely leases his name on buildings nowadays.

Trump won *because* of the disdain of the GOP establishment and without the support of Wall Street, which backed its friend Mrs Clinton, who had made more from a couple of speeches to Goldman Sachs than many earn in a lifetime. Although his buccaneering business empire sailed on a sea of debt, Trump was very good at suggesting he didn't need other people's money and the strings attached. As a very rich man, and an entertainer who generated his own publicity, Trump did not even bother to attend rival casino owner Sheldon Adelson's Republican beauty contest to solicit funding in return for ironclad support for Israel. 'I don't need your money,' Trump quipped to an uncomfortable audience at a Jewish Republican fundraising event. How strange to see the *Wall Street Journal* criticizing Trump's statist interventions at Carrier before he was even in the White House. 'Big Spender' is a term of abuse and not a song in their lexicon.

•

The President's administration picks were in line with the recent habit of packing the cabinet with the super-rich, though Team Trump are billionaires. Trump is the CEO, though at least one chief executive has wryly commented that any board or shareholders would have forced Trump out of his job already. Commerce Secretary Wilbur Ross is an asset-stripper who helped bail out Trump's own casinos. The Goldman Sachs scion-cum-Hollywood film producer, Treasury Secretary Steven Mnuchin, is a long-time Democrat supporter who would have been as at home in an Obama or Clinton administration. Many of these figures are protectionists, who regard trade deficits as a zero-sum game, with Mnuchin opposing even a routine inclusion of the desirability of free trade at a Finance Ministers' meeting prior to the July 2017 Hamburg G20 summit.

Then there are the older men. The CEO of ExxonMobil, Rex Tillerson, may have real experience of complicated places, and knows the links between energy and national security, but as

'CEO' of the State Department he wants cuts, on the bizarre grounds that with fewer wars overseas, the US needs fewer diplomats. Several key State Department posts remain unfilled and the US is fifty ambassadors light at the time of writing. Tillerson is also shy of the media and may not be long in his job. The monkish 'Mad Dog' Mattis is just the latest iteration of an ageing general busy in politics, something that Israel has suffered from for years, though that analogy is rarely mentioned. Another former general (Kelly) headed Homeland Security until he was moved to replace Reince Priebus as White House Chief of Staff. Although Mattis and Kelly are apparently sensible men, there is genuine concern among senior officers about the abandonment of an apolitical military ethos, as well as among civilian officials about the creeping influence of soldiers obsessed with the Middle East in making US foreign policy.[66] More 'funky' picks included Stephen Bannon – ejected in August – as senior counsellor. The maverick (registered Democrat) Flynn had earlier been replaced as NSA on the second throw of the dice by General H. R. McMaster after a former Navy Seal turned admiral compared the post to a 'sick sandwich'. McMaster endorsed Trump's Darwinian 'elemental' and transactional dismissal of the ideal of a global community in a *Wall Street Journal* op-ed that even that paper found it necessary to refute.[67] Senator Jeff Sessions, the new Attorney-General, is another Trump loyalist – though it is not reciprocated – whose Alabama background worries the civil rights lobby. The most senior woman is a multiple billionaire, Betsy DeVos, who took over education, a field Trump has no discernible interest in. Steve Mnuchin forgot on his confirmation-hearing pro forma the odd $100 million in the Cayman Islands, and DeVos the $200 million her family's trust has donated to the Republicans. Shedding assets collectively worth a billion so as to avoid future conflicts of interest has been a problem for this special administration. The dignity of the presidency has been damaged, not just by the lumbering and inarticulate incumbent, but by official spokesmen like Sean Spicer and the overnight sensation Anthony Scaramucci, who are like cartoon figures.[68]

•

Foreign governments now complain that Henry Kissinger's old quip about not knowing who to call when he wanted to speak to Europe has been thrown into reverse. No one knows who really counts in the White House and Washington as a whole for the Trump administration is essentially a royal court in which Trump's personal bodyguard (a former NYPD detective) may have more influence than a more exalted official, an experience common enough if one is dealing with Brunei. Rivalries are so endemic that the whole gang have to travel as a caravanserai lest anyone knife anyone left holding the fort in the West Wing. The family-conscious Chinese have got the measure of things by simply going straight to Jared Kushner, the first son-in-law. Not least with a $400 million debt-relief deal from Anbang Insurance Group to aid a problematic Trump high-rise project on Fifth Avenue though adverse publicity meant this was quietly shelved, and Donald Junior has caused other embarrassments in this family of Comedy Corleones.[69] The world of business provides other clues to what we can expect.

We are witnessing a culture clash between Team Trump and how the Washington foreign policy elite usually views the world. First, they will strip out the concerns about human rights and democracy promotion, which cynics claim camouflages America's assertion of national interests under a cloak of idealism and which from Clinton onwards was highly selective anyway in the case of China. More importantly, they will break with the orderly arrangement of foreign powers into concentric circles. That means Australia, Britain and Canada in the inner zone, other NATO allies, Israel, Japan and South Korea next to that, partners such as Jordan, Saudi Arabia, Taiwan and so on beyond, and then the adversaries and rivals, China, Iran, North Korea and Russia.

Businessmen like Trump or Rex Tillerson do not see the world that way. Their map of the world consists of those who collaborate with or reject deals that can take them to Chad, China, Guinea, Russia, Scotland or Turkey. Trump's team also includes three former generals, scarred by more than a decade of gruelling fighting in Iraq and Afghanistan. Their worldview will include elements of the traditional Washington way, but some of them are idiosyncratic and they are expert technicians in using violence.[70] Whether their expertise is used seems doubtful since Trump says he will not require the intelligence presidential daily briefings (PDAs) which are tailored to suit each new incumbent. They gave LBJ (known as 'Big Ears') much gossip, Ronald Reagan films to view and Obama dense detail that presumed his background knowledge. Trump says he 'watches the shows'.[71]

Were he true to his words on his campaign trail, then Trump would focus on restoring American national greatness by rectifying the adverse effects of globalization and investing in America itself. To that end he has already issued warnings to US and foreign corporations operating or thinking of off-shoring production. Both Carrier and General Motors ditched plans to create jobs in Mexico on the back of warning tweets from the President-elect. Alibaba, Softbank and Toyota were among those to get the message and invest in the US. But that surely won't solve structural problems. While Wall Street is thriving under Trump, Main Street still languishes, with both wages and consumption stagnant. His proposed tax cuts will focus 80–90 per cent of the benefits on the highest-earning 10 per cent. It is probably harder than he thinks to revive the domestic US coal industry, even if environmental concerns are swept aside, and one cannot transform semi-literate unemployed furniture or toy producers into fracking-rig crews or software engineers. Educational reform, especially in STEM subjects, does not figure much in his discourse. With the exception of billionaire Peter Thiel, Trump is no friend of Silicon Valley. He does not own an Apple iPhone (he uses Samsung) and he eschews hackable PCs, as does Vladimir Putin. In addition to claiming these internet giants are merely neutral conduits for the views of the citizenry (which enables them to evade press and TV regulation), some of these concerns own mainstream media (for example Amazon and the *Washington Post*) that Trump regards as hostile.

Although on his Twitter feed Trump sometimes sounds like a hoary Democrat trade unionist, not unlike Martin Sheen's rendition of the noble aircraft-factory foreman Carl Fox in the 1987 movie *Wall Street*, in reality that is not quite what is happening below the radar. Trump's new Strategic and Policy Forum includes the CEOs of Blackstone, GM, IBM, JP Morgan, BlackRock, Walt Disney and Boeing. They might like Trump's promise to slash corporation tax from 35 per cent to 15 per cent, but they won't like protective tariffs.[72] Plans for $1 trillion of infrastructure spending will be whittled down by the Republican-led Congress, in favour of revenue-neutral tax cuts and probably external tariffs. He has no ideological animus towards Medicare and Social Security, and undoing 'Obamacare' has proved tortuous.

Some conservatives who should know better have been busy with the equivalent of putting lipstick on a pig, often projecting their own agendas onto Trump's new administration. Seventy-year-olds do not change their minds, and Trump is no geopolitical thinker but rather a capricious bullying narcissist. He is a creature of the age of Twitter, a perfect 140-character vehicle for his impulses.

So what can we reasonably say about Trump at large? Let us assume he is not impeached, and that we should be more focused on Vice-President Mike Pence than Trump. The big danger is that the elderly President is erratic, vengeful and easily bored to the point where his aides have to drag him away from cable TV or fill his days to avoid him letting loose on Twitter. Cramming sessions on foreign countries apparently involve many maps, since he is a visual person, while documents have to regularly mention Trump himself to guarantee he is paying attention. Every press conference is going to be a nightmare for officials who may find their line undermined and an investor opportunity as even his Tweets have sent stocks up and down. As Eisenhower discovered with his cabinet of five millionaire golfing cronies and a plumber, running a corporation like General Motors is not like being in politics and GM are not necessarily exemplary for the virtues of capitalism. America's and the world's problems require knowledge, patience and thought – for some are intractable – rather than the breakthrough macro- and micro-deals that Trump is accustomed to from the world of real estate. Putin and Xi are not corporate rivals, though both are multimillionaires, but figures formed by

very alien cultures and life experiences to those of Trump. There
is not some 'basic human nature' to be discovered by this nar-
cissistic genius. All of which should be qualified by the fact that
since Bush Senior (1989–93), a former Congressman, Ambassador to both the UN and China, and Chief of the CIA, US
presidents have not had much prior expertise in foreign affairs.[73]

Trump admires strongmen, including Erdoğan, Putin and
Sisi, belatedly adding the 'gentlemanly' Xi Jinping – the strongest of them all – to his list along with the Filipino killer
Roderigo Duterte, who Trump claims knows how to tackle
drug-traffickers. He's a fan of disruptive insurgents such as Nigel
Farage and Marine Le Pen too, though as losers that enthusiasm
may wane. Anyone acting like a doormat will be stepped on too.
President Macron's strong grip got more of Trump's attention
than Mrs May's gentle hand. Trump will also have to deal with
ISIS and not in the transactional sense. Trump's off-the-cuff
solutions include a combination of carpet-bombing and tortur-
ing the families of terror suspects, which no CIA or military
personnel will countenance for fear of legal bills, if nothing else.
However, it is probable that Trump will welcome Russian cooperation in eliminating ISIS, with trade-offs over Crimea and
Ukraine. This will have major consequences in Iraq and Syria,
which one suspects the President does not anticipate, such as
clashes between Syria and Turkey and Baghdad and Erbil after
ISIS melts away. His appeasement of Putin will also cause major
ructions inside the Republican Party and with America's European allies while complicating intelligence sharing arrangements
lest the materials drift via the Russians to the Iranians. Worst of
all, Trump seems to be still campaigning while governing,
directly reaching out to his angry supporters through Twitter
and holding what amount to rallies of the faithful. This is why
any fitful signs that Trump is reverting to a 'normative' Establishment foreign policy are being constantly undercut whenever
he decides to play to his populist base as some of his inner circle
want him to do. That is why he gave a curmudgeonly address
at the opening of a new NATO headquarters and why he suddenly pulled the US out of the Paris Agreement on climate

change, though some of the inner circle such as his daughter Ivanka were not happy about this.

In the same week as Trump's bombastic 'America First' inaugural address on 20 January 2017, President Xi of China spoke at the World Economic Forum in Davos. One could have imagined that his hymn to free trade and global security institutions was the real US presidential address, since it sounded more like what US presidents have said throughout my lifetime. Trump's descriptions of the US itself in his 'American carnage' inaugural, 'the crime, the gangs, the drugs', sounded like Mogadishu, or at least somewhere one would pay good money never to visit. It did not resemble any America familiar to anyone who has spent much time there.

Trump almost immediately engineered spats with China, taking a call from Taiwanese President Tsai-Ing-wen, though he rapidly reverted to the One China, Two Systems line when Xi froze him. It seems to be Trump who is investing most in repairing the relationship. Trump's abandonment of the Trans Pacific Trade Pact was like an early New Year gift to China, since any alternative partnerships will lack US involvement and China will dominate. But China would come off worse in a trade war. According to the World Bank, China's trade-to-GDP ratio is 41 per cent whereas it is 28 per cent for the US.[74] If Trump imposes tariffs to curb China's huge trade surplus ($350 billion) then Beijing will retaliate against US firms with Chinese production and supply lines. China could also dump its $1.115 trillion of US Treasuries so as to punish the dollar. German industry should also worry about their own $43 billion surplus with the US. Trump tried to intimidate BMW (and Japanese Toyota) over a plant project in Mexico. His first meeting with Chancellor Angela Merkel was not entirely happy either after he reminded her of money for NATO that Germany does not 'owe'. A promise to raise defence spending to 2 per cent of GDP by 2024 is not a 'debt' to be settled. Germany brings us back to China. Rhetorically, Trump will fulminate about China's island-building, but using an enlarged navy to halt this will result in a military clash in which others may not take the US side. Will Germany relinquish the title 'Europe's China' or the UK abandon the 'golden era' for the sake of Trump? Many of the US's smaller Asia-Pacific allies will be making their peace with China (as the Philippines have already done), though this will also mean that India and Japan may draw closer to the US. Tension with China, it will be explained, will also complicate management of North Korea's nuclear arsenal. For that Trump needs China as a kind of subcontractor on a troublesome construction site, and Beijing knows this. He will also need Chinese help in managing Afghanistan.[75]

Trump wants to replace the 'terrible' nuclear deal with Iran with something better, though every ninety days he has reported to Congress that Iran is honouring the deal by the lights of the IAEA. Instead, the administration is seeking to tighten sanctions on Iran for breaking the 'spirit' of the JCPOA agreement in other areas which were excluded from the deal. It is also flirting with regime change, without having a clue as to what this might unleash. Unilaterally enhancing sanctions on Iran seems pointless and one doubts whether US big business will enjoy watching the likes of Anglo-Dutch Shell, CNPC, Sinopec, Tatneft or Total scoop up oil and gas contracts. It is worrying that Trump has delegated so much policy to a military he has effectively let off the leash. Mattis and McMaster have dark personal experience of their troops being hit by Iranian-supplied explosively formed penetrators which streamed molten copper through armoured vehicles. While Mattis says he regards the nuclear deal as binding, he also insists that a 'dangerous' Iran has to be contained, a line of thought that the Emiratis, Israelis and Saudis encouraged when Trump visited Riyadh in May 2017. The nuclear deal is not just an American affair either, but a solemn international treaty endorsed by the UN, China, Russia and the EU. Trump may also learn that Iran, Hizbollah and the Iraqi Shia militias are tearing strips off ISIS, so he may postpone tampering with the nuclear deal while meddling in Iran's internal affairs by encouraging separatist movements and a Green Movement which nowadays seems to support Rouhani. Blaming Tehran for international terrorism also sits oddly with ISIS carrying out terror attacks in the middle of Tehran.[76]

Trump once strongly averred that the Saudis and Emiratis should cough up for their own defence, as if they are the equivalents of the deadbeat Europeans. In reality, the money they pay *in advance* covers large chunks of the capital costs of building major defence platforms, which US corporations cannot solely afford. If the US withdrew its support for these countries, there would be a real risk of rampant nuclear proliferation, the containment of which would entail even more US expense, never mind the fact that few Americans wish to die for the Emiratis or Saudis. Trump's visit to Riyadh in May 2017 was extraordinary. He simply ingested the local line on Iran, before moving on to the real business of a $100 billion arms deal and Saudi investment in the US. Perhaps the most bizarre spectacles were Trump moving from foot to foot while waving a sword or when he, King Salman and Egyptian President Sisi booted up banks of computers in a new counter-extremism centre – hastily concocted by Saudi Aramco – by laying their hands on a glowing orb. Melania Trump watched with an inscrutable slight smile. One immediately unfortunate by-product of this regal love-in was that in order to deflect attention from their own role in propagating extremism, the Saudis highlighted the two-faced role of Qatar, which even as it secures itself by buying assets in the West plays host to the leaders of Hamas and their friends in the Muslim Brotherhood, perhaps with US encouragement so as to establish back channels. Further black marks included the role of the Doha-based Al-Jazeera TV station (1996–) before and during the Arab Spring, and the huge ransom Qatar paid to both Islamist terrorists and Iran after a Qatari hunting party was abducted in Iraq. Emboldened by Trump, the Saudis and the UAE have imposed an air, land and sea blockade of Qatar. Both Iran and Turkey (also a supporter of the Muslim Brotherhood) have rushed to aid the embattled Qatari Emir Tamim bin Hamad Al Thani. Israel is not entirely happy either as it ponders whether it might have to pick up the large tab the Qataris have been paying in Gaza.[77]

US policy has been to support a two-state solution to the Israeli–Palestinian dispute, despite Israel's malicious settlement policy and Palestinian terrorism. Trump imagines that his deal-making skills will result in a final deal of deals between Israelis and Palestinians. The hard-right Bibi Netanyahu is

Trump's kind of guy, assuming Netanyahu does not fall victim to one or other domestic corruption scandal afflicting himself and his wife, or come a cropper by alienating Israel's far-right wing by overly accommodating Trump's megalomaniac wish to seal the deal in the Middle East. For sure, Trump likes tough Likud-supporting Israeli Jews, and the 15 per cent of (mainly Orthodox) US Jews who voted for him. They are family, after all. But many of his Orthodox intimates are not keen on the wet, liberal, culturally Jewish crowd, exemplified by the candy-floss-haired critic Leon Wieseltier and his like, and during the campaign some of Trump's supporters seemed to indulge in anti-Semitic attacks on George Soros, William Kristol and Anne Applebaum. A closing Trump campaign ad showed three Jews, Soros, Janet Yellen and Goldman CEO Lloyd Blankfein, to illustrate Clinton's involvements with an alleged 'global power structure'. This should worry everyone.[78]

Trump's plans for a 'huge' wall on the Mexican border are in denial of complex topography, not to mention Native American and ranchers' rights in Arizona and Texas. This project has not simply alienated Mexicans, a proud people who resent being identified with drug-trafficking murderers. Especially since Mexico has recently acted as a giant filter to stop 150,000 people from really troubled places in Central America from making the 3,000km trip northwards to the US. In response to Trump's protectionist threats (tariffs on Mexican assembled car imports), the governments of Colombia and Peru immediately declared their solidarity with the Mexicans and Trump is despised as far away as Chile by all shades of opinion. China has been highly active in Latin America recently, and it is not solely interested in beef, soybeans, copper and coal. It is investing in banks, infrastructure and mines, and selling military equipment to countries like Argentina.[79]

Trump's desire to do right by his European populist admirers cuts across the need to maintain relations with elected national governments and their normative diplomatic apparatus. Britain is a case in point, especially after the Brexit vote in June 2016 gave limited impetus to Trump's own campaign. An acquaintance joked that the UK Foreign Office probably had better contacts with Hizbollah than it did with the incoming Trump administration and Nigel Farage seemed to have better access to Trump than the UK Ambassador in Washington, though this may simply reflect the illusions conjured up by two mavens of self-publicity. While both sides repeat the usual flattering bromides about a special relationship, most British people realize that they are not uppermost in American minds, nor in that of President Trump especially after seeing him glorying in his reception at France's Bastille Day on 14 July 2017.

Since Trump thought Belgium is a city, it is unsurprising that he did not bother to mention the EU in his listing of valuable US allies, though the hopeless EU Commission President Jean-Claude Juncker offered to correct his ignorance. In reality, Trump will not be very interested in Europe, since it lacks collective agency on the world stage though he has offered to do a trade deal before he does one with his special British Brexit friends. After listening too much to Farage he convinced himself that the EU is doomed, with more 'exits' on the way, though in reality no more dominoes fell. But by late February 2017 he pronounced himself happy the EU was happy: 'I do, sure. I have very good relations with the EU. But I thought that the UK would pull out with Brexit and I was right . . . But the EU, I'm totally in favor of it. I think it's wonderful, if they're happy. If they're happy – I'm in favour of it.' We will see how he fares with the duo of Macron and Merkel.[80]

Team Trump would be advised to be wary of some of the other insurgent forces abroad in contemporary Europe, which include anti-Americans on both the far left and the right who admire Putin for giving the US a bloody nose, or whose anti-Semitism is the close cousin of their anti-Americanism. What flamed brightly under the wild 'cowboys' Reagan and Bush, but went into abeyance with Clinton and Obama, is reigniting with the election of Trump, and not solely because Chancellor Merkel regards him as a passing nightmare and herself as the last defender of liberal values still standing.

The German Alternativ für Deutschland, for example, includes leading figures who explicitly wish to revive the late-nineteenth-century imperial alliances with Russia, and who detest the crass materialism of modern American consumer civilization that Trump personifies. The leftist *Der Spiegel* depicted Trump as an orange asteroid hurtling towards 'the end of the world', while its liberal Hamburg stablemate *Die Zeit* saw in Trump the end of the Enlightenment project. Spain's leftist *El País* described Trump's victory as a 'rebellion against reason and decency . . . [on the part of] people of simple faith, oblivious to irony; people who choose their truths not based on facts but on their beliefs or prejudices; people who live far from the ocean and the rest of the planet Earth, of which they are afraid. I've never experienced a similar sense of disconnection in Europe, Africa, Latin America. Just inside the United States.'[81]

While European governments may have no choice other than to work with whatever cards the US electorate dealt, it is not difficult to foresee a very rapid estrangement between Europe and the US under this President though the British will soak up any indignity to grip his hand. This could lead to a compensatory consolidation of Europe (particularly in defence if Trump weakens NATO) and – because of the combination of Putin, Trump and Brexit – a reorientation towards Xi's cool and reasonable-seeming China, for as we are constantly told, physical distance is not what it was. This brings us to the crises afflicting what bills itself as an empire of virtue, though as we shall see one should not confuse Europe with the economic and political Union.

8

Empire of Virtue: The European Union

It is widely believed that in 1938 CBS radio caused mass panic in the US by broadcasting Orson Welles's dramatization of H. G. Wells's *War of the Worlds* in the form of news flashes about a Martian invasion. In reality about 2 per cent of all radio listeners even heard the show, whose alleged hysterical effects were ramped up by newspapers worried that they might be commercially displaced by wireless. Nobody died of shock either, as the newspapers did not report.[1]

Ten years ago Belgium allegedly had such a moment when the Francophone or Walloon national station RTBF broadcast a programme called *Bye Bye Belgium*. Flemish-speaking viewers were watching a football match on their main channel, blissfully unaware that they had just seceded from Belgium amidst scenes of violent chaos. There were 30,000 complaints about the documentary after it showed real Flemish politicians apparently declaring independence in parliament and the 'King' fleeing abroad. Half an hour into the programme, RTBF had to repeat the opening disclaimer that it was a work of fiction. A month later, polls showed that 45.8 per cent of Flemings did indeed want to declare Flanders independent.

The Belgian capital, Brussels, is home to the EU Commission, the European Parliament and the headquarters of NATO. Belgian politicians have played leading roles in European politics, from Paul-Henri Spaak to Guy Verhofstadt. A relatively small capital city of 1.4 million, it has nineteen different borough or communal mayors, each serving between 20,000 and 150,000 residents. Until recently, each commune had its own police force, though these have now been consolidated into six forces. The Metropolitan Police or NYPD they are not.

A bilingual enclave, Brussels has huge social contrasts, between plush Uccle, where the bureaucrats and French tax-dodgers dwell, to Molenbeek near the railway station, home to 95,000 mainly North African migrants. As those investigating the Paris terror attacks in late 2015 discovered, guns as well as drugs are easily trafficked in these sleazy streets.

Due to sheer incompetence, links between two petty criminal brothers with long records, Salah and Brahim Abdeslam, and the terror mastermind Abdelhamid Abaaoud, were missed. The police computers were thirty years old and a search involved twenty-four separate databases, while no one bothered to examine flash drives found hidden behind the radio of the brothers' car after it crashed. Salah evaded capture by hiding inside a sofa; at the time French magistrates said the Belgian police were 'rubbish'.[2]

Belgium holds the world record for not managing to form a government. For 589 days during 2010–11 the country was ruled by its civil servants, though this caused minimal disruption. Belgium's primary linguistic divide (there is a German-speaking minority too) has resulted in a very fragmented society. The French-speaking Walloons (32 per cent of the population) inhabit the poorer, deindustrialized south, while the Flemings (55 per cent) are in richer, northern Flanders. Many would like to see Antwerp as the capital of their independent state rather than polyglot Brussels. National stereotypes thrive, with spick-and-span Flemings deriding allegedly dirty, feckless Walloons.

Belgian politics involves servicing client constituencies with official jobs. Every public-sector post is an opportunity for patronage on the part of Belgium's rival socialist and liberal parties, which reflect the linguistic divide so none of them are nationwide or federal. Party patronage covers every post from school caretaker to the boss of the (defunct) national air carrier, Sabena.

The headlock these parties have on local and municipal government also means that corruption is endemic. After twenty years in power, in 2005 the socialist head of the Walloon regional government had to step down because of dubious refuse-collection contracts, and money being diverted to sports clubs, though the case is still being heard ten years later. The sordid case of serial child-murderer Marc Dutroux also high-lighted corruption in Belgium's criminal justice system.

Given these inter-ethnic rivalries, and pervasive disbelief in Belgium as a state, it is unsurprising that the children of immi-grants feel there is nothing to integrate with. Jobs in mines or steel plants are long gone too. It does not help that the Grand Mosque in Brussels is a Saudi-sponsored nest of Salafist funda-mentalism, whose last director was expelled for preaching hatred of Israel and the West.

But ten years after *Bye Bye Belgium* was shown, even Flem-ish nationalists do not want secession any more. There are two Flemish nationalist parties. Vlaams Belang (Flemish Interest) is the new-fangled version of Vlaams Bloc, the far right anti-Islamic Eurosceptic Party. It has three out of 150 seats in Bel-gium's federal Lower House, and six of 124 seats in the Flemish parliament. It is excluded from every Belgian coalition govern-ment as a kind of pariah.

By contrast, Nieuw-Vlaamse Alliantie (New Flemish Alli-ance) is Belgium's biggest party, with thirty-three seats in the federal parliament and forty-three in the Flemish one. It is the largest element in Prime Minister Charles Michel's centre-right coalition, along with two other Flemish parties and Michel's own Walloon Liberal Party.

In general, Flemings vote right and Walloons vote left. Since Flemings are so generously represented in government, demands for secession have fallen. Voters are more exercised by the econ-omy, job creation, education and, since the mayhem caused in Molenbeek in 2016, by Islamist terrorism, which exposed the glaring deficiencies of Belgium's police and security forces. Many Belgian spies were focused on Chinese, Iranian or Russian agents trying to infiltrate the EU or NATO, for Brussels is known as 'spy central'. There was a disconnection between beat officers and spies, and very few of them knew either Arabic or Turkish. More recently, a prospective trade deal with Canada revived communitarian differences, with the pro-business Flem-ings eager while the protectionist Walloons feared job losses.

Belgium is not the only European country with linguistic

divides that are also political. Belgians are watching to see whether the Catalans dare to hold a referendum on secession from Spain on 1 October 2017. The regional government in Barcelona is committed to this, since pro-independence parties dominate it. As Spain's richest region, Catalonia resents paying more in taxes to Madrid than it receives in services. People in Madrid really resent the Catalans, even though they have not gone in for the bombs-and-ballot combo of the Basques. The conservative PPE national government of Prime Minister Mariano Rajoy is opposed to this vote, arguing that Spain's constitution is heavily devolved anyway, and that such a step is unconstitutional. The conservative-dominated Constitutional Tribunal agrees. That is why Spain's government has rejected holding the kind of referendum that Scotland had in 2015, and which supporters of independence lost. Less than half of Catalans voted in a non-binding referendum that year, though 80 per cent believe in holding a real one.

Support for Catalan independence is finely balanced against those who wish to remain in Spain. Were Catalonia to become independent, it might trigger a similar poll in Belgium.

The EU is watching these bids for independence with trepidation. The breakup of Belgium, one of the founding 'Benelux' states, would be especially unfortunate. Egged on by Rajoy, the EU intimated to the Scots they should not assume automatic 'readmission' – or rather admission – to the EU under the cross of St Andrew, and the same message has gone to those waving the stripey Catalan Senyera Estelada. In June 2017 the Catalans announced they would ignore the Spanish courts so as to hold a referendum on independence, to which Madrid's response was to threaten to tell officials to strike (notably teachers in schools where the poll would be held) and that the central government might assume central command of the police.

The June 2016 Brexit vote further complicated matters within a British asymmetric union consisting of four distinctive political cultures that differ in their sense of dual European identity. Along with England, Wales voted overwhelmingly in favour of Brexit, while majorities in Scotland and Northern Ireland voted to remain in the EU. Conceivably they could hold referenda not to join England in the mother of all divorces, though this is only semi-realistic for Scotland, and even that ambition waned after the 2017 British general election saw the triumphal SNP lose seats to the Conservatives and Labour.

Regional separatism is probably not the highest priority for the EU at present. After the political earthquakes of 2016, that would be sheer survival, though the loss of 13 per cent of the EU's population, one of its two credible military powers, and one of the big three economies is surely traumatic. But before turning to a present in which the edifice's foundations are shaking, we should look more deeply into how something so apparently solid came into being. The glass and steel of the Commission's Berlaymont headquarters and the EU Parliament buildings in Brussels and Strasbourg appear as metaphorically cracked as the baroque palaces of the long-gone Habsburg Empire or the ruins of ancient Rome. If the US has been compared (by the Chinese) to a shooting star, darting across an ample sky, what has happened to Europe's Empire of Virtue?

•

A noble story of the European Union has often been told, sometimes at the expense of ones involving darker attempts to unite Europe with imperial violence. Polyglot empires were common until 1918, despite the ascendancy of nation-states like Germany and Italy; thereafter the nation-state predominated in eastern as well as western Europe. Then the darkness descended. Nationalism's association with belligerent imperialist 'isms', which had thinly veiled the chauvinism of Germany, Italy and Russia, led to the idea of a new, beneficent kind of 'empire', involving the free association of liberal Western nation-states for commercial and idealistic reasons. This was the spiritual descendant of the Holy Roman Empire, which philosophers like Leibniz had extolled as the ideal solution to the religious and political complexities of central Europe. This lives on in the Kantian Europe of perpetual peace.[3]

The key figure in the creation of the EU was the businessman, civil servant and technocrat Jean Monnet, who had extensive experience of Britain and the US, in war and peace, as well as his native France. Possibly his main insight, derived from a Swiss philosopher, Henri-Frédéric Amiel, was that: 'Each man's experience starts again from the beginning. Only institutions grow wiser; they accumulate collective experience, and owing to this experience and this wisdom, men subject to the same rules will not see their own nature changing, but their behaviour gradually transformed.'[4]

This meant finding solutions to real-world problems through durable institutions, bound by law as enforced by courts of impartial judges. Monnet mistrusted transient politicians, inter-governmental bargaining and, above all, after dismal experience, the unwisdom of democratic elections, plebiscites and referenda. Democratically elected parliaments had granted absolute authority to Hitler and Pétain in 1933 and 1940. Monnet admired British pragmatism and the reach of US federal government across a vast continent, so much so that de Gaulle called him 'a great American', which was not meant as a compliment. Monnet was the driving force behind the Schuman Plan, which looked backwards and forwards to find a solution to a major problem, so as to turn Germany's reindustrialization to the common good. Germany was more than prepared to see its power diluted, if this meant a way back to being a sovereign actor; the alternative being French seizure of its industrial heart-lands in perpetuity. But the British and Americans did not wish anything so punitive as they simultaneously discovered 'good Germans' who were useful allies against the Soviets.[5]

The European Coal and Steel Community formed in 1951 pooled and rationalized the war-making heavy industries of France, West Germany, Italy and the Benelux states. The Italians ensured it was the first experiment in labour mobility for their superfluous miners and steel workers. The ECSC began the process of each step forward requiring further steps, sometimes sideways, but generally towards a goal whose justification was the end of major intra-European wars and general peace and prosperity. The transcendence of Franco-German enmity was at the heart of this. Chancellor Helmut Kohl holding hands with President François Mitterrand in 1984 at Verdun, where more than 130,000 French and German dead lay buried from the

Great War, was the symbolic apogee of Europe as peace project. Anything else is inconceivable. When David Cameron, in 2016, tried to justify Britain remaining in the EU to prevent 'World War III' this was rightly dismissed as risible scaremongering, while his attempt to eject the (Brexit-supporting) editor of the most popular newspaper was scandalous.[6]

The ECSC/EEC/EU was never meant as a limited functional agency, like the International Monetary Fund or the World Bank. The Treaty of Paris, which created the ECSC, also established four institutions: a Council of Ministers, a High Authority, a Common Assembly and a Court of Justice to resolve disputes. Monnet became head of the Authority, burning his French diplomatic passport and acquiring one of the new European documents.

These ECSC institutions were the future European Commission, as the High Authority was restyled in 1957, the European Court of Justice, and a (until 1979 indirectly elected) European Parliament in embryo. Although one might imagine it busied itself only with mining or steel issues, the Authority's statistical agency soon began collecting broader data, for example on consumer purchasing power.[7] Monnet also sought to include nuclear energy within a similar framework, as the energy source of the future.

The Community also acquired symbolic expression, once more involving Verdun, partly to mask the smell of it being a Christian Democrat club of which four of the original six were paid-up members. But this Verdun was in 843 rather than 1916. In that year, a Treaty of Verdun divided the Emperor Charlemagne's simulacrum of the ancient Roman Empire. From 800 onwards, from his capital at Aachen, Charlemagne ruled the eponymous Carolingian empire, based on west and east 'Frankish' tribes and conquered Saxons, who under his heirs mutated into what became France and Germany. Here indeed was a proto-European, the simplified history claimed, leaving out the Emperor's extermination of the Saxons. Verdun remains a potent symbol. The most powerful EU civil servant, the German lawyer Martin Selmayr, who is Chief of Staff to EU Commission

President Jean-Claude Juncker, likes to reminisce that when he was a boy his grandfather took him to the 1916 battlefield.[8]

Nor was the European court idle. It was more persistently self-assertive than the oft-derided Commission, which for long periods really was a subordinate agency. The European Court of Justice discovered creative ways of ensuring that the 'spirit' of the founding treaties overrode national law on the grounds that member states had limited their sovereign rights under a Community that had precedence in international law. National judges sought clarification from Luxembourg on issues affecting their own nationals. *Van Gend & Loos* v. *Nederlandsee Administratie der Belastingen* involved a Dutch haulier that did not want to pay import tariffs on imported German urea-formaldehyde used in plastics. *Costa* v. *ENEL* resulted when an Italian refused to pay his (increased) electricity bill to the newly nationalized supplier. Though Mr Costa lost, both judgments claimed that European legal rulings could override national law because lawyers said the 'spirit' said so. Ironically, the greatest resistance to the ECJ's creative judicial imperialism would emanate from Germany's Constitutional Court at Karlsruhe. This was because this court saw itself as the guardian of fundamental and inalienable German rights, which their own politicians were infringing through decisions taken in their dual European capacity.

The High Authority/Commission proposed policies and then monitored their implementation. But the decision to adopt these policies rested with the Council of Ministers, which for practical reasons – they had countries to govern – devolved day-to-day responsibility to a Committee of Permanent Representatives of the Member States who, from 1958, convened weekly in Brussels. The big stuff was reserved for the Council of Ministers. Depending on the size of their own countries, and their commitment to the project, Europe became either a wider stage or a distracting nuisance.

The crucial question of whether decisions could be taken by majority, and whether individual states could exercise a veto, as happened when de Gaulle cut up rough and left France's chair empty, was eventually resolved by the January 1966 Luxembourg Compromise. This is partly why European decision-making is so tortuous (especially with today's twenty-eight or twenty-seven member states rather than the original six). Horse-trading is inevitable in order to *prevent* any state exercising its national veto. Initially, chairmanship of the Council rotated every six months among the six members. From 1974, regular tri-monthly meetings replaced summits.

Unusually, no single foundational event created the EU; rather it was the result of incremental, some would say stealthy, steps known as the *méthode Monnet*. Since there was no European federal state, or European *demos*, the democratic element in these arrangements and practices was deliberately and manifestly short-changed, other than as an aspiration. The original Common Assembly consisted of seventy-eight MEPs, nominated by national parliaments, who had very limited powers. The figure doubled under the Treaties of Rome, though they remained indirectly elected until 1979. Full-time MEPs were elected for five-year terms to a 410-seat assembly, on the basis of national population size. In the first election 190 million people voted, though differing enthusiasms resulted in a 91 per cent turnout in Belgium and 32 per cent in Britain. The European Parliament acquired its own President (Simone Veil being the first and after Martin Schultz, Antonio Tajani is the current incumbent) and with progressive enlargement has mushroomed to 751 members. Its powers have substantially increased too. It has its own internal democratic deficit. While 70,000 voters elect each Maltese MEP, it requires nearly 827,000 Germans to do so. Moreover, the EU does not clearly separate executive, legislature and judiciary, since the Commission is part of the executive and initiates legislation.

With its overseas empire and transatlantic links, Britain regarded quickening signs of continental amity with benevolence, though it was careful to scupper anything that might have undermined NATO, founded in 1949 as the main vehicle for keeping the Americans locked in, the Russians out and the Germans down, as General Ismay put it. NATO superseded the 1948 Brussels Pact. After the Communist coup in Prague that year, this pact united France, Britain, Belgium, the Netherlands and Luxembourg for defence purposes and with a vow of joint military support. Successive US governments of either complexion regarded a united Europe as a desirable goal, its liberal prosperity being a constant rebuke to the ailing and unfree Soviet empire.[9]

The Korean War complicated things, one of many external developments that impacted on the European venture throughout its evolution. Whereas the French were focused on integrating the divided and occupied West Germany into the coal and steel community, the US wanted rapid German rearmament and political unification. This would simultaneously allow the US to repulse Stalin's Korean client in Asia, and deter any thoughts he might have had for a similar incursion into West Germany.[10]

The French Prime Minister, René Pleven, proposed a European army, with one Defence Minister and troops in a single uniform, largely to thwart American plans for a rearmed West Germany. The Germans would be subordinate players in the French plan. Anything that meant the Europeans were ready to defend themselves met US approval, especially as Eisenhower, the US supreme commander of NATO, would remain in overall charge of the new European Defence Community (1952). The renascent Churchill, who returned to power in 1951, scuppered any idea of Britain joining the EDC, but more importantly so did French Gaullists, who needed their own troops to fight colonial wars in Algeria and Indochina. Instead, the German Federal Republic was founded, with its capital in Bonn, and in 1955 the new republic joined NATO.[11]

In the same year, the six decided to give 'Europe' a further push, but this time towards a common market. These talks took place against the failure of the nefarious Anglo-French-Israeli intervention at Suez in 1956. The combination of American disapproval and the resulting undermining of sterling, with Soviet threats to nuke London and Paris, made it brutally clear that the US and USSR were in charge. This also gave a spur to further European integration.

Under the 1957 Treaties of Rome, the original six created the European Economic Community (EEC), consisting of a customs union and common market. It assumed responsibility for external trade policy and aspects of competition, and spawned the common agricultural and fisheries policies and an atomic energy authority. There was no mechanism for a member seceding if it changed its mind, and an amusing incident parodied the style of decision-making.

It happened during the protracted transitional talks that shaped the Community. With negotiations stalled, on New Year's Eve the incoming French rotating President stopped the clock to enable a fortnight of talks, whereupon he started the clock again, and on 14 January took over as President with a deal done. If even time itself could be manipulated, what might be done by creative lawyers? For reasons that need not detain us, the EEC was subsequently renamed the European Community (Maastricht Treaty in 1993) and then the European Union, after the 2007 Lisbon Treaty. By then Europe's peoples had membership of the EU printed on their passports.

The EEC might have remained merely a trading area under common supervision by national politicians sometimes wearing European hats. But ideological federalists always worked in accordance with more expansive teleology, meaning the direction of travel towards an ultimate goal. The prime mover here was the French socialist Jacques Delors, who in January 1985 became President of the Commission.[12]

Successive acts of accession expanded the EEC to include new members. The costs of empire, messy de-colonial wars and increased trade with Europe meant that the British finally decided to join the club. The Belgians and Dutch were enthusiastic advocates of British membership, if only to stymie French dominance of the ECC. For obvious reasons the French were not keen, partly because of Gaullist hostility to Anglo-Saxons, Britain being regarded as a Trojan Horse for the US. Incredibly, one night in 1963, after de Gaulle pronounced *Non*, the other members contemplated refounding the union with the British but without France. This daring thought had passed by morning.[13] By 1973 de Gaulle had gone, and the strength of the German economy was sufficiently worrying for France to want the British included. The aspiration to political union was announced as a decennial objective, for after every landmark decision the sights were raised higher.

Along with the Danes and Irish, Britain joined the EEC in 1973, though a more sceptical Labour government would hold a referendum on membership two years later, in which two-thirds of Britons voted to remain. I did too, in my first exercise of my right to vote (as I also voted, with few illusions about the EU or the UK, in June 2016). Any reader wanting to learn about the EEA, EFTA and the Council of Europe should consult the footnote, since an alphabet soup of acronyms and overlapping institutions would distract from the essence of things at this point.*

In successive waves, countries that had been regarded as backward and peripheral joined the EEC/EU as if it was a merit badge of a higher civilization. Those without experience of war and foreign occupation should not treat their idealism lightly. Successive enlargements took in the former autocracies of Greece (1981), Spain (1986) and Portugal (1986). Such neutrals as Austria, Finland and Sweden joined next, and then in 2004 the liberated Communist states of central and eastern Europe, including the German Democratic Republic, after the revolutions of 1989–90 had vanquished Warsaw Pact communism and reunited Germany into a powerful nation of 80 million people. Monetary union was the price the French exacted for Germany becoming much more potent. The bold Helmut Kohl did not play to the usual cautious type of the ever-penitent German, using Washington and Moscow to outflank London and Paris in his hour of destiny.

It seemed churlish to deny that Estonia, Hungary or Poland, let alone the birthplace of Aristotle and Plato, were in some

---

* After their own referendum, the Norwegians elected to remain outside the EEC, together with Iceland and Liechtenstein in what after 1992 became the European Economic Area. Together with Switzerland, which rejected membership of the EEA and EU, they confusingly also belong to EFTA, the European Free Trade Association. This was established in 1960 as a loose free-trade group, which included Britain, Austria, Denmark, Norway, Portugal, Sweden and Switzerland. There is also the earlier and much larger Council of Europe, established in London in 1949, and including forty-seven nations and 800 million people, with its own European Court of Human Rights in Strasbourg. Its focus is on what might be called soft power.

fundamental sense part of European civilization, though the insidious elision of a great classical, Christian and Enlightened civilization with a bureaucratic and legal project was soon to become problematic. Those used to a familiar Western club were sometimes unenthusiastic about admitting East European states, which Moscow had kept in line, though few were so lacking in taste as to say so openly. Not every nationalist revolution was velvet either. It bothered few that in Latvia, for example, a substantial russophone minority were denied citizenship rights since Stalin had planted them there in 1940. Many of these new members had indigenous or imperial parliamentary traditions which Nazism and communism had suppressed, as well as experiences of authoritarianism which some are revisiting, and 'deep' Greece was more Balkan than those who had studied Aristotle and Plato in their youth could conceive of.

The process of enlargement – and in 'Europe' process rather than 'events' drove the project – is ongoing. Croatia has been an EU member since 2013, and the plan is that Balkan states such as Albania, Bosnia, Macedonia, Montenegro and Serbia will eventually join. A Union of thirty-five members is not inconceivable. A much-enlarged EU was inevitably also a much-changed one. In its original form, three large powers (France, Germany and Italy) balanced three small Benelux states. But in the enlarged version, twenty-one small states outweighed six large ones (France, Germany, Italy, Spain, Poland, and – until the invoking of Article 50 – Britain). This necessitated much institutional re-engineering, and small but rich core countries like the Netherlands are not happy about their loss of weight in an EU packed with east Europeans, and nor is President Macron of France, who senses the moment for the original Franco-German axis to be reborn is nigh.

Enlargement eventually forced the EU to ponder its geographical limits, after a brief hiatus in which the Soviet leader Gorbachev had imagined Russia in the 'common European home'. One solution was to opt for association agreements with North Africa, Turkey, Georgia and Ukraine, for otherwise the EU could theoretically range over Russia to Japan. As we have seen, plans to deepen EU association with Turkey and Ukraine went badly awry in 2016. Events near and far, from the Balkan Wars to 9/11, also demanded a collective response that in the first case was conspicuously delayed while tens of thousands died. This was one of the main drivers behind a common foreign policy (resisted by Britain and France, which had distinguished foreign services, strong militaries and seats on the UN Security Council) and behind the creation of a permanent Council presidency to present the world with a single face. The first was that of the genial former Belgium PM Herman Van Rompuy, the current incumbent is former Polish PM Donald Tusk.

The British were the keenest advocates of enlargement, if only from a Machiavellian desire to dilute the Franco-German 'axis' that lay at the heart of the European project. The conservative, Atlanticist, east Europeans would see to that, while the Muslim Turks would diversify a Christian Democrat club. Germany agreed with the British on eastern enlargement, so as to stabilize its neighbours as a buffer against Russia. The French preferred to deepen the existing union, but lost the argument. Two things soured Britain's relations with the rest of the club, apart from an aloof distaste for backslapping and glad-handing foreign politicians and fear that steely French ENA-trained bureaucrats might outmatch Whitehall's Oxbridge-educated, 'Rolls Royce' civil servants.[14]

First, a Thatcherite desire for deregulation and free markets clashed with the dirigiste welfarism of Jacques Delors, the capably activist French President of the European Commission who became a monster in the eyes of the British press. Britain, he was told, had not abolished socialism to see it creep back through an EEC window in the shape of guaranteed workers' rights. The British also took a mercantile, transactional approach, which confirmed the view that they were a nation of shopkeepers banging on about 'their' rebates. Another problem was that enthusiasm for Europe in Britain was associated with the claret-toned faces and condescending plummy drawls of the likes of Roy Jenkins and Chris Patten, who would become Commissioners, not to mention the less illustrious Kinnock dynasty.

Second, the revival of the German Question in 1989–90 increased demands for the deeper integration of Europe (through

political and monetary union) so as to tie down this not so
guilt-ridden Gulliver-like powerhouse of 80 million people. Germany may have retained its peaceful, provincial air, with its
artists, film-makers, historians and writers narcissistically and
tediously revisiting the Nazi past as a malign treasure trove, but
others noted its enormous contemporary economic power. How
else could all those German billionaires afford so many gloomy
Anselm Kiefer scenes from Wagner or his lead U-Boots on their
mansion walls? German piety made many people sick.*

British Germanophobes, lawyers worried about sovereignty,
and ideological free traders and libertarians who thought the
project had gone far enough became a dogged presence on the
Conservative front and back benches, while various smart-alecs
born in remote climes manifested their ultra-British patriotism.
Minority elements in Labour agreed with them, though with
Tony Blair and Peter Mandelson at the helm, an ostentatious
cosmopolitanism prevailed from 1997 onwards among those
who preferred rigatoni to jellied eels. Blair's insincere grin made
him especially popular in European circles, where his lawyerly
gift of the gab injected a high-flown tone of which many of his
fellow leaders were incapable.

Before continuing to the present, where, for example, the
financier George Soros sees the eurozone and European Union
collapsing like the Soviet Empire in the 1990s, we need to highlight some further aspects of the same story to explain why we
have come to this pass.[15]

In some senses we are suffering from a mass optical delusion.
The Gothic, Renaissance, Baroque, Rococo and Modernism all
existed long before there was 'Europe', save as a geographical
concept, and they involved different regional styles, sometimes
involving states (ducal Burgundy for example) that have long

---

* Study of Nazi Germany is so ubiquitous in the UK that British universities
have imported an entire generation of German historians to teach the sins of
their grandparents. Another wave went to work as researchers on TV programmes about Nazis, some of whom progressed to being big bosses in the
industry. A recent German film has addressed the careerism involved, while
being itself symptomatic of the same problem.

ceased to exist. When we go to Norway or Switzerland we are indubitably in Europe, as if we were in France, Italy or Spain, yet the first two are not part of the economic, legal and political construct called the EEC/EU. Nineteen members use the euro, but citizens of the outside nine do not feel less 'European' because they use kronor, forints or Swiss francs.

But there is also this tangible Europe. 'Europe' consists of physical edifices, filled with internationally minded civil servants on their various career paths. Like the UN, it is a gravy train for the Bismarck and Metternich scions who attend ENA or the LSE, not to mention a lot of common or garden Eurosceptic populists who cannot get enough of Brussels, as a dining experience. Since the 1950s these have been called 'Eurocrats' by their detractors. The buildings include the Berlaymont headquarters of the Commission in Brussels, where the EU sprawls into sixty further buildings, with twenty-eight Commissioners who meet on the thirteenth floor and a total headcount of 23,000 permanent civil servants (though the EU directly employs about 48,000 people in total). Because twenty-eight Commissioners involve considerable areas of overlap in their portfolios, for example one for the internal market and another for competition, Juncker has added seven supervening Vice-Presidents.[16]

The Louise Weiss building in Strasbourg, with its hemicycle chamber, is home to the EU's Parliament, served by a further 6,500 staff, plus 2,000 more working directly for MEPs. Fifteen hundred people work for the Court of Justice, 3,500 for the Council of Ministers and nearly 3,000 for the External Affairs service, either in Brussels or abroad. Apart from being like the Tower of Babel, with every document having to be translated into not just national languages but Basque, Catalan, Irish and Welsh, at a cost of more than €1 billion a year, some of these institutions progress (like medieval abbots and bishops) around various locations, also at enormous cost. This is supposed to symbolize a general buy-in, at least in the Benelux–French heartlands.[17]

Nowadays the EU has five presidents, rather than the two we have mentioned so far, as well as a High Representative for External Affairs. The extra three are the presidents of the Eurogroup of Finance Ministers (Jeroen Dijsselbloem), of the European Central Bank (Mario Draghi) and of the European Parliament (Antonio Tajani). Foreign leaders find this bewildering.

The quality of senior EU leadership generally reflects, to put it charitably, how competitive politics are in the member states, especially when former prime ministers of, say, Luxembourg are required ex officio to cut a dash on the European or world stage as Commission President. Cynics might say that the EU is a useful backup career for those who have not distinguished themselves in national politics, which in many cases resemble the parish pump. How arduous can it be to run Malta? The obscure baroness Catherine Ashton, who went from being a Labour Party social affairs panjandrum, via Commissioner for Trade to High Representative of the External Service, is an example of an overpromoted 'garden gnome', as some in Whitehall uncharitably put it. What is the point of an EU global network of embassies when some countries have outstanding foreign services of their own? The career civil servants are recruited by open competition, though those with good language skills have a head start. Belgians speak many languages; the British do not. While the pay is modest, compared with a banker or commercial lawyer in the City of London or Frankfurt, the perks are many, with EU taxation cancelled by 'expatriation allowances' and generous transitional payments on retirement back to life at home.[18]

Since 1986 the EU has had a logo, which many call a flag, depicting a frozen twelve stars on a blue background to symbolize a union that nowadays includes twenty-eight or twenty-seven nations and an official anthem, Beethoven's 'Ode to Joy'. These symbols are redolent of the 'nationalization' process that most European states underwent in the nineteenth century, whereby elementary education, conscription, a national press, monuments and so forth converted 'peasants into Frenchmen' or which, after notional unification, 'made Italians'. One difficulty with this is that most modern nations are pre-formed, and used to their own cultural, symbolic and institutional lives, and hence regard another as superfluous. That could, of course, change if their rights are threatened by the nation-state.

It was impossible to cite mythical progenitors, such as

Romulus and Remus or Hengist and Horsa, for something half a century old, and national heroes such as Napoleon, Garibaldi and Bismarck were contentious too. This became clear with the euro coinage, which had a common face bearing the map of Europe and a national design on the obverse. Banknotes were especially contentious. One could choose Sir Francis Drake as a notable adventurer, an English Columbus, but in Spanish eyes he was a pirate, and Napoleon would raise even more hackles. Better to stick with figures like Erasmus (in whose name 2 million students have been funded since 1987) or better yet, generic buildings. Europe's universities have dutifully trodden the same path.

The EEC/EU has systematically seeded universities with Jean Monnet chairs, lectureships or fellowships, usually occupied within dedicated European institutes. There is also a European University Institute in Florence for scholars on secondment. It would be fair to say that the prevailing tone is hardly Euro-sceptic, for hungry mouths don't tend to bite hands that feed them. The fact that English is a universal language also means that far more European-born academics work in the UK than in Germany or Poland. Universities are the tip of an iceberg whose submerged bulk consists of hundreds of NGOs which also act as an 'ersatz civil society', receiving major funding from the EU, and which shape environmental or overseas aid policies.[19]

But such rackets for those admitted to the charmed circle pale into insignificance compared with Europe's greater forms of outdoor relief, namely for farmers and disadvantaged regions. The two are interlinked.

Let's start with the earthiest of the real people. The Common Agricultural Policy subsidizes farmers and landowners, partly to guarantee food supply (this a wartime legacy) but also to secure a way of life, for the vast majority of Europe's 10 million farms are very small. But it is striking that the average farm size in the Czech Republic has shot up from 80 to 130 hectares in recent decades. Because since 1999 subsidies are paid according to acreage or hectarage, too much grain is produced (roughly 300 million tonnes) and not enough (labour-intensive) fruit and vegetables. Imports of fruit and vegetables from Chile or Morocco have doubled since 2000, not to mention flowers flown in from Colombia or Kenya. Although lobbyists for farmers and fishermen talk a good game, perhaps it would have been better had EU funding been more evenly spread on other no less deserving constituencies? What made sense in 1958, when 20 per cent of the workforce in Europe worked on the land, does not make sense when by 2010 the full-time farming workforce had shrunk to around 5 per cent. Large cereal farms do not employ many people, and the trend is for farms to grow larger using automation.[20]

Since some countries have efficiently modest farming sectors, Britain being an example, they sought compensation for their CAP contributions through regional funds to address urban dereliction, of which the UK has many examples to choose from. Much money has also sloshed through Brussels on its way to Greece, Italy and Spain and then latterly Eastern Europe. A regulation-sized sign making clear that the blue-spangled banner was responsible marks each example of European munificence, from bridges to hospitals. The subversive political intention, eurosceptics suspect, is to draw these regions closer to Brussels and away from their national capitals. Since 1992 there has been an EU Committee of the Regions, a pseudo-parliament for sub-national politicians, served by a secretariat of 500.

Finally, the European Coal and Steel Community's according of rights and protections to mobile Italian miners and steel workers in the 1950s has been vastly generalized through freedom of movement throughout the Union. In practice this advantaged those on the down slope of weak currencies and low wage rates, as highly unequal economies were rammed together. Manifestly any footloose person with sense would prefer to earn £400 a week cleaning houses in London than the same in a month as a manager or teacher back in Bucharest or Sofia. The proverbial Polish plumbers earn that in a day.

The accession of Bulgaria, Latvia, Poland and Romania meant the arrival of a reserve army of labour, often ready to work long hours in jobs that the idle natives were too grand to touch. Sensible countries imposed 'transitional arrangements' to limit the local impact of this influx; heedless ones like Britain or Ireland did not, and have moaned about it ever since. In Tony

Blair's case, the joke was that he so despised the British working class that he got a Polish substitute, though this may be apocryphal. Access to income supplements and social benefits has also proved contentious, to the point where the presence of these migrant beneficiaries of free movement of labour has itself led to mass alienation from the EU among those who also feel their identities are under threat.

Now these are select clienteles, even if we add investment bankers, patent lawyers, translators and the like. Every now and then the EU offers more general public goods. Climate-change amelioration and energy consolidation are among them, to prevent us looking out on palm trees while the Russians switch the lights off. Rejection of the EU constitution in 2005 by Dutch and French voters was one occasion to revisit pan-European benefits. In 2006 the Commission President, José Manuel Barroso, accordingly urged a 'citizens' agenda' consisting of reducing mobile telephone roaming charges from the extortionate to the domestic rate in a traveller's home country, something that finally happened in 2017. The current President, Jean-Claude Juncker, has responded to evidence of popular disaffection from the project with a public–private stimulus package to combat youth unemployment. All too little, too late, some would say, and they are right.

The EEC/EU has always been an idealistic project, eschewing the power politics that, in reality, have permeated every stage of this story. Along with almost seventy years of intra-European peace was a desire for the EU to be a powerful actor on the world stage. Specifically, it was to be an Empire of Virtue, attracting others to its self-evidently good self. Inspired by its 'cultural, religious and humanist inheritance', the European Union stood for 'the universal values of inviolable and inalienable rights of the human person, freedom, democracy, equality and the rule of law', as the Lisbon Treaty proclaimed in 2007. How could a union that was the handiwork of so many lawyers be otherwise? The problem here was partly that China, Russia and the US generally worked to the old rules, actively rejecting democracy and human rights in the first two cases, though America fully signed up to the same idealistic agenda too, apart from executing murderers.

By 2015–16 the Empire of Virtue was in trouble, though those who merely manage the EU failed to notice that things were falling apart around their ears. The 2008 financial crisis generally subverted the belief that those who seem to master money and numbers actually know what they are doing, other than to make themselves vastly rich. Rigidities in a common currency compounded problems exacerbated by globalization and led to angry leftist populisms in Greece and Spain that evolved from Occupy street movements into neophyte political parties.

The British Labour Party is undergoing a regressive version of the same process even though the tactic of building a surging extra-parliamentary movement benefited Jeremy Corbyn in the election in June 2017 despite every effort to smear him. A weak and divided Conservative government managed the considerable feat of alienating older voters while never attracting the young, though its Prime Minister Theresa May scraped back wounded into Downing Street. But before addressing Europe's populist waves, it is worth identifying other problems that have put the project in jeopardy. If the insurgents come to power, then many of them want referenda on eurozone membership. They differ as to what happens if they win. The French Front National wanted a restored franc for ordinary folk while the euro would be retained for big business engaged in international trade. The Alternativ für Deutschland wants a hard northern euro to include Austria, Germany, Finland and the Netherlands, while France, Greece, Italy, Portugal and Spain either join a soft euro or go their separate ways.[21]

•

Many European nations have proud military histories. Think randomly of the Vikings, Spanish conquistadores, Napoleon's Imperial Guards, the French Foreign Legion and British Royal Marines Commandos. Collectively, 'Europeans' have been formidable, though we would probably celebrate the Roman legions more than the multinational Waffen-SS that invaded the Soviet Union in 1941 along with regular forces from Germany, Finland, Italy, Spain and Rumania that bulked out the Wehrmacht.

Any or all of this figures often on the Yesterday or History channels. Skimming through them it seems to always be the Blitz, D-Day or some ghastly massacre in Poland. As a victor nation, which was never conquered and occupied, the British are particularly prone to this form of nostalgia. War may be part of the European entertainment imagination, but it is retreating as a common experience or concern. War happens elsewhere, also overwhelmingly experienced through TV, and usually in the failing Middle East.

Various reasons have been advanced for this collective transformation, including the end of conscription and advent of professional armed forces. Europe's ageing population does not help either, since fighting is customarily done by superfluous young males in their twenties and thirties. As so often, following the money is a good precept.

In this case, defence spending has been a shrinking portion of national budgets, and significantly less than most post-Second World War states spend on education, health and welfare. Leaving aside the US (3.62 per cent), only four of NATO's European members meet the 2 per cent of GDP spending target promulgated at the 2014 Newport summit. The virtuous boys are Estonia (2.04 per cent), Greece (2.46 per cent), Poland (2.18 per cent) and the UK (2.07 per cent), though the latter achieved this by lumping spending on intelligence with defence. Conspicuous laggards include Germany (1.18 per cent), France (1.8 per cent) and Turkey (1.69 per cent).

In effect, the armed forces have moved from being central to the identities of nation-states to being another service that protects a civilianized way of life, much like firefighters or police officers. In some countries they retain a vestigial presence at the apex of the constitutional order, notably in Britain, where every state occasion sees bearskin hats, greatcoats, medals and swords. That Ruritanian flummery apart, most civilians are still humbly grateful to those men and women who are prepared to die in dusty places, even if the generals leading them are duffers. Most European countries have less ostentatiously post-imperial versions of the same.[22]

The fact that most people are increasingly unlikely to accept their own national governments' decisions to go to war, except if the nation is attacked, means they are highly disinclined to see that decision pass to any supranational entity like the European Union. Most people grasp that terrorism has few military remedies, since asymmetric opponents living among us present few opportunities for a decisive engagement. Terrorists are better fought by the intelligence services and the police, something Europol is supposed to address at the supranational level.

National governments are loath to surrender the right to go to war, or to do anything that needlessly duplicates what NATO has done for over sixty years. That is why NATO almost gets a free pass in the conservative press, though there is plenty of duplication and profligacy there too. Countries may choose close defence partners, as the British and French did with the Lancaster House treaties of 2010, but that is well short of relinquishing control to a European common army. This means that attempts to create joint European forces have not yielded very much, beyond the occasional joint Dutch–German brigade, or France and the UK sharing aircraft carriers, but even here 'Europe' lacks such fundamental assets as heavy-lift aircraft, shared networked intelligence, combat jets and missile systems to make modern war-fighting conceivable. That dovetails nicely with how the Empire of Virtue regards itself. Hence Europe's emphasis on crisis management, conflict resolution and stabilization missions, where troops are more like heavily armed social workers.

Europe also suffers from pointless duplication of equipment, the result of each country insisting on maintaining its own defence industries, largely to reap export sales. Much of the equipment, such as transport planes or helicopters, is old, and readiness rates are deplorable. German Tornados have a 44 per cent readiness rate and their Eurofighters are 52 per cent combat ready. If one reads the German press, hardly a day passes without some fresh equipment and procurement scandal, even down to malfunctioning infantry assault rifles, though the UK has also managed to acquire new warships whose engines fail in warm water despite Britain's strategic reorientation to the Gulf. In

China they would jail whoever was responsible for such a fiasco; in the UK they tend to be given a CBE.

As in other areas, Europe never gives up. As of 2016, member states will contribute to a European Defence Fund, to be used to purchase drones, helicopters and warships, offsetting these loans against their contributions to EU budget targets. A new European Defence Research Programme will use existing funds (€90 million) and money borrowed from the European Investment Bank, totalling €3.5 billion, to fund work on drones and cyber defence. Work already being funded includes German research into mini-drones to patrol EU borders, and Portuguese research on sensors to detect movement inside buildings. Franco-German tank manufacturers have merged, and both countries wish to cooperate on a new fifth-generation combat fighter to replace the Eurofighter and Rafale, bringing Italy in to make a new Euro-drone. Despite British and Polish opposition, EU defence ministers have established a new joint command headquarters to coordinate military operations in North Africa and the Sahel where Nato has little interest. Were President Donald Trump to observe his value-for-money approach to NATO, or decide not to assist containing Russia in the Baltic, then European joint defence efforts might be given a fillip, but this would not change the civilianized mentality in Europe. Trotsky said many stupidly vicious things, but pointing out that one cannot ignore war since it comes looking for you was not among them.[23]

•

Germany is a large country, and what it does affects the whole of Europe, as we have already noticed in the eurozone crisis and its aftermath. A glaring example of the autism of great powers involved the migration crisis that began in 2014. Its most dire effects were felt not by Germany, but in Italy and Greece. Germany's stolid Chancellor Merkel displayed the panicky, reckless streak she had earlier revealed in the wake of the Fukushima nuclear accident in 2011 when she ordered the closure of all German atomic reactors, though clearly her East German background and religiously motivated compassion also played a role.

Merkel's blithe declaration 'we can do it' licensed more than

1.2 million migrants' arrival in Germany. One ex post facto rationalization was that migration would counteract Germany's secular demographic decline though surely migrants become dependent old people too. Germany needed more fecund working-age people to support an ageing population that was not having children. The problem was that training and integrating these people to work in such an advanced economy was a labour of Sisyphus, as the Swedes have also discovered. The Bavarian authorities were also especially overstretched by refugees from Austria and Hungary, and had to hire extra border guards, policemen, translators and teachers even to cope with the flow.

The vetting of refugees and migrants had to be conducted retroactively on people who had often deliberately destroyed their identity papers. That meant it was impossible to discover whether an unaccompanied 'child' of fifteen was a young man of twenty-four, or that 15 per cent of the 'Syrians' were not from Syria at all. A handful of such migrants turned out to be ISIS terrorists, including two of the Bataclan Theatre attackers in Paris on 13 November 2015, as well as the Tunisian Anis Amri, who had come to Italy by boat in 2011. After moving to Germany to evade deportation, Amri murdered twelve people at a Berlin Christmas Market with a marauding truck in December 2016. Apart from terrorists there were Syrian criminal clans who have successfully terrorized the police in sleepy towns like Naumburg.[24]

The ensuing European migrant crisis highlighted the gulf between elite and popular opinion, though those who helped refugees hailed from every class of person. It also exemplified how many people resented being told what to feel and think by the liberal elites. The more the media (and in particular TV) sought to highlight individual tragedies, as hundreds died in capsized boats or lived in squalor in the Calais 'Jungle' waiting to leap aboard a truck to Britain, the less many of their audiences were disposed to have their emotions manipulated by reporters who abandoned any obligation of objectivity. 'You've made it!' one BBC reporter congratulated a migrant coming ashore. Instead of addressing why people felt their identities under threat, liberals tried to avoid this 'conversation', moving swiftly on to how this or that study or report showed why such views were wrong, both factually and implicitly in the moral sense. Viewers divided their attention – and their responses – between drowned infants and angry young men storming flimsy Balkan border posts or attacking long-distance truck drivers entering the Channel Tunnel with clubs and knives.

The inability of governments to grasp the problem strained governing coalitions (notably the German CDU and its more conservative and Catholic Bavarian sister party, the CSU) and benefited insurgent parties that exploited anti-migrant sentiment. In many cases this issue displaced the insurgents' foundational economic Euroscepticism, to the extent that parties of single-issue-obsessed professors became much more 'populist' under alternative leadership. Italy's anarchic Eurosceptic Five Star Movement (5SM) is currently undergoing a similar transformation, with its comedian leader Beppe Grillo demanding repatriation of all illegal migrants, presumably to make 5SM a more attractive future coalition partner for the stridently anti-migrant Lega Nord should Italy hold a general election in 2018.[25]

In no particular order, these parties include France's Front National, Germany's Alternativ für Deutschland, Britain's UKIP, the Dutch Freedom Party, Denmark's People's Party, the Finns Party, the Swiss People's Party, Norway's People's Party, Greece's Golden Dawn and the Lega Nord. We will deal with some of their different ideologies separately, as well as why some became so potent. A few are already in power, either singly or in coalitions, while others expected to benefit in major national elections in March, May, June and September 2017.

Mishandling of the migrant crisis opened major regional rifts within the EU, whose institutions reacted in their customary dilatory way. The European border agency, Frontex, whose HQ, for pork-barrel reasons, was located in Warsaw, hundreds of miles from the Aegean and Mediterranean coasts, was completely overwhelmed. At a conference-cum-therapy session in Bratislava Castle to discuss the impact of Brexit, EU leaders deleted the word 'chaos' from the part of Donald Tusk's speech dealing with the migrant crisis. That said it all, really.[26]

The most obvious fault-line involved the Visegrad Four, the informal alliance of the Czech Republic, Hungary, Poland and Slovakia, formed at Visegrad in Hungary in 1991. These states had no experience of overseas empire and decolonization, but had historically viewed themselves as the external bulwark against 'the Turk'. Hungary and Poland had religious nativist parties in power too. From September 2015 they resisted a German-inspired EU Commission proposal for mandatory migrant quotas to distribute the burden evenly throughout the EU, a proposal accompanied by the veiled threat that their structural development funding might be cut off if they did not comply. Their obstructionism resulted in a shift to closing borders and shutting down migrant routes from the Balkans into Austria and Germany. Blocking the flow of refugees and migrants resulted in the human equivalent of traffic jams, and a new rift involving the two countries worst affected. Greece and Italy felt they were being used as vast holding pens to alleviate the pressure of migrants on Germans and Swedes.[27]

The migration crisis also played havoc with mainstream political parties throughout Europe. While conservative governments could tack right, at least in a rhetorical sense, to stem the exodus of their supporters to the insurgent right, no such option existed on the left, if one discounts such exceptions as Slovakia. The left's traditional alliance of metropolitan intellectuals and the blue-collar working class had collapsed, with immigrants often filling the vacuum, though they could resent illegal migrants too. The European left sought to have its cake and eat it, by opposing globalized multinational capitalism while rejecting any checks on free movement of peoples, since multicultural societies are 'good'. It did not help that their forecasts were out of whack. Labour imagined that 13,000 migrants would come to Britain from new EU accession states; instead, they got over a million. The mainstream left could not address any of this since, as the indigenous industrial working class declined, or migrated to the insurgent right, their own vote depended on urbanized immigrants, and what the British Labour Party clumsily calls 'globally oriented networked youth'. As a result of this, the traditional working class sometimes went 'walkabout', towards the populist right or the cosmopolitan values of metropolises became unmoored from the rest of the country. The Left was always in denial that it would pay that price.

Humanitarian and realist accounts of the migration crisis competed for attention and there was much sloppy invocation of the lessons of the 1930s. Huge numbers of migrants are fleeing war zones such as Iraq, Syria and Somalia, and many of them have a legitimate case to claim asylum, as their lives are menaced in their own country.

By no means all refugees want to go to Europe. In the case of Syrians, an estimated 1 million did so, but the vast majority (4.8 million people) elected to stay in their own part of the world – in Jordan, Lebanon, Turkey and the Kurdistan region of Iraq. These places are coping heroically, despite their own chronic youth unemployment and sectarian tensions, with millions of refugees who want to return home when it is safe to do so. Another 6.6 million Syrians are internally displaced. The enormously wealthy Gulf Arab states have taken no migrants at all even as their money sustains Islamist rebels fighting Assad.

Much of the above would also apply to Afghanistan, though many of its refugees seem to live well enough in neighbouring Iran without venturing further to Europe. Afghanistan is a failed country, afflicted by corruption and multiple rival tribalisms that are not strong enough to dominate the whole, as well as by the zealous Taliban who from 2001–2 onwards the US tried and failed to destroy. The concept of safety is always relative in Afghanistan too since the Taliban are resurgent, besieging Kunduz far from their Pashtun heartland. The country also has a 35 per cent unemployment rate. Under a deal concluded in October 2016, Afghanistan agreed to take back 88,500 failed asylum seekers in return for €3.75 billion in thinly disguised EU 'development aid'.

But not all refugees are fleeing war zones. Many are from North and sub-Saharan Africa. For sure, Eritrea in the Horn of Africa is a despotic place in which military conscription can entail forced labour for life. The EU has given Eritrea €312 million to crack down on people-smuggling, as part of the Khartoum

Process through which further millions also go to the dictatorship of Sudan's Omar al-Bashir.

Most African countries are not hellholes like Eritrea. Nevertheless Burkina Faso, Chad, Gambia, Ghana, Mali, Mauritania, Morocco, Niger, Nigeria, the Republic of South Africa, Senegal, Sierra Leone, not to mention Kenya and Uganda, all produce economic migrants, even though there are plenty of places – from Lagos to Nairobi and down to Johannesburg – where they could find work in highly entrepreneurial economies.

Formerly known as Upper Volta, Burkina Faso has 3,200km of land borders with six neighbours. It has just nineteen fixed border-posts and 300 frontier police, earning $200 a month and with no money for fuel or spare parts for their jeeps. I've seen more adequately equipped personnel protecting elephants and rhinos from poachers. Since a smuggler can earn $5,200 by packing thirty migrants into a bus for a single trip, he can easily afford small bribes that represent a fortune to a policeman.

Europe could get tough with Burkina Faso. It could force the government in Ouagadougou to act by diverting aid towards a proper, well-equipped border force and threaten to cut off aid altogether unless the government cracks down on smugglers. This can be done. President Mahamadou Issoufou of Niger, which will have received €600 million of EU aid by 2020, introduced thirty-year jail sentences for people-smugglers, and under new laws, owners of buses and trucks who collude in smuggling will forfeit them, too.

People-smuggling is big business, worth an estimated $5 to $6 billion a year to the smugglers, according to Europol. It is dominated by loose criminal networks, with drivers, escorts, boat crews, forgers, scouts and other facilitators. Sometimes the smugglers do not move people themselves, since by forging applications for family reunion in half a dozen cities, one can legally import six women who pay for the privilege. Smuggling generates other forms of crime, such as bribing officials and rinsing the cash proceeds into legitimate businesses, and it is sometimes affiliated with financing terrorism.[28]

Aided by smugglers, many migrants crossed Turkey into the western Balkans by land. They could either move north to such preferred destinations as Germany, Sweden and the UK, where they often have family and friends, or try to reach Greece directly via the Dodecanese islands adjacent to the coast of Turkey. Bewildered European holidaymakers found benches and parks filled with refugees and migrants, whose treatment in Greece left much to be desired. It also enabled a genuinely neo-Nazi movement, Golden Dawn, to posture as security guards in edgy neighbourhoods, before going on to establish a welfare network, rather as if it were Hizbollah with swastikas.[29]

The migrant crisis resulted in unilateral abrogations of the Schengen Agreement, which after the 1999 Treaty of Amsterdam had become part of European law, abolishing Europe's internal borders, though Britain and Ireland opted out. Traversing the Balkans to reach Austria was made harder as many of the governments along the route rapidly constructed border fences, sometimes using convicts to do so. Hungary erected razor-wire fences along its borders with Croatia and Serbia. The number of refugees treated for police dog bites rose exponentially. After the EU offered the Turks the equivalent of Anglo-Saxon 'Danegeld' in the shape of €6 billion, President Erdoğan agreed to block this Balkan/Aegean route. As we have seen, he is an emotional fellow and he has also threatened to release the flow if the EU frustrates Turkish EU accession talks. He might soon be able to get his way inside the EU if a united federalized Cyprus becomes his Trojan Horse with Turkish Cypriot veto rights over every national decision.

The refugee crisis has been compared with squeezing a balloon into different shapes. Block one route, and the flow goes elsewhere. With the Balkans closed, in 2016 the majority chose the route across the Mediterranean, travelling from west, central and east sub-Saharan Africa to Libya's long coast. Following US-backed Anglo-French intervention in Libya in 2013, which resulted in the death of Colonel Gaddafi, this militia-dominated failed state became the epicentre of the people-smuggling business. Libya's desert land borders are vast and porous; those with Algeria and Chad are each 1,000km. There are 800,000 migrants waiting for the chance to cross the Mediterranean from Libya. Half a million migrants have already reached Italy in the last three years. So far (June 2017) some 85,000 migrants have crossed from Libya to Italy, though the final number is likely to exceed the 2016 record of 181,000. The largest contingent are Bangladeshis, followed by Nigerians.

In Gaddafi's day, the smugglers were under his control and the seas were patrolled by his coastguard and navy. He earned himself millions – the Italian government under his friend Silvio Berlusconi happily stumped up – just by threatening to allow migrants into Italy, thereby 'turning Europe black', as the Colonel charmingly put it.

With Gaddafi gone, Libya became a paradise for people-smugglers. Migrants pass via extensive chains of Eritrean, Ethiopian and Sudanese middlemen into the hands of Libyans who keep them in warehouses. One is at Sabratha, a former Roman amphitheatre on the outskirts of Tripoli, where migrants languish like numbered livestock until they cough up more money for the sea voyage. Local militias protect the smugglers, especially the big men, like Eritrean-Ethiopian Ermias Ghermay or Libyan Dr Mosaab Abu Grein. In Khartoum, the smuggler kingpins consort openly with the army.

Libyan smugglers dispatch migrants to sea with rudimentary navigational instructions and a mobile phone, to which they text a number for the Italian coastguard after ten hours have elapsed. There is an acute shortage of boats since these are intended to be one-way trips. That is why dirigibles that could safely carry twenty people are crammed with a hundred, as well as rackety old wooden boats that soon sink. An estimated 5,000 of these Mediterranean migrants drowned in 2016 alone, 3,770 the year before, though these figures are probably underestimates since many drownings go unreported.

Once in Italy, the migrants pass into the hands of local factors of the criminal networks. They are stored in houses, often sleeping upright, if greed dictates it. We know a lot about this since Sicilian prosecutors with extensive experience of the Mafia know how to intercept their phones and use surveillance cameras. The migrants are moved to Bologna and then take trains to Rosenheim in Bavaria. The Italians have discovered that as the Germans denied the Italian Mafia existed (until people were shot in German restaurants), so they are in denial about organized people-smuggling, even though much of the cash proceeds is laundered by pseudo-migrants living openly in Germany, such as Ghermay's wife Mana Ibrahim, who lives in Frankfurt.[30] Since attempts to stabilize Libya are a very tortuous process (Italy is the only country with an embassy there), the Italian government is trying to implement a domestic quota programme requiring cities to house migrants who are no longer able to move north to Germany or Sweden.[31]

Any money the EU slowly disburses to diminish the push factors in Africa has to compete with the cash being made by the unscrupulous. Local smuggling networks in Africa offer pay-as-you-go and full package options for would-be migrants. The former involves a migrant travelling in stages, stopping – often for a year – to earn enough money for the next leg of the journey. The latter can cost anything up to $40,000 and involve entire families, including members already in Europe, making an investment in a single large payment on the promise that, once successful, the migrant will remit money home from the El Dorado that is Europe. Human nature ensures that the new home, however cold, shabby and unwelcoming, is depicted as wonderful.

Smugglers also offer credit options which can lead to a migrant being in perpetual debt and forced to work in prostitution or as slave labour in the black economy in order to get his or her passport back. Strictly speaking, this is coercive and criminal human trafficking rather than people smuggling, which relies on the active complicity of entire families.

Several things could usefully be done to prevent the migrant crisis becoming perpetual, for there is no shortage of people fleeing war zones, drought or desertification, or simply wanting a better life.

There should be a European debate about whether the 1951 UN Refugee Convention should now apply to economic migrants from other continents. The point is that the current crisis is not a one-off event like the Second World War, which saw West Germany absorb millions of ethnic German expellees, or more pertinently, the exodus of 300,000 Hungarians after the failed

1956 uprising. As Christian Europeans, the latter were easily absorbed by host nations that shared their visceral hatred of communism. By 1959, 38,000 Hungarians were resettled in the US, 25,000 in Canada and 20,000 in Britain. Rightly or wrongly, many people in Europe sense that the current million-plus migrants are an advance guard of tens of millions of refugees and migrants, both actual and potential. What happens, for example, when the regime of the ailing Abdelaziz Bouteflika in Algeria expires, or if Yemen runs out of water, as its capital is projected to do in four years' time? If Iraq or Syria fragment, how long before bouts of ethnic cleansing generate more refugees, not to mention any war involving the Kurds, Iraqis and Turkey?[32]

At present a European maritime Operation Sophia (and land-based training programme for coastguards and police in Libya) is costing €35 million per week. Aid money should also be spent on sending European policemen to these countries in Africa to focus the minds of the local police on the problem. There should be a massive public information campaign in the migrants' home countries to puncture delusions about life in Europe. This should highlight the deadly risks that illegal migrants take, pointing out that many drown, their bodies ending up at the bottom of the Mediterranean, and that the local economic and political climate is unwelcoming.[33]

If Europe were serious about this problem, it would also introduce draconian penalties for domestic employers of illegal migrant labour, or those who cram dozens of them into tiny basements or garden extensions and sheds. As the Italians have urged, freelance NGOs should deliver any migrants they rescue from inshore waters either back to Libya, or if rescued further out, to more EU countries, so as to relieve the strain on southern Italy.

The entire process of repatriating failed asylum-seekers should be accelerated, only allowing them to appeal decisions once outside the EU area in defiance of lawyers who see these clients as a gravy train as well as a humanitarian cause. The Italians have ordered 30,000 failed asylum-seekers to leave, but only 5,000 have done so. They are opening sixteen detention centres to hold these people prior to deportation. There are half a million failed asylum-seekers languishing in Germany.

Measures like these would diminish the opportunities for human-rights lawyers and humanitarian NGOs to prolong anti-deportation proceedings at public expense and for their own enrichment. Current EU policy is to push the migration issue outside Europe by paying Libya €200 million to staunch the flow of migrants, while affording Jordan and Lebanon the kind of deal that was concluded with Turkey to encourage refugees to remain in their home region. The trouble here is that once word of a crackdown circulates, would-be migrants will make even more effort to get to Europe before it becomes impossible.[34]

While European states should respect international obligations to those fleeing war zones, they are not under any obligation to redress the world's economic inequalities. Middle-class writers often extol the virtues of multicultural inner-city areas, but empathy is quickly exhausted in those who have to compete with migrants for basic services. Uncontrolled illegal migration impacts unfairly on benefits, education, health, housing services, private-sector rents and public transport in ways that destroy any notion of the contributory element that lies at the heart of Europe's generous welfare states, not to mention the link between taxes and basic services. This is before we briefly raise less tangible issues like 'trust' (for example that migrants will not corrupt the electoral system) or the desirability of separate multicultural enclaves in which indigenous 'outsiders' are resented. Apart from the importation of foreign intra-group hostilities, nothing new among Greek and Turkish Cypriots or Kurds and Turks, many European societies have had to struggle with the antediluvian attitudes of some Muslim males towards women in general, from Cologne to Rotherham.

As we have witnessed in various European countries as well as the US, the anger queue-jumping engenders quickly assumes political forms. What on earth do Europe's leaders imagine is driving this angry 'populism', including that of established legal immigrants who have patiently made a new life in a sometimes hostile environment? It is not rage at the common fisheries policy or at such abstractions as 'neoliberalism'.

Illegal migration is an insidious problem that strips desperately poor countries, remittances apart, of precisely the enterprising young who ought to remain there, while oppressing the poorest sections of our own societies (notably earlier migrants) with people who compete for diminishing resources while expectations are rising.[35]

Migration also raises the questions of whether one can simply uproot people from entirely different cultural universes and expect them to thrive in societies that may subscribe to other values, with radically different expectations of their citizens, attitudes to women being a conspicuous case in point. Demonstrations of humanitarian liberality seem strange when the beneficiaries sometimes prove to be highly illiberal themselves. Above all, voters would have liked to have been asked about the rapid transformation of their own societies, though this has never explicitly been the case. A reasonable argument could be made for Europe to emulate the US as a land of industrious immigrants, but until voters are given that choice and the information that contradicts as well as supports that case, they will resent this being done without their consent by elites who themselves use none of the same services but who benefit from cheap migrant labour.

•

Migration clearly fuelled various manifestations of populism that enabled fringe parties to cross over into the mainstream, while dragging the discourse of mainstream parties their way. When the migrants were Muslim, including some who refused to assimilate, this also reinforced various latent anxieties about fundamental European cultural identity that secularism had contributed to with its purposive uncertainties. Though Europe is often depicted, by secularists, as the summation of Enlightenment and liberal virtues (although these are not evenly spread), it is also a venerable Judeo-Christian culture, and some of that is neither liberal nor soft, however much faith leaders aver otherwise. A couple of examples, France and Hungary, can serve to illustrate some of the historical forces at work here.

The French far right has very deep roots going back to

conservative reactions to the Enlightenment and the French Revolution. The nationalist thinker Charles Maurras and his Catholic, monarchist *Action Française* magazine and movement represented one stream, which was a reaction to left-wing support for Alfred Dreyfus in the late 1890s. Maurras was an agnostic, but he regarded Catholicism as vital to the integration of nation and society. This strain of the French Right may have been damaged by Vichy's record of collaboration, but it has not disappeared. Resentful former Pétainistes were one contributory element in the post-war far right, but it also appealed to many former wartime resisters like Pierre Poujade, who in the 1930s had been a fascist. Poujade founded a shopkeepers' protest movement in 1956, one of whose members was Jean-Marie Le Pen. He was one of those who hated de Gaulle for handing Algeria back to the Arabs, and for the earlier loss of French Indochina. Many of these tough former soldiers had supported the terroristic Secret Army Organization or OAS.

Founded in 1972, the Front National combined neo-pagan mumbo jumbo and nationalism with a virulent hatred of Jews. Since this mixture lacked broad electoral appeal, by the late 1970s it was downplayed in favour of attacks on the Establishment 'gang of four' main political parties, and opposition to primarily North African Arab immigration. This had little to do with Islam, for at that time religion hardly figured in discussion of migration anywhere, not least because Islam had yet to enter its pathological phase. The chief slogan was 'One million unemployed is one million immigrants too many'. Jobs and welfare were to be subject to 'national preference', meaning benefits should be restricted to what are known as 'French people from the stump'.

FN policy proposals initially combined elements of Anglo-Saxon deregulatory liberal economics with strategic nationalizations and stringent external protectionism. They acquired depth after its new leader, Marine Le Pen (Jean-Marie's youngest daughter), met a bright young ENA graduate, Florian Philippot, in 2009. He had admired the left-wing Gaullist nationalist Jean-Pierre Chevènement, who resigned from Mitterrand's cabinet in 1983 and who opposed the EMS, Maastricht and the euro. He also wanted France to revert to its semi-detached stance in NATO. Le Pen adopted both Philippot and his brand of economic nationalism in her presidential campaign. This programme was further to the left than anything offered by most mainstream social democrats. She wanted a plan for strategic renationalizations, tariff walls, a separation of investment and retail banking, a transactions tax on shares, a cap on credit-card charges, no further welfare cuts and no privatization of public services, a free health service and an end to open borders. In a nutshell, all benefits were to be focused on native French people and Europe was to revert to a happy assemblage of sovereign nation-states, shorn of the EU's federalizing goals.[36]

Opposed to GATT and CAP, the Front National also wants to protect traditional rural French life. It is big on ecology and animal welfare, too. The actress Brigitte Bardot is a fervent FN supporter. In fact, Marine Le Pen went on a 2017 tour inspecting cows and cuddling dogs, cats and rescued Guyanese sloths.[37] Pets were the last straw in Marine's troubled relations with her father after one of his Dobermanns killed her favourite Bengal cat, Arthemys, and she moved out of the family's residential complex. Other policies are aggressively philoprogenitive (more French babies for mothers staying at home) or seek to purge education and culture of the dominant left which highlights the Occupation, Vichy and colonialism at the expense of all else. Disneyland Paris, Hollywood and US cable TV imports won't thrive under the Front either.

Although it goes unremarked, a kind of cultural Christianity is mixed in with the populist right. In Denmark, the anti-Islamist People's Party was created by a Lutheran pastor, Søren Krarup, after Muslim migrants complicated the reciprocal trust on which a system that fused high taxes and generous welfare payments was based. Since 1905 France has formally separated Church and state, though culturally France is a Christian country, with Jewish and Muslim minorities. This was a problem for the FN. The party included fascistic neo-pagans who worshipped pre-Christian Celtic symbols, secular supporters of laicity and an influx of conservative Catholics who detested the reforms of the Second Vatican Council, notably the new vernacular liturgy.

One solution was to find a common symbol that would keep everyone happy. In 1978 the Front alighted on Joan of Arc, the humble (i.e. non-elite) shepherdess who vanquished and then was martyred by the English. Jean-Marie's daughter closely identified herself with Joan (the clue is in gender), whose day the FN took to celebrating on 1 May to provoke the left, though after Brexit the English are not so villainous as that legend insists.[38]

Although Catholic support for the FN was initially lower than from the rest of the population, this changed, for like extreme parties of the left that mutated into chichi Eurocommunists, those on the far right could also change their spots. Marine Le Pen sought to make the FN a more normal part of French democracy, ostensibly marginalizing the skinhead thugs whose company her father had not declined, given his own frisson of violence (one eye was damaged in a fight). She disavowed Papa's overt racism, usually delivered with malicious subtlety rather than in the argot of the sergeants' mess. A number of French Jews joined the party and Le Pen's partner Louis Aliot was keen to recruit them. A 2014 poll put Jewish support for the FN at 13.5 per cent, though since Jews are 1 per cent of the French population they are electorally insignificant.[39]

The idea that 'Europe' is under external attack by an aggressive politico-religious ideology, call it Islamism, salafism and so forth, has become axiomatic in some circles. Fear of 'Islam's' European ambitions has been pumped up by books like *Eurabia: The Euro-Arab Axis* (2005), by Swiss-based Bat Ye'or (the pseudonym for Gisele Littman), which claims Europeans are sliding into *dhimmitude*, a cultural cringe akin to the actual legal status of non-Muslims in the historic Muslim world. A dozen other books do the same thing in less strident tones though often with diminishing insight, and claims that 'Europe' is facing its 'end' are as ridiculous as saying that 'Africa' or 'Asia' are bound for the scrapheap. Maybe this kind of thing works best as fiction? The French novelist Michel Houellebecq described this collective fate in imaginative form in his *Submission* (2015), confirming him as the writer with the greatest instinctual feel for these times.

The more Marine Le Pen turned to attacking creeping Islamization the more younger Catholics she attracted, especially when she emphasized France's Catholic roots and deplored the proliferation of minarets and mosques. This was despite some tensions. Le Pen is a keen supporter of laicity, who wants to ban yarmulkes and veils as well as halal and kosher food. She regards modern churches as infected with pro-migrant liberal multiculturalism. Catholics with traditional views on abortion and same-sex marriage – who were increasingly mobilized – could not fail to notice her relaxed attitude to the former, and that she was divorced and surrounded by an increasing number of openly gay neo-fascist supporters who had registered that crazed Islamists in Mosul or Raqqa hurl gays from tall buildings. Reflecting a process of *'homonationalism'*, 33 per cent of gay couples voted FN in the 2015 regional elections.[40]

French religious sociology makes religion tricky terrain for the FN. While Marine Le Pen plays well in the post-industrial, secular North of France, her niece Marion Maréchal-Le Pen, the apple of Grandpa's eye, plays better in the more religious southeast and is spoken of as a future leader.[41] She took part in Catholic protests against same-sex marriage and adoption. But one should not underrate Marine, a confident, relaxed and open-faced blonde born in 1968, and whose background was as a lawyer, with the stolidity of an office manager in a provincial accountancy firm. Having survived a 1976 bomb attack on her parents' apartment at eight years of age, her mother walking out at fifteen, and being shunned by lawyer colleagues who called her a whore and spat on the floor in the cafeteria, Marine Le Pen is a very tough woman. Her final gambit was to drop all reference to the Front National in her election campaign in 2017 and then to resign as head of her own party, offering voters herself 'for France'.[42]

The existence of a large and militant silent Christian majority was revealed when François Fillon, a Thatcherite and socially conservative Catholic, defeated Bordeaux mayor Alain Juppé and Nicolas Sarkozy for the presidential nomination for the Republicans in late 2016 after tapping into the militancy of the Catholic lay organization Sens Commun. In the event,

Fillon's candidacy was immediately holed below the waterline by 'Penelopegate' – his wife had been paid large amounts of public money for a job whose nature was obscure – and other revelations about cash for access and gifts of expensive bespoke suits which made him the best-dressed man in French politics.[43] The French Left was also bitterly divided between a lacklustre Socialist Party candidate (Benoît Hamon) and the ageing Trotskyite firebrand Jean-Luc Mélenchon. The awful nightmare arose of a run-off between a fascist and a Trotskyite before French voters recovered their sanity.

This created a space for an untried populist centrist, the young banker Emmanuel Macron, who after deserting President Hollande's unpopular government founded a movement En Marche that drew support from across the political spectrum. Although Macron won a convincing victory over Le Pen in the presidential election final round in May 2017, after she showed her darker colours in a TV debate, it was worrying that half the electorate had also voted for two anti-globalist, anti-EU, protectionist candidates (Mélenchon and Le Pen) in either the first or second rounds. Whether Macron's presidency will be a temporary reprieve or permanent salvation from France's miserabilist mood remains to be seen. In June 2017 he won an overwhelming majority – on a very low turnout – in the 577–seat National Assembly, comprised of a new presidential bloc based on moderate conservative supporters of Alain Juppé and the 'Blairites' he coaxed from the Socialist party and a large number of political neophytes. Whether the labour unions will collaborate with his reforms remains to be seen, though it is worth recalling that only 11 per cent of workers are union members. While the largest union is willing to cooperate, the more leftist CGT will not. Its 'tankie' members will prefer the Leninist maxim 'the worse the better'. If one includes the high abstention rate, Macron has less than 20 per cent popular support in a system which gives him a royal flush in terms of institutional power. His efforts to restore the dignity of the presidency have also led to jibes about the 'Sun King' or 'Manupiter' in a word-play on 'Jupiter', which was how Louis XIV was dubbed by his critics. That very dominance may propel opponents onto the streets, for in any inclusive democracy, 'stones are converted into ballots' as Engels put it. Macron's plans to reform the EU are contingent on proving to the Germans that he has successfully reformed France, and even then Berlin is likely to remain sceptical about any fiscal transfer union. Still, following on from elections in Austria and the Netherlands, Macron's election stalled a supposedly ineluctable populist insurgency, and it may restore the Franco-German axis that lies at the heart of the Union.[44]

•

The venerable roots of the far right are also apparent in Hungary, where a right-wing populist authoritarian is Prime Minister. In a sunny field near Hungary's beautiful Lake Balaton one August day last year, a heavy metal band called Kárpátia was thrashing away, with the usual crowd of hirsute youth swilling beer and banging their heads. So far we could be anywhere in the twenty-first century, though a huge banner depicting Attila the Hun might be unusual at Glastonbury. Many of the audience also had tattoos of the Turul bird, a falcon-like mythological creature that fought off eagles belonging to enemies.

But what were those banners which the young crowd unfurled? They were not the red, white and green Hungarian flag, but a modified version, in which two angels prop up a coat of arms from the first Kingdom of Hungary. These were the Magyar Árpáds, whose first Christian scion, King-cum-Saint Stephen, founded Hungary on Christmas Day 1000. The rock fans waving this flag almost certainly knew that the last people to use it were the Arrow Cross fascists, who in the final year of the war helped the Nazis to deport Hungary's Jews, of whom half a million perished.[45]

Many of Kárpátia's songs celebrate the much larger Hungary which disappeared after the Treaty of Trianon in 1920 gave away almost two-thirds of the Hungarian part of the old multinational Dual Monarchy. The Carpathian mountains, referred to in the band's name, are nowadays part of Romanian Transylvania.

Hungary, which joined the EU in 2004, is a pretty secular country. The communist regime crushed the life out of Hungary's churches, turning the Catholic Cardinal József Mindszenty into an international martyr. About 38 per cent are nominally Roman Catholic, but there is a sizeable Calvinist minority, which includes the current Prime Minister, Viktor Orbán, and a smaller Lutheran one. Orbán was first Prime Minister in 1998–2002, though he returned to power in 2010 with a super majority that enabled his party, Fidesz (the Hungarian abbreviation for Federation of Young Democrats), to alter the constitution in 2011.

Fidesz has internal and external agendas. A football-mad former student radical who saw the right light in the early 1990s, Orbán positively revels in being 'illiberal'. Under his regime there has been some nostalgia for Admiral Miklós Horthy, the authoritarian who ruled Hungary as Regent from 1920 until the Germans defenestrated him in 1944. Fidesz has used state funds and media control to rig the political system against the opposition, and an unrepresentative consultation of under a million people to rewrite the constitution. The judiciary were purged and the remit of the Constitutional Court restricted. As the rule of law atrophied, the unexamined power of Hungarian oligarchs flourished, often in corrupt ways.

Though a member of the conservative European People's Party bloc in the European Parliament, Fidesz also seeks to consolidate a sense of nationhood by attacking the European Union and globalization. By granting Hungarian citizenship to 3 million Hungarians in the former Greater Hungary, Orbán is pandering to dreams of a 'Hungarian Euroregion'. The hostility to the EU is simply explained. It involves contrasting Hungarian democracy with a 'preachy and paralysed' EU liberal universalism, thereby enabling majority national governments to pose as persecuted minorities themselves. Thus conservative Hungary, Poland or Russia can be victims of 'Gayropa'. Orbán meets Putin once year, crafting gas and nuclear deals with the Russians and collaborating on how to combat civil-society lobbyists. Although a decade ago Orbán was a critic of Russia, nowadays there are multiple shady links and the 1956 Uprising is described as a CIA plot. A new statue by a Russian artist commemorating the Red Army's role in suppressing it has appeared in Budapest.[46]

Hungary is unusual in having a further right-wing party of some scale. This is Jobbik Magyarországért Mozgalom, or the

Movement for a Better Hungary, Jobbik for short, which polls around 17 per cent of the vote. Jobbik was founded by conservative students in 2002. Originally it focused on Hungary's Roma (Gypsy) minority as the source of all social evils. In 2007 it established a uniformed paramilitary Hungarian Guard that bore a close resemblance to the old Arrow Cross. But Jobbik has a bigger target in its sights, namely the Jews, whom it blames for the ill effects of globalized capitalism on Hungary, after the bumpy transition from communism in the 1990s.

Unlike the Roma, who number anywhere between 450,000 and a million people, Hungary's 100,000 Jews are not a large or visible minority in a country of 10 million. Yet a remarkable number of Hungarians think Jews control the country (a third), a quarter argue Jews are too influential, and 15 per cent want Jews to leave.[47] Asked to name one, many would alight on George Soros, the New York-based financier and philanthropist, who is denounced as a CIA stooge, even though Fidesz originally benefited from his Open Society NGO's largesse. In 1989 Orbán himself received a Soros grant to study at Oxford's Pembroke College, though he is now trying to close Soros's Central European University and used disgusting anti-Semitic posters of Soros to attack him in July 2017.[48] If detestation of the market makes the Hungarian far right unusual, so does its attitude to Islam. Whereas Fidesz is avowedly Islamophobic, Jobbik is pro-Arab (and anti-Israeli) and pro-Turkish. The Hungarian Guard leader, Gábor Vona, dreams of a great 'neo-Turanian' alliance including Hungarians, Turks and the peoples of the Turkic oil- and rug-stans.[49]

Until recently religion did not play a major role in Hungarian politics. Originally Fidesz was anti-clerical and Jobbik neo-pagan, with the least religious supporters of any political party. But both parties have recognized that cultural Christianity can be a powerful shaper of national identity. In fact, Christianity can become part of a new political religion, which fuses the Christian heritage (St Stephen) with the Turul bird of prey, which is pagan and tribal in origin. Fidesz and Jobbik are not tools of powerful religious interests, like the PiS (Law and Justice party) in Poland, which represents a reactionary strand of

Polish Catholicism that is busily taking Poland backwards and eastwards. The three churches have been co-opted to run Hungary's education and health services, while religious studies became part of the elementary school curriculum in 2013. So did books by anti-Semitic authors from the interwar period, while statues of Horthy began to appear too.

In effect, there is a growing fusion between Fidesz and Jobbik. This is reflected in what the co-founder of Fidesz wrote about Roma in a friendly newspaper: 'A significant part of the Roma are unfit for coexistence. They are not fit to live among people. These Roma are animals, and they behave like animals . . . These animals shouldn't be allowed to exist. In no way. That needs to be solved – immediately and regardless of the method.'[50] Jobbik has other targets. In late 2013 it proposed to register all Hungarian Jews so as to 'evaluate' the danger of any in government or parliament, and although this blast from the European past was soon rescinded, the World Jewish Congress was rightly alarmed. Since 2015 the influx of migrants has led Fidesz and Jobbik to defend Hungary aggressively (with border fences), all in the name of what a Christian Europe should do. Hungary was probably the sole country in the EU where the Catholic Church declined to help migrants and refugees alongside NGOs. As Orbán told the European Parliament in May 2015, he wanted 'to keep Europe for the Europeans, and . . . Hungary as a Hungarian country'. He is an admirer of the new bilateral and nationalistically assertive era of Trump, Putin and Xi.

•

The Front National, Fidesz and Jobbik are part of a much broader pan-European 'populist' insurgency, though only some of those parties that have achieved power can be reclassified as authoritarian nationalists. For reasons that seem overly defensive, the term populist occasionally raises hackles, especially among populists, for whom the history of North or South America is not a strongpoint. A Mexican would find it unexceptional when contemplating the leftist Andrés Manuel López Obrador, a name one does not encounter in the British tabloid press. There the term is attacked as snobby liberal code for calling ordinary people bigots and racists though the term surely means far more than that. In fact the term populism is fairly neutral, but it is also clumsy, for it seeks to describe many things that may not consort easily. A good way of thinking about it is in terms of family portraiture, in which all members share big ears or the loping 'Habsburg' jaw.

A dictionary definition of a populist is 'a member of a political party seeking to represent the interests of ordinary people'. This is not entirely correct since there have been populist movements which never became parties. In the late 1940s Italy had Guglielmo Giannini's Fronte dell'Uomo Qualunque (Common Man's Front) and more famously, for it lent itself to a new political category, 'Poujadism', named after Pierre Poujade, who launched a Shopkeepers and Artisans' Defence Union in 1956 to protest sales taxes and department stores. It was one of the streams that flowed into the Front National.[51]

The people can be variously described as epitomizing the *volonté générale* (general will), *Volksgeist* (spirit of the Volk) or the 'silent majority'.[52] Sometimes they have common sense on their side, but at other times not. The obvious danger here is that sizeable minorities will be dismissed and traduced as 'the other people' as Trump puts it, along with all the non-elected elites, such as central bankers, judges, and professional experts of one kind or another, without whom our democracies and societies cannot smoothly function. Some data from the US indicates why we may need experts. In what was not a joke, in 2015 Democrat and Republican voters were asked their views on the US bombing Agrabah. A third of Republicans were eager to do this, as were 19 per cent of Democrats. The problem was that Agrabah is a fictional place in the 1992 Disney cartoon film *Aladdin*. The year before only one in six Americans could place Ukraine on a map, the median response being to locate it in Latin America or Australia. That is what experts are for. The notion that we can arrive at an informed view, of brain surgery, engineering or gas geopolitics after a brief review of Wikipedia seems to have become as pervasive as the belief that there is some democracy of opinion which would surely not extend to our dentist or heart surgeon.[53]

This is not to deny that populists have justifiable reasons for their revolt against Established elites. The ruling elites are no longer merely national either, but hidden behind such acronyms as the ECB, EU, IMF and so on, acronyms that can have the fate of nations in their hands.

Populism suggests that something has gone very wrong with the elites, as the American social historian Christopher Lasch noted a few decades ago. Without being overly nostalgic, an earlier generation of politicians often had direct experience of ordinary people, whether through service in the armed forces or as trades unionists, which enabled them to communicate in the same language. One might not have liked what was being said, but the person's experience down a coalmine, on a farm or a D-Day beach encouraged respect. They had a sense of public service rather than of personal entitlement, if only because opportunities to turn political office into money were not so great while deference was higher. Imagine now a kind of new meritocratic aristocracy with none of the virtues of old aristocracies, and which has sealed itself off from public services. For sure they call their foreign cleaners 'love' and donate to the world's starving, but most of their serious energy goes into self-cultivation and guaranteeing their children's membership of the new elites. The current political class are the cumulative products of very similar backgrounds, the same elite schools and universities – whose major selling point is their cosmopolitan difference from the country they are in – followed by stints in think tanks or as aides to more senior politicians. It is telling that only 2 per cent of deputies in France's National Assembly come from working-class backgrounds. This class become a blur of earnest young men (and women) in identical suits and open-necked shirts, toiling over their computer screens and slightly intoxicated by 'ideas' and trained in the same media skills that enable them to avoid giving honest answers. In some cases they have also become a hereditary caste, as have such occupations as journalism or TV where nepotism is even more rife among those who have graduated from conscientiously writing clever undergraduate essays to weekly columns though the difference is often not discernible. Having been 'rivals', superannuated politicians join together chummily on the sofas of TV programmes with political themes. Instead of anything as quaint as public service, these people regard politics as an entry on their CV before they get on with the real business of earning serious money, for many are out of politics by their late forties. An inadvertent insight into this mentality was provided by Samantha Cameron when, on launching a new range of designer dresses, she remarked in a magazine profile that since 'Dave' had done 'his thing' for many years, it was now time for her to 'do her thing'. Eleanor Roosevelt she was not, speaking of whom, FDR himself (a product of Groton and Harvard) had a burning commitment to social reform as well as being a great war leader. One can safely assume that whereas a statue of FDR watches over Grosvenor Square in London, there will be no statue commemorating David Cameron. Perhaps just a selfie of his and Samantha's toes in a villa bedroom, which the former Prime Minister thoughtfully shared with his social media followers in the week an election was held to clear up the mess he left behind.

Critics of populism, which means most of those writing about it, scarcely mention political corruption or the thriving democratic cultures of most populist movements. Many European countries have undergone major political scandals involving money (the 2009 '£1,600 duck house' parliamentary expenses scandal exposed by the *Daily Telegraph* in the UK and sundry sordid episodes in France, Germany, Italy and above all Greece and Spain) which, unsurprisingly, have left many citizens angry and disdainful towards all politicians who become 'the caste' or 'class'. Nor do people appreciate the unseemly revolving doors through which senior politicians like José Manuel Barroso, Gerhard Schröder, Tony Blair, and David Cameron have passed in order to make a lot of money, whether with Gazprom, Goldman Sachs or JP Morgan, though Cameron's services seem restricted to the hospitality and tourism sectors.

The critics also underestimate the internal democracy of most populist parties (which seem to enjoy perpetual leadership elections) and the fact that all those who have joined coalition governments are willing to be voted out of office when the time comes. The internal affairs of populist parties resemble what the Germans call *Vereinsmeirerei*, meaning the procedural obsessiveness of a stamp-collecting club. Moreover, many populist parties seek more Californian- or Swiss-style referenda to transmit the popular will. If some of them had their way, we would be perpetually voting, a nightmare to most sensible people who already balk at two or three elections per year, as the French showed in June 2017 when only 49 per cent of them voted. The computer mastermind Gianroberto Casaleggio, the muse to Beppe Grillo, who made the Italian 5SM movement such a success online, believed (he died in 2016) that by 2054 there would be a world government under an enlightened despot, with constant voting on every issue via the Internet.

Unlike fascism, or such 'demobilizing authoritarians' as Franco and Salazar, populism can be a means of extending democratic representation to marginalized groups. In some countries swathes of people have been deliberately politically excluded by ruling elites. Think of how Erdoğan's AKP galvanized the pious so-called Black Turks of Anatolia against the ruling Kemalist elites. As an Aymara Indian, Evo Morales similarly mobilized indigenous Bolivians as did Hugo Chávez with Venezuelans in the countryside. There is a similar problem in developed societies with the walking wounded of globalization in depressed areas where time seems to have stood still, though they are notionally politically represented. The elites are no longer merely national either, but part of a free-floating global class. They are 'rootless cosmopolitans' (old code for Jews), 'citizens of everywhere and nowhere' or 'Davos Man', habitués of the annual Alpine gathering of movers and shakers.

Populism is not solely the fault of failing elites but of structural trends in all developed societies which are likely to accelerate. We can see growing divides between the metropolis and the country 'hinterland' in many countries. In the 1920s and 1930s many European capital cities were equally politically and culturally out of sync with their rural hinterlands, for example Red Vienna or Red Berlin and Madrid. Something like that is happening today, except the division is almost like the early modern one between 'court' and 'country' that led to civil wars and insurgent regional oppositions, as in the seventeenth century, when parts of the aristocracy united with the labouring classes to oppose both absolutist courts and the urban middle classes. Poland has been one of Europe's outstanding success stories. In 1991 its GDP was 10 per cent of Germany's, but twenty-six years later it has risen to 53 per cent. Yet Poland too has depressed and neglected regions, known as 'Polska B', which contrast with the bustling capital. There are a lot of British, French, German, Italian and Spanish 'Bs' too and not much of an idea about how to fix them.[54]

Many developed countries have also witnessed a retreat from belonging and membership, as political parties and trades unions go the way of Christian Churches. People become lonely atoms trundling around Aldi, Carrefour, Lidl or Waitrose, to be cashed out by imperious machines, and then captives of a plastic screen in their living rooms showing endless 'news', reality TV and police dramas. Many don't read a newspaper, with the civically important local versions vanishing even more rapidly than the nationals. Civic engagement shrinks while mass migration has undermined social trust which relies on familiarity with customs and agreed norms.

The state of political parties is worth examining, too. Mass parties, including those called People's this or Volks that, represent a few hundred thousand activists, although the British Labour Party currently boasts 600,000 members. Worse, a pervasive professionalization of politics led to a choice between small differences, akin to that between Coca-Cola and Pepsi. Marine Le Pen combined the Gaullist UMP and the Socialist PS into a single UMPS to signify this fusion of what her colleague Beppe Grillo calls *la casta*. The political class all employ the same policy jargon, disconnected from how real people actually discuss things, while the incestuous gossipy doings of a tiny bunch of special advisers and the media that latch on to them become a form of entertainment in their own right. All of which is virtually incomprehensible to anyone outside these bubbles. Why vote for politicians who won't even talk about your concerns, or who seek to dismiss them with reasoned factual evasions lest they subvert the presumed wisdom of increased immigration and multiculturalism? Or who spout nostalgic patriotic platitudes, and the verities of trickle-down economics, that are obviously at variance with either the reality of where power in the modern world lies or who controls enormous wealth.[55]

Populism does not solely consist of parties of the nationalist nativist Eurosceptic right. Europe has also witnessed a collapse of mainstream social democracy and the rise of insurgent challengers from the far left. Greece's Syriza and Spain's Podemos are good examples of these radical insurgents. Both were inspired by what they imagined had happened in Chávez's Venezuela though under his successor it has sunk into anarchy, poverty and repression. Indeed, Caracas was revealed to have subsidized think-tank jobs for Podemos leaders. These movements severally gained momentum from the 2008 financial crisis, which spawned a number of occupy movements that mutated into political parties or consolidated fringe left-wing factions. They identified 'neoliberalism' as the chief ideological culprit, while accusing mainstream social democratic parties of being the bankers' collaborators in a more moralized Blairite version of the capitalist status quo. The young populist leaders had all the fervour of the seminar room, and like students seemed to relish debates that went through the night. In the Greek case while the country they ruled went to hell in a handcart, though not the hell of Venezuela.

Unsurprisingly, such parties did best in weak southern economies where mandatory austerity had blighted so many young as well as old lives. In Greece, in January 2015 Syriza was elected with a mandate to defy the international financial institutions managing the country's debt crisis as well as to clean up the Augean stables of corruption. In the event, Syriza's gamesmanship – as practised by its absurdly self-confident Finance Minister Yanis Varoufakis – merely irritated its northern creditors, while it did little to curb the power of the oligarchy or to break the clientelism which lies at the heart of Greece's problems. How could it, since Syriza had its own clients among radical students, many of them well into middle age, and bullying Communist trades unionists in the bloated public sector? They were as much a part of the Greek 'deep state' as the bankers and shipowners the left denounced with such moralizing fervour. Ironically, once Syriza's posturing had reduced Greeks to withdrawing a maximum of €60 a week from ATMs, Podemos quickly distanced itself from the fraternal party. Neither it nor the ailing PSOE managed to prevent Prime Minister Mariano Rajoy, his PPE party the subject of multiple corruption allegations, from winning a second term. As for Greece, it drifted back to the out-of-sight-out-of-mind position it occupied on the Balkan peripheries of Europe, albeit now as a holding pen for huge numbers of migrants.[56]

It is impossible to predict where this story will end, though Europe is surely going to experience some rough seas. That is about as useful as saying there will be hurricanes in the Caribbean next October. The political revolt has already claimed the scalps of David Cameron, Matteo Renzi and the hapless François Hollande, on whom it seemed to rain even when he visited a tropical island. Theresa May narrowly dodged a bullet too. Yet this wave is not irreversible and the fortunes of populist parties are very mixed. Support for Alternativ für Deutschland and the Finns Party has waned, after the former's links to Russia became too blatant, and when the latter found being in government too onerous. Whether the AfD will recover by replacing the strident Frauke Petry with the lesbian former investment banker Alice Weidel seems doubtful.

The liberal conservative Dutch Prime Minister Mark Rutte survived a challenge from the anti-Islamist Geert Wilders, though only after telling migrants who refused to assimilate to 'piss off' on live TV, and more generally by adopting a coarser tone more redolent of a Rotterdam docker. A major row with Turkey's President a few days before the election helped Rutte too. The UKIP vote has also imploded, with those who defected from Labour turning to the triumphant Brexiteering Conservatives or rather to the 'stable and secure' Theresa May who then effectively forfeited power after a disastrous election that left her a captive of her own backbench Brexit boys and the Northern Irish DUP. UKIP's sole MP, Douglas Carswell, also abandoned the sinking ship. Italy remains the chief source of concern. The new Italian Prime Minister, Paolo Gentiloni, may feel obliged to seek a new mandate before spring 2018 too, since none of his three predecessors had one at all, and Gentiloni's cabinet is that of Matteo Renzi in all but name. Indeed in a remarkably rapid comeback, on 30 April 2017 Renzi won a convincing victory (70 per cent of the ballot) in the Democratic Party's leadership elections. Whether he can return to power largely depends on how many Italians agree that in a country with so many world class firms it is the political system that is holding the country back from its real potential.[57]

New insurgent parties have joined truculent regions in complicating smooth EU governance. At national or regional level they can block what they do not like, for example the Dutch rejecting the EU–Ukraine trade deal, or the Walloons another with Canada. This results in a vicious circle that further lowers respect for EU institutions and leaders as they struggle to manage the migration crisis. If the EU is preoccupied with its own survival, how will it cope when the ECB decides to halt its huge exercise in quantitative easing? Can it unravel the colossal mistake represented by the euro? While many are eagerly awaiting a final bout of creative destruction, like patriotic liberals in the 1848 'springtime of nations', they should not underestimate the tenacity of the status quo, for judging by the paltry concessions won by Cameron in 2015–16, deep reform is improbable, since the EU lacks a reverse gear.[58]

The sceptics should expect scepticism themselves, though their confidence in their own opinions and talents is a marvel to behold. Geert Wilders's election manifesto in 2017 consisted of one side of paper in a country where these normally bulky documents are costed by independent experts to within 0.5 per cent during each election. French savers were presumably alarmed when Le Pen belatedly entertained the wheeze of two parallel currencies, one of which (called the franc) would be massively devalued the day after she introduced it. UKIP seemed to want to curb EU migration while opening the country up to all-comers from Africa and South Asia, a prospect their Eurosceptic supporters may only have welcomed in theory rather than reality.

This is before we contemplate the chaos of a Europe of sovereign nations, which would certainly only resemble 1848 in terms of turmoil. How much bureaucratic energy and mental

effort would have to be expended in establishing new relationships if more -exits followed Brexit, though without a trace of
self-awareness UK Brexit Secretary David Davis has conceded:
'I don't think anybody is likely to follow us down this route.' It
would be like some gigantic energy-annihilating black hole, benefiting only lawyers, rather than the dawning of a new galaxy.
It would distract from such problems as educational reform,
youth unemployment and the cost of living, let alone adapting
our societies to the under- and unemployment which the Fourth
Industrial Age will surely cause. Reviving coal or steel is like
being nostalgic for bows and arrows in the age of the F-22.
Europe might also end up with insurgent leaders who are too
incompetent to deliver what their supporters hoped for, or who
regard politics as the gateway to media celebrity, and then a
politics that we might all regret as voter anger is refuelled, all
under the malign shadows of Putin and Trump.[59] But discussion
and expertise are for the birds, or rather the 'elites', at a time
when the masses want action above all else, or else. 'And with
one leap Jack was free,' goes the story, until chaos engenders
nostalgia for the much-traduced Established elites.

Conclusion

The roller-coaster start of the Trump administration may provide clues for how it might end. The dignity of the presidency has nosedived with a man who promiscuously Tweets and uses visiting foreign statesmen as walk-on entertainment for the dining millionaires at his Florida complex Mar-a-Lago, diners whose membership fees doubled after Trump entered office as did the room rates for foreign delegations at his hotel in Washington. There is no clear dividing line between the tycoon President and family members who act as advisers while running his empire, as one can see from Jared Kushner and his wife Ivanka Trump. The court-like informality of the administration has already seen the ousting of the America First ideologue Steve Bannon (for mishandling the entry ban on nationals of six Muslim countries) by the National Security Advisor H. R. McMaster, only for the latter to be cut out after blazing rows with Trump about language that undermined the military's desire to win Muslim allies. The ubiquitous John Bolton fancies himself as the general's replacement. Bannon was back up when the President rejected the Paris Agreement on climate change. His stylistic fingerprints were all over Trump's address in Warsaw on 6 July 2017, with its images of barbarians massing at the West's gates. By August, Bannon was out. Sundry 'influential' billionaire acquaintances and friends of Trump enjoy informal access to the President, whose respect for constitutional proprieties, expertise, institutions and regular process is scant. When the Russian foreign minister Lavrov paid his first visit to the White House (accompanied by the ambassador who had been allegedly instrumental in suborning members of Trump's team) in May 2017 he did not bother to conceal his glee at the chaos enveloping the administration. 'You're kidding me' was a comment not just applicable to the dismissal of FBI director Comey. Even the humourless Russian President openly joked about the daily farce being played out in the White House, offering Russian transcripts of meetings between Trump and Lavrov.

The daily synthetic noise from the Trump administration will continue, damaging US soft power as the Ugly American returns as a figure of fear and fun, while visitor numbers to the US have collapsed since Trump's inauguration by a third at a cost so far of $11 billion to the tourism industry. US domestic politics remains so toxic that it has become a form of entertainment for foreigners, having long ceased to be something any sane person would seek to emulate. Not all the noise comes from Trump of course, for the culture has degenerated into a kind of cacophony of bombastic, discordant and meaningless sound. Constant protests and the media barrage may paradoxically consolidate Trump's support base, enabling him to pose as the hapless victim of elite conspiracies involving the CIA and FBI and the *New York Times* and *Washington Post*. Making America Great Again will prove a labour of Sisyphus. More (white-collar) jobs are likely to be lost to the Fourth Industrial Revolution than will be created to satisfy the former blue-collar constituencies which voted Trump into power. Protective tariffs will push up prices (with massive borrowing to build big stuff compounding inflation) while wages fail to keep pace. Because of the strong US dollar, other countries' goods will be even cheaper, thereby forcing more tariff rises to compensate. The US internal market is huge, so this does not affect America as much as countries much more fatefully dependent on exports.

The administration already suffers chronic divisions among those vying for the favour of a President who is capricious and erratic and mainly preoccupied with his (abysmal) 'ratings'. Attempts to cow the free press and the independent judiciary will ultimately fail for both are tenacious opponents, while Trump's claque at Fox News have been hit by sexual harassment scandals. The non-fake media may unearth dubious business activities involving Trump, dealing with which will sap the energy of the administration that is easily distracted. These revelations are likely to include Azerbaijan, Russia, Saudi Arabia and Turkey. Living for sensation, Trump is already bored with the daily complexity and grind of government, preferring to watch cable TV at any opportunity, and surprised by the gulf between his 'Make America Great Again' simplicities and intractable domestic (and international) realities. Oddly for an international businessman, Trump detests foreign trips, even if they provide temporary respite from his domestic tribulations as the 'most persecuted president in history', a self-pitying conceit that ignores four who were assassinated. The most neglected problem is how to reform the US education system for a world in which regular work itself may not be taken for granted and in which the social media and cable TV culture are creating a sofa-bound 'idiotocracy'. By 2020 the choice may be between Mike Pence and a Democrat 'Another', though how Trump's presidency will end remains a matter of intelligent speculation by the likes of the bright *New Yorker* journalist Evan Osnos.

Much big talk about how Trump will do this or that on the world stage will come to nothing, while urban mayors, governors and entire regions will pursue their own foreign relations despite the Trump administration and regardless of whether they are 'Red' or 'Blue'. Trump will fail to divide China and Russia, or Russia and Iran. He may lose Turkey, Pakistan and Egypt to this camp too, with Turkey not only giving up on the EU but possibly also leaving NATO, especially if Trump persists in arming the Syrian Kurdish YPG. Although Trump will win a few 'new' friends in India, Israel and Japan, he will alienate many US allies, including Australia, Europe and Latin America, where Trump's fantasy Mexican wall pushes even enemies and rivals together. As a self-styled unpredictable disrupter, Trump contributes to the view that President Xi's China is a more stable and predictable ally, especially because for China everything is ultimately about business beyond a few core regional interests. The $1.6 billion per day of trade between China and the EU will reinforce that perception as talk of trade wars rumbles in the US. Trump himself is fuelling that perception since after lengthy sessions with Xi at his Mar-a-Lago complex he pronounced China's leader a 'gentleman', whose indispensable advice on North Korea he valued. China will also act as a good citizen within international institutions, which it will reshape in accordance with its own will, while Xi will consolidate his domestic power at the next Congress. Trump's enthusiasm for strongmen also means that the likes of Erdoğan, Putin, Duterte and Sisi – to whom he has been warmer than to the likes of May or Merkel – have less to worry about from human-rights activists.

Putin will remind everyone of Russian greatness by dialling up and down interventions in frozen conflicts on Russia's peripheries, while acting boldly in the Middle East, where following the failure of Trump's Israeli–Palestinian peace gambit, Putin's diplomats will step in. Russian dabbling in Western domestic politics will continue, if only to remind Russians of the blessings of Putin's autocracy. In 2018 the Russian economy will be in sufficiently healthy shape for Putin to win re-election for another six-year term, though he is adamant that it will be his last. Some claim he is weary of high office, though getting out of it will be even harder than getting in. Entertainment, infotainment, electronic surveillance and patriotism will continue to keep most Russians stoically docile, and they will vote for the President. Since Russians do not know that the pollsters are not connected to the FSB, Putin will continue to enjoy suspiciously high approval ratings. His real problem will be that, like many Russian leaders in the past, he cannot simply relinquish power. By investing in Big Defence, rather than information war and lightweight and coercive agility, the West will continue to fail to check communications subversion by Russia, notably by not highlighting what is wrong with life for ordinary people in Russia itself or how their own conservative (and sometimes liberal) media are bound up with Russian business interests. Much pointless effort will be expended on checking 'hybrid warfare', while quite openly Putin will continue to develop his links with European populist parties, even as Trump seems to have had doubts about them. A Europe competing for their favours, like twenty-seven whores under a lantern with only two punters, to put the matter very crudely, suits both men, though they may be disappointed should Europe's centre hold.

A general anxiety about the state of the world in 2017 may give the EU a reprieve, though it will almost certainly be unable to agree which way to go at the fork in the road of its sixtieth anniversary, and the euro remains a glaring problem. Sensible suggestions, for example from Dutch Labour politicians, that Brussels should cut back what it does by 40 per cent, will be ignored, while Macron's ambitious reform proposals depend on his first reforming France itself in a manner that convinces the Germans to support limited debt mutualization, eurobonds and outright financial transfers, though without a common system of taxation. His huge parliamentary majority may turn into a curse, first since only 49 per cent of the French voted in June 2017, and second because the feeble opposition in the National Assembly propels dissent out onto the streets. Is 'Kim Jong Macron', as French wits have dubbed him, man enough to take on the CGT? As usual, the EU will try to do two things at once, pushing for deeper integration while placating populists with some cosmetic repatriation of powers to a national level. A two-speed Europe, which some have countenanced to enable the like-minded to push ahead with for example defence cooperation, will surely aggravate those left in the slow lane. As the distinction between mainstream and populists blurs, some may prove less amenable to consensual EU 'Diktat' than was once assumed, and the Visegrad states in the East will not cooperate either, especially if the EU accuses them of violating the bloc's core democratic and legal values.

Trump has already damaged by association one of his European admirers, Geert Wilders in the Netherlands, a budding celebrity who, like Nigel Farage, prefers international stardom to the responsibilities of power. Lauding Trump did Marine Le Pen no favours in May 2017. By late September 2017, Germany's new Chancellor will be a supporter of the EU, and most likely it will be a fourth term Angela Merkel.

Although Italy does not have to hold an election until 2018, it is not inconceivable that the Five Star Movement could win and govern in alliance with the far-right Lega Nord. A major European country would be ruled by people from an online outfit with almost zero experience of governing, which again is promising to hold a referendum on eurozone membership. This also threatens to collapse the eurozone, or at least see it retreat into a Hanseatic mode. The British will continue to obsess about Brexit, which has eclipsed every other political issue, although the prospect of a second Scottish independence referendum has receded, the only bright light in a June 2017 election which Prime Minister Theresa May comprehensively botched. The effect of this self-imposed fiasco brought about by the person a leading German newspaper dubbed 'The Woman Without Qualities', in an echo of novelist Robert Musil, was to potentially increase the prospects for a softer Norwegian- or Swiss-style deal, especially if public opinion turns against a hard Brexit. Hope will continue to spring eternal about trade deals far and wide among the über-British patriots born in Peru or South Africa, in denial of the reality that 1 per cent of British exports go to Australia. The imperatives of buccaneering Brexit Britannia will ineluctably clash with many of the delusions Britain has about its role promoting democracy, the rule of law and human rights. The British, they are told, share common values with the (murderous) President of the Philippines as well as the autocratic sheikhs of the Gulf. Measures adopted to blunt the sharp-edged effects of globalization on those who voted for Brexit may clash with the needs of employers and the City, while the effects of impending Brexit (for example a 96 per cent fall in EU nurses coming to Britain) may not please those who voted Leave to curb immigration since their substitutes are likely to be more Muslims from Bangladesh and Pakistan.

Throughout Europe it is hard to decide whether populist parties are durable or evanescent, and how they will fare if migration abates and European economies recover as they are beginning to do. Finland's Finns Party and Germany's Alternativ für Deutschland are in the 'here today, gone tomorrow' casualty ward already. Mainstream parties will collude to exclude them from power, though this will entail assembling complex coalitions which take an inordinate time to form as can be seen in the Netherlands, which four months after its election still lacked a government. Since any single party can flounce out, such governments will be fragile, and confirm populist suspicions that the elites are conspiring to deny voters a real choice. While migration can be contained in some places and for a limited time, for example in the Balkans, but not from Libya, in the long-term one has to be pessimistic about how desertification, drought, war and bad governance in the 'push' societies will result in this problem getting worse over future decades. What happens if Algeria collapses when President Bouteflika is pronounced dead? Will this mean a further gaping hole alongside the one left in Libya?

ISIS's physical caliphate has been virtually destroyed, with the fall of Raqqa following that of Mosul. But ISIS, or a future iteration, will continue to present a terrorist threat in Africa, China, Europe, the Middle East and the US, with its leadership diffused or relocated to some failed state, from which it will emit virtual pulse beats. Jihadism can be contained but it cannot be eliminated since its underlying pathological causes lie beyond anything non-Muslim outsiders can cure. Iraqi Arabs and Kurds may go to war over Kirkuk once ISIS is no more, and Iraq and Turkey may clash too should Erdoğan seek to realize irredentist dreams. Iran will continue to increase its regional power, while Saudi Arabia will undergo a succession crisis. Grand reform schemes will be abandoned by Riyadh as the price of oil recovers, as has already happened through the reversal of cuts to subsidies in early 2017, once the social media weather had been read, even though the oil price had not moved by very much. Russia will doubtless play a more important role in the Middle East than the US, though China will make its presence felt too. Perhaps the one certainty in that region is that Putin will fail in his Israel–Palestine peace bid, as will Trump with his delusion that personal chemistry will work wonders in a conflict that has taxed the world's best political minds for decades.

Elsewhere, the West will gradually abandon Afghanistan to management by China, Russia, Iran, India and Pakistan even if it retains a small force there to combat Al Qaeda and ISIS. Profound differences among these managers will ensure that Afghanistan never finds peace. Several national liberation regimes will finally exhaust their legacy of political capital. This will be true of the FLN in Algeria and the ANC in South Africa, though only the latter has a plausible opposition. If Africans thrive it will be despite their governments. Latin American politics will finally grow out of *Chavismo*, even as this thrives on the European left, and China will increase its influence there too.

In China, Xi Jinping will manage an orderly transition to the next leadership team, identifying a successor at the 19th Party Congress in late 2017 or perhaps soldiering on for a third term. China will cautiously assume a greater role in dealing with climate change and managing international institutions, or joining Russia to help broker bilateral deals in various conflicts around the world. This process will be accompanied by much wishful thinking on the part of those in the West who are appalled by Trump. Rex Tillerson will fade to a ghostly figure, along with a depleted State Department. The US will not be in high demand as an honest broker. Who in their right mind would want the erratic Trump involved in resolving any complex conflict unless their aim was to sabotage it? At the same time, most of China's energies will continue to be bound up with internal economic and social transformation. In a turbulent world, many people will be inclined to ignore the authoritarian features of Communist rule, allowing Beijing to pose as a rock of stability. How can this be otherwise since both American and British voters have done so much to make democracy seem a recipe for chaos? Having squared Trump with minimal effort, China may become bolder in asserting its claims against its neighbours. Since Trump can change his views in seconds, this could result in a test of wills with the US, with fickle Chinese netizens as hostile to Trump as they were once positive. The US will discover that most of its allies would remain neutral in such a conflict, or indeed sympathize with China. America will no longer be the indispensable universal guarantor of world order as regional blocs become more important.

•

For understandable reasons, people (often very young ones) ask what they can do about any of this. In reality, there is very little any ordinary person can do to reverse geopolitical developments that have been in the making for a generation, resulting in power shifting to the three men whose faces are on the cover of this book. That in itself signifies the fact that the West is fading, not as a civilization or powerful assembly of economies, but as the major driving geopolitical force in the world. That is not a counsel of despair, and a world resembling the one in 1890 does not inevitably have to result in another 1914. There are plenty of formerly powerful states that most people would happily live in, and some very powerful ones where we would not.

A period of critical reflection on some of the clichéd thinking that brought the West to this dismal pass would not go amiss; nor would an expansion of teaching of international relations and macro-economics, perhaps with geography and history subsumed into these subjects? National strategy is too important to be left to politicized generals and admirals doing their turns on our media, as if they have some monopoly of the subject. We need to study the mistakes of the past as much as its moral 'lessons' to avoid being trapped into a superficial discourse seemingly imprisoned by the immediate present, or, worse, allowing us to be mentally kidnapped by foreign powers and their lobbyists whose interests are not ours. But as a wise man recently wrote, foreign policy begins at home. There are matters ordinary people can do something about almost everywhere.

Optimists foresee a future in which humans collaborate with increasingly sophisticated machines. A great wave of technology-driven change is already lapping around our feet, or rather absorbing our minds in devices held in our hands. The Fourth Industrial Revolution will have enormous effects on our societies and our individual sense of worth which is largely defined by work. Automation, or rather human anomic alienation, relies on our collaboration, and our consent can be withdrawn. We choose, after all, to check out at machines rather than with the low skilled who sit at tills. We choose to buy books or bank online, with the fiction that we are pressed for time, even as we spend three hours or more per day navigating a two-inch screen reading dross or pretending to 'connect' with total strangers, whereas the reality is that complex algorithms are simply reducing us to a product traded with advertisers. Worse, deep data analysis of social media will allow governments to detect opposition to any given policy before it generates more than a few angry Tweets. We choose not to be civically engaged, whether singing in a choir or buying the local newspaper, or, increasingly, national ones. We are increasingly trapped in a perpetual electronic and virtual present that is turning people into incommunicative idiots capable of little more than a tweet, or into 'slacktivists' who mistake tweets for doing anything.

Scaling the local to the general is much more difficult. If all politicians are the 'same', then encourage some who are not, or create new parties that better address current complexities rather than the old 'tribal' class or religious allegiances of the vanishing past. Though populists have been better at identifying voter concerns than resolving them, it is just about conceivable to imagine a post-populist politics which addressed itself to the most fundamental problems, rather than to a red mist of fact and fantasy. President Macron has shown how that can be done to startling effect with his En Marche movement. While the fashionable self-dramatizing term 'resistance' is overblown, it should be possible to see through the celebrity–media matrix which is hijacking political life, especially since such figures have no solutions to the changes we are about to undergo. For example, what if 'virtual' migration of skilled jobs lowers wages or destroys as much employment as 'real' migrants are claimed to do, though many of our services (and service industries) would collapse without them? All ends of the political spectrum would be advised to revisit even their deepest convictions, for these may not be relevant to the world after 2008. Unless the ultra-rich are planning to live in fortifications or on remote islands, they might be advised to listen to those who want to see a reformed capitalism that no longer rewards croneyism and failure. We should reacquaint ourselves with a politics based on something more than surface noise and more generally learn to tune out noise in general, especially the social media variety which seems to simply create hermetically sealed micro communities of the like-minded. Compared with those changes, the struggle for global mastery is a minority pursuit, fascinating to observe, but ultimately like the froth of events that accompanied the huge and irrevocable transformations of the original Industrial Revolution when the original 'best of times, worst of times' was written.

Acknowledgements

Warm thanks are due to Axel Kaiser, Michael Mandelbaum, William Doino, Christopher Coker, George Walden, William Anthony Hay, Rupert Edis, Howard Davies, Paul Ritchie, Simon King, Luke Harding, Andrew Green, Bruce Anderson, Ian Whitacker, Edward Blair, Tajendra Sudhu, Andrew Wilson, David McDonough, Nicholas Soames, Stephen Glover, Eric Lonergan, Ben Chu, Shmuel Bar, Reagan Reaud, Nick Pyke, Leaf Kalfayhan, Adrian Weale, Edward Luttwak, Brad Jones, Michael Spencer, Jack Straw and Jeremy Warner for help with sources and useful conversations. George Morley made valuable editorial suggestions. No one else is responsible for my views and conclusions.

Michael Burleigh
London, September 2017

A Note on Further Reading

To conserve length, this book does not have a full bibliography though many useful titles can be found in the notes. Instead, I would like to recommend a few sources I found especially enlightening. Among newspapers and journals I read most are the *Financial Times*, *Bloomberg News*, *Le Monde diplomatique*, *Le Figaro*, *Die Welt*, *Deutsche Welle*, *Frankfurter Allgemeine Zeitung*, *Il Sole 24 Ore*, the *Guardian/Observer*, the *Daily Mail* and the *Mail on Sunday*, the *New York Times*, the *Washington Post*, *Survival*, *Al-Monitor*, *Institute of Modern Russia Media Roundup*, *Moscow Times*, the *Wall Street Journal*, *World Politics Review*, *Foreign Affairs*, *War on the Rocks*, the *American Conservative*, the *People's Daily*, the *New Yorker*, *National Interest*, the *American Interest* and the *New Statesman*, which all deserve honourable mentions. The following books are excellent.

FINANCIAL CRISIS

Ron Suskind, *The Confidence Men: Wall Street, Washington and the Education of a President* (New York, 2011)

Howard Davies, *The Financial Crisis: Who is to Blame?* (Cambridge, 2010)

John Kay, *Other People's Money: Masters of the Universe or Servants of the People?* (London, 2015)

David Marsh, *Europe's Deadlock: How the Euro Crisis Could Be Solved and Why It Won't Happen* (New Haven, 2013)

Markus Brunnermeier, Harold James and Jean-Pierre Landau, *The Euro and the Battle of Ideas* (Princeton, 2016)

Padma Desai, *Financial Crisis, Contagion, and Containment: From Asia to Argentina* (Princeton, 2003)

Otmar Issing, *The Birth of the Euro* (Cambridge, 2008)

IRAQ, IRAN, SAUDI ARABIA, ISIS AND TURKEY

Pierre Razoux, *The Iran–Iraq War* (Cambridge, MA, 2016)

Michael Axworthy, *Iran: Empire of the Mind* (London, 2007)

Vali Masr, *The Shia Revival: How Conflicts within Islam Will Shape the Future* (New York, 2006)

Afshon Ostovar, *Vanguard of the Imam: Religion, Politics, and Iran's Revolutionary Guard* (Oxford, 2016)

Christopher Davidson (ed.), *Power and Politics in the Persian Gulf Monarchies* (London, 2011) and *After The Sheikhs: The Coming Collapse of the Gulf Monarchies* (London, 2012)

Andrew Hosken, *Empire of Fear: Inside the Islamic State* (London, 2015)

Fawaz Gerges, *ISIS: A History* (Princeton, 2016)

Çiğdem Akyol, *Erdoğan: Die Biografie* (Freiburg im Breisgau, 2016)

Simon Waldman and Emre Caliskan, *The New Turkey and Its Discontents* (London, 2016)

RUSSIA

Mikhail Zygar, *All the Kremlin's Men: Inside the Court of Vladimir Putin* (New York, 2016)

Charles Clover, *Black Wind, White Snow: The Rise of Russia's New Nationalism* (New Haven, 2016)

William J. Dobson, *The Dictator's Learning Curve: Inside the Global Battle for Democracy* (London, 2015)

Peter Pomerantsev, *Nothing is True and Everything is Possible: The Surreal Heart of the New Russia* (London, 2013)

Luke Harding, *Mafia State: How One Reporter Became an Enemy of the Brutal New Russia* (London, 2012)

Bobo Lo, *Russia and the New World Disorder* (London, 2015)

Vladimir Sorokin, *Day of the Oprichnik: A Novel* (New York, 2006)

Boris Reitschuster, *Putins Demokratur: Ein Machtmensch und sein System* (Berlin, 2014)

CHINA

Julian Gewirtz, *Unlikely Partners: Chinese Reformers, Western Economists, and the Making of China* (Cambridge, MA, 2017)

Esra Vogel, *Deng Xiaoping and the Transformation of China* (Cambridge, MA, 2011)

Gideon Rachman, *Easternisation: War and Peace in the Asian Century* (London, 2016)

Jonathan Fenby, *Tiger Head, Snake Tails: China Today, How It Got There and Why It Has to Change* (London, 2013)

Arthur Kroeber, *China's Economy: What Everyone Needs to Know* (Oxford, 2016)

Minxin Pei, *China's Crony Capitalism* (Cambridge, MA, 2016)

Edward Luttwak, *The Rise of China vs. the Logic of Strategy* (Cambridge, MA, 2012)

George Walden, *China: A Wolf in the World?* (London, 2008)

David Bandurski, *Dragons in Diamond Village: Tales of Resistance from Urbanizing China* (Brooklyn, 2016)

Stein Ringen, *The Perfect Dictatorship: China in the 21st Century* (Hong Kong, 2016)

Kerry Brown, *CEO China: The Rise of Xi Jinping* (London, 2016)

Howard W. French, *Everything Under the Heavens: How the Past Helps Shape China's Push for Global Power* (New York, 2017)

Richard C. Bush, *Hong Kong in the Shadow of China: Living with the Leviathan* (Washington, DC, 2016)

USA

Michael Mandelbaum, *Frugal Superpower: America's Global Leadership in a Cash-Strapped Era* (New York, 2010) and *Mission Failure: America and the World in the Post-Cold War Era* (Oxford, 2016)

Colin Dueck, *The Obama Doctrine: American Grand Strategy Today* (Oxford, 2015)

Trita Parsi, *Losing an Enemy: Obama, Iran, and the Triumph of Diplomacy* (New Haven, 2017)

Thomas Frank, *Listen, Liberal: Or, What Ever Happened to the Party of the People?* (London, 2016)

Michael D'Antonio, *The Truth About Trump* (New York, 2016)

Andrew J. Bacevich, *The Limits of Power: The End of American Exceptionalism* (New York, 2013) and *The New American Militarism: How Americans are Seduced by War* (Oxford, 2013)

John Judis, *The Populist Explosion: How the Great Recession Transformed American and European Politics* (New York, 2016)

Richard N. Haass, *Foreign Policy Begins At Home: The Case for Putting America's House in Order* (New York, 2013)

Christopher Lasch, *The Revolt of the Elites and the Betrayal of Democracy* (New York, 1995)

EUROPE AND THE EU

Luuk van Middelaar, *The Passage of Europe: How a Continent Became a Union* (New Haven, 2013)

Mark Urban, *The Edge: Is the Military Dominance of the West Coming to an End?* (London, 2015)

Tim Shipman, *All Out War: The Full Story of How Brexit Sank Britain's Political Class* (London, 2016)

Yannis Palaiologos, *The 13th Labour of Hercules: Inside the Greek Crisis* (London 2016)

Paul Collier, *Exodus: Immigration and Multiculturalism in the 21st Century* (London, 2013)

Michel Houellebecq, *Submission* (London, 2015)

Jan-Werner Müller, *What is Populism?* (Philadelphia, 2016)

Caroline Fourest and Fiammetta Venner, *Marine Le Pen* (Paris, 2011)

Benjamin Moffitt, *The Global Rise of Populism: Performance, Political Style, and Representation* (Stanford, 2016)

Notes

1. Two Shocks That Made Our World 'Incandescent with Moral Clarity': The Post-Cold War Present

1 John Nixon, *Debriefing the President: The Interrogation of Saddam Hussein* (London, 2016), p. 144.
2 I strongly recommend Pierre Razoux's epic *The Iran–Iraq War* (Cambridge, MA, 2015).
3 Michael Mandelbaum, *Mission Failure: America and the World in the Post-Cold War Era* (Oxford, 2016), p. 4.
4 Justin Marozzi, *Baghdad: City of Peace, City of Blood* (London, 2014), p. 355, is excellent on the impact of war on Iraq.
5 The finest account of the 1980–88 war is Razoux, *The Iran–Iraq War*, and see Charles Tripp, *A History of Iraq* (Cambridge, 2007), pp. 250–54, for the impact of UN sanctions.
6 See the revealing article by Robert Boynton, 'The Neocon Who Isn't', *American Prospect*, 18 September 2005.
7 Mandelbaum, *Mission Failure*, p. 17.
8 Peter Baker, *Days of Fire: Bush and Cheney in the White House* (New York, 2013), p. 135.
9 Andrew Bacevich, *The New American Militarism: How Americans are Seduced by War* (Oxford, 2013), p. 95.
10 Steve Coll, *Ghost Wars: The Secret History of the CIA, Afghanistan and Bin Laden, from the Soviet Invasion to September 10, 2001* (London, 2005), is a brilliant account.
11 Patrick Cockburn, 'Did Iraq Really Plot to Kill Bush?', *Independent*, 3 July 1993.
12 Bob Drogin, *Curveball: Spies, Lies, and the Con Man Who Caused a War* (London, 2007), is a vivid account of deception and incompetence involving several Western intelligence agencies.
13 Text of Blair's Speech, BBC News, 17 July 2003, and, on Rumsfeld, Stephen Glover, 'Obama's Right. There is No Special Relationship . . . and the Sooner We Recognise That the Better', *Daily Mail*, 12 January 2011.

14 Toby Dodge, *Iraq: From War to Authoritarianism* (London, 2012), p. 38.

15 See the important essay by Daniel Mahoney, 'Humanitarian Democracy and the Postpolitical Temptation', in William Anthony Hay and Harvey Sicherman (eds.), *Is There Still a West? The Future of the Atlantic Alliance* (Columbia, MO, 2014), pp. 30–33.

16 This is the main theme of Michael Burleigh, *Small Wars, Faraway Places: The Making of the Modern World* (London, 2013).

17 Ron Suskind, 'Faith, Certainty and the Presidency of George W. Bush', *New York Times* magazine, 17 October 2004.

18 Peter Galbraith, *The End of Iraq: How American Incompetence Created a War Without End* (New York, 2006), pp. 114ff., is comprehensively and justifiably damning. Jeremy Greenstock, *Iraq: The Cost of War* (London, 2016), is full of insight, even if its publication was delayed by a decade.

19 Ibid., pp. 16–17.

20 Marozzi, *Baghdad*, p. 377.

21 Bacevich, *The New American Militarism*.

22 Peter Conradi, *Who Lost Russia? How the World Entered a New Cold War* (London, 2017), pp. 76ff.

23 Michael Mandelbaum, *The Frugal Superpower: America's Global Leadership in a Cash-Strapped Era* (New York, 2010), pp. 70–71.

24 Helga Haftendorn, 'The Post-Cold War Transformation of the Atlantic Alliance', Begin-Sadat Center for Strategic Studies, 1 May 2007.

25 For a devastating critique of R2P see Rajan Menon, *The Conceit of Humanitarian Intervention* (Oxford, 2016).

26 Mandelbaum, *Mission Failure*, pp. 123–4. Samuel Moyn's *The Last Utopia: Human Rights in History* (Cambridge, MA, 2010), is a brilliant analysis of this construct, though it does not deal with how much money is involved for lawyers in their reign of virtue.

27 Ian Bremmer, *Superpower: Three Choices for America's Role in the World* (New York, 2015), pp. 67–76.

28 Toby Dodge, *Iraq's Future: The Aftermath of Regime Change* (London, 2005), pp. 57–63.

29 Martin Wolf, 'The Shifts and the Shocks: What We've Learned – and Still Have to Learn – from the Financial Crisis', Global Strategy Forum lecture, 9 December 2014 (London, 2015), p. 28.

30 See Sebastian Mallaby, *The Man Who Knew: The Life & Times of Alan Greenspan* (London, 2016), p. 504, for the line from Greenspan's speech.

31 Padma Desai, *Financial Crisis, Contagion, and Containment: From Asia to Argentina* (Princeton, 2003).

32   See Ron Suskind, *The Confidence Men: Wall Street, Washington, and the Education of a President* (New York, 2012), p. 63.

33   John Kay, *Other People's Money: Masters of the Universe or Servants of the People?* (London, 2015), pp. 23–4, is superb.

34   'Rolling Stones Play Private Deutsche Bank Gig, Paid $67,500 a Minute', *Huffington Post*, 28 March 2008.

35   Suskind, *Confidence Men*, pp. 83–4.

36   Dan Frosch and Dudley Althaus, 'Nafta-Friendly Texas Guarded About Trump', *Wall Street Journal*, 29 November 2016.

37   The best account of this transformation is Thomas Frank's savage *Listen, Liberal: Or, What Ever Happened to the Party of the People?* (New York, 2016).

38   George Walden, *The New Elites: Careers Among the Masses* (London, 2000), is an unrivalled analysis of the latest addition to the British penchant for ten stock 'characters'.

39   David Cay Johnson, *The Making of Donald Trump* (Brooklyn, 2016), pp. 155ff. on Cinque and pp. 161–6 on Sater.

40   Michael D'Antonio, *The Truth About Trump* (New York, 2016), pp. 333–52.

41   On this see Benjamin Moffitt, *The Global Rise of Populism: Performance, Political Style, and Representation* (Stanford, 2016), especially pp. 70ff.

42   Mervyn King, *The End of Alchemy: Money, Banking and the Future of the Global Economy* (London, 2013), p. 95, and the definitive account by Iain Martin, *Making It Happen: Fred Goodwin, RBS and the Men Who Blew Up the British Economy* (London, 2013), p. 252, for RBS's balance sheet.

43   Cited by Andrew Farlow, *Crash & Beyond: Causes & Consequences of the Global Financial Crisis* (Oxford, 2013), p. 63.

44   'Moody's $864 Million Penalty for Ratings in Run-Up to 2008 Financial Crisis', *Guardian*, 14 January 2017.

45   I thank Bryan Appleyard for drawing my notice to Stephen Fay's *The Collapse of Barings* (London, 1996). See also the more contemporary confessions of a Libor trader, Alexis Stenfors, *Barometer of Fear* (London, 2017).

46   I owe this example to Joseph Stiglitz, *The Roaring Nineties* (London, 2004), pp. 120–21.

47   Cited by Alex Brummer, *Bad Banks: Greed, Incompetence and the Next Global Crisis* (London, 2015), p. 121.

48   Howard Davies, *The Financial Crisis: Who is to Blame?* (Cambridge, 2013), pp. 70–75, is very cogent on these arcane issues.

49   King, *The End of Alchemy*, p. 143.

50 Courtney Comstock, 'Emails Show How Greg Lippmann Built
    Deutsche Bank's $5 Billion Subprime Short: "Duping CDO Fools"',
    Business Insider, 14 April 2011. For the song, see Comstock,
    'A Deutsche Bank Trader Wrote a Song About the Crappy CDO
    Business to a Tune by Vanilla Ice', *Business Insider*, 14 April 2011
    with lyrics.
51 Suskind, *Confidence Men*, p. 402. On banking corruption see
    Laurence Cockcroft, Anne-Christine Wegener, *Unmasked:
    Corruption in the West* (London, 2017), pp. 83–98.
52 Suskind, *Confidence Men*, pp. 25–8, for this story.
53 Ibid., p. 99.
54 Ibid.
55 Andrew Ross Sorkin, 'President Obama Weighs His Economic
    Legacy', *New York Times*, 28 April 2016, is useful on how Obama
    viewed the crisis.
56 Ibid., p. 232.
57 Wolf, 'The Shifts and the Shocks', p. 32.
58 Stiglitz, *Roaring Nineties*, p. 28.
59 David Marsh, *Europe's Deadlock: How the Euro Crisis Could be
    Solved and Why It Won't Happen* (New Haven, 2013), pp. 43–4,
    for these quotations.
60 Markus Brunnermeier, Harold James and Jean-Pierre Landau, *The
    Euro and the Battle of Ideas* (Princeton, 2016), p. 21.
61 Michael Mandelbaum, 'Euromess', *American Interest* (September/
    October 2015) p. 87.
62 Otmar Issing, *The Birth of the Euro* (Cambridge, 2008), p. 49.
63 On this important theme see Andreas Rödder, *21.0 Eine kurze
    Geschichte der Gegenwart* (Munich, 2015), pp. 297–9.
64 Allan Little, 'How "Magic" Made Greek Debt Disappear Before It
    Joined the Euro', BBC News, 3 February 2012.
65 Brunnermeier, James and Landau, *The Euro and the Battle of Ideas*,
    pp. 46–8.
66 Joseph Stiglitz, *The Euro and Its Threat to the Future of Europe*
    (London, 2016), pp. 89–92.
67 George Soros, 'Open Society Needs Defending', *Project Syndicate*,
    28 December 2016.
68 Stiglitz, *The Euro*, pp. 118–99.
69 James Angelos, *The Full Catastrophe: Travels Among the New
    Greek Ruins* (New York, 2015), pp. 69–81. For a good study of
    'Vorsprung durch Cheating' see Paul Taylor, 'The Dishonest
    Germans', *Politico.eu*, 25 July 2017, which includes the emissions-
    defeating-software scandal, car-industry cartels and cost-fixing,

Deutsche Bank and money-laundering and Siemens' sale of gas turbines which ended up in Crimea despite EU sanctions.

70 Andre Tauber, 'EU-Beamter rechnet gnadenlos mit griechischer Statistik ab', *Die Welt*, 17 May 2017.

71 As pointed out by Stiglitz, *The Euro*, p. 81.

72 Henry Foy, 'The Greek Tragedy', *Financial Times* weekend magazine, 21/22 January 2017, pp. 12–19.

73 Stiglitz, *The Euro*, pp. 65–8.

74 Nina Adam, 'German Investment Strays from Home', *Wall Street Journal*, 26 October 2016.

75 Linda Tirado, *Hand to Mouth: The Truth About Being Poor in a Wealthy World* (London, 2014), p. 18.

76 Daniel Finkelstein, 'Why the Left Will Never Understand Populism', *The Times*, 18 January 2017, p. 23, is excellent on this theme.

77 David Goodhart, *The Road to Somewhere: The Populist Revolt and the Future of Politics* (London, 2017). Amanda Craig's novel *The Lie of the Land* (London, 2017) explores the clash of civilizations between London and 'Deep Devon' in a fascinating way too.

78 Frida Ghitis, 'Latin America's Populists are a Cautionary Tale for US Under Trump', *World Politics Review*, 17 November 2016.

79 See Stephen Fidler, 'How Politics is Looking More "Latin American"', *Wall Street Journal*, 21 October 2016.

80 Harry Wilson and James Hurley, 'Odey Staff Sacked After Market Calls so Wrong', *The Times*, 9 January 2017 and Nishant Kumar, 'Odey's Hedge Fund Slumps 49.5% in Worst Ever Annual Loss', *Bloomberg News*, 5 January 2017. On the wider problem of projecting Western experiences onto China by the 'nabobs of negativism' see Stephen Roach, 'Deciphering China's Economic Resilience', *Project Syndicate*, 25 July 2017.

81 The quotation from Wang Qishan speaking to Paulson is from Roger Altman, 'The Great Crash, 2008', *Foreign Affairs*, January/February 2009. John Pomfret, *The Beautiful Country and the Middle Kingdom* (New York, 2016).

82 On this see Mandelbaum, *The Frugal Superpower*, pp. 32–3.

83 The finest account of this shift is Gideon Rachman's *Easternisation: War and Peace in the Asian Century* (London, 2016).

84 Michele Kelemen, '5 Fact Checks from President Obama's News Conference', *NPR Now*, 16 December 2016 citing a YouGov poll which also showed a worsening of Putin's unfavourability among Democrat admirers from –54 to –62 between 2014 and 2016.

2: Gulf Rivals

1 Tim Marshall, *Prisoners of Geography* (London, 2015), p. 144.
2 Mourning his Iranian friend Ghadanfar Rokonabadi, a senior intelligence officer he had met in Beirut, Robert Fisk does not ponder why he was killed in such a hajj stampede, 'The Untold Story of the Deaths at Hajj', *Independent*, 12 June 2016.
3 Hussein Ibish, 'Saudi Arabia's New Sunni Alliance', *New York Times*, 31 July 2015.
4 David Graham, 'Sheikh Nimr al-Nimr and the Forgotten Shiiites of Saudi Arabia', *Atlantic Monthly*, 5 January 2016.
5 Ben Hubbard, 'Cables Released by Wikileaks Reveal Saudis Checkbook Diplomacy', *New York Times*, 20 June 2015 and Jonathan Ferziger and Peter Waldman, 'How Do Israel's Tech Firms Do Business in Saudi Arabia? Very Quietly', *Bloomberg News*, 2 February 2017.
6 Christopher M. Davidson, *After the Sheikhs: The Coming Collapse of the Gulf Monarchies* (London, 2012), pp. 205–9 and 232ff. For a thoughtful take on the current Qatar crisis see Ellen Laipson, 'As Stalemate in the Gulf Crisis Continues, the Costs for the Region Grow', *World Politics Review*, 1 August 2017.
7 Christopher M. Davidson (ed.), *Power and Politics in the Persian Gulf Monarchies* (London, 2011), is a useful guide to each Gulf state.
8 Yaroslav Trofimov, 'Arab Shiites Are Caught in Iranian–Saudi Strife', *Wall Street Journal*, 7 July 2016, and see Kristian Coates Ulrichsen, *Insecure Gulf: The End of Certainty and the Transition to the Post-Oil Era* (London, 2011), pp. 40–41.
9 Bruce Riedel, 'Saudi Arabia Losing Ground to Iran', *Al-Monitor*, 6 November 2016.
10 Khalid Hassan, 'Are Egyptian–Saudi Disputes Just a Passing Crisis?', *Al-Monitor*, 23 October 2016, and Mustafa Saadoun, 'How Oil is Bringing Iraq, Egypt Closer', *Al-Monitor*, 26 October 2016.
11 Christopher Hope and James Kirkup, 'Saudi Middle Man Put Pressure on Government to Drop Investigation into BAE Systems' Funding of Lavish Spending', *Daily Telegraph*, 10 April 2008.
12 Max Fisher '28 Pages: The Controversy Over Saudi Arabia and 9/11, Explained', *Vox*, 20 April 2016.
13 Catherine Ho, 'Saudi Government Has Vast Network of PR, Lobby Forms in US', *Washington Post*, 20 April 2015.
14 'Senate Grants September 11 Victims the Right to Sue Saudi Arabia', Associated Press/*Guardian*, 17 May 2016.
15 See Doyle McManus, 'The Saudi–US Relationship: Shakier than Ever', *LA Times*, 10 January 2016.

16   Andrea Wong, 'Saudi Arabia Holds $117b Worth of US Government Bonds', *Bloomberg News*, 17 May 2016.

17   John Gapper, 'Do Not Bend the Rules for Saudi Aramco', *Financial Times*, 7 June 2017.

18   'Russian President, Saudi Spy Chief Discussed Syria, Egypt', *Al-Monitor*, 22 August 2013.

19   Dominic Evans, Maher Chmaytelli and Patrick Markey, 'How Iran Closed the Mosul "Horseshoe" and Changed Iraq War', Reuters, 7 December 2016.

20   'Bahrain Uncovers Large Bomb Making Factory', Reuters, 30 September 2015.

21   'Arms Seized in Kuwait Came from Iran', Reuters, 16 August 2015.

22   Simon Mabon, *Saudi Arabia and Iran: Power and Rivalry in the Middle East* (London, 2016), pp. 53–4.

23   Robert Lacey, *Inside the Kingdom: Kings, Clerics, Modernists, Terrorists and the Struggle for Saudi Arabia* (London, 2013), p. 65.

24   Yaroslav Trofimov, 'Jihad Comes to Africa', *Wall Street Journal*, 5 February 2016, is an important piece.

25   Ibrahim Warde, 'Saudi Arabia's Unsure Future', *Le Monde diplomatique*, December 2015, pp. 4–5.

26   Bruce Riedel, *The Kingdom of Saudi Arabia* (Washington, DC, 2015) is an expert guide to the royal family. On the demotion of Prince Nayef see Ben Hubbard, Mark Mazzetti and Eric Schmitt, 'Saudi King's Son Plotted Effort to Oust His Rival', *New York Times*, 18 July 2017, and Justin Scheck, Shane Harris and Summer Said, 'Kiss Sealed Saudi Drama', *Wall Street Journal*, 20 July 2017.

27   Caroline Montagu, 'Civil Society in Saudi Arabia: The Power and Challenges of Association', Chatham House Research Paper, March, 2015, pp. 30–34.

28   Theodore Krarasil, 'Nationalism is Taking on a New Meaning in Saudi', *National* (UAE), 7 June 2015.

29   Simon Robinson, 'US Cables Detail Saudi Royal Family's Lavish Lifestyles', Reuters, 28 February 2011.

30   Zainab Fattah, 'Saudi Arabia Enters Homebuilding Business to Tackle Shortage', *Bloomberg News*, 4 April 2016.

31   Paul Aarts and Carolien Roelants, *Saudi Arabia: A Kingdom in Peril* (London, 2015), p. 45.

32   Ibid., p. 26.

33   Geoffrey Gresh, 'China's Emerging Twin Pillar Policy in the Gulf', *Foreign Policy*, 7 November 2011.

34   'Saudi Arabia's Post Oil Future', *The Economist*, 30 April 2016.

35   Jim Krane, 'Revamping Energy Policy in Saudi Arabia: A View to the Future', Baker Institute, Rice University, Issue Brief 9, June

2015; Laura El-Katiri, 'Saudi Arabia's New Economic Reforms', *Harvard Business Review*, 17 May 2016; Mohammed Alyahya, 'Saudi Arabia is a Kingdom on the Cusp of Transformation', *Financial Times*, 12 May 2016; and more sceptically, David Gardner, 'Will Saudi Arabia's Ambitious Reform Programme Work?', *Financial Times*, 25 April 2016, and Shmuel Even and Yoel Guzansky, 'Saudi Arabia's Vision 2030: Reducing Dependency on Oil', *INSS Insight*, no. 819, 6 May 2016.

36 Anjli Raval, 'Saudi Arabia Looks Beyond Oil to Exploit Its Sunshine', *Financial Times*, 7 September 2015. See also (Anon.), 'How Saudi Arabia Plans to Lure Luxury Travelers', *Bloomberg News*, 1 August 2017.

37 Yoel Guzansky, Shmuel Even, 'The Challenge of the Oil Market to the Gulf States', *INSS Insight*, no. 926, 10 May 2017.

38 Ibid.

39 Ibrahim al-Hatlanu, 'Is Saudi Arabia Bringing Sexy Back?', *Al-Monitor*, 27 May 2016.

40 Ben Hubbard, 'Young Saudis See Cushy Jobs Vanish Along with Nation's Oil Wealth', *New York Times*, 16 February 2016.

41 Aarts and Roelants, *Saudi Arabia*, p. 62.

42 Davidson, *After the Sheikhs*, pp. 233–5, entertains this possibility.

43 As pointed out by Frederic Wehrey et al., *Saudi–Iranian Relations Since the Fall of Saddam*. Rand Corporation Report (Santa Monica, 2009), pp. 26–34.

44 See Vali Nasr, *The Shia Revival: How Conflicts Within Islam Will Shape the Future* (New York, 2007), pp. 236ff. Some Wahhabi clergy, including senior members of the ulema, have openly incited murder against the Saudi Shia. For the latest violent clashes see Simon Henderson, 'Simmering Trouble in Oil-Rich Shia Area Complicates Riyadh's Concerns', Washington Institute for Near East Policy, *Policy Alert*, 5 July 2017.

45 Madawi al-Rasheed, 'Saudi Arabia's Islamist–Liberal Divide', *Al-Monitor*, 28 April 2015, is excellent on patronage of rival factions.

46 'Saudi Arabia Unveils 900km Fence on Iraq Border', Al Jazeera, 6 September 2014, and Angus McDowall, 'Saudi Arabia's New Yemen Strategy: Get Behind a Fence', Reuters, 22 January 2015.

47 Frederic Wehrey, 'Saudi Arabia's Anxious Autocrats', in Larry Diamond, Marc Plattner and Christopher Walker (eds.), *Authoritarianism Goes Global: The Challenge to Democracy* (Baltimore, 2016), pp. 105–7.

48 The finest history of Iran is Michael Axworthy, *Iran: Empire of the Mind: A History from Zoroaster to the Present Day* (London, 2008).

49   Hooman Majd, *The Ayatollah Begs to Differ: The Paradox of Modern Iran* (London, 2009), p. 165.

50   Christopher de Bellaigue, *Patriot of Persia: Muhammad Mossadeq and a Very British Coup* (London, 2013), is a fine account.

51   Axworthy, *Iran: Empire of the Mind*, pp. 244–8.

52   'Iran at Forefront of Stem Cell Research', *Washington Times*, 15 April 2009.

53   Akbar Ganji, 'Who is Ali Khamenei?', *Foreign Affairs*, September/October 2013, pp. 53ff.

54   See Steve Stecklow, 'Khamenei Controls Massive Financial Empire Built on Property Seizures', *Reuters Investigates*, 11 November 2013, for the details.

55   Saeed Kamali Dehghan, 'Conservative Cleric Ebrahim Raisi Enters Iran's Presidential Race', *Guardian*, 9 April 2017.

56   On Soleimani see Dexter Filkins, 'The Shadow Commander', *New Yorker*, 20 September 2013, and Afshon Ostovar, *Vanguard of the Imam: Religion, Politics and Iran's Revolutionary Guard* (Oxford, 2016).

57   For this see Abbas Milani, 'Iran's Paradoxical Revolution', in Diamond et al. (eds.), *Authoritarianism Goes Global*, p. 62.

58   For these complex events see Afshon Ostovar, *Vanguard of the Imam: Religion, Politics, and Iran's Revolutionary Guard* (Oxford, 2016), especially pp. 59ff.

59   Axworthy, *Iran: Empire of the Mind*, pp. 162–6.

60   Razoux, *The Iran–Iraq War*; Michael Axworthy, *Revolutionary Iran: A History of the Islamic Republic* (Cambridge, MA, 2015).

61   Mehdi Khalaji, *Tightening the Reins: How Khamenei Makes Decisions* (Washington, DC, 2014), p. vi.

62   Ganji, 'Who is Ali Khamenei?', p. 55.

63   Homa Katouzian, *Iran: A Beginner's Guide* (London, 2013), pp. 210–11.

64   Ghoncheh Tazmini, *Khatami's Iran: The Islamic Republic and the Turbulent Path to Reform* (London, 2009).

65   Axworthy, *Revolutionary Iran*, pp. 340–47.

66   Ibid., pp. 373–4.

67   Steve Stecklow, 'Chinese Firm Helps Iran Spy on Citizens', Reuters Special Report, 22 March 2012.

68   'Le poulet, bientôt interdit à la télévision iranienne?', *Le Monde* Blog.fr, 17 July 2012.

69   This discussion of Iranian taxes owes much to Maysam Bizaer, 'Facing Oil Slump, Iran Moves to Tax Its Way Out of Crisis', *Al-Monitor*, 15 January 2016.

70   On the negative impact of sanctions on France and Germany see

Trita Parsi, *Losing an Enemy: Obama, Iran, and the Triumph of Diplomacy* (New Haven, 2017), pp. 233–4, and on the spies revolt see Natan Sachs, 'Israel's Spy Revolt', *Foreign Policy*, 10 May 2012.

71 Amos Yadlin and Avner Golov, 'Don't Tear Up the Iran Deal, Make It Better', *USA Today*, 12 January 2017. As a younger man, General Yadlin was one of the Israeli pilots who bombed Saddam Hussein's Osirak reactor in 1981.

72 'Kerry Warns Saudi Arabia of Consequences If They Get Nukes', *Business Standard*, 20 January 2016.

73 'Iran Grain Barter Deal Crashes', Reuters, 28 June 2012.

74 Ostovar, *Vanguard of the Imam*, pp. 204–29 is excellent on the Iranian politics of IRGC intervention in Lebanon, Syria and Iraq.

75 For an excellent discussion of Iranian policy see Dina Esfandiary and Ariane Tabatabai, 'Iran's ISIS Policy', *International Affairs* (2015) vol. 91, especially pp. 6–10. On Yemen see Bruce Riedel, 'Iran Outflanking Saudi Arabia in Yemen', *Al-Monitor*, 1 August 2017.

76 Alexander Cooley, 'Countering Democratic Norms', in Diamond et al. (eds.), *Authoritarianism Goes Global*, pp. 120–21.

77 Alex Vatanka, 'Iran Abroad', ibid., pp. 69–70.

78 Gresh, 'China's Emerging Twin Pillar'.

79 Khalaji, *Tightening the Reins*, pp. 41–2.

80 Shmuel Bar, *Iranian Defence Doctrine and Decision Making*, IDC Herzliya Lauder Center paper (Herzliya, 2004), p. 15.

81 Ganji, 'Who is Ali Khamenei?', pp. 65ff.

82 'Polling Gives a Dark Forecast for Iranian President Hassan Rouhani', *Guardian*, 13 July 2016.

83 On the same day we got John Bolton, 'The Iran Deal Can't be Enforced', *Wall Street Journal*, 7 February 2017 and Melanie Philips, 'Our Arms Sales Help Keep Iran's Plots in Check', *The Times*, 7 February 2017. By contrast see Michael Axworthy, 'Regime Change in Iran Would Be a Disaster for Everyone', *Foreign Policy*, 18 July 2017, which systematically refutes the neocon case against Iran.

84 Aaron David Miller and Richard Sokolsky, 'Memo to the Next President: Avoid the "Vision Thing" in the Mideast', *Politico*, 31 October 2016, is an important 'memo' on what to avoid.

3: Islamic State (ISIS): Messages In Blood

1 The best recent account is by Fawaz Gerges, *ISIS: A History* (Princeton and Oxford, 2016), especially pp. 98ff. See also the valuable reportage of Patrick Cockburn, *The Rise of Islamic State: ISIS and the New Sunni Revolution* (London, 2015).

2   Nelly Lahoud, 'The, "Islamic State" and al-Qaeda', in Simon Staffell and Akil N. Awan (eds.), *Jihadism Transformed: Al-Qaeda and Islamic State's Global Battle of Ideas* (London, 2016), pp. 21–2.

3   Jean-Charles Brisard, *Zarqawi: The New Face of al-Qaeda* (Cambridge, 2005).

4   Andrew Hosken, *Empire of Fear: Inside Islamic State* (London, 2015), gives a good sense of the early iterations of AQI and ISI.

5   See Vasilios Tasikas, 'The Battlefield Inside the Wire', *Military Review*, September–October 2009, pp. 64–71.

6   William McCants, *Abu Bakr al-Baghdadi* (Washington, DC, 2015), is a useful biography.

7   As noted by Sami Moubayed, *Under the Black Flag* (London, 2015), p. 111.

8   Christoph Reuter, 'The Terror Strategist: Secret Files Reveal the Structure of Islamic State', *Der Spiegel*, 18 April 2015, exaggerates the role of Ba'athists in ISIS.

9   Alon Rieger, Eran Yashiv, 'The Syrian Economy: Current State and Future Scenarios', *INSS Strategic Assessment*, vol. 20, no. 1 (April 2017), p. 77.

10 Udi Dekel, Nir Boms and Ofir Winter, *Syria's New Map and New Actors: Challenges and Opportunities for Israel* (Tel Aviv, 2016), p. 27.

11 Two fine recent accounts of events in Syria are Leon T. Goldsmith, *Cycle of Fear: Syria's Alawites in War and Peace* (London, 2015), and Charles R. Lister, *The Syrian Jihad: Al-Qaeda, the Islamic State and the Evolution of an Insurgency* (London, 2015). Sardar Mlla Drwish, 'Who is Golani, Nusra's Nr 1 Man?', *Al-Monitor*, 8 August 2016, expertly establishes Golani's background.

12 David Francis and Dan De Luce, 'Hitting the Islamic State's Oil Isn't Enough', *Foreign Policy*, 17 November 2015.

13 Yoram Schweitzer and Zvi Magen, 'The Islamic State, the Caucasus, and the Russian Response', *INSS Insight*, no. 725, 28 July 2015.

14 Abdel Bari Atwan, *Islamic State: The Digital Caliphate* (London, 2015), pp. 150–58.

15 Katrin Kuntz, 'Money and Status Attract Fighters', *Der Spiegel*, 7 January 2015 and Lahoud, 'The "Islamic State"', p. 32.

16 Gerges, *ISIS*, p. 233.

17 'ISIS to Use Saudi School Books for Students in Syria and Iraq', *Muslim Press*, 31 August 2014, and David Kirkpatrick, 'ISIS's Harsh Brand of Islam is Rooted in Austere Saudi Creed', *New York Times*, 24 September 2014.

18 Shiraz Maher, *Salafi-Jihadism: The History of an Idea* (London, 2016), pp. 84ff.

19 Graeme Wood, 'What ISIS Really Wants', *The Atlantic*, March 2015, and William McCants, *The ISIS Apocalypse: The History, Strategy, and Doomsday Vision of the Islamic State* (New York, 2015).

20 Hashmatallah Moslih, 'Iran Foreign Legion Leans on Afghan Shia in Syria War', Reuters, 22 January 2016.

21 Peter Harling, 'Basra, Dystopian City', *Le Monde diplomatique*, August 2016, p. 4.

22 Michael Schmidt and Eric Schmidt, 'As ISIS Loosens its Grip, US and Iraq Prepare for Grinding Insurgency', *New York Times*, 25 July 2016 citing US Army Colonel Christopher Garver.

23 Michael Knights, 'Mosul Battle: Iraq Gaining Momentum Against IS', BBC News, 9 January 2017.

24 Ibid. On Al Qaeda and the Ba'athists see Emily Anagnostos, 'Iraq's Sunni Insurgency Begins as ISIS Loses Ground in Mosul', Institute for the Study of War, 7 February 2017.

25 Catherine Philip, 'Al-Qaeda "Will Take Over from Assad and Isis" in Syria', *The Times*, 29 July 2016, and Michael Georgy, 'After Mosul, Islamic State Digs in for Guerrilla Warfare', *Reuters World News*, 20 July 2017, for the next generation of Ba'athist ISIS commanders and their tactics.

26 Kay Johnson, 'Islamic State Faces Uphill "Branding War" in Afghanistan and Pakistan', Reuters, 14 August 2016.

27 Milo Comerford, 'Isis is Now Waging a Sectarian War in Afghanistan – and Even the Taliban Oppose It', *Independent*, 28 July 2016.

28 Sudarsan Raghavan, 'Taliban in Afghanistan Tells Islamic State to Stay Out of Country', *Washington Post*, 16 June 2015.

29 Hameedullah Khan and Saud Mehsud, 'After Syria and Iraq, Islamic State Makes Inroads in South Asia', Reuters, 7 September 2014.

30 Alexandra Stark, 'To Counter ISIS, Bangladesh Needs to Solve Its Homegrown Violence', *Diplomat*, 16 March 2016.

31 Emma Graham-Harrison and Chris Stephens, 'Libyan Forces Claim Sirte Port Captured as Street Battles Rage', *Guardian*, 11 June 2015.

32 George Mikhail, 'What's Next for Egypt's IS Affiliate After Killing of Leader?', *Al-Monitor*, 14 August 2016.

33 Giada Zampano, 'Italy is Quick to Expel Extremists', *Wall Street Journal*, 2 December 2016.

34 Christoph Reuter, 'Retreat and Delusion: Is the Islamic State Finally Collapsing?', *Spiegel Online International*, 8 August 2016.

35 Jason Burke, 'As Isis Strikes, Al-Qaida Plays the Long Game in Islamist Supremacy Struggle', *Guardian*, 2 July 2016, and Clint Watts, 'It's Not You, It's Me: Al Qaeda Lost Jabhat al-Nusra. Now What?', *War on the Rocks*, 29 July 2016.

36   James Leibold, 'How China Sees ISIS is Not How It Views
     "Terrorism"', *National Interest*, 7 December 2015.
37   See the thoughtful essay by Hal Brands and Peter Feaver, 'Trump
     and Terrorism', *Foreign Affairs* (March/April 2017), pp. 28–36.
38   Sam Jones, 'Intelligence Agencies Fight to Unravel Isis Network in
     Europe', *Financial Times*, 27 March 2016.
39   Yaroslav Trofimov, 'Jihad Comes to Africa', *Wall Street Journal*,
     8 February 2016, is useful on the malign influence of Saudi Arabia.

4: The Sick Man of Europe: Erdoğan's Turkey

1   'Raid Targeted Turkey's President', *Wall Street Journal*, 18 July
     2016 and, 'Warum der Putsch scheitert', *Frankfurter Allgemeine
     Zeitung*, 17 July 2016, for the details. Edward Luttwak, *Coup
     d'Etat: A Practical Handbook* (Cambridge, MA, 2016), is a useful
     primer that has been used in at least one failed coup attempt.
2   This has been suggested by Shmuel Bar, 'Turkey – Quo Vadis',
     Shmuel Bar Consulting and Research Ltd, August, 2016, p. 5. On
     Erol Olcak see Hannah Lucinda-Smith, 'Turkey's Strongman Owes
     All to a Martyr', *The Times*, 15 July 2017.
3   For the Intcen report see Andrew Rettman, 'Gulen Did Not Order
     Turkey Coup, EU Spies Say', *European Observer*, 17 January 2017,
     and Yeliz Candemir, 'Turkish Moves Hit Business', *Wall Street
     Journal*, 4 November 2016, pp. A1–A8.
4   David Gardner, 'Turkey Slips into the Chaos of the Middle East',
     Financial Times, 16 July 2016, and Ozan Demircan and Gerd
     Höhler, 'Turkish Crackdown Hits the Business World', *Handelsblatt
     Global Edition*, 8 August 2016.
5   Erik Zürcher, *Turkey: A Modern History* (London, 2004), pp. 152–63.
6   Eugene Rogan, *The Fall of the Ottomans: The Great War in the
     Middle East, 1914–1920* (London, 2015), p. 395, is outstanding, as
     is Andrew Mango, *Atatürk* (London, 2004).
7   Norman Stone, 'Modernity's First Mistake Was to Take on Religion
     in the July Heat', *Sunday Times*, 17 July 2016.
8   For these and following details of Erdoğan's life see Çiğdem Akyol,
     Erdoğan: Die Biographie (Freiburg, 2016), pp. 44ff.
9   Simon Waldman and Emre Caliskan, *The New Turkey and Its
     Discontents* (London, 2016), pp. 143ff.
10   Michelangelo Guida, 'Founders of Islamism in Republican Turkey:
     Kısakürek and Topçu', in Mohammed Bamyeh (ed.), *Intellectuals
     and Civil Society in the Middle East: Liberalism, Modernity and
     Political Discourse* (London, 2012), p. 119.

11 Zürcher, *Turkey*, p. 263.

12 Akyol, *Erdoğan*, pp. 112ff.

13 Waldman and Caliskan, *The New Turkey*, pp. 150–53, is enlightening.

14 David Kirkpatrick, 'Premier of Turkey Takes Role in Region', *New York Times*, 12 September 2011.

15 Semih Idiz, 'The "Sunnification" of Turkish Foreign Policy', *Al-Monitor*, 1 March 2013.

16 Pinar Tremblay, 'Islamization of Istanbul Continues', *Al-Monitor*, 30 May 2013.

17 Jamie Dettmer, 'Turkey: Erdoğan Condemns Coed Dormitories', *Daily Beast*, 12 November 2015.

18 Zülfikar Dogan, 'The Islamization of Turkey', *Al-Monitor*, 4 June 2015.

19 Pinar Tremblay, 'Who's Telling Turkish Couples to Quiet Down During Sex?', *Al-Monitor*, 28 December 2016.

20 'Ex-"Miss Türkei" wegen Erdoğan-Satire verurteilt', *Die Welt*, 31 May 2016.

21 Akyol, *Erdoğan*, pp. 220–25.

22 Borzou Daragahi, 'Document Reveals What Really Drove Turkey's Failed Coup Plotters', *BuzzFeed*, 28 July 2016, is somewhat undermined by Erdoğan's own earlier breaking off of peace negotiations with the PKK to stymie the moderate Kurdish HDP.

23 Gunnar Köhne, 'Die Akte, "Ergenekon"', *Deutschlandfunk*, 21 May 2011.

24 Dogan, 'The Islamization of Turkey'.

25 'EU's Delayed Report on Turkey Fuels Human Rights Concerns', Voice of America, 21 October 215.

26 Andreas Holzapfel, 'Was passiert, wenn der Türkei-Deal platzt?', *Die Welt*, 7 August 2016.

27 'Özdemir soll zum Bluttest. Erdoğan beschimpft deutsche Abgeordnete', N-TV, 6 June 2016, and Deniz Yücel, 'Erdoğan fordert jetzt Bluttests für deutsche Abgeordnete', *Die Welt*, 6 June 2016.

28 Ece Toksabay and Tuvan Gumrukcu, 'Erdogan Warns Europeans "Will Not Walk Safely" if Attitude Persists, as Row Carries On', Reuters, 22 March 2017.

29 'Russia, Turkey Work to Patch Ties', *Wall Street Journal*, 8 August 2016.

30 Cengiz Çandar, 'Why is Turkey so Focused on Syria's Al-Bab?', *Al-Monitor*, 28 December 2016.

31 Nick Danforth, 'Turkey's New Maps are Reclaiming Ottoman Empire', *Foreign Policy*, 23 October 2016.

32 Mustafa Akyol, 'How Atatürk Became a Model for Erdoğan', *Al-Monitor*, 23 October 2016.

5: Failed Nation? Russia Under Putin

1 As has Julia Smirnova, 'So stehen Sie wie Putin einen Skandal durch', *Die Welt*, 11 April 2016.
2 Nikolai Klimeniouk, 'Freunde fürs Leben', *Die Welt*, 18 April 2016.
3 Bill Browder, *Red Notice: How I Became Putin's No. 1 Enemy* (London, 2015).
4 Andrew Rettman, 'EU and US Duped on Russia Corruption, Film-Maker Claims', *European Observer*, 27 April 2016, and, 'EU Parliament Hosts Russian Propaganda Circus', *European Observer*, 28 April 2016.
5 For this important point see Bobo Lo, *Russia and the New World Order* (London, 2015), pp. 15–16.
6 Vladimir Sorokin, *The Day of the Oprichnik: A Novel* (New York, 2006).
7 Good biographies of Putin include Steve Lee Myers, *The New Tsar: The Rise and Reign of Vladimir Putin* (London, 2015), Angus Roxburgh, *The Strongman: Vladimir Putin and the Struggle for Russia* (London, 2013), and, in German, Boris Reitschuster, *Putins Demokratur: Ein Machtmench und sein System* (Berlin, 2014).
8 Myers, *The New Tsar*, p. 124.
9 Mikhail Zygar, *All the Kremlin's Men: Inside the Court of Vladimir Putin* (New York, 2016), p. 180.
10 Fred Weir, 'Oligarchs Out, "Siloviki" in? Why Russia's Foreign Policy is Hardening', *Christian Science Monitor*, 2 February 2015; see also Yuri Felshtinsky and Vladimir Pribylovsky, *The Putin Corporation: The Story of Russia's Secret Takeover* (London, 2012), pp. 189ff.
11 Luke Harding, *Mafia State* (London, 2012), p. 11; 'The Making of the Neo-KGB State', *The Economist*, 23 August 2007.
12 William Dobson, *The Dictator's Learning Curve: Inside the Global Battle for Democracy* (London, 2012), pp. 13–15.
13 Andrew Monaghan, 'Putin's Removal of Ivanov as Chief of Staff is More About Rejuvenation', *Chatham House*, 15 August 2016.
14 Ben Judah, *Fragile Empire: How Russia Fell In and Out of Love with Vladimir Putin* (New Haven, 2014), pp. 123–4, for this analogy (with Elizabethan England).
15 Peter Hobson, 'FSB Seeks to Classify Information About Russian Officials' Villas', *Moscow Times*, 6 October 2015.
16 Tom Balmforth, 'KGB 2.0? Report Says Kremlin Plan Afoot for Major Security-Service Shakeup', Radio Free Europe, 21 September 2016.
17 Lilia Shevtsova, 'Forward to the Past in Russia', in Larry Diamond, Marc Plattner and Christopher Walker (eds.), *Authoritarianism Goes Global: The Challenge to Democracy* (Baltimore, 2016), p. 47.

See also Mikhail Klikushin, 'Don't Take Russians' Threats Seriously Until You Know Where Their Kids Live', *Observer*, 24 July 2017.

18 Mark Tucker, 'Tycoon Tried to Win Support for Putin', *The Times*, 29 October 2016. It is remarkable that the British allowed a former KGB officer turned oligarch to acquire two national newspapers on the grounds that he was a liberal champion of a free press. On the American–Russian cultural affinities see the interesting study by Rosalind Henderson and Tom Hamburger, 'Guns and religion: How American conservatives grew closer to Putin's Russia', *Washington Post*, 30 April 2017.

19 Alec Luhn, 'Russia Funds Moscow Conference for US, EU and Ukraine Separatists', *Guardian*, 20 September 2015.

20 Neil MacFarquhar, 'Russia, Jailer of Local Separatists, Welcomes Foreign Secessionists', *New York Times*, 25 September 2016, and Casey Michel, 'Why Russia Loves the Idea of California Seceding', *Politico*, 15 January 2017.

21 Celestine Bohlen, 'What Lies Behind French Conservatives' Love of Putin?', *New York Times*, 4 October 2016, and Andrew Rettman, 'Moscow Ready to Sign Pact with Italy's Grillo', *European Observer*, 7 March 2017.

22 Natalia Antonova, 'Marine Le Pen May Have Lost, But the Kremlin is Winning', *European Observer*, 13 May 2017.

23 Karl Schlögel, 'Die gefährliche neue Liebe der Deutschen zu Russland', *Die Welt*, 3 July 2016.

24 See Sijbren De Jong, 'Nord Stream 2: The Elephant in the Room', *European Observer*, 7 February 2017; Andrew Rettman, 'Russia to Build Nord Stream 2 Despite Polish Objection', *European Observer*, 22 August 2016; Sijbren De Jong, 'Is Nord Stream II dead?', *European Observer*, 18 August 2016, 'Empty Gazpromises', *European Observer*, 2 May 2016 and 'Why Europe Should Fight Nord Stream II', *European Observer*, 23 February 2016.

25 Geoffrey Hosking, *Russia and the Russians: A History from Rus to the Russian Federation* (London, 2001), pp. 99ff.

26 See Stephen Kotkin's superb history *Magnetic Mountain: Stalinism as a Civilization* (Berkeley, 1995).

27 Padma Desai, 'Russian Privatisation: The Comparative Perspective', *Harriman Review*, August 1995, pp. 48–74.

28 Ibid., pp. 320–33.

29 Bobo Lo, *Axis of Convenience: Moscow, Beijing, and the New Geopolitics* (London, 2008), p. 21.

30 Shevtsova, 'Forward to the Past', p. 55, note 8.

31 Laura Mills, 'To Fight Grievances, Russian Farmer Takes Road to Vladimir Putin's Kremlin', *Wall Street Journal*, 22 November 2016.

32 John Browne, *Beyond Business: An Inspirational Memoir from a Visionary Leader* (London, 2010), p. 145.

33 Zygar, *All the Kremlin's Men*, pp. 91–107.

34 Julia Famularo, 'The China–Russia NGO Crackdown', *Diplomat*, 23 February 2015, and, for the background, Thomas Carothers, 'The Backlash Against Democracy Promotion', *Foreign Affairs*, March/April 2006, p. 62 for the quotation.

35 Zvi Magen, Sarah Fainberg and Vera Michlin-Shapir, 'Russia in Conflict: From the Homefront to the Global Front', *INSS Strategic Assessment* (October 2016), vol. 19, p. 10, for these numbers.

36 On investor interest see Eduard Steiner and Holger Zschäpitz, 'Das grosse Kapital ist auf Putin's Seite', *Die Welt*, 24 November 2016, and Sergey Aleksashenko, 'Is Russia's Economy Doomed to Collapse?', *National Interest*, 1 July 2016.

37 Nicholas Eberstadt, 'The Dying Bear. Russia's Demographic Disaster', *Foreign Affairs*, November/December 2011, p. 96.

38 George Walden, *China: A Wolf in the World* (London, 2011), pp. 105–6.

39 Lo, *Russia and the New World Disorder*, pp. 141–50.

40 Tim Marshall, *Prisoners of Geography* (London, 2015), p. 10.

41 Peter Pomerantsev, *Nothing is True and Everything is Possible: Adventures in Modern Russia* (London, 2015).

42 Fred Weir, 'Maybe the Soviets Weren't so Bad? Russian Nostalgia for the USSR on the Rise', *Christian Science Monitor*, 29 January 2016.

43 For the above see Charles Clover's remarkable *Black Wind, White Snow: The Rise of Russia's New Nationalism* (New Haven, 2016).

44 Mark Hollingsworth and Stewart Lansley, *Londongrad: From Russia with Cash: The Inside Story of the Oligarchs* (London, 2010).

45 Anton Barbashin and Hannah Thoburn, 'Putin's Philosopher. Ivan Ilyin and the Ideology of Moscow's Rule', *Foreign Affairs*, 20 September 2015.

46 'Putin Celebrates Unrepentant Fascist Zhirinovsky', *World Affairs*, 25 April 2016.

47 Tor Bukkvoll, 'Russian Special Operations Forces in the War in Ukraine – Crimea and Donbas', in Bettina Renz and Hanna Smith (eds.), 'Russia and Hybrid Warfare – Going Beyond the Label', University of Helsinki Aleksanteri Institute online working paper no. 1/2016; www.stratcomcoe.org/bettina-renz-and-hanna-smith-russia-and-hybrid-warfare-going-beyond-label. See also Sarah Fainberg, Viktor Eichner, 'Russia's Army in Syria: Testing a New Concept of Warfare', *INSS Strategic Assessment*, vol. 20 (July 2017), for an Israeli analysis of Russia's 'new generation warfare'.

48 Richard Herzinger, 'Putins Traum von einem russisch dominierten Europa', *Die Welt*, 5 February 2016, and Dirk Banse, 'So schwächen Putins Psychokrieger Europa', *Die Welt*, 4 April 2016.
49 I am indebted here to a fine study by Michael Kofman, 'A Comparative Guide to Russia's Use of Force: Measure Twice, Invade Once', *War on the Rocks*, 16 February 2017.
50 Christopher Fettweis, 'Misreading the Enemy', *Survival: Global Policy and Strategy* (2015), vol. 57, pp. 149–72, is thoughtful.
51 Regular news on military activity in the Arctic can be found on the Norwegian website Barents Observer. The editor, Thomas Nilsen, was sacked after the FSN allegedly nobbled its owners.
52 A charming BBC nature series, 'Arctic Live' in 2016, on polar bears in the Arctic, managed to give an overoptimistic version of the Russian economic presence.
53 Friedrich Schmidt, 'Propaganda von Panama nach Palmyra', *Frankfurter Allgemeine Zeitung*, 5 May 2016.
54 Julia Smirnova, 'Die russische "Wagner-Einheit" zieht in den Syrien-Krieg', *Die Welt*, 10 May 2016.
55 Michael Reynolds, *Shattering Empires: The Clash and Collapse of the Ottoman and Russian Empires 1908–1918* (Cambridge, 2011).
56 US Energy Information Administration (EIA) data on Turkey's energy sources on 7 July 2015.
57 Jacopo Barigazzi and David Herszenhorn, 'Russia's "Crescent of Instability" Spreads West', *Politico* Europe, 3 February 2017, and Yury Barmin, 'Jordan Eyes Center Stage in Russia's Anti-Terrorism Policy', *Al-Monitor*, 1 February 2017.
58 Dobson, *The Dictator's Learning Curve*, p. 61.
59 Jake Rudnitsky, 'Russians Marvel at Anti-Corruption Cop's $131 million Cash Pile', *Bloomberg News*, 14 September 2016.
60 Lo, *Russia and the New World Disorder*, pp. 129–31.
61 Peter Eltsov, 'What Putin's Favorite Guru Tells Us About His Next Target', *Politico*, 10 February 2015.

6: China: A Country for Old Men

1 Evan Osnos, 'Born Red', *New Yorker*, 6 April 2015 for the polling figures. People were less enthused by Xi's stewardship of the economy.
2 Tom Phillips, 'Democracy is a Joke, Says China – Just Look at Donald Trump', *Guardian*, 17 March 2016 for examples of Chinese commentary. By contrast, despite Trump's unreciprocated praise of Putin, the Russian leader may have preferred the entirely

predictable Clinton, even if Russian agencies dabbled in the election. See also Mareike Ohlberg and Bertram Lang, 'How to Counter China's Global Propaganda Offensive', *New York Times*, 21 September 2016.

3 Osnos, 'Born Red', quoting He Weifang.

4 Palash Ghosh, 'Thieves, Conmen, Kidnappers, Rapists and Killers: Welcome to the Parliament of India!', *International Business Times*, 4 August 2014.

5 See Stein Ringen, *The Perfect Dictatorship: China in the 21st Century* (Hong Kong, 2016), pp. 32–4.

6 Edward Luttwak, *The Rise of China vs the Logic of Strategy* (Cambridge, MA, 2012), pp. 6–7.

7 Andrew Browne, 'China Hones Its Passive-Aggressive Diplomacy', *Wall Street Journal*, 31 August 2016, p. A2.

8 A Rand Corporation report commissioned by the US Army by David Gompert, Astrid Stuth Cevallos and Cristina Garafola, *War with China: Thinking the Unthinkable* (Santa Monica, 2016), is suitably chilling.

9 Ben Chu, *Chinese Whispers: Why Everything You've Heard About China is Wrong* (London, 2013), pp. 24–7, for a brilliant account.

10 For a thoughtful discussion of contested memories in Asia see 'The Unquiet Past', *The Economist*, 15 August 2015, pp. 47–52. Rana Mitter's *China's War with Japan 1937–1945: The Struggle for Survival* (London, 2013), brilliantly succeeds in restoring China's place in this epic struggle.

11 Two indispensable accounts are Frank Dikötter, *Mao's Great Famine: The History of China's Most Devastating Catastrophe, 1958–62* (London, 2010), and his *The Cultural Revolution* (London, 2016). An outstanding general history of China is Jonathan Fenby's *History of Modern China: The Fall and Rise of a Great Power, 1850–2008* (London, 2008).

12 For an excellent account of these machinations see Jonathan Fenby, *Tiger Head, Snake Tails: China Today, How It Got There and Where It is Heading* (London, 2012), pp. 165–9, one of the best books too on contemporary China.

13 Ezra Vogel, *Deng Xiaoping and the Transformation of China* (Cambridge, MA, 2011), p. 304, and the important book by Julian Gewirtz, *Unlikely Partners: Chinese Reformers, Western Economists, and the Making of Global China* (Cambridge, MA, 2017).

14 Arthur Kroeber, *China's Economy: What Everyone Needs to Know* (Oxford, 2016), pp. 164–6.

15 Vogel, *Deng Xiaoping and the Transformation of China*, p. 541.

16 The best account is Kroeber, *China's Economy*, pp. 22–3.

17 Vogel, *Deng Xiaoping and the Transformation of China*, pp. 394–422.

18 Agnès Andrésy, *Xi Jinping: Red China, the Next Generation* (Lanham, MD, 2016), pp. 15–23.

19 Kerry Brown, *The New Emperors: Power and Princelings in China* (London, 2014), p. 116.

20 See the fascinating account by David Bandurski, *Dragons in the Diamond Village: Tales of Resistance from Urbanizing China* (Brooklyn, 2016).

21 John Pomfret, *The Beautiful Country and the Middle Kingdom: America and China, 1776 to the Present* (New York, 2016), pp. 570–72.

22 Ringen, *The Perfect Dictatorship*, pp. 15–16.

23 Fenby, *Tiger Head, Snake Tails*, pp. 180–81.

24 Dominique Fong, 'China Puts Property Tax on Back Burner', *Wall Street Journal*, 20 March 2017.

25 Robert Lawrence Kuhn, *The Man Who Changed China: The Life and Legacy of Jiang Zemin* (New York, 2004), pp. 308–9.

26 Ibid., pp. 537–40, for SARS and submarines.

27 Pomfret, *The Beautiful Country and the Middle Kingdom*. pp. 624–5. For 'volunteer vigilantes' see Willy Wo-Lap, 'Beijing Harnesses Big Data & AI to Perfect the Police', Jamestown Foundation, 21 July 2017.

28 Zi Yang, 'Rural China and the Asian Methamphetamine Trade: A Case Study of Lufeng', Jamestown Foundation *China Brief*, vol. 17, no. 2, 6 February 2017, for details and photos of the meth haul and the worried suspects.

29 Ringen, *The Perfect Dictatorship*, p. 82. See also Willy Wo-Lap, 'Beijing Harnesses Big Data & AI to Perfect the Police State', for the details of uses of AI and facial recognition technology.

30 David Shambaugh, *China's Communist Party: Atrophy and Adaptation* (Washington, DC, 2009), p. 46.

31 Kroeber, *China's Economy*, pp. 205–8, is convincing on this.

32 Minxin Pei, *China's Crony Capitalism: The Dynamics of Regime Decay* (Cambridge, MA, 2016), pp. 71ff.

33 Te-Ping Chen, 'Xi Jinping's Corruption Trap', *Wall Street Journal*, 22 December 2016, pp. A1–A3.

34 Jonathan Pollack, 'Unease from Afar', in Kenneth M. Pollack et al. (eds.), *The Arab Awakening: America and the Transformation of the Middle East* (Washington, DC, 2011), pp. 298ff.

35 Bandurski, *Dragons in Diamond Village*, pp. 58ff.

36 As underlined by Kroeber, *China's Economy*, pp. 230–31.

37 Jonathan Watts, *When a Billion Chinese Jump: Voices from the Front Line of Climate Change* (London, 2010), p. 348.

38 Andrew Nathan, 'China's Challenge', in Diamond et al. (eds.), *Authoritarianism Goes Global*, p. 27.

39 David Shambaugh, *China's Future* (Cambridge, 2016), pp. 61–4, is one distinguished advocate of the disorder thesis; Will Freeman, 'The Accuracy of China's "Mass Incidents"', *Financial Times*, 2 March 2015, is a sceptic.

40 The best history of the CCP is Richard McGregor, *The Party: The Secret World of China's Communist Rulers* (London, 2012).

41 Chris Buckley, 'Xi Jinping May Delay Picking China's Next Leader, Stoking Speculation', *New York Times*, 4 October 2016.

42 Zi Yang, 'Meet China's Emerging Number 2', *Diplomat*, 5 May 2017, with biographical details of Li Zhanshu.

43 Benjamin Kang Lim and Ben Blanchard, 'Xi Set to Consolidate Power in China by Curbing Communist Youth League', Reuters, 30 September 2016.

44 Kerry Brown, *CEO, China. The Rise of Xi Jinping* (London 2016), p. 56.

45 R. W. McMorrow, 'Membership of the Communist Party in China: Who is Being Admitted Now?', DailyJStor.Org, 19 December 2015.

46 Willy Wo-Lap Lam, 'Xi Jinping Promotes Protégés to Top Positions in Run-up to 19th Party Congress', Jamestown Foundation, 9 June 2017.

47 Andrésy, *Xi Jinping*, p. 31.

48 Osnos, 'Born Red'.

49 Brown, *The New Emperors*, especially pp. 148–86, makes the important distinction between rigid alleged 'factions' and the much more liquid reality of perceptions and relations.

50 Shambaugh, *China's Future*, pp. 72–4.

51 Kroeber, *China's Economy*, p. 75.

52 Xinning Liu and Tom Hancock, 'Shanghai Loosens Housing Policy after Rare Protests', *Financial Times*, 13 June 2017.

53 As cogently discussed by Anja Manuel, *This Brave New World: India, China and the United States* (New York, 2016), pp. 129–33.

54 Kroeber, *China's Economy*, p. 172.

55 Gabriel Wildau, 'China's State-Owned Zombie Economy', *Financial Times*, 29 February 2016.

56 Tom Mitchell, 'Xi's China: The Rise of Party Politics', *Financial Times*, 25 July 2016. On Wang see Tom Mitchell, Gabriel Wildau and Henny Sender, 'Wang Qishan: China's Enforcer', *Financial Times*, 24 July 2017.

57 Andrésy, *Xi Jinping*, p. 98, for the PBOC estimate.

58 Patti Waldmeir and Gabriel Wildau, 'China Graft Probe Uncovers Falsified Revenues at Large SOEs', *Financial Times*, 29 June 2015 for the lottery.

59 Ting Shi, 'Xi Calls for a China in 2016 Where "Nobody Dares to be Corrupt"', *Bloomberg News*, 13 January 2016, and Macabe Keliher and Hsinchao Wu, 'How to Discipline 90 Million People', *Atlantic*, 7 April 2015.

60 Sherry Fei-Ju and Charles Clover, 'Reality Check. Chinese TV Cashes in on Corruption Hit Drama', *Financial Times*, 29/30 April 2017. On the fall of Sun Zhengcai see Tom Phillips, 'Man Tipped as China's Future President Ousted as Xi Jinping Wields "Iron Discipline" ', *Guardian*, 25 July 2017.

61 Charles Clover, 'Xi Warns China Military Amid Anti-Corruption Purge', *Financial Times*, 20 July 2015.

62 Charles Clover, 'Xi's China: Command and Control', *Financial Times*, 26 July 2016, and Zi Yang, 'Xi Jinping and China's Traditionalist Restoration', *Real Clear World*, 21 July 2017, is a comprehensive account of the new emphasis on the 'soul of the nation' and the revival of philosophies and legalism that served the emperors very well for centuries. This doctrine is being taught in schools, the PLA and among Party cadres.

63 Nathaniel Taplin, 'China's Gradualist Reform Approach Reaching Bitter End', *Wall Street Journal*, 6 March 2017.

64 Manuel, *This Brave New World*, pp. 70–71.

65 Dalia Marin, 'Was die Roboter-Revolution für uns bedeutet', *Frankfurter Allgemeine Zeitung*, 22 February 2017.

66 Joseph Hammond, 'Morocco: China's Gateway to Africa?', *Diplomat*, 1 March 2017, and Juan Pablo Cardenal and Heriberto Araújo, *China's Silent Army: The Pioneers, Traders, Fixers and Workers Who are Remaking the World in Beijing's Image* (London, 2013).

67 Points made by Mexico's former Deputy Foreign Minister, Andres Rozental, in an interview: 'Good Neighbor', *Octavian Report*, vol. 3, no. 3, May 2017, pp. 4–9.

68 Frida Ghitis, 'Why Trump's Rise is Sending Latin America into China's Arms', *World Politics Review*, 2 February 2017, and Christopher Sabatini, 'Could Trump Succeed Where Chavez Failed and Unite Latin America Against the US?', *World Politics Review*, 22 February 2017.

69 Richard Bitzinger, 'Does China Have What It Takes to Become a Global Security Power?', *World Politics Review*, 9 May 2017.

70 Bernhard Zand, 'China's High Seas Ambitions', *Der Spiegel*, 9 August 2016, and Erich Follath, 'Beijing's New Silk Road to Europe', *Der Spiegel*, 31 August 2016.

71 Brahma Chellaney, 'China's Debt-Trap Diplomacy', *Project Syndicate*, 23 January 2017.

72   For Xi's speech see, 'President Xi's Speech to Davos', World
     Economic Forum, 17 January 2017.

73   Tom Philipps, 'China Orders GPS Tracking of Every Car in
     Troubled Region', *Guardian*, 21 February 2017.

74   Andrew Small, *The China–Pakistan Axis: Asia's New Geopolitics*
     (London, 2015), pp. 69–76.

75   Michael Sheridan, 'China's Great Leap Backwards', *Sunday Times*
     magazine, 16 May 2016, pp. 12–19. On Hong Kong see Richard
     Bush, *Hong Kong in the Shadow of China: Living With The
     Leviathan* (Washington, DC, 2016), and on its economy compared
     with Shenzen see Andrew Browne, 'A Less Shiny Hong Kong Is
     Easier to Control', *Wall Street Journal*, 5 July 2017. On Liu Xiaobo
     see Josh China, 'China Activist Sought Peaceful Change', *Wall
     Street Journal*, 14–16 July 2017.

76   Tanguy Lepesant, 'Taiwan Breaks Free of China', *Le Monde
     diplomatique*, June 2016, p. 10.

77   An excellent guide to these subjects is Howard W. French's
     *Everything Under the Heavens. How the Past Helps Shape China's
     Push for Global Power* (New York, 2017), pp. 142ff.

78   There is an interesting online film about the *Sierra Madre*, *Mission
     to Ayungin Shoal. On Board the BRP Sierra Madre* (ABS/CBN
     New.com date unknown).

79   Jonathan Fenby, 'The Great Wall of Sand', *New Statesman*, 13–19
     May 2016, p. 32.

80   On this see François Godement, 'Expanded Ambitions, Shrinking
     Achievements: How China Sees the Global Order', European
     Council on Foreign Relations Report, March 2017, pp. 7–10.

81   See Zhang Hongzhou, 'Chinese Fishermen in Troubled Waters',
     Diplomat, 23 October 2014; Lucy Hornby, 'Chinese Fishermen
     Caught Up in Asian Geopolitical Conflict', *Financial Times*, 22
     August 2016; and Luttwak, *The Rise of China*, pp. 103–5, for the
     Chinese maritime agencies described. See also Emma Graham-
     Harrison, 'The Islands on the Frontline of a New Global
     Flashpoint', *Observer*, 5 February 2017, pp. 15–16.

82   Nathan, 'China's Challenge', pp. 30–31.

83   Kazunori Takada and Chris Buckley, 'Japan Brand Name Firms Shut
     China Plants After Protest Violence', Reuters, 17 September 2015.

84   Chu, *Chinese Whispers*, pp. 211–17, is a thoughtful account of
     'nationalist-democratic' Angry Youth. See the fascinating piece by
     Te-Ping Chen and Josh Chin, 'West Loses Allure in China', *Wall
     Street Journal*, 27 July 2017. As one remarked, 'If you don't go
     abroad, you don't actually know how great China is.' They were
     not impressed by how special interests dominate US politics, or by

beggars on the streets, or 'insecurity', which included two Chinese graduate students randomly killed while they sat in their car near a campus.

85 Alain Peyrefitte, *The Immobile Empire* (New York, 1992).

86 Luttwak, *The Rise of China*, pp. 72ff.

87 David Shambaugh, *China Goes Global: The Partial Power* (Oxford, 2013), p. 19.

88 'The Brains of the Party', *The Economist*, 10 May 2014.

89 Nathan Beauchamp-Mustafaga, 'Chinese Public Opinion and North Korea: Will Anger Lead to Policy Change?', Jamestown Foundation *China Brief* vol. 15, no. 1, 9 January 2015.

90 Shannon Tiezzi, 'China Backs Russia on Ukraine', *The Diplomat*, 4 March 2014.

91 As pointed out by Ramesh Thakur, 'Is the Sun Setting on the US Imperium?' in *Japan Times*, 14 May 2017.

92 Small, *The China–Pakistan Axis*, pp. 57–60.

93 Ibid., p. 155.

94 Clare Phipps, 'China Military Commemorates Second World War Victory', *Guardian*, 3 September 2015. See also Adam Ni, 'Why China Is Trimming Its Army', *Diplomat*, 15 July 2017. In 1985, one million troops were cut; half a million more in 1997; 200,000 in 2003, and a further 300,000 cut was announced in 2015. Current force strengths are unknown, but in 2013 the Ministry of Defence reported an army of 850,000 personnel.

95 Jane Perlez, 'China to Raise Military Spending, But Less Than in Recent Years', *New York Times*, 4 March 2017.

96 See Damen Cook, 'China's Most Important South China Sea Military Base', *Diplomat*, 9 March 2017, which includes aerial photos of this complex.

97 Colum Lynch, 'China Eyes Ending Western Grip on Top UN Jobs with Greater Control of Blue Helmets', *Foreign Policy*, 2 October 2016. See also Kyle Haddad-Fonda, 'How Serious Are China's Offers to Mediate Conflicts in the Islamic World?', *World Politics Review*, 31 July 2017, for a sceptical view of China's attempts to mediate between Israelis and Palestinians or Iranians and Saudis.

98 Nathan, 'China's Challenge', pp. 34–5.

99 Gideon Rachman, *Easternisation: War and Peace in the Asian Century* (London, 2016), pp. 88–9.

100 Henry J. Kenny, 'Vietnamese Perceptions of the 1979 War with China', in Mark Ryan, David Finkelstein and Michael McDevitt (eds.), *Chinese Warfighting: The PLA Experience Since 1949* (Armonk, NY, 2003), p. 231.

101   Tom Hancock, 'China Drive to Relocate Millions of Rural Poor Runs into Trouble', *Financial Times*, 13 June 2017.

7: The USA: The Noisy Nation

1   Michael Mandelbaum, 'A New American Foreign Policy?', *American Interest*, 14 November 2016.

2   For a very good account of the Clinton years see Colin Dueck, *Reluctant Crusader: Power, Culture, and Change in American Grand Strategy* (Princeton, 2006), p. 114.

3   Maurice Lemoine, 'Panama Gets Its Canal Back', *Le Monde diplomatique*, August 1999.

4   Michael Mandelbaum, *Mission Failure: America and the World in the Post-Cold War Era* (Oxford, 2016), p. 83.

5   Colin Powell, *My American Journey* (New York, 1995), p. 561.

6   Dueck, *Reluctant Crusaders*, pp. 141–2.

7   Colin Dueck, *The Obama Doctrine: American Grand Strategy Today* (Oxford, 2015), p. 43.

8   Mark Landler, *Alter Egos: Hillary Clinton, Barack Obama, and the Twilight Struggle Over American Foreign Policy* (New York, 2016), pp. 75ff.

9   Dueck, *The Obama Doctrine*, pp. 140–41.

10   Since the Pentagon categorizes these as strikes, far more multiple bombs may have been involved. See Micah Zenko, 'How Many Bombs Did the United States Drop in 2016?', Council of Foreign Relations blog post, 5 January 2017.

11   Chris Woods, *Sudden Justice: America's Secret Drone Wars* (London, 2015), p. 221.

12   William McGurn, 'The War That Dare Not Speak Its Name', *Wall Street Journal*, 30 November 2016.

13   Ed Morrissey, 'Obama: Rise of ISIS Caught Me by Surprise', *Hot Air*, 8 December 2016.

14   Hugh White, 'What's so Great About American World Leadership?', *Atlantic Monthly*, 23 November 2016.

15   John Pomfret, *The Beautiful Country and the Middle Kingdom: America and China, 1776 to the Present* (New York, 2016), p. 593.

16   See John Bolton, 'Obama's Parting Betrayal of Israel', and Brett Stephens, 'Obama's Fitting Finish', *Wall Street Journal*, 28 December 2016, pp. A10–A11.

17   Jeffrey Goldberg, 'Netanyahu Says Obama Got Syria Right', *Bloomberg News*, 22 May 2014, and Eli Lake, 'Israel Helped

Obama Skirt "Red Line" on Syria,' *Bloomberg News*, 15 June 2015.

18 Edward-Isaac Dovere, 'James Baker Blasts Netanyahu', *Politico*, 23 March 2015.

19 Goldberg, 'The Obama Doctrine'.

20 Mandelbaum, *Mission Failure*, p. 305, citing Alan J. Kuperman, 'A Model Humanitarian Intervention: Reassessing NATO's Libya Campaign', *International Security* (2013), vol. 38, pp. 116–23, for the comparative figures.

21 Landler, *Alter Egos*, p. 205.

22 Andrew J. Bacevich, *The New American Militarism: How Americans are Seduced by War* (Oxford, 2013), pp. 39–48.

23 Michael Peck, 'Why is America Wasting the F-22 Raptor on Bombing ISIS?', *National Interest*, 30 September 2016, and Robert Beckhausen, 'Report: US F-22 Raptor Stealth Fighters Flew to Commandos' Rescue in Syria', *National Interest*, 21 August 2016. My interest in the F-22 Raptor was piqued by Mark Urban's *The Edge: Is the Military Dominance of the West Coming to an End?* (London, 2015), pp. 20ff. Tim Hepher and Leigh Thomas, 'France and Germany to Develop New European Fighter Jet', *Reuters Business News*, 13 July 2017.

24 Tim Broderick, 'Coming Soon: F-22 Raptors and F-35 Stealth Fighters Armed with Super Lasers?', *National Interest*, 13 December 2016; Dave Majumdar, 'Revealed: China's Radars Can Track America's Stealthy F-22 Raptor', and 'America's F-22 and F-35 Stealth Fighters Versus Russia's S-300, S-400 and S-500. Who Wins?', *National Interest*, 19 February and 19 September 2016.

25 Dina Smeltz and Ivo Daalder (eds.), *Foreign Policy in the Age of Retrenchment: Results of the 2014 Chicago Council Survey of American Public Opinion and US Foreign Policy* (Chicago, 2014), pp. 1–5. On Trump and the UN see Steven Metz, 'Will Trump Choose Revolution or Reform for Dealing with the UN?', *World Politics Review*, 10 February 2017.

26 Richard N. Haass, *Foreign Policy Begins At Home: The Case for Putting America's House in Order* (New York, 2013), is a very impressive statement of the issues.

27 See Pomfret, *The Beautiful Country and the Middle Kingdom*, for the ebb and flow of these mutual enthusiasms.

28 See the fascinating account by Lynne Olson, *Those Angry Days: Roosevelt, Lindbergh, and America's Fight Over World War II, 1939–1941* (New York, 2013).

29 Robert Taft, 'Shall the United States Enter the European War?' address on 17 May 1941 Congressional Record 19 May 1941 cited

in Ronald Radosh, *Prophets on the Right: Profiles of Conservative Critics of American Globalism* (New York, 1975), p. 128.

30 T. J. Jackson Lears, 'Pragmatic Realism Versus the American Century', in Andrew Bacevich (ed.), *The Short American Century: A Postmortem* (Cambridge, MA, 2012), p. 100.

31 Stephen E. Ambrose, *Eisenhower: The President 1952–1969* (London, 1984), p. 612.

32 Daniel McCarthy, 'Why is John McCain Accusing Rand Paul of Working for Russia?', *National Interest*, 23 March 2017.

33 See Ian Bremmer, *Superpower: Three Choices for America's Role in the World* (New York, 2015), pp. 65–8.

34 See the fascinating article by T. X. Hammes, 'The End of Globalization? The International Security Implications', *War on the Rocks*, 2 August 2016.

35 Walter Russell Mead, 'The Jacksonian Tradition and American Foreign Policy', *National Interest*, Winter 1999/2000.

36 Paul Pilar, 'Anti-Semitism in the US: Its Foundations and Recent Surge', *National Interest*, 18 March 2017.

37 For a fair description see Walter Russell Mead, 'Donald Trump's Jacksonian Revolt', *Wall Street Journal*, 11 November 2016, and 'The Jacksonian Revolt', *Foreign Affairs*, 20 January 2017. See also Felipe Fernández-Armesto, *Our America: A Hispanic History of the United States* (New York, 2014), for an important corrective to the usual, 'Anglosphere' view.

38 Stephanie Kirchgaessner, 'If Berlusconi is Like Trump, What Can Italy Teach America?', *Guardian*, 21 November 2016.

39 Michael Kazin, 'Trump and American Populism', *Foreign Affairs*, November/December 2016, pp. 18–20.

40 John Judis, *The Populist Explosion: How the Great Recession Transformed American and European Politics* (New York, 2016), is excellent on the US background. See also Hugh Rockoff, 'The "Wizard of Oz" as a Monetary Allegory', *Journal of Political Economy*, vol. 98 (1990). The famous film starring Judy Garland was made in 1939.

41 As pointed out by Serge Halimi in 'Trump, the Know-Nothing Victor', *Le Monde diplomatique*, December 2016, p. 2.

42 Ruth Ben-Ghiat, 'An American Authoritarian', *Atlantic Monthly*, 10 August 2016.

43 David Cay Johnson, *The Making of Donald Trump* (Brooklyn, 2016), pp. 70–76, for his 'Polish Brigade'.

44 Seema Mehta, 'Transcript: Clinton's Full Remarks as She Called Half of Trump's Supporters "Deplorables"', *LA Times*, 10 September 2016.

45 Jerome Karabel, 'The Year of the Outsider', *Le Monde diplomatique*, December 2016, p. 5, for a fine analysis.

46 Daniel Henninger, 'The New Trump Democrats', *Wall Street Journal*, 18 November 2016.

47 See Nicholas Eberstadt, *Men Without Work: America's Invisible Crisis* (West Conshohocken, PA, 2016), and Tyler Cowen, *Average is Over* (New York, 2013).

48 For a brilliant portrait of this steel-, Democrat- and Mafia-dominated town in advanced decay see Justin Gest, *The New Minority: White Working Class Politics in an Age of Immigration and Inequality* (Oxford, 2016), pp. 74ff.

49 Arthur Brooks, 'How Trump Filled the Dignity Deficit', *Wall Street Journal*, 11–13 November 2016, and Lenny Bernstein, 'US Life Expectancy Declines for the First Time Since 1993', *Wall Street Journal*, 8 December 2016, though obviously a one-year profile is not a trend.

50 A point ably made by David Bromwich in his contribution to 'Election-1', *New York Review of Books*, 10 November 2016, p. 6.

51 Karabel, 'The Year of the Outsider', p. 5.

52 See the interesting anthropological monograph by Jonathan Rieder, *Canarsie: The Jews and Italians of Brooklyn* (New York, 1985), which highlights white reactions to War on Poverty policies that benefited African-Americans.

53 Cited by Arlie Russell Hochschild, *Strangers in Their Own Land: Anger and Mourning on the American Right* (New York, 2016), p. 224.

54 Joan Williams, 'What so Many People Don't Get About the US Working Class', *Harvard Business Review*, 10 November 2016.

55 J. D. Vance, *Hillbilly Elegy* (London, 2016), p. 146.

56 Jeff Gue, 'A New Theory for Why Trump Voters are so Angry – That Actually Makes Sense', *Washington Post*, 8 November 2016, and Kathy Cramer, *The Politics of Resentment: Rural Consciousness in Wisconsin and the Rise of Scott Walker* (Chicago, 2016).

57 Hochschild, *Strangers in Their Own Land*, pp. 136–40.

58 One book which turns the approach of academy back on itself is Gest's *The New Minority: White Working Class Politics in an Age of Immigration and Inequality,* pp. 29ff.

59 See the very subtle analysis by Shelby Steel, 'Trump, Clinton and the Culture of Deference', *Wall Street Journal*, 9 November 2016. See also the valuable Colin Woodard, *American Nations: A History of the Eleven Rival Regional Cultures of North America* (New York, 2011).

60 Danielle Kurtzleben, '4 Reasons Mormons are More Skeptical of Trump Than Other Religious Conservatives', npr.org, 25 October

2016, and on the results Jana Riess, 'Most Mormons Planned NOT to Vote for Trump. What the Heck Happened?', Religion News Service, 15 November 2016. On Roman Catholics see Mathew Schmalz, 'It Remains to be Seen Whether Trump Will Deliver the Vision They Hope He Will', Fortune.com, November 2016, and Bradford Richardson, 'Catholic Comeback Helps Propel Donald Trump to White House Win', *Washington Times*, 10 November 2016. My friend Bill Doino helped with research on the US Catholic vote. On 'apocalyptic geopolitics' see James Politi, 'Papal Allies Attack Bannon's "Apocalyptic" Vision', *Financial Times*, 15 July 2017.

61 Douglas Schoen, 'Hillary Clinton, Underdog', *Wall Street Journal*, 1 August 2016. Forty-three per cent of those polled by CNN/ORC trusted Trump.

62 See the thoughtful piece by Andrés Martinez, 'Americans Have Seen the Last Four Presidents as Illegitimate. Here's Why', *Washington Post*, 20 January 2017.

63 This paragraph owes much to the lucid analysis of Jonathan Rauch, 'What's Ailing American Politics?', *Atlantic*, July/August 2016, pp. 51–63.

64 See Francis Fukuyama, 'The Failed State', *Prospect*, January 2017, p. 31, and Ben McGrath, 'The Movement. The Rise of Tea Party Activism', *New Yorker*, 1 February 2010, from a huge literature we need not explore. Josh Corless familiarized me with the Freedom Caucus.

65 See the excellent analysis by Ryan Lizza, 'Occupied Territory', *New Yorker*, 20 June 2016, pp. 26–32.

66 Matt Cavanaugh, 'The Mike Flynn Problem is Actually a Profession of Arms Problem', *War on the Rocks*, 16 March 2017. See also the important article by Missy Ryan and Greg Jaffe, 'Military's Clout at White House Could Shift US Foreign Policy', *Washington Post*, 28 May 2017. On Trump himself see Lucy Marcus, 'Donald Trump, CEO', *Project Syndicate*, 26 July 2017, as well as Peggy Noonan's devastating profile, 'Trump is Woody Allen Without the Humor', *Wall Street Journal*, 27 July 2017.

67 William Galston 'A Turning Point for Trumpinology', *Wall Street Journal*, 8 June 2017.

68 Gerald Seib, 'Trump Shuffles America's Ideological Deck', *Wall Street Journal*, 6 December 2016.

69 David Kocieniewski and Caleb Melby, 'Kushners Set to Get $400 Million from Chinese Firm on Tower', *Bloomberg News*, 13 March 2017.

70 Michael Klare, 'The World as Seen by Donald Trump', *Le Monde diplomatique*, January 2017, pp. 2–3.

71 Derek Grossman, 'Adapting the President's Daily Brief to Trump', *War on the Rocks*, 6 January 2017.

72 Philip Delves Broughton, 'Corporate America Wonders Which Trump to Believe', *Financial Times*, 7 January 2017, hits the nail on the head.

73 As said by the estimable Andrew J. Bacevich, 'Get Ready for a Wild Ride', *The Spectator*, 7 January 2017.

74 Isabel Hilton, 'Citizen of the World', *Newsweek*, 10 February 2017, p. 31.

75 Klare, 'The World as Seen by Donald Trump', p. 3.

76 On Mattis see Dexter Filkins, 'The Warrior Monk', *New Yorker*, 29 May 2017, especially pp. 41–3.

77 See David Gardner, 'Qatar pays the price for betting on the Brotherhood', *Financial Times*, 7 June 2017 and Kobi Michael, Yoel Guzansky, 'Qatar under Siege: Regional Implications and Ramifications for the Palestinian Area', *INSS Insight*, no. 935, 12 June 2015.

78 Adam Garfinkle, 'Donald Trump's Excellent Middle East Adventure', *Foreign Policy*, Research Institute (Philadelphia) E-Notes, 7 December 2016, and Dana Milbank, 'Anti-Semitism is No Longer an Undertone of Trump's Campaign. It's the Melody', *Washington Post*, 7 November 2016.

79 Frida Ghitis, 'Why Trump's Rise is Sending Latin America into China's Arms', *World Politics Review*, 2 February 2017.

80 'Highlights of Reuters Interview with Trump', Reuters, 24 February 2017.

81 Soeren Kern, 'Donald Trump and the Return of European Anti-Americanism', Gatestone Institute, 21 November 2016.

8: Empire of Virtue: The European Union

1 Jefferson Pooley, Michael Socolow, 'The Myth of the War of the Worlds Panic', *Slate,* 28 October 2013.

2 A view confirmed by Belgium's own investigation. See Valentina Pop and Mark Maremont, 'Belgium Botched ISIS Cell Hunt, Secret Report Shows', *Wall Street Journal*, 6–8 January 2017, pp. A1 and A6.

3 Maria Rosa Antognazza, 'What Would Leibniz Say About the Schisms in Europe Today?', LSE Brexit Blog (7 December 2016).

4 Cited in 'Jean Monnet', in Anthony Teasdale and Timothy Bainbridge (eds.), *The Penguin Companion to the European Union*, 4th edn (London, 2012), p. 595.

5   Jan-Werner Müller, *What is Populism?* (Philadelphia, 2016),
    pp. 94–5.
6   Tim Shipman, *All Out War: The Full Story of How Brexit Sank
    Britain's Political Class* (London, 2016), pp. 235–6.
7   Luuk van Middelaar, *The Passage to Europe: How a Continent
    Became a Union* (New Haven, 2013), p. 45. This is without doubt
    the most intelligent book on the genesis of the EU.
8   David Herszenhorn, '"Monster" at the Berlaymont', *Politico
    Europe*, 22 November 2016.
9   For an excellent discussion of these national perspectives see
    Brendan Simms, *Britain's Europe: A Thousand Years of Conflict
    and Cooperation* (London, 2016), pp. 176–8.
10 James Sheehan, *The Monopoly of Violence: Why Europeans Hate
    Going to War* (London, 2008), pp. 158–63.
11 Van Middelaar, *Passage to Europe*, pp. 143–51.
12 The best biography of Delors is by Charles Grant, *Delors:
    Architecte de l'Europe* (Paris, 1995).
13 Van Middelaar, *Passage to Europe*, p. 171.
14 On attitudes to enlargement see Andreas Röder, *21.0: Eine kurze
    Geschichte der Gegenwart* (Munich, 2015), pp. 310ff.
15 George Soros, 'Open Society Needs Defending', *Project Syndicate*,
    28 December 2016.
16 Markus Brunnermeier, Harold James and Jean-Pierre Landau, *The
    Euro and the Battle of Ideas* (Princeton, 2016), p. 19.
17 For these statistics see Teasdale and Bainbridge (eds.), *The Penguin
    Companion to Europe*, pp. 271–2. They may not be quite up to
    date.
18 Herszenhorn, '"Monster" at the Berlaymont'.
19 James Heartfield, *The European Union and the End of Politics*
    (Alresford, 2013), pp. 116–20.
20 'The Common Agricultural Policy', in Teasdale and Bainbridge
    (eds.), *The Penguin Companion to Europe*, p. 108. Calculating the
    size of the rural workforce (on roughly 12 million farms in the EU)
    taxes even the Commission. See, 'How Many People Work in
    Agriculture in the European Union?', *EU Agricultural Economics
    Brief No. 8*, July 2013. On farm sizes and CAP see Nicolas Kayser-
    Bril, 'EU Farming Policy: The Damage Done by 20 Years of Inertia',
    European Observer, 31 January 2017.
21 'AfD träumt vom Euro ohne Frankreich', *Die Welt*, 10 January
    2017.
22 Sheehan, *The Monopoly of Violence*, p. 223.
23 Corey Cooper, 'How a Middle Ground on EU Defense Can

Complement NATO, Not Weaken It', *World Politics Review*, 19 May 2017.

24 Loretta Napoleoni, *Merchants of Men: How Jihadists and ISIS Turned Kidnapping and Refugee Trafficking into a Multi-Billion Dollar Business* (London, 2016).

25 Philip Willan, 'Italy Prepares Mass Deportations as Half a Million Migrants Arrive', *The Times*, 2 January 2017, pp. 26–7.

26 Eszter Zalan, 'EU 27 Agree "Roadmap", But Italy Spoils the Party', *European Observer*, 16 September 2016.

27 Eszter Zalan, 'The Rise and Shine of Visegrad', *European Observer*, 30 December 2016.

28 See Europol/Interpol Joint Report: 'Migrant Smuggling Networks', May 2016.

29 Yannis Palaiologos, *The 13th Labour of Hercules: Inside the Greek Crisis* (London, 2016), p. 194.

30 Alexander Bühler, Susanne Koelbl, Sandro Mattioli and Walter Mayr, 'On the Trail of African Migrant Smugglers', *Der Spiegel* online, 26 September 2016.

31 James Politi, 'Surge in Sea Migrants Dashes Italy Hopes on Deal with Libya', *Financial Times*, 13/14 May 2017.

32 Malise Ruthven and Nick Thorpe, 'On Today's Refugee Road', *New York Review of Books*, 24 November 2016, pp. 27–30, for the comparison with Hungary in 1956.

33 Wendell Steavenson, 'A London Bubble', *Prospect Magazine*, September 2016, pp. 36–45, is typical.

34 Eszter Zalan, 'EU Leaders to Push Migration Issue Outside of Europe', *European Observer*, 4 February 2017.

35 Paul Collier, *Exodus: Immigration and Multiculturalism in the 21st Century* (London, 2014), and Douglas Murray, *The Strange Death of Europe: Immigration, Identity, Islam* (London, 2017) are the best recent accounts.

36 Caroline Fourest and Fiammetta Venner, *Marine Le Pen* (Paris, 2011), pp. 159ff.

37 For FN policy see Jonathan Marcus, *The National Front and French Politics: The Resistible Rise of Jean-Marie Le Pen* (London, 1995), pp. 108ff.; Marion Solletty, 'Marine Le Pen's Animal Instincts', *Politico* Europe, 4 January 2017.

38 Judis, *The Populist Explosion*, pp. 100–101.

39 Cnaan Liphshiz, 'More French Jews Drifting to National Front Party', *Times of Israel*, 26 September 2014.

40 Sébastien Chenu, 'Le FN séduit de plus en plus d'homosexuels', *Les InRocks*, 12 April 2016.

41 Olivier Roy, 'The French National Front: From Christian Identity to

Laïcité', in Nadia Marzouki, Duncan McDonnell and Olivier Roy (eds.), *Saving the People: How Populists Hijack Religion* (London, 2016), pp. 79–93.

42   Fourest and Venner, *Marine Le Pen*, pp. 25ff, and Emmanuel Galiero 'Marine Le Pen, au nom de la rose bleue', *Le Figaro*, 17 November 2016.

43   For the flavour of Fillon see Judith Weintraub, 'François Fillon: "Je veux vraiment réformer la France et la diriger avec dignité" ', *Le Figaro*, 17 November 2016.

44   From the many profiles of Macron see Sylvanie Chassany, 'A Providential Man on the Move', *Financial Times*, 29/30 April 2017. For an excellent study of Orbán see Martin Fletcher, 'The Long March from Freedom', *New Statesman*, 28 July to 10 August 2017. pp. 43–7.

45   Evelyne Pieller, 'Hungary Looks to Its Past for Its Future', *Le Monde diplomatique*, November 2016, pp. 8–9.

46   Péter Krekó, 'Putin–Orbán Axis Assails the EU', *European Observer*, 30 January 2017. For a subtle analysis of how the concentration of power does Macron few favours see Carlo Invernizzi-Accetti and Francesco Ronchi, 'The Dangers of the Macron Model', *Wall Street Journal*, 14–15 July 2017.

47   Marton Dunai, 'Anti-Semitism Taboo Under Threat in Hungary', Reuters, 21 May 2014, for the results of this survey.

48   Robert Tait, 'Civil Activists Fear New Crackdown in Hungary After Trump Election', *Guardian*, 10 January 2017.

49   Zoltán Ádám and András Bozóki, '"The God of Hungarians", Religion and Right-Wing Populism in Hungary', in Marzouki et al. (eds.), *Saving the People*, p. 138.

50   Keno Verseck, 'Hungarian Leader Adopts Policies of Far-Right', *Der Spiegel*, 30 January 2013.

51   Harvey Simmons, *The French National Front: The Extremist Challenge to Democracy* (Boulder, CO, 1996), pp. 27ff.

52   Müller, *What is Populism?*, p. 29.

53   Tom Nichols, 'How America Lost Faith in Expertise', *Foreign Affairs* (March/April 2017), p. 60.

54   For an excellent synoptic view see Timothy Garton Ash, 'Is Europe Disintegrating?', *New York Review of Books*, 19 January 2017, pp. 24–6, which includes Polish GDP figures compared with German.

55   See the excellent analysis by Tim Wigmore, 'Bonfire of the Elites', *New Statesman*, 28 November 2014, pp. 30–31.

56   The best account of Syriza and the problems of modern Greece is Yannis Palaiologos, *The 13th Labour of Hercules: Inside the Greek Crisis* (London, 2016).

57 Mark Gilbert, 'The Comeback Kid: What Renzi's Return Means for Italy's Stormy Politics', *World Politics Review*, 8 May 2017.

58 Simon Nixon, 'Governing, Not Elections, is EU's Challenge', *Wall Street Journal*, 9 January 2017 is characteristically astute.

59 For the failure of a Brexit-inspired domino effect on the Continent see Adam Bienkov, 'David Davis on Brexit: "I don't think anyone is likely to follow us down this route" ', *Business Insider*, 12 July 2017.

Index